The Complete
CBT Guide for

Depression and
Low Mood

The Complete CBT Guide for

Depression and Low Mood

Lee Brosan and David Westbrook

ROBINSON

ROBINSON

This edition published in 2015 by Robinson

Copyright © Leonora Brosan and David Westbrook, 2015

1 3 5 7 9 8 6 4 2

The moral right of the authors has been asserted.

Important Note
This book is not intended as a substitute for medical advice or treatment.
Any person with a condition requiring medical attention should consult
a qualified medical practitioner or suitable therapist.

Quotation from *Rachel's Holiday* on page 24 copyright © Marian Keys, 1998
Wherever You Go, There You Are by Jon Kabat-Zinn, quoted with the permission of
Hachette Books
Coming to Our Senses by Jon Kabat-Zinn (Copyright © by Jon Kabat-Zinn, 2005)
reprinted by permission of A.M. Heath & Co. Ltd.

Every effort has been made to trace and contact copyright holders. If there are any
inadvertent omissions we apologise to those concerned, and ask that you contact us so
that we can correct any oversight as soon as possible.

A CIP catalogue record for this book
is available from the British Library.

ISBN 978-1-78033-880-4 (paperback)
ISBN: 978-1-78033-881-1 (ebook)

Typeset in Palatino by Initial Typesetting Services, Edinburgh
Printed and bound by CPI Group (UK) Ltd, Croydon, CR0 4YY

Robinson
is an imprint of
Little, Brown Book Group
Carmelite House
50 Victoria Embankment
London EC4Y 0DZ

An Hachette UK Company
www.hachette.co.uk

www.littlebrown.co.uk

This book is dedicated to David Westbrook, who sadly died before it was completed. David will be remembered as a tremendously compassionate and skilled therapist, an inspirational colleague, and a wonderful family man. He is greatly missed by all who knew him. We hope that this book will stand as a fitting tribute to his memory.

Acknowledgements

Writing is almost always a mixture of pleasure and pain, and when I began this book I was anticipating much pleasure from doing so with an old colleague; sadly the pleasure was abruptly broken off by David's tragic death. So my first acknowledgement is to David as the author of much of Part 1, especially the elegant figures scattered throughout it; as the first editor of those chapters that came in during his lifetime; and for the hopeless task of trying to introduce me to Dropbox. Needless to say, any errors in the final product are mine alone.

I am indebted to the many people who have been so sympathetic to the process of continuing alone, and so tolerant of the fact that the book has taken so long to see the light of day.

I would also like to thank Fritha Saunders and Andrew McAleer for their endless patience and encouragement as editors, and Andrew for taking over so brilliantly. Many thanks also to Chris Irons for his comments and advice.

I am more indebted than I can say to the authors who contributed chapters. Depression continues to be a major problem for our times, and all the contributors are playing an important part in developing our understanding of it, and improving our ability to help. It's probably impossible to describe the extreme busyness of everyone who has been involved, but it's astonishing they have time to breathe, never mind to contribute their chapters. I am deeply thankful, and to bring the range of their expertise together has been a complete privilege.

Contents

Introduction: Making the most of this book   xv

PART 1
Introduction to depression and CBT – the basics
David Westbrook and Lee Brosan

Understanding depression   1

1. What is depression?   3

2. Are you depressed?   16

3. Myths and facts about depression   22

4. Why do people get depressed?   27

5. Can depression be treated?   34

Understanding CBT   41

6. The CBT model of depression   43

7. Starting to help yourself through CBT   62

8. Helping yourself by becoming more active   69

9. Identifying negative thoughts   79

10. Tackling negative thoughts   88

11. Solving problems   111

12. Relapse prevention: how to stop depression coming back   119

PART 2
Further strategies for tackling depression

Introduction   127

13. Using activity to combat depression: more about behavioural   129
     activation – *David A. Richards*

14. Thinking too much: dealing with rumination in   162
     depression – *Edward Watkins*

15. Using images to help with depressing memories –   186
     Jon Wheatley and Ann Hackmann

16. Compassion-focused therapy for depression – *Paul Gilbert*   216

17. Mindfulness: befriending depression – *Willem Kuyken and*   247
     Halley Cohen

PART 3
Tackling common problems in depression

Introduction   281

18. How to tackle low self-esteem – *Melanie Fennell*   283

19. Overcoming sleep difficulties – *Colin Espie*   316

20. Couples and depression: improving the relationship and   357
     improving depression – *Donald H. Baucom, Tamara G. Sher,*
     Sara E. Boeding and Christine Paprocki

PART 4
Tackling different types of depression

Introduction   389

21. Bipolar disorders and problematic mood swings –   391
     Warren Mansell, Phillip Brawn, Robert Griffiths, Ben Silver
     and Sara Tai

22. Postnatal depression – *Peter J. Cooper and Lynne Murray*   437

23. Depression in physical illness – *Stirling Moorey, Kathy Burn and Lyn Snowden*   471

24. Depression in later life – *Ken Laidlaw and Dichelle Wong*   512

Appendix 1: Further reading, references and other resources   539

Appendix 2: Blank worksheets   557

Index   603

Preface

This book is based on an approach to therapy called *cognitive behavioural therapy* (usually shortened to CBT, and also sometimes known just as cognitive therapy – they all mean much the same thing). CBT was developed for treating depression back in the 1970s and has been shown to be highly effective – at least as effective as antidepressant medication. CBT can be carried out face-to-face, like any other therapy, but it can also be very useful for people who are not seeing a therapist. There is good evidence to suggest that the ideas and techniques of CBT can work well when used by people on their own, in a self-help format such as this book. Good self-help books will explain the principles behind CBT, and suggest ways of making changes. This approach is what this book is all about.

Since its first development CBT has kept changing and progressing. Clinicians and researchers have continued to look at ways to make it more effective and to develop new ideas and techniques that will help those with psychological problems such as depression. We have been very lucky that the people responsible for many of these developments in CBT have agreed to write the chapters describing their approaches.

This book is split into four parts. In Part 1 we will start with the basics: what depression is and what causes it, and the ideas and techniques of CBT that have made such a big impact on how people deal with depression.

Part 2 gives more detailed information about techniques for tackling depression, such as becoming more active, or learning to be kind to yourself.

Part 3 looks at specific problems that are common in depression, such as sleeping difficulties and low self-esteem.

Finally, Part 4 considers the treatment of depression in a number of special cases. One of these is where people experience marked swings between low mood and extremely high mood. Others include depression in the elderly, in people with poor physical health, and in the time around childbirth.

We hope we have included everything that you will need to overcome your depression.

Introduction: Making the most of this book

In this section we are going to talk a lot more about CBT and how you can use it to help yourself. Before starting, it may be helpful to think a bit about what you want to get out of this book. You might just want to get some information about depression, or about CBT. Alternatively, you might want to work through it in a systematic way as if you were seeing a therapist.

Some people find that it is most helpful to read through everything before making a start, while others want to get straight to the most relevant bits, and still others like dipping in and out according to what grabs their attention. There's no right or wrong way, except that it would probably be useful to read through the introduction to CBT (pages 1–39) before you begin your self-help. For some people it will be clear that maybe one or two chapters are most relevant, while others may need to read more.

If you are worrying about a self-help approach, it's worth remembering that even when people work with a therapist, CBT puts a lot of emphasis on self-help. The therapist will explain things to you, and will show you ways of thinking or doing things differently. This book will try to do exactly the same thing – explain what is going on, and help you to work out what you can change.

Having said that, there is also evidence that people benefit more from a self-help approach when they have some support from someone else. The person supporting you can encourage you to keep going, and be there for you to bounce ideas off. Your supporter can be a partner, family member or friend – any of these may be helpful, provided that it is someone you can trust to be supportive. You will see tips for supporters dotted throughout this book, designed to assist them in helping you. If you don't have anyone to support you, though, don't worry; you can still benefit – and the tips can help you, too.

Here are some further ways of making the most of self-help.

- *Put aside a regular time to work through this book,* just as you would if you were seeing a therapist. Try to find a time when you can have half an hour or an hour to yourself, when you can really concentrate on yourself and what you need. This could be once or twice a week, depending on how you feel. You will get the most out of this book if you work through it on a regular basis, so be realistic about the best time to do this, and stick to it.

- *Get a notebook* – whether paper or electronic – where you can write down ideas and notes about what you are reading and keep track of what you are doing. Many of the self-help exercises involve writing things down, so having somewhere dedicated to do it will make it much easier.

- *Keep track of how you are doing,* so that you don't lose sight of changes you've made. As a first step, you could fill out and make a note of your score on the brief questionnaire about depression (Table 1: PHQ-9, shown on page 16) and the one about anxiety, if that's relevant to you (Table 2: GAD-7, shown on page 20), so you can come back to the scores later and see how you've improved.

- *Try things out.* It is very important that you try out the suggestions in this book. Just reading the exercises, without doing anything different, will not help nearly as much as actually doing them. You wouldn't expect to get fitter by reading a book about exercise, but not actually doing any. Obviously that won't work! The same is true here. You need to put our suggestions into action if they are going to do any good.

- *Don't worry if you find it difficult at first.* Sometimes making changes can be very difficult, and it can be hard to believe that it is going to work. CBT can take a bit of time and repeated practice before you start to feel different. Again, as with exercise, you need to persevere.

If you went to the gym once and then went home and said, 'I don't look any different, so that doesn't work,' most people would tell you that you need to keep going. It's a bit like that with CBT – you need to persevere for a while before you see the benefits.

- *Remember that everyone is different,* so what works for you may be different from what works for someone else. The best approach is to pick one of the techniques and try it out for yourself for a reasonable period of time, perhaps a week or two. If it helps, even a little bit, then it is worth continuing, and perhaps adding another technique. If it does not help after a reasonable trial, then try a different technique. But remember, self-help isn't always for everyone, so if you have given this a good try and it doesn't seem to be making any difference, don't feel disheartened. Instead, visit your GP and discuss what you've been doing and they will be able to discuss other options with you. They may suggest that you try one-to-one therapy or a different treatment approach altogether.

Key messages

- The self-help approach can sometimes work better if you have someone to support and encourage you, so think about whether you'd like to find someone to be your supporter as you work through the book.

- Remember that making changes can be difficult at first, but as you go on it will get easier.

- Like starting to exercise, you need to keep at it. Don't give up if it doesn't seem to work immediately – keep going and you will begin to see changes.

- If you've given it a good try but still don't feel different, then don't feel disheartened. Self-help isn't for everyone, and your GP can help you to think about alternatives.

Tips for supporters

- Help the person you are supporting to organize themselves with a notebook, and to make a time for their therapy.

- Decide between the two of you exactly what you are going to do. Will you be present at every session? Or are you only going to be there when the person you're supporting needs help? Or something in between?

- Make clear what time you will have available. If you don't live with the person you are supporting, decide on a way of making contact that suits both of you.

- Encourage them to make a note of the symptoms they have been experiencing and their score on the questionnaires (if they want to use them).

- Help them to decide whether they need to have any discussions with their GP before they start. This will be particularly important if they are having suicidal thoughts, or if they aren't sure what is wrong with them. Finally, it would probably be a good idea if you could read this book, too.

PART 1

Introduction to depression and CBT – the basics

Understanding depression

1 What is depression?

What depression can feel like

Mark is a young man of thirty-two whose family have had a business for generations. Recently, however, the business has been in difficulties and they are struggling to keep going. To make things worse, an innovation Mark tried lost them money. Mark feels a complete failure. He thinks that he is completely responsible for the business, and he cannot think what to do to keep it. He knows that he is going to let everybody down.

Sally is a forty-six-year-old woman with two teenage children. She used to work as a teaching assistant, but left when her new boss made it clear that she didn't like her. She feels completely useless – the children don't need her any more, and she can't even contribute financially. Once the children go to school she sits on the sofa and cannot make herself move to do anything. She has started to think that no one likes her or wants her around, so has stopped contacting her sisters and friends.

Barry is a twenty-year-old who has just gone to university. He was having a fantastic time in his first term, staying up late and going to every party he could find. But a few weeks into term he found that people were keeping away from him, saying they just couldn't keep up. Even so, he felt fantastic. He had loads of energy, and in tutorials was full of brilliant ideas. He talked and talked, and got very irritable if people didn't seem to listen – but he talked over them anyway. He hardly slept because there were so many interesting things to do, and didn't bother to eat much either. After a couple of weeks like this, he was surprised to find that his tutor was worried and asked him to see the college nurse. He thought it was ridiculous!

If you have picked up this book, then the chances are that you already know something about depression. You may know what it feels like for you, and how it affects you. You may know how it is affecting someone close to you, and see the sorrow and frustration that it brings. Or you may be working with people who get depressed, and you want to explore more about how to help.

Although you may have some previous knowledge of depression, we aim in the next few chapters to describe it clearly, and to separate some of the myths from the facts. We will discuss why some people get depressed and what keeps depression going, and we will talk about effective ways to treat it. Finally, we will help you to think about whether you are depressed and, most importantly, how you can use this book to improve your mood.

What do we mean by depression?

What is depression? Is it an illness? Is it different from being unhappy, or being in a mood? Why does the title of the book include 'low mood' as well as depression? We use the word 'depression' in so many different ways that it can be very confusing, and can lead to misunderstandings. We will try to reduce some of this confusion.

First, the word 'depression' can be used just to mean a mood – it describes how we feel. For instance, someone might say she felt depressed if she looked out of the window and saw that it was still raining, so she couldn't go out, or if she hoped a friend would ring but they haven't. In this situation many of us might say 'I'm so depressed!'

Now imagine Clare, who has moved job to a new town, and doesn't know anyone. The job is going OK, but she is very lonely and can't seem to make friends. After a few weeks she realizes that she is actually feeling low a lot of the time. She feels OK at work, but once she's at home she doesn't know what to do with herself, and life starts to feel very bleak. Next, imagine what might happen if Clare lost her job in the new town, and couldn't move because she couldn't sell her new house. Now she constantly feels very bad. She spends a lot of time just sitting on the sofa staring into space. She can't summon up the energy to do anything, and there doesn't seem any point anyway. She can't see a way out of her predicament, and is starting to believe that she'll never be able to do anything right, and it's probably what she deserves anyway.

In these examples, it is clear that in the first case the person is not depressed – it's just a bad day. In the third case, it's easy to see that Clare is depressed. The depression is severe, it goes on all the time, and she's stopped being able to function. We could describe this state as a 'major depressive disorder', if we wanted to use psychiatric terms. Some people might also refer to this as being 'clinically depressed' (but see below about the use of this term). If we used a questionnaire to look at her symptoms, we might categorize her as severely depressed.

The second case is a bit trickier. The depression hasn't yet taken over, but Clare is being affected by it, and feeling low quite a lot of the time. This case wouldn't fit into the psychiatric definition of a major depressive disorder, but she would probably get quite a high score on the questionnaire. We could describe her as being unhappy, but we could also describe her as having a mild or moderate level of depression.

Depression or unhappiness?

When we are thinking about the difference between depression and unhappiness, there are three things to consider:

- *The severity of the low mood*: how bad it feels. Do you feel very upset and in emotional pain a lot of the time? Do you find yourself crying, or start to think that life is not worth living? The worse these feelings get, the more it may be sensible to think of how you feel as depression rather than as unhappiness.

- *The persistence of the low mood*: is it there all the time, and does it go on and on without letting up? For instance, if you got a new job or made new friends, would you feel better? If not, then again it may be more sensible to think of how you feel as depression.

- *The extent to which it affects you*: as depression gets worse, you are likely to have more and more different symptoms, beyond just low mood – for example, your body and your behaviour are affected, and you find it increasingly difficult to function. We describe the symptoms of depression below, and if you experience more than a few of these, it is more likely that you are suffering from depression than normal unhappiness.

Does it matter what it's called?

The simplest way to think about this is that unhappiness may just be a different way of describing milder levels of depression. But does it matter what we call it? Most of us accept that at some point in our lives we are likely to be unhappy. Things sometimes go wrong, and life is not always easy. Regardless of what we call it, though, we should remember two things: it *is* natural to feel low sometimes, and you *can* do something to improve how you feel, and to tackle the problems that may be causing you to feel that way.

In the end it probably doesn't matter too much what we call it. We will talk later in this section (page 16–18) about how to identify depression for yourself, but the ideas and strategies that we will show you will be relevant whether the problem is low mood, unhappiness, or depression. So no matter how bad your feelings, the ideas in this book should help you. If you are quite badly depressed then you may need additional help (we will talk more about this on page 18) but hopefully there will still be things in this book that will enable you to cope with it better.

Symptoms of depression

Once people are depressed there are a whole range of symptoms that accompany the changes in mood. It is helpful to think of these in four different groups (we will come back to this in Chapters 4 and 6, which look at what keeps depression going).

- Emotional symptoms – the feelings you get inside
- Cognitive symptoms – your thoughts and beliefs
- Behavioural symptoms – the things you do and say
- Physical symptoms – the way your body reacts

Let's look in a bit more detail at each of these.

Emotional symptoms

The most obvious emotional symptom is of course feeling depressed. You may feel low, blue, down, fed up – people have many ways of describing their low moods. Another part of the picture is that you don't feel good any more – you may lose interest in things, and lack any sense of enjoyment, even of things that you would previously have enjoyed. Some depressed people find that their emotions are almost entirely absent: everything just feels flat and grey all the time.

Cognitive symptoms

There are two aspects to depressive thinking.

First, there can be problems with the *process of thinking*. You might find it hard to concentrate, or to make decisions; you might feel that you can't focus on a topic, or notice that you are reading the same sentence in a magazine or book over and over. You might have trouble remembering things.

The second category is to do with the *content of your thoughts*. This is at the core of depression, and we will come back to it throughout this book, since it is here that much of CBT focuses. The content of depressive thinking is very negative: about yourself ('I'm a complete failure – nothing I do is any good'); about the world in general ('Life is difficult and nothing ever works out well'); and about the future ('It's always going to be like this'). Depression makes you see everything in the most negative light.

Sometimes these negative thoughts can be so bad that you start to have thoughts about death and suicide, even to the extent of starting to plan how you might do it. *If this is the case with you, then please go straight to page 18–19 where we talk about what to do if you feel like this.*

Physical symptoms

This category of symptoms is to do with the way that our bodies react when we get depressed. When the symptoms get bad, it really is like having an illness. There are a number of ways in which your body can be affected:

- *Tiredness, low energy and fatigue.* This is one of the most common physical symptoms of depression, and can make it very difficult for you to do anything.

- *Sleep difficulties.* You may find it difficult to go off to sleep, wake up frequently throughout the night, or wake up very early in the morning and not get back to sleep. You may find that you seem to sleep OK, but that you don't feel refreshed. You may also find that you sleep *more* than usual – you might fall asleep in the day, or sleep for unusually long periods at night.

- *Diurnal variation.* This means that your mood may be consistently better or worse at some times of day. The most common pattern is for people to feel worse in the morning, and then to pick up as the day goes on. *Early-morning wakening* is when people wake up very early, and feel very low indeed. Some people experience different patterns of variation over the day, but this is the most common.

- *Appetite and weight problems.* Like sleep, this can go either way. You may find that you have no appetite and that you lose weight without meaning to. Or you may find that you are unusually hungry, craving food. This is usually unhealthy food, high in fat and carbohydrate, rather than healthy food. You may find that you are putting on a lot of weight, which then makes you feel even worse about yourself.

- *Sexual problems.* It is very common for people to lose any interest in sex when they are depressed. Depression can also make it difficult for your body to function sexually. This can cause additional problems for partners, which we will come back to later (Chapter 20) and again it may make you feel worse.

- *Being slowed down or agitated.* People with severe depression may find that their whole body slows down. They find it hard to walk at more than a snail's pace, and take a long time answering the most simple question. This is sometimes called *psychomotor retardation*. It can also go the other way, so that people can be physically overactive, and find it difficult to sit still. You may find that you are pacing around the room, or pulling your hair, or wringing your hands. We call this state *psychomotor agitation*.

Behavioural symptoms

This category of symptoms refers to what we do when we are depressed. Remember that when you are depressed you may have little energy or confidence, and get little pleasure from anything. This means that it can be very hard to make yourself do anything. Typically, people start to withdraw from activities that they used to do. You might find yourself making excuses not to take part in something you've agreed to do, not returning phone calls from people, not managing to get to the shops or tidy up at home. You might avoid doing things that need doing, like paying bills or mending the car. As the behavioural symptoms get worse, you may find that you have stopped doing almost anything and that you are spending a lot of time sitting or lying around. You might stop taking care of yourself physically and find it hard even to get up and wash.

Classification of depression

We said earlier that it does not matter exactly what name we give to how you are feeling. Nevertheless, mental-health professionals who work with people experiencing depression often use a system that helps them to gain a more objective view of the problems their patients are describing. There are two such systems in common use. The American Psychiatric Association's system is called the Diagnostic and Statistical Manual of Mental Disorders, or DSM-5. The other, which is used more in the UK, is called the International Classification of Diseases, or ICD-10. The numbers refer to the number of times that the systems have been revised, which shows that classifying mental disorders is not a straightforward task.

DSM-5 looks at a list of symptoms that includes depressed mood, loss of pleasure, weight changes, sleep changes, being agitated or slowed down, loss of energy, feelings of worthlessness, concentration difficulties and thoughts of death or suicide. It defines a 'major depressive episode' as having five or more of these symptoms most of the day, nearly every day, for a continuous period of two weeks or more. In addition, the symptoms must cause the sufferer significant distress or affect how they are able to function.

Similarly, ICD-10 looks at the key symptoms of low mood, loss of interest or pleasure, and fatigue, and then considers further symptoms including: disturbed sleep; poor concentration or indecisiveness; low self-confidence; poor or increased appetite; suicidal thoughts or acts; agitation or slowing of movements; and guilt/self-blame. These ten symptoms define the degree of depression, which could be:

- Not depressed (fewer than four symptoms)
- Mild depression (four symptoms)
- Moderate depression (five to six symptoms)
- Severe depression (seven or more symptoms)

ICD-10 also says that the symptoms need to be present for most of every day, and should be there for a month or more.

Dysthymia

Dysthymia, or dysthymic disorder, refers to a more 'grumbling', low-level form of depression, in which you do not have the full range of symptoms that make a major depressive disorder, but you still feel very low and may not function as well as you could. In order to meet the diagnosis for dysthymia these symptoms have to go on for a long time – at least two years before the diagnosis is made. It may not be as intense as major depression, but it affects your ability to function and makes life difficult for you.

Bipolar depression and cyclothymia

These terms refer to people who do not just get depressed but also have times when the pendulum swings the other way. At these times their mood is unnaturally high, and they become excessively energetic and optimistic – sometimes very unrealistically so. These high periods are known as *mania*. At other times the high mood can be more agitated and irritable than excited and happy. This problem of mood fluctuations between extreme highs and extreme lows used to be known as *manic depression*, but these days it is more often referred to as *bipolar disorder* (because your mood can be at either 'pole', or end, of a scale). As with depression/dysthymia, there is also a less extreme version of bipolar disorder, when your mood fluctuates from high to low in a less exaggerated way: this is known as *cyclothymia*. (Chapter 21 later in this book talks in more detail about these problems.)

A word about terminology

Throughout this book a number of authors have used the term 'clinical depression' to describe major or severe depression. However, clinical depression is not a diagnosis in itself – it's really a shorthand way of referring to these severe depressions.

Other problems that go with depression

As if depression on its own were not enough, many people who get depressed also experience other problems with their mood. Two of the most common are anxiety, and irritability or anger.

Anxiety

Anxiety very often accompanies depression, but it can also be a problem in its own right. So how can you tell which is which? Are you anxious because you are depressed, or depressed because you are anxious? Which should you try to tackle first? In order to work this out, there are a couple of questions you might ask yourself:

- Which came first? If you started to suffer from anxiety, have not got better, and have found life increasingly difficult and limited, then it is not surprising that you would get low in mood as a result. In this case, it is probably sensible to tackle the anxiety problems first, since it is likely that the depression will improve when the anxiety starts to get better.

- Which is more prominent at the moment? If the anxiety is there some of the time, but the depression never goes away, it may be a good idea to focus more on the depression.

Sometimes it can be very difficult to tell which is worse, or which came first, and in this case professionals normally operate by the rule that depression 'trumps' anxiety. In other words, if you're not sure, focus on depression first.

As in depression, it can be helpful to think of anxiety symptoms in these four categories:

- *Emotional*: feeling tense, edgy, nervous, anxious.

- *Cognitive*: your attention is drawn to things that might present a risk or threat to you. You may have thoughts like 'Something terrible is going to happen', 'I'll die', or 'I'll make a terrible fool of myself'.

- *Physical*: these are particularly prominent in anxiety and include racing heart, shortness of breath, light-headedness, 'butterflies' in the stomach, trembling, dry mouth, sweating, muscle tension and many others.

- *Behavioural*: when people are anxious they tend to avoid the things that make them feel worse, sometimes to the extent that they can't go out at all, or can't face dealing with life's problems. People also use 'safety behaviours' a lot – ways to make themselves feel safe if they do have to confront the situations they fear.

On page 20 there is a brief questionnaire that you can use to help you decide how big a problem anxiety is for you.

If you remain unsure about which to tackle, then your GP should be able to help you think about it and can refer you to the right places for help, if that is what you need. If you want to tackle anxiety yourself, then some useful contacts are listed in the Other Resources section of Appendix 1. You could also have a look at the companion book to this one – *The Complete CBT Guide for Anxiety* (see page 540).

Anger and irritability

Of course people can be angry and irritable for a variety of reasons, but these emotions are often a part of depression. Again, let's describe the symptoms in our four groups:

- *Emotional*: angry, furious, irritable, tense, wound up, 'having a short fuse'.

- *Cognitive*: you may be preoccupied with seeing yourself as having been badly or unfairly treated, or about wider injustice. You may be angry about big things, such as the abuse and cruelty that we see in the world, or about small things: your partner should not leave their coffee cup for you to wash up; your children should not leave their toys all over the house; that driver should not have cut you up on the roundabout. The angry thoughts may be worse if you feel the unfair behaviour shows that people are disrespecting you.

- *Physical*: you may be aware of churning feelings in your stomach, feelings of heat in your body, tense and painful muscles, tears of rage. People sometimes talk about a 'red mist' coming over them.

- *Behavioural*: at milder levels of anger and irritability you may be snapping at people around you, telling them off, or cutting them off and ignoring them. It can mean banging doors and slamming things around. More seriously, though, people can become violent to those close to them, or cause fights and accidents outside the home. Anger and irritability can cause problems with relationships, particularly if families or work colleagues are not aware that it is a result of depression.

If these symptoms ring a bell, especially if you are afraid that you cannot control your anger and may cause harm to someone else, then it would be good to go and talk to your doctor. On pages 539–40 there is a list of books and other resources that may help you.

When the anger is a part of depression, it may help to accept that you *are* depressed. Sometimes anger can mask depressive feelings that we don't want to acknowledge to ourselves or to others because we are ashamed of them. If you can admit that you are feeling depressed, you may initially feel that you have let yourself down. In the long run, however, it will be much better. You will know what the problem is, and will be able to get the right help, or use the right self-help resources. Furthermore, when you are angry it is very difficult for other people, especially people you are close to. It will be much easier for them to cope with your anger if they understand that you are depressed.

If you think you are feeling excessively anxious and/or angry, don't worry too much, because when you start to work on your depression you will probably find that the other problems start to improve too. See how it goes when your depression starts to get better, and then if there is still a significant problem with anxiety or anger you can consider trying to address them more directly.

Key messages

- The word depression covers a wide range of different states, from quite mild upset to serious and debilitating conditions.

- The ideas and techniques of cognitive therapy outlined in this book are relevant no matter how serious your depression is, or what exactly it is called.

- It is helpful to think of any kind of depression in terms of four types of symptoms: emotional, cognitive, behavioural and physical.

- Sometimes depression is accompanied by other kinds of feelings, typically anxiety or anger, which may need to be understood and helped as well.

Tips for supporters

- As we've seen, depression can be quite a complicated mixture of feelings, thoughts, behaviours and physical problems, and anxiety and anger are often a part of it.

- When people are depressed it is very difficult for them to think clearly about what's happening to them.

- Help the person you are supporting to think about whether they are depressed, or whether they might be suffering from anxiety or anger. The questionnaires at the start of Chapter 2 should help with this, so encourage the person you are supporting to fill them out.

- You could also help the person to think about how they feel in terms of the four groups of symptoms – this will be very useful later.

2 Are you depressed?

Since you are reading this book, it's likely that you are wondering if you are depressed. One way to decide is to go back to the symptoms described in the first chapter. If you recognize yourself in these descriptions then it is likely that you are suffering from some degree of depression.

There are also questionnaires that can help you to think about it. One of the most commonly used of these is the Patient Health Questionnaire, or PHQ-9. This is a quick questionnaire used by many GPs and psychology services to help decide whether someone is depressed (and also to measure progress once therapy has started). Table 1 below shows the PHQ-9. Use the questionnaire yourself by reading each of the statements and putting a circle round the number that best describes the degree to which you agree with it. A zero would mean that you don't feel or experience what is being described at all; a three would mean that you feel it most of the time or all of the time. Once you've circled the numbers in the columns, add up each column and write the total at the bottom, then add these together to get your total score.

Table 1:
Patient Health Questionnaire (PHQ-9) to assess depression

Over the last 2 weeks, how often have you been bothered by any of the following problems?	Not at all	Several days	More than half the days	Nearly every day
1. Little interest or pleasure in doing things	0	1	2	3
2. Feeling down, depressed or hopeless	0	1	2	3

3. Trouble falling or staying asleep, or sleeping too much	0	1	2	3
4. Feeling tired or having little energy	0	1	2	3
5. Poor appetite or overeating	0	1	2	3
6. Feeling bad about yourself – or that you are a failure, or have let yourself or your family down	0	1	2	3
7. Trouble concentrating on things, such as reading the newspaper or watching television	0	1	2	3
8. Moving or speaking so slowly that other people could have noticed; or the opposite – being so fidgety or restless that you have been moving around a lot more than usual	0	1	2	3
9. Thoughts that you would be better off dead, or of hurting yourself in some way	0	1	2	3
Add each column's scores:				

Add together all column scores to get TOTAL SCORE: _____

Finally, if you checked off **any** problems, how difficult have these problems made it for you to do your work, take care of things at home, or get along with other people?	Not difficult at all ❑	Somewhat difficult ❑	Very difficult ❑	Extremely difficult ❑

If you scored at least 'Somewhat difficult' on that last question, then your score can be interpreted as follows:

0–4   No depression

5–9   Mild depression

10–14   Moderate depression

15–19   Moderately severe depression

20 or more Severe depression

It is important to say that your score on the PHQ-9 is not by itself a psychiatric diagnosis, but a high score is an indication that you may need help. You can also use the PHQ-9 again as you work through the book to see how you are doing – when things start to improve you should see your score drop.

What if my depression is very bad?

This book contains many ideas and techniques that will be helpful for all sorts of depression. But sometimes a self-help book is not enough, particularly if your depression is quite severe, and you may need additional help. This could be either psychological therapy or medication – we talk more about the latter in Chapter 5 – or maybe even both. Psychological therapies, particularly CBT, are now much more widely available on the NHS than they used to be. The main way to get access to psychological therapies is to visit your GP, tell him or her how you are feeling, and ask for a referral. Your GP will also be able to discuss various treatment options, and will discuss with you whether medication could help. Another option is to call NHS 111, who can give advice about what to do in your particular case.

A special note on thoughts about harming yourself or ending your life

Question 9 in the questionnaire above asked if you have thoughts about harming yourself, or if you have thoughts that you would be better off dead.

Sometimes when your mood gets very low you can start to think that there really is no hope and no escape, and that you and other people might be better off if you were not around. If you recognize these thoughts, and fear that you are feeling suicidal, please get help straight away. If there is someone around whom you trust, then let them know how you feel, so that they can help you to keep safe. You can make an

appointment with your GP or physician, and don't let the reception-
ists tell you that you will need to wait – you are a priority. If it is out
of hours, then your local Accident and Emergency department (A&E)
has people who can help. You don't have to live with these thoughts
and feelings on your own. The right assistance for recovery is available. We will say a little more about dealing with these thoughts
on page 109.

Symptoms of anxiety

Another useful questionnaire, also used by GPs and other professionals, is called the Generalized Anxiety Disorder questionnaire (GAD-7),
which is shown below in Table 2. As we said earlier, it is very common
for people who are depressed to experience problems with anxiety,
too. This questionnaire can give you an idea of how bad the anxiety
problems are. If you are scoring in the moderate or severe range (a total
score of 10 or more on the questions below), then you may need to get
professional help for the anxiety as well. If you are not sure whether
anxiety or depression is the main problem for you, then go to your GP
and talk it through with him or her, so you can be confident of what to
tackle first.

Table 2:

Generalized Anxiety Disorder Questionnaire (GAD–7) to assess anxiety

Over the last 2 weeks, how often have you been bothered by any of the following problems?	Not at all	Several days	More than half the days	Nearly every day
1. Feeling nervous, anxious or on edge	0	1	2	3
2. Not being able to stop or control worrying	0	1	2	3
3. Worrying too much about different things	0	1	2	3
4. Trouble relaxing	0	1	2	3
5. Being so restless that it's hard to sit still	0	1	2	3
6. Becoming easily annoyed or irritable	0	1	2	3
7. Feeling afraid, as if something awful might happen	0	1	2	3
Add each column's scores:				

Add together all column scores to get TOTAL SCORE: _____

Finally, if you checked off any problems, how difficult have these problems made it for you to do your work, take care of things at home, or get along with other people?	Not difficult at all ❑	Somewhat difficult ❑	Very difficult ❑	Extremely difficult ❑

If you scored at least 'Somewhat difficult' on that last question, then your score can be interpreted as follows:

0–4   No anxiety

5–9   Mild anxiety

10–14   Moderate anxiety

15 or more Severe depression

Key messages

- In order to help you think about whether you are depressed and/ or anxious, try filling in the PHQ-9 and GAD-7.

- If you can't work out the best way forward, then go and talk to your GP or to someone else you trust, to ask for their help in making the decision.

- If your depression is very bad, and you are having thoughts about ending your life, then get yourself to a doctor or mental-health professional as soon as possible, so that you can start to get the help you need.

Tips for supporters

- Hopefully the person that you are supporting has filled in the questionnaires by now, so help them with scoring and making sense of the scores – it can be quite muddling for someone who's not feeling great!

- If you or the person you are supporting are not clear what the main problem is, or if either of you is worried that the depression or other problems are very severe, then help them get to the doctor. It may only need a single appointment and then you can both go back to working with this approach.

- Sometimes people are worried about going to the doctor in case they are whisked off to hospital. Reassure the person you are supporting that this is very unlikely. Only people with the most severe problems are taken to hospital, and then only after other things have been tried.

3 Myths and facts about depression

It can be very hard for people to talk about depression, and they often suffer on their own. Sometimes people feel too ashamed to admit to feeling depressed, and worry about what other people will think. Often people have been encouraged to keep things to themselves. This has been getting better over the last few years, but for a lot of people there is still a great deal of shame. Because people have not talked openly about depression, it has been easy for myths about it to develop. Happily there does seem to have been a shift in attitudes in recent years, and a number of prominent people have openly spoken about their own problems with depression: for example Alistair Campbell, who worked very closely with ex-Prime Minister Tony Blair, and Steven Fry, the author and TV personality.

The myths about depression may make it harder for people when they are depressed, so we will talk about some of the main ones below.

Myths

'It's weak and pathetic – only losers get depressed.'

This used to be a common view. Many of us have been told to keep a stiff upper lip, or pull our socks up, or snap out of it. You may have tried to take this tack yourself. The problem is that it doesn't work very well. The British government spends hundreds of millions of pounds a year helping people with depression. If it was just a matter of snapping out of it, we could save a lot of money! And remember that more and more people now feel able to say that they get depressed – and they are certainly not people you would think of as weak and pathetic losers. Winston Churchill famously talked about the 'black dog' of his depression, and since he led Britain to victory in the Second World War he could hardly be described as a loser! Another person clearly not a loser is J.K. Rowling, the author of the amazingly popular Harry Potter books. Seven years after graduating from university, Rowling said she saw herself as a failure. She was diagnosed with depression and has described how she contemplated suicide. As everyone knows, she went on to become one of the most successful and well-known authors in the world!

'I don't deserve to get help.'

You may believe that you don't deserve to get help, and that it's right that you feel the way you do. You might believe that this is a punishment because you are such a bad person, or have done so many terrible things. This can make it very difficult to accept help and to take the steps you need to take to get better. But thoughts like this are really the depression talking. Guilt and self-blame are recognized symptoms of depression, and shame is extremely common too. So believing that you don't deserve help is itself a symptom of depression. Try to put these thoughts aside so that you can concentrate on getting better. Chapter 10 will show you how to start doing this.

'Depression is biological – only pills can help.'

We are going to talk in the next section about the causes of depression and we will see that for some people there is a biological factor. But this does not mean that there is nothing you can do. Diabetes is biological, but sufferers can be helped enormously by adapting their diet and lifestyle. No matter what the cause of your depression, there is a great deal that you can do to help.

'This isn't depression – it's just me, and there's nothing that anyone can do.'

This myth is often particularly strong for people who have spent much of their lives feeling depressed. It may be because they have had difficult lives from a very early age, and have never had a chance to feel OK about themselves or about the world. But actually what this means is that you may have been depressed for a very long time – we recognize now that children do become depressed – and your depression can still respond to treatment. Although it can be very difficult to believe that things *can* change, we know that people can improve enormously if they start to understand depression and what keeps it going. It is not a life sentence!

'Other people can cope with their lives; I should be able to cope with mine. It's my fault.'

When you are depressed it is very easy to think that you are the only one, and that everyone else can cope. But take a look at the statistics in the next section, 'Facts'. Depression is much more common than you may think, and you may know a lot of people who are depressed. Remember that people are often ashamed of it, and will try to hide it. It may be that if you haven't seen someone around for a while it's because they're depressed and are withdrawing from things they used to do. Or maybe you see them but don't realize they are not coping – maybe they don't acknowledge you when you see them, which has made you assume that you've done something to offend them, not realizing that they are depressed. A character in the novel *Rachel's Holiday* by Marian Keyes says, 'The trouble with us is that we compare our insides to other people's outsides' – and it's true. We only see other people's outsides, and we often don't know how they feel inside.

You may have noticed that most of these myths concern the shame, self-blame and hopelessness that depression can cause. But these thoughts are themselves symptoms of it – it's the depression making you think this way. In Chapters 9 and 10 we will look more closely at thoughts in depression, and consider different ways to tackle these.

Facts

Having read about some of the myths surrounding depression, what about the facts?

Depression is much more common than many people imagine. Different studies have used different ways of measuring how many people are affected, but most estimates suggest that around one in six people will be depressed enough to require treatment at some point in their lives and that women are more likely to be affected than men. That means that if you know fifty people, around eight of them are likely to be significantly depressed at some point.

The majority of people who get depressed get better within a year, but approximately one in five don't completely recover. Although they may have experienced an improvement in their mood, they still have some symptoms and difficulties. Approximately half of those who have had a period of depression will experience another episode within the following two years. This means that getting the right help, and learning how to manage your symptoms, is crucial. CBT is particularly important because it has been shown to reduce the risk of repeated episodes of depression.

Key messages

- Depression is very common but it has been shrouded in secrecy and fear for a long time, so there are a lot of myths about it.

- These myths go against what we know about depression and how it can be helped.

- Believing the myths can make it harder to go for therapy.

Tips for supporters

- Help the person you are supporting to think about these myths. Do they share them? Do you? Carefully consider your own views about depression.

- Try to have an honest discussion about your thoughts on depression. It's much better to get things out in the open.

4 Why do people get depressed?

Why do we get depressed? Is it biological? Is it to do with our lives? Our parents' genes? The bullies at school? There is no one answer to this question: many different factors can be involved, and we will describe the major ones here.

Biological factors

Heredity

It is thought that people inherit genes that make them more or less likely to develop depression, just as they inherit genes that determine the colour of their eyes, or whether they are tall or short. If you have ever spoken to a doctor about depression, you may have been asked whether other people in your family have been depressed. If you have a family history of depression, especially in your siblings or parents, then you may be at higher risk. However, just because you have depression in the family, it does *not* mean that you are definitely going to get it. And if a parent was depressed when you were growing up, that may have affected you through its impact on family life, rather than because you have inherited certain genes.

Brains and biology

When you are depressed there are a number of physical changes in the brain, both in levels of chemicals called *neurotransmitters*, which carry messages around the brain, and the levels of electrical activity. However, when you recover from depression these changes are reversed and the brain goes back to normal. It's difficult to say whether these changes cause depression, but they certainly accompany it.

Other physical problems may also contribute to depression. Having an underactive thyroid gland, or *hypothyroidism*, can cause depression. Because there is a connection between depression symptoms and other medical conditions, a doctor may ask for blood tests, especially if there are other reasons to suspect that you may have one of these problems. Furthermore, people who experience a lot of physical pain are susceptible to depression, and so are people with long-term illnesses. Being physically run down can play a big part in bringing your mood down, which can lead into a vicious circle. As you get depressed, you may get more run down physically, making it harder to cope, which may worsen the depression.

Difficult life experiences

Early life experiences

It is possible that you had a difficult life from an early age. Your parents may have separated or died when you were young, or they may not have known how to look after a young child. Sometimes parents don't look after children properly because they are preoccupied with their own problems, and sadly sometimes because they are actively cruel. Or perhaps your parents had very high expectations of you, and you never felt that you were good enough. Perhaps things were all right when you were very young, but you were bullied later in childhood.

All these experiences may make us more likely to develop depression as we grow up. Chapter 15 talks about how we can combat the memories from our early experience which can contribute to this process, and Chapter 18, on tackling low self-esteem, also gives us tools to overcome the impact of early experiences.

Life events

Things may have been going reasonably well, but then something major happens in our life – what is sometimes called a 'major life event'. Maybe we lose our job. Maybe someone very important to us has died, or we have separated from or divorced our partner. Such difficult experiences increase the risk of becoming depressed.

Ongoing stress or 'hassles'

Sometimes it doesn't take a big event to make us depressed. Instead, it can be brought on by smaller problems that just seem to go on and on, with no end in sight. Maybe we have financial problems, or we are living in very bleak circumstances. Maybe we are in a difficult relationship that we don't feel able to leave or in which we often feel put down. Maybe we have terrible neighbours who keep us awake all night and we fear they will never move away.

Whichever kind of problems in life we are talking about, it is our view of ourselves and the world around us that is crucial in depression.

What we are talking about here are things that make you *vulnerable* to developing depression: they make depression more likely. If you have a vulnerability to depression, for whatever reason, it doesn't mean that you will *definitely* get depressed. If your life goes well then you are likely to be fine. It just means that if things go wrong, then you are more likely to get depressed than someone who doesn't have the same vulnerability.

These various factors also add up. If you have a genetic vulnerability, *and* your early life was difficult, *and* you have problems later in life, then the chances that you will get depressed are greatly increased.

Different factors affecting the development of depression

All the above factors can contribute to depression in different ways, which we can put together like this:

Predisposing or vulnerability factors

These are the things that make us vulnerable to depression, possibly from a very early age. Our genetic make-up and our early experiences are both examples of vulnerability factors. They make us vulnerable to depression but do not necessarily in themselves cause it.

Precipitating factors or triggers

These are things that happen to us later in life, which turn that vulnerability to depression into an actual problem. Major life events or ongoing stresses are common examples of factors that might turn vulnerability into a reality. Physical illness might also be a trigger.

Maintaining factors

Maintaining factors are processes that keep the depression going once it has started. Sometimes these maintaining factors can be external – life events and stresses. For example, it may be that you started to get depressed because you split up from your partner, but even though you start to get over that, the depression is maintained because in the past your partner made all your social arrangements, so you now feel isolated and lonely.

Very often, however, maintaining factors are things that we do or think. You might tell yourself that no one wants to talk to you now you are on your own, and so you withdraw from any kind of social event. Those thoughts and behaviours mean that you don't see old friends or make new ones, and as a result become more and more lonely and isolated. Understanding these maintaining factors is a major part of CBT, and we will talk about this in detail later on, in Chapter 6.

Protective factors

Finally, there is one other important aspect. These are not factors that *make* us depressed but those that protect us, or help us *not* to become depressed. Having someone who is close to you, to whom you can talk when things get difficult, is a strong protective factor. Having a job that you enjoy, and which makes you feel valued, can also be a protective factor. Sometimes the protective factors are not enough to stop depression completely, but they do keep it in check and help to stop it getting as bad as it might otherwise do.

How these factors fit together can be seen in Figure 3 below.

Figure 3: What makes people depressed?

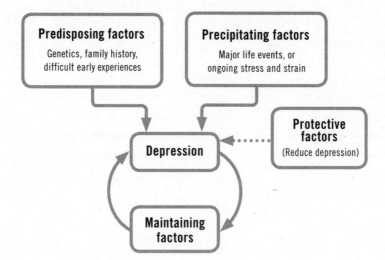

We can see, therefore, that how and why people get depressed is complicated; there is no single easy answer. To get a full picture we need to understand what is happening in each of these areas.

Using this understanding in therapy

Understanding why we are depressed can help greatly to make sense of our experience, and to stop us blaming ourselves, so it can be a very useful exercise. However, although this may sound a bit contradictory, it's not absolutely necessary. CBT is particularly interested in working out and tackling the *maintaining* factors, because if we understand what keeps the depression going then we can make changes that will stop it. We will talk in more detail about this later in Part 1.

Key messages

- Depression has no single cause, but is brought about by a combination of many different factors. These include:

- *Predisposing factors* – things that make you vulnerable to developing depression. These can be both inherited and from life experiences.

- *Precipitating factors* – things that trigger depression, such as difficult life events, or ongoing problems.

- *Maintaining factors* – processes that keep the depression going.

- There are also *protective factors*, which help to guard against depression.

Tips for supporters

- Help the person you are supporting to think about the key things in their own lives that might have made them vulnerable to depression.

  ◊   Did many of their family members have depression?

  ◊   Was their early childhood very difficult?

  ◊   Have they had a lot of stressful events going on in their lives in recent years?

- Help the person to think about what is keeping the depression going at the moment. This is often a very important place to start making changes, so if you can identify maintaining factors that will be a great help.

- Are you aware of protective factors that the person may have forgotten about? Try to remind them of times they have coped, or ways they can help themselves. Remember that you may well be a protective factor yourself, particularly if you are a friend or family member!

5   Can depression be treated?

The short answer to this is 'Yes'! You may have heard of the National Institute for Health and Clinical Excellence, or NICE for short. It is NICE's job to produce guidance about treatment for a whole variety of physical and mental conditions. NICE reviews the available evidence and makes recommendations about what the NHS should offer people. If you want to know exactly what NICE says, then you can find their depression guidelines on the internet at: *www.nice.org.uk/CG90*, or look at their website at *www.nice.org.uk*.

NICE recommends the following interventions for depression.

Physical treatments

Antidepressant medication

There are a number of different types of antidepressant medication. The first of these were developed some time ago, and are known as the *tricyclic antidepressants*. The best known of these are probably amitriptyline, clomipramine and imipramine. Another common category from this time comprises the *monoamine oxidase inhibitors* (MAOIs). These drugs are effective, but for some people they have unpleasant side effects. More recently, other types of antidepressants have been developed. These are *selective serotonin reuptake inhibitors* (SSRIs) and *serotonin norepinephrine reuptake inhibitors* (SNRIs). All antidepressants need a prescription from a medical doctor, so if you are interested in taking them, make an appointment with your GP. The SSRIs are generally the ones that are tried first, but your GP will help you to decide which would be best for you.

There are a number of common questions that people have about anti-depressants:

Are they addictive?

No, they are not. When we talk about a drug being addictive we usually mean that when you take it for a while its effects start wearing off and you need to take bigger and bigger doses to get the same effect. Addiction also means that you may suffer bad side effects if you try to stop taking the drug. Antidepressants do not work like this – you can take the same dose over long periods of time and you will still get the same effect. However, some people do experience problems if they stop taking the drug suddenly and can feel a bit unwell. If you wish to stop taking your antidepressant medication, it's much better to do it gradually. Talk to your doctor about it, and s/he will be able to help you decide how to do it most sensibly. On the whole, although some people experience withdrawal effects (particularly if they stop suddenly), these are nothing like the major upheaval of coming off addictive drugs, and are much less likely to happen if you stop gradually.

Will I have to take my medication for ever?

Again, for most people, the answer to this is 'No'. Depending on how severe your depression is, the type you are suffering from, and whether it's the first time you've had it, you might be prescribed medication for a few months or years, but rarely for ever. Your doctor will be able to offer you individual guidance. If your depression has been severe, or if you've had more than one episode, then it's much better to stay on the medication for at least a year, even after the depression has improved, to reduce the likelihood of it coming back.

Do antidepressants just mask the problems that made me depressed in the first place?

It's helpful to think of antidepressants as a kind of chemical leg-up. It makes it easier to get back on the horse, but you still have to ride! Remember that when you are depressed your brain chemistry changes, and your thinking becomes much more negative. In this state, it can be difficult to solve the problems that made you depressed. Taking anti-depressants can put you into a stronger frame of mind so that you feel more able to tackle problems and make changes that are then likely to help prevent the depression from returning.

Non-prescription drugs

All the medications that we have described above need to be prescribed by a medical doctor. There are other things that you don't need a pre-scription for, but there is less reason to be confident that they will make a difference. For example, St John's Wort can be bought over the coun-ter at the pharmacy, and is thought to work in a similar way to SSRIs. However, you should always talk to your GP before taking St John's Wort as it can seriously alter the effect of other drugs you might be tak-ing (including the contraceptive pill).

Exercise

There is some evidence that physical exercise can help depression. It is probably not so helpful for people with the most severe types of depres-sion, but for milder cases it can make a huge difference. Assuming you don't have significant physical health problems, half an hour of physical exercise, three to five days per week, could be very beneficial.

Light therapy

For some people depression seems to come on only in the winter, when there is less natural light, and they recover in the spring when the days start to lengthen. This type of depression is known as Seasonal Affective Disorder, or SAD.

Light therapy is a way to treat SAD by exposure to artificial light. During light therapy, you sit or work near a device called a light therapy box; the box gives off bright light that mimics natural outdoor light. Light therapy is thought to work by directly affecting brain chemicals that may be linked to mood, thereby easing SAD symptoms. There are a number of devices on the market that can be bought without a prescription, but if you think that you may be suffering from SAD it is very sensible to talk to your doctor, or to someone who knows you well, so that you can be sure that this is the right way of understanding your depression.

Electroconvulsive therapy (ECT)

In ECT an electric current is passed through the brain to produce an epileptic fit. Nobody knows quite how this works, but for a minority of patients it has been shown to be very helpful. It is only ever used on people with the most severe depression where other interventions have not worked.

Keeping physically well

Although this isn't a treatment for depression, looking after yourself properly can be very important. If you are physically run down then you become more vulnerable to depression. So trying to eat sensibly, maintaining regular patterns of eating and going to bed, and keeping reasonably fit can help.

Psychological treatments

Psychological treatments have been found to be very effective in the treatment of depression. The most well-known of these is CBT, on which the advice in this book is based.

Research has shown that CBT self-help is especially effective if you have someone who can support you while you are doing it. This is why we suggest that you might like to involve a family member or friend as your supporter while you work through this book.

CBT is not the only psychological therapy that can help depression. One alternative is called Interpersonal Psychotherapy, or IPT. Like CBT, this is a structured therapy that is relatively brief, usually between twelve and sixteen sessions. (See pages 43–4 for more detail of the structure of CBT.) IPT takes as its starting point the idea that people are likely to get depressed when important relationships in their lives go wrong. The main focus of IPT is to help people understand and tackle relationship difficulties. Some forms of CBT can also help with this (see Chapter 20) but all IPT therapy concentrates on these issues. IPT is comparatively new in this country, so at the moment it can be harder to find an IPT therapist. If you think that this may be an approach you'd find helpful, then you could talk to your GP. There are also self-help books using the IPT approach which are listed in the Other Resources section on page 540.

Key messages

- There are many effective treatments for depression. The National Institute for Health and Clinical Excellence (NICE) publishes guidance on what the most effective treatments are – see *www.nice. org.uk.*

- There are two main categories of effective treatment: medication (antidepressants) and psychological therapy (such as CBT, which is the basis of this book).

- There is also evidence that exercise can be helpful in combating depression, particularly for milder kinds.

Tips for supporters

- If the person you are supporting wonders about taking medication, then encourage them to make an appointment to see their GP to discuss it.

- Remember that medication is not necessarily an *alternative* to self-help – it could make it easier to benefit from self-help.

- Encourage the person you are supporting to think about exercise.

Understanding CBT

6 The CBT model of depression

As we said in the introduction, this book is based on a form of therapy known as cognitive behavioural therapy (CBT). In this section we will look at some of the basic ideas of CBT, and how it can help with depression.

The basic ideas of CBT

The fundamental problem for most depressed people is *feeling* bad – feeling sad, low, flat, blue, down and so on. Not only do people suffer these bad feelings, but they also never feel any good or positive ones – this is known as *anhedonia*, or lack of pleasure. There are other important symptoms of depression as well, as we saw in Chapter 1, but fundamentally most depressed people want to change this emotional state and live a 'normal' life. Sadly, you can't just flip a switch and make yourself feel differently, but there are things that you can do. In order to understand this, we need to talk about two of the other key parts of depression which we described in Chapter 1: cognition and behaviour. This is why this approach is called cognitive behavioural therapy – it helps you to change your feelings by changing your cognitions (thoughts) and behaviour.

Just to recap, when we think about mental-health problems it is helpful to consider four groups of symptoms.

- *Emotion* refers to the *feelings* you have when you are depressed – the sadness, misery or desperation that you feel.

- *Cognition* means thoughts, beliefs, images and so on: the processes that go on in your head all the time (and therefore obviously cannot be known by other people unless you tell them). So it might be thoughts like 'Oh dear, I've made a mess of this'; beliefs like 'I am not worthwhile'; or images such as seeing yourself as ugly and unattractive.

- *Behaviour* means what you do: your actions, what you say, how you interact with other people and the world in general (so unlike cognition, behaviour is in principle observable by other people).

- *Physiology* refers to changes in your bodily state – for example, in depression this would include what are sometimes called *biological* symptoms, such as changes to your sleep and eating patterns, loss of energy, loss of sexual interest and so on.

The central idea of CBT is simply that our thoughts and behaviour have a powerful role in determining how we feel, and that therefore changing them can be an effective way to change our feelings. Let's look more closely at these two crucial systems.

Cognitions (thoughts)

Let's look at the role of thoughts first. Many of us tend to think that the way we feel is a simple result of what happens to us. For example, I lose my job and therefore I feel upset. In CBT we believe that this misses out a crucial step. If it was just the event that directly caused the feeling, then the same event should cause the same feeling in everyone – everybody who lost their job would feel the same way about it. But we know this is not true. Different people can have very different reactions to similar events. Many people would feel sad or anxious about losing their job, but some might be more angry than upset, whilst others might even be quite positive. CBT therapists take the view that what makes this crucial difference is the individual's interpretations of the event. It is not the event itself that makes me feel upset, but rather what I think about it – what I take that event to mean. In other words, events are always filtered through my own individual thoughts and beliefs about them. If I had different thoughts about the event, I would end up feeling a different way. If I thought 'How dare they, after all I've done for them!' I might feel angry, whereas if I think 'I wasn't enjoying the job anyway, and the redundancy money will help me make a new start', then I might feel quite positive about it.

Let's illustrate this with another simple example. Suppose you are walking along the street, and someone you know passes by without saying hello. What would you feel in this situation? A number of different reactions are possible, depending on what you think is happening. Table 4 below shows some possible reactions.

Table 4: Thoughts and feelings

Scenario: you walk past someone you know who doesn't acknowledge you	
Thoughts	Resulting feelings
'Oh dear, I wonder what I've done wrong. No one ever seems to want to talk to me – I always lose friends like this.'	Sadness, depression
'Oh no, what if she saw me and thinks I ignored her? She'll think I'm really rude.'	Worry, anxiety
'Why is she being so rude and stand-offish?'	Irritation
'She must still be hung over from that party last night!'	Amusement

Note that the actual event here is the same in every case: your friend has not acknowledged you. But your feelings can be very different, depending on what kind of thoughts you have about the event. It is the particular thoughts that make all the difference to how you feel. By *thoughts* here, we mean the way that we see events, our interpretations, the meanings we take from them – these are all different ways of talking about our cognitions.

Behaviour

The behavioural part of CBT suggests that what you do, or don't do, also strongly affects your thoughts and feelings. Suppose in the above example your reaction was one of the first two, resulting in sadness or anxiety. If that was the case you probably wouldn't talk to your friend. But then you'd be likely to go on thinking that she did not like you, or thought you were an idiot. As a result you might continue to feel depressed or anxious. On the other hand, if you decided to find out what was really happening and went up to talk to your friend, you might find that actually the 'hangover' explanation was the correct one. As a result, your feelings might change. Changing what you *do* can make a big difference to how you think and feel – for example, by allowing you to find out whether your thoughts are accurate or not.

Interacting systems

The four systems we have described don't exist in isolation – they constantly interact with each other. A change in one system can produce changes, for better or worse, in all the others. For example, my thoughts affect my behaviour, my emotions produce changes in my body, and so on. If I think my friend doesn't like me anymore (thoughts) that may stop me from talking to her (behaviour), which may interfere with our relationship and make me more sad (emotion). When I'm depressed (emotion), I may lose energy (body), which makes it difficult for me to do anything (behaviour), thus further worsening my mood (back to emotion). One of the key ideas in CBT is that psychological problems can arise when the interaction between systems gets stuck in a pattern that is unhelpful. We shall talk a lot more about this in the next section.

Finally of course, we all constantly interact with the outside world; we are affected by other people and events, and in turn our behaviour has an impact on those people and events.

Putting all this together, we can illustrate these ideas in a diagram (Figure 5 below). This is often known as the 'hot cross bun' because it looks a bit like one.

Figure 5: The hot cross bun

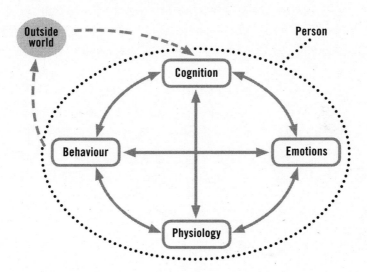

Key messages

- In CBT we view emotions, such as depression, as arising not simply from events or situations, but from our thoughts (or cognitions) about those events – what we take them to mean.

- Emotions, thoughts, behaviour and physiology are all tied together in constantly interacting systems. Each can affect, and be affected by, all the others.

Tips for supporters

- It can be very difficult to grasp these ideas, especially when you are depressed, so the person you are supporting may not 'get it' straight away.

- Can you think of something that he or she has said that you can easily see another side to? Can you use this example to show that it's possible to interpret the same situation in different ways? Watch out for them saying, 'Even my thoughts are wrong; that shows how stupid I am!' Remind them that that is just another example of a negative thought, and can be interpreted in a different way – in this case, that they are thinking like that because they're depressed, not because they're stupid.

CBT and depression

So the CBT model suggests that sometimes the way the different systems interact can be unhelpful and counter-productive. For example, when we have strong feelings like being depressed, or anxious, our thoughts may mislead us and make things seem worse than they really are. They can then lead us into behaviour that keeps us stuck rather than helps us to get better.

In depression, the main feature of our thoughts and beliefs is that they tend to be excessively *negative*. When we are depressed it's as if we're seeing the world through dark glasses. We can easily see the clouds, but there doesn't seem to be much in the way of silver linings!

So, faced with the kind of event with a friend that we discussed above, a depressed person tends to see the most negative interpretation. In the example above, it wasn't just that your friend didn't see you, or was preoccupied; you are likely to think that they were ignoring you because they don't like you – and you may even go on to think that no one else does either. Then, as we have seen, you might walk on without saying anything, so you wouldn't find out what was going on. Because you are feeling low your body might be affected; for example, you don't sleep well, which makes you tired, so you don't feel energetic enough to go out and see friends. And then it's quite likely that as your social life grinds to a halt because you are going out less and less, you may think you don't have any friends. In other words, all these different systems of depression would hang together to make you feel worse and worse.

People who are depressed tend to show this negative bias towards every aspect of their lives: towards themselves ('I'm bad', 'I'm useless', 'I'm incompetent', 'I'm unlovable'); towards the world around them ('nothing ever goes right for me', 'no one likes me', 'everything is just miserable and pointless'); and towards their future ('it will always be like this', 'there is nothing I can do to change things').

It is important to note that in CBT we do not view negative thoughts as always wrong, and CBT is not about 'positive thinking'. Of course it is possible that things *are* negative for you. Life is sometimes difficult, and people do have real problems. However, when you are depressed, it is likely that you will see things as even worse than they really are. One aim of CBT is therefore to help you stand back and examine such ideas, and come to a reasonable judgement about whether they are or are not accurate. CBT is about *realistic* thinking, not blindly positive thinking. If you decide that you are in fact being excessively negative, you can look for more accurate and more helpful ways of seeing things. On the other hand, if you decide that there is a real problem, you can look for a solution to it (hence the role of problem-solving in CBT, discussed later in Chapter 11).

The processes involved in depression

So what makes someone depressed and keeps them depressed? The CBT model has several steps. We saw earlier that there are a number of different factors responsible for depression, including bad experiences in childhood. The CBT view is that these experiences make you vulnerable not just because they were so horrible, but because of the way they taught you to *think* about yourself. For example, if you were treated badly as a child, you may come to believe that you must have done something to deserve such treatment. You may therefore end up believing that you are bad or unlovable. Or if you were frequently criticized for getting things wrong, you may end up believing that you are incompetent, or that you will always be rejected if you do not do everything perfectly.

Depending on their strength, such beliefs may not cause any obvious problems for a long time. However, if you later meet a 'trigger' situation – for example, if someone important to you criticizes or rejects you – the beliefs may be 'activated'. You may be dominated by negative thoughts about being useless, worthless, unwanted and so on. These thoughts then lead to your becoming depressed. This kind of thought is called a 'negative automatic thought' or NAT. 'Negative' because that's what it is (e.g. 'I'm useless'), and 'automatic' because it usually pops into your head without any effort on your part – often dozens of times a day. See Figure 6 for a diagram showing how these processes may develop. This is very similar to Figure 3 earlier in this book, but now we are focusing specifically on a CBT view.

If the NATs become frequent or powerful enough, they have a strong influence on your mood. If someone else were to follow you around all day, whispering in your ear 'You're useless, nobody likes you, you're a bad parent, you're no good at your job . . . ' you can imagine that it would probably be pretty upsetting. Yet when you are depressed, this may be exactly what you are doing to yourself.

It can be even more upsetting because we typically take our own thoughts as the truth. We might reject this kind of criticism if someone else said it, but we tend not to question our own thoughts. We just assume that this is how things really are. One of the crucial first steps in recovery is learning to recognize that such thoughts *might* be true, but are not necessarily so. These thoughts are *opinions*, not facts, and like all opinions they can sometimes be mistaken.

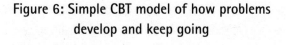

Figure 6: Simple CBT model of how problems develop and keep going

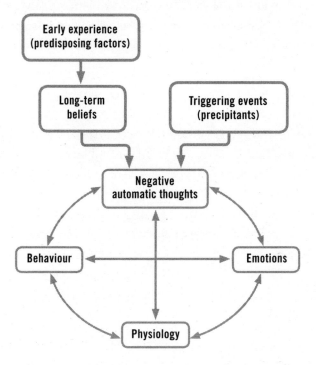

Note that this is very similar to the diagram on page 31, but we have put into the picture the way that early experience affects our beliefs, and the maintaining factors are shown in more detail using the 'hot cross bun'.

Think about your own experiences, and see how they might fit into the model. Below we give further examples of vicious cycles, and then show how Carol, in the story below, filled in the model to explain her own depression.

Vicious circles

The negative thoughts and low mood can easily make each other worse, in what we call a *vicious circle*: in other words a process in which two or more factors amplify or reinforce each other in a way that drives the process round and round in a self-perpetuating way. Low mood increases negative thinking, which further lowers mood, which ... Figure 7 below shows how this vicious circle can work to keep you stuck in depression.

Figure 7: Vicious circle – negative bias

Note two important characteristics of this kind of vicious-circle process.

First, it doesn't matter what starts it off. Whether we think that the first step is low mood that then produces negative thinking, or whether we think it's negative thinking that then produces low mood – in either case, once the process has started it will tend to maintain both the low mood and the negative thinking.

Second, no matter what made it start, this kind of process will not stop unless one of the components changes (e.g. you start thinking less negatively). It's a bit like an arms race between two nations. Nation A fears attack, so builds up its forces; Nation B feels threatened and builds up *its* forces; that makes Nation A even more fearful ... and so on. Such an arms race can only stop when one of the nations decides to do something different. In the same way these vicious circles in depression can only be stopped by changing one or more of the processes involved.

Let's look at a few other vicious circles that are common factors in keeping depression going.

Activity

A very common consequence of depression is that you become less active, and this can maintain the low mood (see Figure 8). Low mood increases negative thoughts in general, and specifically thoughts about activity. Previously satisfying activities may be seen as too difficult, as they require more energy than you feel you have, or you may not enjoy them as much. Under this barrage of negative thoughts you may stop doing some or all of your previous activities. As a result, you lose many of the rewards that give life meaning – activities that used to lead to a sense of achievement, or doing something enjoyable, or having social contact, or whatever. Those losses then serve to maintain the low mood. In severe cases this kind of process can result in an almost complete loss of activity, when someone ends up doing almost nothing most of the time. This is a very important aspect of depression, and we will talk much more about it in Chapters 8 and 13.

Figure 8: Vicious circle – activity

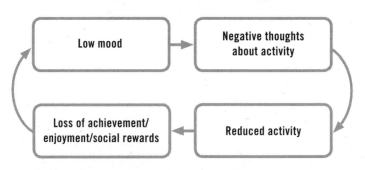

Social activity

You may have particular difficulties with social relationships if you get locked into a 'self-fulfilling prophesy'. This means that your thoughts can lead you into behaving in ways that seem to confirm how you think (see Figure 9). For instance, if you believe that people don't like you, you might start to avoid everyone you know, and never return their phone calls or texts. They might start to think that you don't want to be with them, and stop trying to contact you. So you have 'proved' that you are right, and that other people don't like you.

Figure 9: Vicious circle – social activity

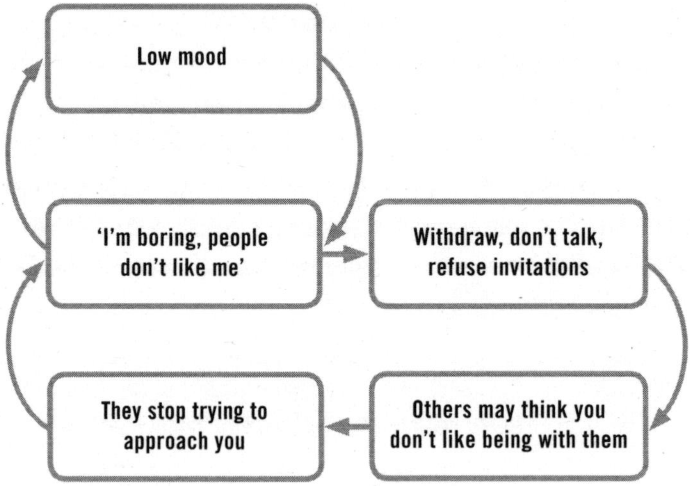

```
            ┌─────────────────┐
            │    Low mood      │
            └─────────────────┘

┌─────────────────┐         ┌─────────────────────┐
│ 'I'm boring, people │ ──→  │ Withdraw, don't talk, │
│  don't like me'  │         │  refuse invitations  │
└─────────────────┘         └─────────────────────┘

┌─────────────────┐         ┌──────────────────────┐
│ They stop trying to │ ←── │ Others may think you  │
│   approach you   │        │ don't like being with them │
└─────────────────┘         └──────────────────────┘
```

Hopelessness

Another kind of self-fulfilling prophesy is shown in Figure 10. Hopeless thoughts lead to your making less effort to cope or change things for the better, which means things are now less likely to change, which seems to confirm your hopelessness.

Figure 10: Vicious circle – hopelessness

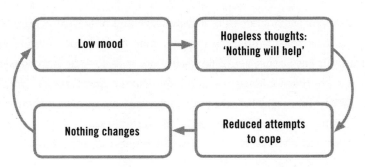

Depression about depression

Another common vicious circle is shown in Figure 11 below. As we have noted before, depression has many effects on your emotions, your thoughts, your behaviour and your body. You may get into a cycle where you start blaming yourself for these symptoms. You think they mean that you're lazy, useless, that your marriage is on the rocks, and so on. In reality it may be that these are just symptoms of depression that will fade away as you begin to recover. But being self-critical about them can keep you locked into this cycle.

Figure 11: Vicious circle – depression about depression

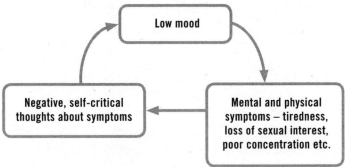

Conflict with other people

Not all vicious circles happen within one person. It is also possible to have vicious circles happening between two or more people. Figure 12 illustrates one way this might happen. Low mood is often accompanied (maybe sometimes caused) by low self-esteem (see Chapter 18). Such low self-esteem, in combination with depression's general negative bias, can lead people to become extremely sensitive to any perceived criticism from other people: if I am feeling bad about myself, I can't bear anyone pointing out anything bad. So imagine you are Joe in the diagram, and Sally (perhaps your partner, or a friend) says something that could be interpreted as critical. Because of your sensitivity you may overreact with excessive anger; that then leads Sally to be more angry and critical, which then reinforces your low mood and low self-esteem. It's just like the arms race we talked about earlier in relation to negative bias (see page 52).

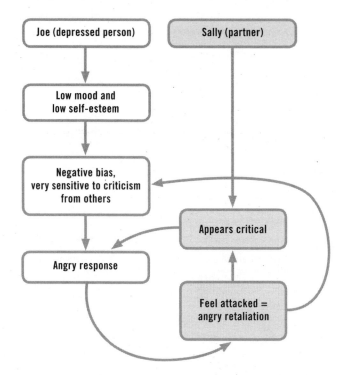

Figure 12: Vicious circle – conflict with others

Understanding your own vicious circles

You may find it helpful to start considering how these ideas apply to you. As a first step, think about whether any of the common vicious circles described above fit with your own experience of depression. If so, draw them in a way that describes your own thoughts, emotions and so on. For example, draw a circle that shows your own individual negative thoughts about activity, and what effects those thoughts have on which activities.

In doing this, it is important to realize that the examples we have given are just some common patterns. They will not be found in everyone. You may not have any of these; furthermore, you may be able to identify particular vicious circles for yourself that are not among those we have described here. That's fine – it's all about adapting these ideas to your own specific case.

So look for any areas where you seem to be stuck in a dead end, where you just seem to keep repeating the same mistakes over and over again. Can you see some ways in which thoughts, emotions, behaviour and bodily changes are feeding into each other in unhelpful ways? If so, see if you can draw out the vicious circle on a piece of paper or in your notebook. Figure 13 on page 59 is a completed example.

Carol's story

Carol is a thirty-two-year-old woman who is married with two sons of seven and four. Her husband Barry works very long hours trying to build up his own business. Carol works to help out financially, and because she is good at what she does she has just been promoted to a management job in the shop that she works in.

Carol has noticed that over the last couple of months she has felt tired and low. She is having trouble getting off to sleep at night, and lies awake in bed thinking about all the things that might go wrong. The crunch came when school asked to talk to her about her seven-year-old son, Jamie, after he had been in a fight with two other boys in his class. She blames herself for being a bad mother, and for not being around enough for the boys. She has started to think that her workmates don't seem to like her so much any more, and she finds it hard to keep up with all the demands of her busy life.

Carol and her sister were brought up by a single mother who was very preoccupied with problems in her own life. With hindsight Carol thinks her mother may have been depressed herself, but at the time all she knew was that her mother didn't seem to care very much about her and her sister, and would often ignore them and leave them to fend for themselves. Carol remembers thinking that there must be something wrong with her, because surely mothers were meant to love their children, weren't they? She vowed that if she ever had children she would never neglect them like that.

Development

We could describe the development of Carol's depression like this:

- Carol's early experiences were of not feeling wanted or loved by her mother. This led her to certain long-term beliefs – that she was not worth much, and that she was unwanted and no good. Despite these beliefs she managed well for a long time. She got married and had children, and although she hadn't done very well at school she found that she was quite bright and could

take on a lot at work. The long-term beliefs might have sat somewhere at the back of her mind, but they certainly didn't stop her
doing things.

- The problems came when there were two important precipitants.
  Jamie started to have problems at school, which she thought was
  her fault because she was no good as a mother. And when she
  was promoted her workmates seemed to change, so she started to
  think that no one liked her.

The diagram below illustrates how Carol's depression developed.

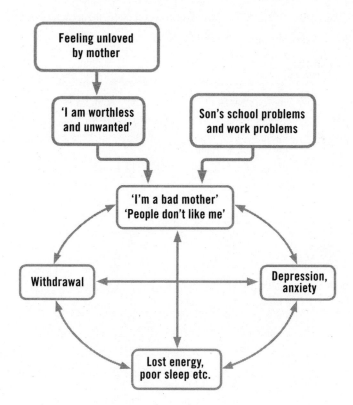

Figure 13: Carol's problem development

Maintenance

Once Carol started to feel depressed and think negatively, the vicious circle took over. She always used to go out with her friends for a drink after work on a Friday night, while Barry looked after the children. But now she is afraid that they don't want her to go with them, and tells everyone she is going home and can't join them. So there is a vicious circle like that of 'social activity' above; Carol's version is shown in Figure 14.

Figure 14: Carol's 'social activity' vicious circle

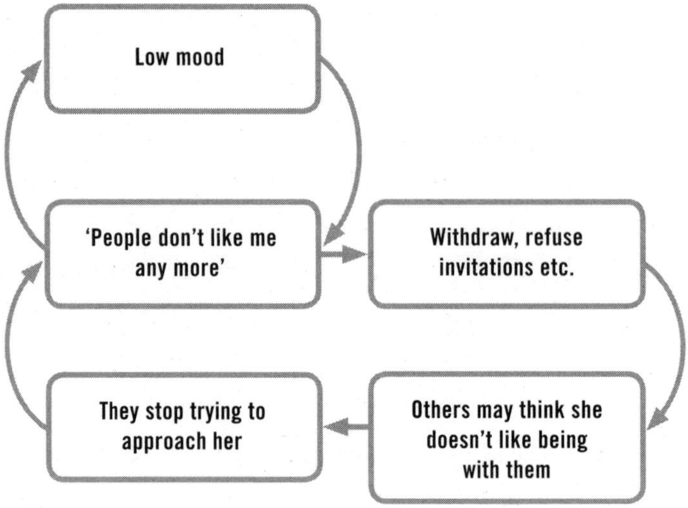

The worse she feels, the more she starts to remember how she vowed she would never neglect her children, and thinks what a failure she is as a mother. She thinks she will damage her children, and that they would be better off without her. Not surprisingly, therefore, her mood gets lower and lower. She is going round and round the feelings and thoughts cycle demonstrated in Figure 15.

Figure 15: Carol's 'negative thinking' vicious circle

Key messages

- The CBT view sees depression as being driven by negative thoughts and beliefs, and their effects on your behaviour and emotions.

- Difficulties you may have experienced in the past may result in a tendency to think negatively now, especially when emotions are strong.

- A key factor in understanding why depression persists is the recognition of vicious-circle processes, where different systems feed into each other in ways that keep the problems going, no matter what started them off in the first place.

- You might want to take a first step towards recovery by trying to understand your own vicious circles.

Tips for supporters

- Help the person you are supporting to draw up a map of their own vicious circles, using the guidelines above.

7 Starting to help yourself through CBT

So now that we have some ideas about what is keeping your depression going, what can you do about it? That is the question that the next few sections of the book aim to answer.

The simple – but not by itself very helpful! – answer is 'break the vicious circles'. Since it is the vicious circles that are keeping you stuck, you need to disrupt those cycles in order to break free of them. As we noted above, that means taking steps to change one or more of the factors involved. And since we are talking about CBT here, it is probably no great surprise that we will be talking about ways to change your thoughts and your behaviour, so as to stop those processes from just rolling along.

One step at a time . . .

Before beginning to make changes, it is important to be aware that it will probably feel quite challenging at times. In particular, some of the features of depression make it hard to start, or to keep going. As we have already seen, people who are depressed commonly feel hopeless, unmotivated, pessimistic and lacking in energy. These feelings can obviously make it difficult to keep up the effort needed to overcome the depression. Indeed, when you try the techniques set out in this book, you may find yourself plagued by thoughts that tell you it's too hard, it won't work, it's pointless because you're a hopeless case . . . or a dozen other negative reactions. These thoughts are perfectly normal, but it is important to remember that they are a product of your depression, not necessarily an accurate reflection of reality. Try not to let the negative thoughts put you off. Instead, notice them, then put them on one side for the moment, rather than paying them a lot of attention: 'OK, there's one of those unhelpful negative thoughts . . . I'm not going to pay it any attention right now; I'm going to move on with what I'm doing.' See Chapter 17 on mindfulness for much more about this kind of approach to negative thoughts.

Partly because of these problems, the golden rule in helping yourself is 'one step at a time'. In other words, don't set yourself targets that are too difficult to reach. If you have not been out of the house for a week, it is not likely to be helpful to set yourself the goal of returning to full-time work, going out most evenings and taking up a new hobby, all by next week. If you are too ambitious it is likely that you won't achieve your goals, which will lead you to become more self-critical. It is a better idea to work towards your long-term targets by following a series of smaller, more achievable steps. That way, you are more likely to succeed, as each smaller achievement will encourage you and help to rebuild your confidence. There is an old proverb: 'A journey of a thousand miles begins with a single step.' Your journey out of depression also needs to begin with single, small steps.

In planning such steps towards recovery, it is also important to start from where you are now. It will not usually be helpful in the early stages to set your goals according to what you *would* have been able to do before you were depressed, or what you think you *should* be able to do. Ambitious goals might have been realistic once, and they will be again; but whilst you are depressed, you will not be able to do everything as easily as you once could. Think of it as similar to recovering from physical problems. If a marathon runner broke his leg badly, he would not be able to run marathons as soon as the cast came off. He'd need to learn to walk again. He'd need to increase the distance he could walk in careful stages, and he might be quite frightened about starting to run. He would not get very far if he said, 'What's the point of trying to walk 100 yards when I used to run marathons?'

This principle of being realistic about what you can manage is also important when it comes to reviewing your efforts. It is very easy to fall into the trap of belittling small achievements because you would previously have been able to do them easily. Again, you need to judge your efforts by how difficult it is for you *now*, not by what you or other people can *usually* do. It is important to reward yourself for doing a *bit* more or feeling a *bit* better – don't wait for full recovery before giving yourself a pat on the back. For someone who is severely depressed, getting up before ten o'clock in the morning can be a huge achievement, and seriously deserving of congratulation. Depression is a real problem, which causes real disability, even if it is not as visible as a broken leg.

Finally, you might want to refer back to 'Making the most of this book' on page xv, and in particular remember the message about *doing* exercise versus just reading about exercise. It is no use just reading the book and then carrying on with your life as before. If you want things to change then you need to *do* something different, not just read about it. You need to use the techniques in real life, and gradually find out what works for you.

Identifying your goals for therapy

Now that you have decided you are going to make a start to tackle your depression, it will be helpful to work out exactly what that will mean for you. How will you know that your depression is better? In what ways will your life be different? What do you want to change? Of course, in some senses the answer is obvious. You probably want to feel better, and to go back to being able to do what you were doing before you got depressed. But what exactly does that mean for you? If you can be more specific about your goals you stand more chance of being able to work towards them. So think about what you would *do* differently if you weren't depressed. For instance, you might want to go back to getting up in the morning and making breakfast for the family. You might want to be back at work. You might want to be able to get through the day without bursting into tears.

When you are thinking about goals it can be helpful to remember the SMART rule. SMART goals are as follows:

Specific – you say exactly what you want to achieve rather than having a vague or general goal. For instance 'feeling better' is rather vague. 'Getting up in the morning and getting out of the door without crying' is a much more specific one.

Measurable – this means that you will know when you have achieved your goal. If your goal is not to cry, you can count the number of times in a day that you do, and hopefully see that it decreases as you go on with this book.

Achievable and reasonable – don't set goals that you know you won't be able to reach. For instance, don't aim to be the next David Beckham, unless you have very good reasons to think that you might be. But you might say, 'I want to increase my activities and start playing football again, so I'll find out about local clubs.'

Timed – it will help you to work towards your goals if you set a time limit on them. Give yourself a deadline, and then work towards this. For instance, if you want to find out about local football clubs, give yourself a week to look them up on the internet or buy a local paper.

Final preparations for self-help

By this point you hopefully have some understanding of CBT and how it can help you. You will have done a certain amount already, including:

- Thinking about whether you'd like to involve a supporter.
- Deciding where and when you are going to have your self-help sessions.
- Getting a notebook, paper or electronic, to record self-help exercises and progress.
- Getting a clear idea of your symptoms.

- Looking at the vicious circles and thinking about how they apply to you.

- Thinking about your goals and what you'd like to accomplish through therapy.

Structuring your time

When you start to use CBT for yourself you might find the number of things you need to think about a bit overwhelming. Some people find the following format helpful:

1. How am I doing? This means thinking a bit about how you feel, and the progress you've made. Did you manage to do the things that you planned? How did it go?

2. What's the most important thing to concentrate on? You can't solve all your problems at once, so decide which one you want to tackle today. If you get distracted by other problems, then just say, 'OK, I know that's important too, but I'll get to that another day.'

3. What's the next step? Is there something that you can try to do differently over the next few days?

4. Concentrating on the here and now: you may find that you want to spend a lot of time working out exactly why you are depressed, where things went wrong and so on. Although that is natural and can sometimes be helpful, it could also be unhelpful and unproductive (see Chapter 14).

CBT tends to focus mainly on the maintaining processes: the current vicious circles that are keeping you stuck. This is because although the origins of the problem are of interest, once depression has taken hold the vicious-circle processes tend to dominate and keep it going, whatever the origins were. Therefore we focus on those factors as the best place to make a difference. Imagine you came across a fire in your home or office. What is the first thing you would do? Probably not go and look for the match that started the fire! Your first priority is to put the fire out. In the same way, our first priority is to help you get the depression under control.

We can see this with Carol, in the example above. Although we understand Carol's early experience and the long-term beliefs that it led to, we can see that she managed very well for a great deal of her life. It was only when things started to go wrong for her that the long-term beliefs kicked in. Thinking about her early life would not help much in the present. The important thing for her is to break into the vicious circles that keep her depression going.

Key messages

- CBT self-help approaches can begin to make a difference to your depression.

- Certain features of depression can make it difficult to fight back. It is important to be prepared for these difficulties, so as to give yourself the best chance of succeeding.

- Try not to be put off by negative thoughts about your efforts to help yourself.

- Tackle recovery in small steps, one step at a time.

- Judge your efforts according to how you are now, not according to what you can do when you are well or what you think you ought to be able to do.

- Specify your goals in SMART terms, so that you will have a good idea of how you are getting on.

Tips for supporters

- Go through the 'Final preparation points' on pages 65–6 with the person you are supporting.

- If some of the points have been left out, then encourage the person to spend time thinking about them.

- As we go on from here, you will need to find the delicate balance between encouragement and pushing too hard! As we've said, it's very difficult for people with depression to make a start and keep going. If you push too hard they may react by getting angry or demoralized. On the other hand if you don't encourage them enough they may not have the motivation to change their behaviour. So encourage, but don't force it.

8 Helping yourself by becoming more active

For many people, the best place to start to tackle depression is by looking at your level of activity. We talked earlier (around Figure 8, page 53) about the vicious circle that leads to you becoming less active than usual, because you feel too tired, or it doesn't seem worth the effort, or you don't enjoy things any more. We also talked about how the broad strategy for overcoming depression is to break or disrupt those vicious circles. So here is our first example of that: you can begin to overcome depression by increasing your activity levels. Because different people will start in different places, you will need to tailor these broad guidelines to set your own more specific goals (but bear in mind the section above on the importance of being *realistic*).

There are several steps in learning about and possibly changing your activity.

Getting a clear idea of how you are spending your time

The first step is to gather more information about your own pattern of activity, and how it affects your mood. It is best to do this in a careful, detailed way, using the methods described below, so that what you write will not be too influenced by depressive ways of thinking. If you just sit down and think about what you did last week, the negative bias of depression may make you think that you did nothing worthwhile, or that nothing gave you any satisfaction. As always, that *might* be true, but it also might not. To get a more accurate picture, you need to record your activity close to the time you did it, so that there is less room for negative memory biases to mislead you. The best way to do this is using a form like that shown on the following page. This form is known as a Weekly Activity

Schedule (WAS). It's really just a timetable, with a box for each hour of each day. To complete it, you fill in two bits of information for each hour:

1. A brief description of how you spent your time during that hour.

2. Two numbers, labelled **P** (for Pleasure) and **A** (for Achievement). Use these numbers to say how much you *enjoyed* what you did during that hour (**Pleasure**) and how much you felt you'd managed something it was *hard* for you to do (**Achievement**). These numbers can be anywhere from 0 (none at all) to 10 (the most enjoyment or greatest sense of achievement possible). So P1 would mean it was only slightly enjoyable. P8 would mean it was very enjoyable. In rating your pleasure and achievement, remember to use your current activity level as the standard. When you are well, it might not be much of an achievement to get up and dressed (it might rate only A0 or A1), but it might well be a considerable achievement when you are depressed (maybe even A8 or A9 on some days).

As an example, Table 16 shows a part of a completed Weekly Activity Schedule for Sammy, who was very depressed and finding it extremely hard to do anything at all.

Table 16: Part of a completed Weekly Activity Schedule

Time	Monday	Tuesday	. . .
7–8 a.m.	Got up, dressed P0 A5		
8–9 a.m.	Breakfast for children, to school P1 A6		
9–10 a.m.	Walked the dog P3 A4		

Draw up your own form or copy the blank one on page 72, and try it for a while. A few important tips for filling in your own Weekly Activity Schedule:

- Try to fill in the Weekly Activity Schedule as close as possible to the actual time of the activity. A couple of hours later probably won't matter too much, but the sooner the better. If you leave it until the end of the day, that may already be enough time to let negative thinking creep in and influence your memory and therefore your record.

- Note that 'P' and 'A' don't necessarily go together. Some activities are pleasurable, but don't give much sense of achievement (e.g. eating a bar of chocolate); some are achievements but not necessarily pleasurable (e.g. doing a necessary chore); some activities may give you both (e.g. going to a social occasion when you didn't feel like it, but ending up enjoying it). These are perhaps the most helpful to your mood, but don't worry if there aren't many – or any – of these at the moment.

When you have completed the record for a reasonable time (perhaps a week or so), look at it and see what you can learn from it. There are three main things to look for.

1. You can use your form to get a better picture of how active you really are. For some people, it may be helpful to realize that you are doing more than you thought you were. On the other hand, the record may show that you aren't doing very much. If so, then you may need to think about planning to increase your activity – see below.

2. The record can help you see which activities, if any, do give you at least *some* sense of achievement and pleasure. When you start to think about changes, these are the activities it may be worth increasing.

3. Finally, you can use the information you have gathered to plan changes. What does it suggest you need to change? Are you spending long periods doing very little except feeling low? Does it look as if there are lots of chores that must be done, but very little enjoyable activity? Are there any activities that you enjoy at least a bit, or which improve your mood even a little, and which you might do more of?

Worksheet 1: Weekly Activity Schedule (WAS)

Time	Monday	Tuesday	Wednesday	Thursday	Friday	Saturday	Sunday
5–6 a.m.							
6–7 a.m.							
7–8 a.m.							
8–9 a.m.							
9–10 a.m.							

10–11 a.m.	11–noon	Noon–1 p.m.	1–2 p.m.	2–3 p.m.

Time	Monday	Tuesday	Wednesday	Thursday	Friday	Saturday	Sunday
3–4 p.m.							
4–5 p.m.							
5–6 p.m.							
6–7 p.m.							
7–8 p.m.							

8–9 p.m.	9–10 p.m.	10–11 p.m.	11–midnight	Midnight–1 a.m.

Changing your pattern of activity

The next step is to use what you have learned to plan future activity. There are two common aims. First, to increase your overall level of activity if it is low. Second, to focus specifically on doing more of the things that give you at least some sense of pleasure and achievement. If you can keep active, and do more things that give you a feeling of pleasure or achievement, this will begin to lift your mood. Trying to find things you enjoy is particularly important because anhedonia, or lack of pleasure, is an important part of depression. It's not just about stopping feeling low, it's about starting to be aware of the good feelings too, even if that's only a tiny bit to begin with.

In planning what to do, you will use the same worksheet as a plan instead of as a record. Move on from just recording what you have been doing to using the WAS to plan what you will do.

Write in times to do things that might be rewarding in terms of pleasure or achievement. Remember these do not have to be very special events. Even small pleasures like having a relaxing bath, or sitting down with a cup of coffee and a magazine can contribute to maintaining a better mood. Think about things you used to enjoy, and plan to restart some of those. It is important to realize that, at least in the early stages, it is not likely that you will immediately enjoy anything as much as you did before you were depressed. The return of enjoyment often takes quite a while. So at first you will probably have to force yourself to do things even though you are not enjoying them that much. It is worth persevering. Increasing what you do should at least give you some sense of achievement. Try to keep at it, and slowly the enjoyment should return as well.

Similarly, achievements do not have to be huge to be worthwhile. You don't have to wait until you have become world-famous before you recognize any achievements! Just spending ten minutes tidying up a messy kitchen drawer that has been annoying you can help you feel you have done something useful today.

Look for your own individual way of approaching chores and pleasures. One person would do the chores he hated most when he was feeling lower in mood. His view was that he was feeling rotten anyway, so he might as well do something that would only spoil a good mood. At least he could then feel a sense of achievement that he had got that job done, and he didn't have to worry about it again for a while. Other people might save such tasks for when they are feeling more energetic and motivated. Whatever works to lift your mood is what is right for you.

In planning activities in this way, it is better to be specific. In other words, don't just say to yourself, 'I must do more.' Instead, schedule in a specific activity at a specific time, e.g. 'Go and buy that birthday card on Wednesday morning.' Always remember the golden rule of setting yourself small, achievable targets when you are planning what to do. Remember also to give yourself a pat on the back whenever you manage to do what you planned.

Before we finish talking about activity, we should mention the benefits of physical exercise. There is some research evidence suggesting that exercise (e.g. walking, running, swimming or other sports) can have a direct therapeutic effect on mood. Even if it does not directly affect mood, exercise is clearly helpful to your general fitness, which may in turn make you feel better in yourself. So it is worth including in your activity-planning some reasonably demanding physical exercise on a regular basis.

One last point. Remember that Negative Automatic Thoughts (NATs) can intrude at any point when you are working on your activities. They make it hard to give yourself credit, to enjoy yourself, or to make any changes. So watch out for them, and don't allow yourself to be knocked off course. In the next section, we will introduce some ways of dealing with NATs.

And finally, as we said earlier, the issue of activity is really important in depression and Chapter 13 talks about this in much more detail.

Key messages

- One of the main ways depression keeps itself going is by reducing your activity, so you lose the benefits of doing things that used to give you pleasure or a sense of achievement.

- You can help yourself by using carefully planned approaches to increasing or modifying your daily activity, so that you increase things you enjoy, or which make you feel worthwhile.

- Use the Weekly Activity Schedule first to record, then to plan, activities.

- Don't be harsh in judging your efforts. Encouragement for even small successes is more helpful than being self-critical about not managing everything that you hoped for.

- Try to incorporate some physical exercise into your activity plans.

- See Chapter 13 for a specific approach to depression called 'behavioural activation' that makes changing your activity its main target.

Tips for supporters

- Ask the person you are supporting whether it would be helpful for you to prompt them about keeping their WAS record, or later on about sticking to their WAS planning. Go by what they say! Unasked-for prompting may be seen as unhelpful nagging or criticism, which may make them feel worse rather than better.

- Help them to develop realistic and specific goals in their activity plan.

- Congratulate them on any degree of success in sticking to their plan, and encourage them not to set themselves too-high standards.

9 Identifying negative thoughts

We have already mentioned that Negative Automatic Thoughts, or NATs, play a central role in keeping your mood low. It follows that to tackle the low moods, you need to work with the NATs. As with the activity methods we just talked about, the first step is 'getting to know the enemy better'. In other words, to tackle depression effectively, you need to know in detail what your own individual pattern of NATs is.

NATs have several characteristics:

- As the name suggests, they are *negative*. They involve seeing the downside of everything: thinking that you have failed in some way, or that other people disapprove of you, or that you are lazy, useless and so on.

- They are *automatic* in the sense that these are not thoughts you *try* to have or deliberately think – they just pop into your head.

- They are often *brief* and, when you're depressed, *frequent*. It only takes a second to think, 'I've made a mess of this', and you may have such thoughts dozens of times a day or more.

- They are often *plausible* – they may seem obviously true to you: they appear to be a simple description of reality, rather than just a thought. One of the crucial steps in coping better with NATs is recognizing that 'thoughts are like opinions, not facts'. In other words, like opinions, thoughts *might* be true, but they may also be inaccurate and unhelpful. Therefore, again like opinions, each one needs evaluation to decide whether it is accurate or not. Another way of putting this is the motto: 'Don't believe everything you think!'

- They 'match' the depression in the sense that anyone who thought like that would be likely to feel depressed. For instance, most of us would get depressed if we genuinely believed that we were useless at everything and no one liked us.

The best way to find out more about your NATs is again to keep some records for a while, writing down your thoughts and feelings close to the time that they happen. There is a blank thought record (Worksheet 2) after this section, which you can copy for your own use, and an example below showing part of a thought record that Carol filled out. Some people find it much easier to do this recording electronically, with a tablet or smart phone – it certainly solves the problem of where to keep the notebook.

Table 17: Part of Carol's completed thought record

Date/time	Situation	Emotion/ Severity (0=not at all – 100=worst it can be)	Thought/Belief (0 per cent=don't believe it at all – 100 per cent=believe it completely)
1 June, 8 a.m.	Kids playing up	Angry (50) Sad (80)	'They always play me up' (75 per cent) 'It's my fault, I'm a useless mother' (100 per cent)

Let's go through how you use this kind of record, step by step:

- Draw up a worksheet along the lines shown above or photocopy the one on pages 84–5. Carry it around with you so that you can write thoughts down as quickly as possible after they happen.
- Look out for any significant *worsening* of your mood. Whenever that happens, get out the worksheet and try to write down what

happened. If it happens lots of times every day, just write down the worst few times, or record two or three typical examples.

- You might want to focus particularly on any thoughts you identified in the vicious-circle exercise as playing a part in maintaining your own vicious circles (see page 57).

- Record thoughts as close as possible to the time when they happened. If you can't do it immediately – for example if you're driving, or you're with other people – then at least make a mental note, or scribble a note at the first opportunity. Then fill in the form as soon as possible later. The reason for this is these thoughts can be hard to remember accurately even a few hours later. They may also get distorted by negative memory biases.

- In column one, write down the date and time it happened.

- In column two, write down the situation you were in when you started to feel worse (who you were with, if anyone; what happened; what you were generally thinking about at the time, etc.).

- In column three, write down what emotions you felt (sad, angry, guilty, anxious . . .), and how strong each one was on a scale from 0 to 100 (0=not at all, 100=the worst ever). Note there may be more than one emotion – if so, name and rate each one separately.

- In column four, make a note of the thoughts that went through your mind just as, or just before, you started to feel bad.

- One of the common difficulties in trying to do this for the first time is distinguishing between thoughts and feelings. This is not helped by the fact that in English we often say 'I *feel* such and such' when what we really mean is 'I *think* such and such'. For example, 'I feel that interview went badly' really means 'I think it went badly'. A simple rule of thumb you can use is that feelings can usually be described with just one word: 'sad', 'angry', 'scared', 'happy', etc. If what you're trying to express clearly needs more than that, then it's probably a thought, not a feeling.

- Sometimes the thoughts may be more like pictures in your mind's eye, rather than words. If so, write down what the picture seems to say to you (for example, if you get a mental picture of yourself all alone, you might write down 'I am alone and unloved').

- Try to make sure that you write down the thought as it occurred to you, not some summary of it. For instance, it is more accurate to record 'I am useless – I have let everyone down' rather than 'I thought about being useless'. The second, summarized version hides the emotional impact of the original thought, which is what you want to capture. For the same reason, it's important to write down your thoughts even if you can quickly see that they are exaggerated or untrue.

- When you've written your thought down, put another number to say how much you believed that thought *at the time it happened*, from 0 per cent (not at all), to 100 per cent (absolutely certain it is true). The reason for rating your belief *at the time* is that many people find that when they think about it later, they can easily see that the thought was not true. But it may have been very convincing at the time, and that's what explains its power over your mood.

- Sometimes NATs occur in the form of questions: for example, 'Why does no one like me?' It is helpful to turn these into a direct statement of the substance of the thought, e.g. 'No one likes me'. There are two reasons for doing this. First, when you come to rate your degree of belief in the thought, it doesn't make much sense to ask how much you believe a question. You can't rate how much you believe 'Why does no one like me?'. But you can rate how much you believe 'No one likes me'. Second, when we come later to trying to step back and evaluate whether your NATs are true, considering the evidence for or against them, again it doesn't make much sense to look for evidence for or against a question.

- Although for most people writing thoughts down like this is a good approach, it is not absolutely essential. The important point is just to identify and note the NATs in some way. Exactly how you do that can vary. Instead of writing, perhaps you could make an audio record of them on your mobile phone or other device. There are even mobile phone apps available to help you these days, especially for smart phones.

Don't worry if you find this exercise difficult at first and don't blame yourself for being 'stupid' or 'useless'. Looking at your own thoughts in this way is very unfamiliar to most people, and it takes practice to get better at it. Persevere for a week or two, and you should find that you start to get more 'tuned in' to the NATs, and it gets easier.

One of the problems about spotting NATs can be that you think, 'But that's not a NAT, it's just the way things are.' If you catch yourself thinking like this, then it's a good indication that it's the depression talking. The rule should be that if the thought is negative, you can write it down and carry out the steps above. We hope that after doing this a few times you may learn to recognize that it's depression talking, not just 'the way things are'.

Worksheet 2: Basic thought record

Date / time	Situation	Emotion and severity (0–100)	Negative thoughts and belief at the time (0–100 per cent)

One other problem may occasionally arise from recording your thoughts. Some people might find that focusing on their NATs may make them feel worse. This is particularly likely if you have coped with depression by trying to avoid your thoughts. If you do feel worse for a while, remember that this is nearly always a short-term problem. As you get used to thinking about and tackling your thoughts, things will start to improve. It's understandable that if you have been avoiding thinking about your problems, it can be distressing to turn round and face up to them. On the other hand, you do need to know what you're dealing with, so this temporary worsening may be a price worth paying in order to overcome the depression. Remember that however distressing the thoughts may be, they are not necessarily true: 'thoughts are opinions, not facts'. On the other hand, if you keep trying for a couple of weeks and still feel worse, then it may be worth trying another approach – perhaps one of those described in the following chapters of this book.

Key messages

- Negative thoughts (NATs) are central to what keeps you depressed.

- The first step to fighting back against them is to know more about them. Spend some time identifying them using the recording methods described in this section.

Tips for supporters

- Encourage the person you are supporting to record their NATs, using the worksheet on page 84. If writing is difficult, help them find some other way of recording, perhaps speaking into a smart phone if they have one.

- If they are finding it hard to spot the NATs, you may be able to help. Ask them what would be helpful, but one possible approach is to help them revisit a recent upsetting situation in their imagination. Have them close their eyes and try to imagine what happened as vividly as possible. This may help to bring the NATs back to mind.

- Check that the NAT makes sense of their depression. A simple rule of thumb is to ask yourself, 'If I had that thought, would I feel that bad?' If the answer is 'No, not really' then the thought they've identified probably isn't the one making them depressed, and it would be helpful to ask a bit more.

10   Tackling negative thoughts

In this chapter we cover three main ways of tackling negative thoughts:

- Distracting yourself from the thoughts

- Testing the thoughts out

- Experimenting to see if the thoughts are realistic or not

Tackling negative thoughts by distracting yourself from them

When you've recorded your negative thoughts for a week or two, you should have a clearer picture of the kind of NATs that trouble you most often. Now we need to think about how to deal with them. The first and easiest technique is simply to try to distract yourself. This may be most useful if you have many NATs throughout the day. By doing other things that keep your mind busy, you leave less room for the NATs to occupy your mind. Increasing your activity levels is a good way to distract yourself: read a book or magazine, go for a walk, listen to music or talk to a friend.

Activity is not the only way of distracting yourself from the NATs. You can also use a range of other methods, even in situations where activity is difficult. Here are some that people have found useful:

- Count all the red objects you see around you, or the number of bricks in a wall, or anything else you can see.

- Describe to yourself in your mind, in great detail, what you can see, hear, smell or feel around you. 'The room has white walls; there's a blue carpet; there are one, two, three chairs in the room; the first chair has a check pattern on the fabric; I can hear the neighbour's vacuum cleaner . . . ' and so on.

- Repeat the words of a song in your mind. Try to go through the whole song, imagining the music in as much detail as you can.

- Think of an object, such as a flower. Hold the image in your mind and really concentrate on it. Picture the petals, the colours and the shape of it. Try to imagine what the flower's fragrance is like.

You can distract yourself by thinking of anything that is pleasant, funny, or that will keep you occupied. Remember you should *really concentrate* on whatever it is you think of for it to be effective.

Distraction can be a good short-term way of coping with NATs. However, as it does not actually change the thoughts, it is not a long-term solution. We will look at more effective ways of tackling negative thoughts in the next section of this chapter.

Key messages

- A simple way to fight NATs is to do something to distract yourself, so that you just leave less room for them to buzz around in your brain all day.

- Distraction can be anything that will engage your mind and take attention away from the NATs.

Tips for supporters

- Help the person you are supporting to come up with ways of distracting that might work for them. For example, what kinds of activity do they find absorbing?

Tackling negative thoughts by testing them out

Although distraction can be a helpful short-term coping strategy, *thought-testing* is a much more effective way to tackle negative thoughts. The aim of thought-testing is to bring your NATs out into the daylight and take a good look at them to see whether they may be misleading you.

This is *not* the same as 'positive thinking'. Simply seeing every situation as positive may be no more realistic than seeing every situation as negative. Sometimes life *is* negative, and bad things do happen (for example see Chapter 23 for some ideas about depression in the face of physical illness). What we are looking for is *realistic, helpful* thinking.

The first step in testing negative thoughts is to identify them. When you have monitored your negative thoughts for a while (see Chapter 9), you should have an idea of the kind of NATs that trouble you.

Remember that, as with identifying the thoughts, it is perfectly normal to find thought-testing hard at first. Indeed, some people find this one of the hardest CBT techniques. Take it one small step at a time, keep practising for a while and it should become easier.

It is best to start off this kind of exercise by using a pen and paper to write down the thought you are going to test. Writing a thought down can be a useful first step in taking a more objective look at it.

There are several ways of testing thoughts to see if they are accurate and helpful. We will try to illustrate some of them using the NATs from Carol's example worksheet above. Her thoughts were 'The kids always play me up' and 'I'm a useless mother'.

Thinking errors

One good way of getting NATs into perspective is to try to identify 'thinking errors': ways of thinking that can easily mislead us to excessively negative conclusions. These are common patterns that all of us can fall into, especially if we're feeling down or anxious. See if you can spot any of these in your own thinking.

Over-generalizing

This means drawing large, general conclusions from small, specific events – for example, if I make one mistake and then conclude 'I am stupid'. Often you can spot this error by looking for words like 'always', 'never' and so on. In the example thoughts, Carol may be over-generalizing when she thinks 'They *always* play me up'. Even the worst-behaved children aren't *always* difficult, 24 hours a day, 365 days a year!

All-or-nothing thinking

This means seeing everything in extremes. Things are either good or bad; people are nice or nasty, clever or stupid; if I am not perfect, then I am completely useless. The problem with this way of thinking is that real life is made up of shades of grey. Most people are neither perfect parents nor wicked and uncaring: they are somewhere in between – sometimes good, sometimes not so good. Even if it is true that Carol was not handling her children well on this particular morning, that doesn't mean she is a useless mother.

Emotional reasoning

This involves believing that because you feel a certain way, that must be how things actually are. If I *feel* inadequate, that must be because I *am* inadequate. If I feel frightened, there must be some danger around. In many areas of life, we are easily able to see that a feeling is not necessarily true. If I run into some bad traffic when I am late for work, I may *feel* as if everyone is deliberately trying to hold me up, but in calmer moments I know this is not true. NATs may more easily fool us into believing that they are facts. In our example, it may be that emotional reasoning is playing a part. Carol feels useless at the moment and that leads her to believe she must be a useless mother. Don't trust emotional reasoning when you are depressed: stick to factual evidence.

Fortune telling

This refers to the mistake of thinking you know for sure what will happen in the future, without actually testing it out. For instance, you might decide against going to a social occasion because you 'know' it will be boring, or you might not bother trying any of the self-help techniques in this book because you 'know' they won't work. Unless we have a great deal of evidence, based on actual experience, we don't *know* what will happen in the future. We can only guess, and our guesses can be wrong. Even when we have tried something before, it is important to remember that things can change, and the future is not always exactly the same as the past.

Mind reading

This means thinking we know what is in other people's minds, without necessarily having any good evidence. For instance, you may think you 'know' that someone else doesn't like you, or disapproves of you, or is cross with you, even though they have not said or done anything to you. This mistake is similar in some ways to fortune telling: we can't actually *know* what someone else is thinking unless we ask them and they tell us. Otherwise, it is just a guess and we may be mistaken. Usually, if you are concerned about what someone else is thinking, it is best to ask them!

What is the evidence?

One of the most useful approaches to testing NATs is to look for what *evidence* is available. This is based on the principle that NATs are more like opinions than facts. They are one possible way of viewing a situation, and they may be accurate, but they also may not. Using the 'evidence' approach, you try to suspend judgement for a while. Then you decide objectively whether the thoughts are true, by looking for evidence for and against them. What information do you have that supports the thought and makes it believable to you? On the other hand, is there any information you may not have noticed or remembered that does *not* support the thought?

This approach is a bit like holding a trial in court. In a trial, the magistrates or jury are asked to put aside any prejudices and make no assumptions about whether the defendant is innocent or guilty. They then have to decide on the most likely version of events, using the evidence presented to them. That evidence has to be hard facts, not just personal opinion – we'd be startled if a judge put someone in prison just because she *felt* they were guilty, with no other evidence!

In the same way, you need to put your NATs on trial. You, the judge, have to decide whether they are true or false, accurate or misleading. And to do this properly, just as in court, you need to look for hard, factual evidence, not feelings or hunches. Yet again, it is best to learn this approach by writing things down, at least at first.

Worksheet 3 is a sheet you can use to test your thoughts. This is how to use it.

- Fill in the first four columns as before. Let's suppose it's about Carol's thought in our example: 'I'm a useless mother'.

- In column five, write down all the evidence that *supports* this view – in this case Carol would need to try to think of any evidence suggesting she is indeed a bad mother. Remember that this must be as close as you can get to good, solid, objective evidence, not just feelings or intuition.

- In column six, write down all the evidence that suggests the thought is *not* completely true. For most people, this will probably be harder

Worksheet 3: Testing the evidence about NATs

Date / time	Situation	Emotion and severity (0–100)	Negative thoughts at the time (0–100 per cent)	Evidence that supports the thought	Evidence that counts against the thought	Balanced thought

than the previous step, because we tend to start off assuming that our negative thought is true. Imagine you had an ace defence lawyer, or a good friend, who wanted to defend you in court: what evidence would they bring *against* the negative thought? Again, try to come up with objective evidence. In this case, Carol would need to think of any time she had not been completely useless, anything suggesting that at least sometimes she is an OK mother.

• Try to weigh up the evidence on each side fairly, as you would want a judge to do if you were on trial. Which side seems to have more evidence? Does it seem that the original negative thought is entirely supported, or is there at least some good evidence that it is not completely true?

• If you decide in the above step that there is at least some room for doubt about the NAT, try to work out a more accurate or realistic version of it, and write it down in column seven. In Carol's example, perhaps it might be something along these lines: 'I'm not a useless mother. Like most people, I sometimes handle the kids well, sometimes not so well (particularly when I'm feeling down). Overall, I'm probably pretty OK – and I'm working on getting better.'

In the following example (Table 18) you can see how Carol might fill in her worksheet after receiving a phone call about her son getting into a fight at school.

Table 18: Carol's completed thought–testing worksheet

Date / time	Situation	Emotion and severity (0–100)	Negative thoughts at the time (0–100 per cent)	Evidence that *supports* the thought	Evidence that counts *against* the thought	Balanced thought
Tuesday afternoon	Got a phone call at work asking me to go and talk to Paul's school because he's got into a fight.	Shame, absolute misery – about 80.	Oh no, he's probably done something awful and will be in terrible trouble. It's all my fault because I neglect them – I'm a useless mother, even worse than mine was because I should know what I'm doing. 100 per cent!	I do work hard, and there are times when I'd rather do something for work than for them. I can be really ratty sometimes. Paul is in trouble at school so there must be something wrong.	Well, I suppose Paul's not the first person in his class to be told off for fighting – the school are pretty hot on it, and I know other mums who've thought it was really silly that they've had to be told off too! I do love them, and I do try to do things right. We have lovely times sometimes, and at least when I'm ratty I tell them I'm sorry – I don't pretend it's not happening, or that it's their fault.	I'm not perfect, but I don't think I'm useless. I love them, and even though I get snappy and work too hard I think they know that I love them – I don't think they feel neglected.

Sometimes you may find that you really don't have much evidence either way. If that is so, the 'pros and cons' approach may be more helpful, or you can use 'behavioural experiments' to gather more evidence. Both of these are described below.

Pros and cons

Sometimes it is not possible to use evidence to decide whether a NAT is accurate – like the old saying about optimists seeing half a glass of water as half-full, whilst pessimists see it as half-empty. Sometimes the evidence does not support one view more than the other. They may be equally true because they are just different ways of describing the same situation. For example, Peter has recently moved to a new country, where he has made two or three good friends. A pessimistic view would be 'I'm really isolated; apart from Ben and Jeff I don't know anyone in this country.' An optimistic view would be 'I'm so lucky to have met them; I really feel like I'm starting to belong.' Even though there is no right or wrong way of describing the situation, the beliefs may still differ in their *consequences* – for example in how they make you feel. If there really is no difference in the truth of two different views, it seems sensible to go with the one that has the best effects, on you or on other people. So it can be useful to ask yourself what the pros and cons are of a particular way of seeing things. What are the pros – the advantages or pay-offs – of thinking like this? And what are the cons – the disadvantages or downside? If Peter thought the pessimistic way, then there might be a big 'con' – he might get demoralized and give up trying to meet other people, or be very tense when he met them. If he thought the optimistic way then he'd be much more relaxed and chatty, and more likely to make other friends too, so thinking in that way has the 'pro' effect of making things better for him.

As usual, write down a list of each. Try to think about the effects on you, or on other people you care about, and consider long-term as well as short-term effects. When you have written down as many pros and cons as possible, try to weigh them up. Does it seem that on balance this way of thinking is useful or not? If it's not helpful, try to think of an alternative view that might be more helpful.

What alternative views might be possible?

The basic idea of this approach is simply to drive home the fact that thoughts and beliefs are *possible* ways of viewing a situation, but are rarely the *only* possible way. You try to generate ideas about alternatives: what *could* someone think when faced with this situation? If you can imagine anyone at all facing it and not feeling the same way about it as you do, then there must be at least one other possible view.

To work on this, it can be useful to try to shift your viewpoint by asking yourself different questions. For instance, what would someone else – preferably someone you like or respect – think when faced with this situation? How would you yourself see the situation at a time when you were *not* depressed? What would you say to help a close friend if it was them rather than you who was having your thoughts and feelings in this situation? When you have come up with at least one alternative view, you can use the 'evidence' or 'pros and cons' methods above to compare your original NAT and the alternative(s). Which seems most likely to be true, or helpful? You can also use 'behavioural experiments' (the next section) to test out your NAT against the new alternative.

Key messages

- The most important approach to NATs is to stand back and test them to see if they are really true or helpful. Various methods can be used to do this, including spotting thinking errors, looking for evidence, weighing up pros and cons, and looking for alternative views.

- When trying to decide whether a NAT is accurate, stick as far as possible to considering only clear, observable evidence, not feelings or hunches. Be a fair judge when your NATs are on trial!

- This approach will probably seem difficult and unfamiliar at first, but should get easier if you persevere. As always, try it and find out which methods work best for you after a reasonable period.

Tips for supporters

- You can help best not by giving your partner answers to their NATs, but by asking questions that help them come up with their own answers. The whole point of this exercise is for them to find new ways of thinking that are helpful and believable to them. Those may not be the same as your answers, and just using someone else's answers won't help them get better at questioning thoughts for themselves.

- Examples of questions that may be useful include:

  ◊   What makes you think that?

  ◊   Is there anything that does not fit with that thought?

  ◊   The current thought is one way of looking at the situation, but what other ways might there be?

  ◊   How might someone else see it?

  ◊   What would you say to a close friend who had this thought?

  ◊   How would you have seen this before you became depressed?

  ◊   Is it possible this may look different in a few days/weeks/ months? If so, how do you imagine you might look at it then?

Tackling negative thoughts using behavioural experiments

'Behavioural experiments' are just ways of testing out thoughts and beliefs through action. They have that name because they are like scientific experiments, only instead of testing out a scientific theory you are testing out your own thoughts or beliefs. The point is that whilst thinking and talking about NATs can undoubtedly be very useful, often the best way to prove something to yourself is to *do* something, not just think about it. Mark Twain, the American writer of *Huckleberry Finn* and other books, is supposed to have once said, 'A man who carries a cat by the tail learns something he can learn in no other way.' In other words, real experiences can give us information that no amount of talk can provide. There are two main areas where this kind of approach can be helpful.

First, as we noted above, there can be times when you just don't have enough good factual evidence to come to a decision about whether a particular negative thought or belief is accurate or not. For example, suppose Carol is thinking she is a bad mother because she sometimes gets cross and shouts at her children. It might be helpful to know whether this is unusual, or whether all parents do that from time to time. But unless she has happened to see such incidents, or has talked to other parents about them, she may not know how other people react. So a useful behavioural experiment might be to set out to talk to or observe other parents and find out the facts. We sometimes call this kind of experiment a 'survey' experiment, because it involves surveying what other people think or do. Other examples might include:

- Jill was concerned that her conversation with other people was too boring. She had an expectation that she always had to be clever and witty, and because she couldn't manage that all the time, she often ended up saying nothing at all. She found it useful to do a survey experiment of observing other people's conversations in ordinary life – on buses, in pubs, cafés or shops – to see what they were really like. She soon discovered that actually most conversations are pretty humdrum, which helped her to feel less pressure.

- Bill was convinced that other people must think badly of him because he was looking after the kids at home whilst his wife was working. He assumed they would be thinking he was lazy or 'not a real man'. He felt too embarrassed to ask people directly what they thought, but was able to sit down with an old friend and devise a couple of questions about this, which the friend then took to various contacts without mentioning Bill's name. Doing the survey anonymously through a friend also helped Bill feel more confident that the answers would be honest, rather than just trying to make him feel better. In fact, most people were entirely accepting of his role in the family.

The second use of behavioural experiments is to use real life to test out NATs versus alternative thoughts, to see which seems to be more accurate or to work best. For example, suppose that whilst reading this booklet you have been having common NATs such as 'It won't work for me'. You might have recognized that as a NAT, and you might have come up with some alternative thought such as 'Maybe it will work if I try'. How can you tell which of these thoughts is right? The best way might be to set up a behavioural experiment – don't just guess, but try it out in action. Using this approach you don't have to rely on just faith or hope – you can *show* yourself what the answer is. How might you do that? Try using these steps:

1. Get a clear summary statement in your mind of what thought the experiment is designed to test (or even better, write it down in column two of Worksheet 4 on page 104.

   In this case, it seems to be something like 'These self-help approaches won't make any difference to my mood'.

2. Then, think how to test this out. What could you do that would tell you whether your belief is true or not (column three)?

   In this case, perhaps you could make a plan that over the next week you will *not* try any of these approaches. Record your mood each day to see what it's like without doing anything special. Then for the following week, try your best to put into action at least one of these self-help approaches consistently. Again, record your mood from day to day.

3. Next, predict as clearly as you can what the results will be if your thought is true – and if it is false (column four).

    In this case, the prediction would be that if your NAT is right there will be no difference between the two sets of ratings (or maybe the second ones will actually be worse); on the other hand if the second set of ratings is better – even a little better – then that would suggest the NAT may not be true.

4. Now reflect on what actually happened: does it support your belief/ prediction, or is the result different from what you expected (column five)?

    In this case, you could compare the two sets of mood records as above. Is there any difference at all (even a small one)? If there is, which approach produced the best mood? You may also need to take account of any factors that might have distorted the results. For example if during the second week you won the lottery, or had some bad news, the ratings might be better or worse for reasons that really have nothing to do with what you're trying to test – so you may need to do it again some other time.

5. Finally, take a bit of time to reflect on the implications of your experiment. What do the results suggest? Are there reasons to modify your original thoughts or beliefs? If so, what would be a more realistic and accurate version (column six)?

    In this case, suppose your mood was a little better during the 'self-help period' (and there were no obvious distorting factors). It might imply that your belief that it wouldn't make any difference is at least not completely true. Perhaps you might modify that thought to something like 'Maybe self-help can make a difference if I try to apply it' and you might think about trying another part of the programme.

Worksheet 4: Behavioural experiments

Date	Target cognition(s)	Experiment	Prediction	Outcome	What I learned
	What thought or belief are you testing? Is there an alternative perspective? Rate belief in thoughts (0–100 per cent).	Design an experiment to test the thought/belief (e.g. facing a situation you might avoid, behaving in a new way, finding something out).	What do you predict will happen?	What actually happened? What did you observe? How does the outcome fit with your predictions?	What does this mean for your original thought/belief? How far do you now believe it (0–100 per cent)? Does it need to be modified? How?

Below is an example of how you might fill in this worksheet.

This example also illustrates some of the most important factors in making behavioural experiments effective:

- Start off with a clear question, and a reasonably clear idea of what should follow according to each point of view, so that the experiment can tell you which is more accurate. In our example, the question is whether using CBT self-help approaches will make any difference. The NAT predicts that using these approaches won't have any effect on mood. The alternative thought predicts that giving it a good try *will* make a difference.

- Try to have a reasonably clear idea of how you will judge the results, using the best measure you can find. In our example, it is probably better to rate your mood each day, rather than just think back after the whole experiment has ended. The negative biases may make it difficult to judge accurately if you just think about it afterwards.

- Take some time to review the results of the experiment and what it tells you. If there is something that has made it difficult to reach a conclusion, work out what might make a better experiment and have another go.

- You need to be aware that behavioural experiments are by their nature unpredictable. Sometimes things do go wrong, and it's good to be prepared for this. For instance, you might predict that no one will talk to you if you join your friends at the pub, and then find that they *don't* talk to you very much. The temptation here is to conclude that you were right, and they don't want you around. But keep in mind that even if the experiment didn't go the way you were hoping, there might be things you can learn from it. In this example, you might look back and realize that you spent your whole time staring into your beer mug and not looking at anyone, making it very difficult for them to talk to you. Keep in mind that you can always learn something useful, even from 'failed' experiments. If

Table 19: A completed behavioural experiment worksheet

Date	Target Cognition(s)	Experiment	Prediction	Outcome	What I learned
	What thought or belief are you testing? Is there an alternative perspective? Rate belief in thoughts (0–100 per cent).	Design an experiment to test the thought/ belief (e.g. facing a situation you might avoid, behaving in a new way, finding something out).	What do you predict will happen?	What actually happened? What did you observe? How does the outcome fit with your predictions?	What does this mean for your original thought/belief? How far do you now believe it (0–100 per cent). Does it need to be modified? How?
Monday 11th	These self-help approaches won't make any difference to my mood – about 70 per cent The alternative is that they will, but it's hard to believe given how long I've been depressed (10 per cent).	I won't do anything for a week, and see how I feel at the end. Then I'll do everything I can manage for the next week, and see how I feel at the end of that week.	If I'm right, there won't be any difference between the two weeks. If they do make a difference I suppose I'd conclude that the approaches do help.	I felt absolutely dreadful for the first week – it was a really bad week anyway – and when I started trying to do something the next week it did get a bit better. I actually had one quite good day.	Maybe it was because the second week wasn't so bad for other reasons, but I did feel a bit better. It's hard to believe this will really make a difference, but I guess my belief it won't has gone down to about 50 per cent, and the idea that it will has probably gone up to 25 per cent. It's just about enough to make myself keep trying at it.

something negative happens, you can try to understand more about what made it happen – and maybe there's something you could do different next time.

- If something doesn't go the way you'd have liked it to, you may find yourself more convinced that you're a failure. But remember that this too is a negative thought, and can be dealt with in the same way as others can. We like to think that there is no such thing as a truly failed experiment – either it goes well, and you can start to change your views, or it doesn't and you can use it to understand what's going on – particularly whether there is a vicious circle involved that needs to be understood. Getting your supporter's views at this point could be a very good thing to do – it will be much easier for them to see the reason things didn't go so well.

Key messages

- Behavioural experiments are useful for generating evidence that may not be available just by sitting and thinking or talking about something. They involve planning some kind of extra experience, so that you can see how things work in the real world.

- Survey experiments involve observing something or asking people about something, in order to get a better idea of what other people actually do, say or think.

- Other experiments involve figuring out what your NATs say should happen if you do something, then trying it out in the real world to see if that prediction is right. Don't just ponder in your mind what might happen but try it out in action and *see* what happens. If it does not work out as badly as you feared, what can you learn? How might your thinking change?

Tips for supporters

- Almost by definition, behavioural experiments tend to be scary. They involve testing out a NAT, and the person you are supporting will naturally tend to worry about how awful it will be if the NAT turns out to be true. Be supportive about these difficulties.

- Help them to think through what would be the best way to test their thoughts. If a survey, exactly what questions should be asked? If trying something out to see what happens, what exactly should they do, and what do they need to observe?

- Help the person you are supporting be prepared for, and cope with, an experiment going 'wrong'. What can they learn from such experiences, so as to help it go better next time?

Suicidal thoughts

As noted on page 18, suicidal thoughts are a common aspect of depression. These can vary from vague ideas that you would not mind not living any longer, all the way up to specific and detailed plans for how to kill yourself. At the lower end of this spectrum, you may be able to dismiss the thoughts fairly easily. But at the more severe end, you need to get help to avoid the risk of acting on them. Most depressed people do not commit suicide, and most people who have suicidal thoughts do not act on them, but it is important to take the risk seriously if your suicidal thoughts are getting more severe. People recover from depression and when they do, they are happy to be alive: don't take the risk of blocking out that possibility for ever by acting on suicidal thoughts.

If you have frequent or severe thoughts about suicide, and particularly if you have started to plan details of how you would actually carry it out, then you need to tell someone and get help as soon as possible. If you are not already seeing a mental-health professional whom you can tell about these thoughts, then contact your GP.

You might also find it easier to cope with suicidal thoughts by *postponing* any action, rather than committing yourself to *never* acting on them. Rather than trying to think how you can get through the rest of your life, it may be easier to plan just to get through the next day without hurting yourself.

In a crisis you might also consider contacting Samaritans. Samaritans' volunteers listen in confidence to anyone in any type of emotional distress, without judging or telling people what to do. You can phone them twenty-four hours a day (08457 90 90 90 in the UK); email on *jo@ samaritans.org* (they aim to reply within twelve hours); or write to them at Chris, PO Box 9090, Stirling, FK8 2SA. See *www.samaritans.org* for more information.

11 Solving problems

'For every problem under the sun
There is a remedy, or there is none.
If there be one, try and find it.
If there be none, never mind it.'

Anon

It may seem strange to have a section on problem-solving in a book on CBT. After all, you have been solving problems all your life, and are probably pretty good at it. You do it without thinking, and without even noticing you are doing it most of the time. So why do you need to be told? It's because when you get depressed, your natural problem-solving abilities break down, and the skills that you used automatically before you got depressed may disappear. When problems come, as they inevitably will, they may seem overwhelming and impossible to deal with. So in this section we are going to describe the steps you can take to solve problems and get on top of things more easily, and thus stop things feeling so overwhelming.

Before we talk about how to solve problems, we need to think about whether there *is* a problem to be solved. This is important because we have spoken a lot about negative thinking, and the way that depression makes you see everything in the worst possible light. But we also know that not *all* problems are in your mind. Sometimes there are real difficulties that need to be dealt with.

For any problem that we experience when we are depressed, we need to be able to tell the difference between (a) our negative thoughts about the situation, which we need to tackle as we have already seen, and (b) the problem itself, which we need to tackle in the practical way described here.

Imagine that you have been made redundant from work. This is likely to be a problem for many people (although as we pointed out earlier, some people may feel that it has created a great opportunity for change for them!). You might be worried about paying the mortgage, or about ever finding another job; you might be worried about what other people think of you. Dealing with difficult situations when you are depressed often requires two stages:

1. What are your negative thoughts about the situation? In this example, it's the idea that everyone will despise you, and you'll never get another job. You can use the techniques on questioning NATs to help you manage these thoughts – so you may end up reminding yourself that no one despised your friends when they were made redundant, and that one of them has got a new job and the other has set up a new business.

2. What are the practical aspects of the situation that you need to tackle? In this case, it's working out the best way of finding a new job, and asking for help, such as from the Citizens Advice Bureau (CAB – see page 541) to manage your finances in the meantime.

There is another aspect of thinking about problems that we need to bear in mind. There are times in life when things happen that make us sad and low, but such feelings are natural and normal. Imagine that a pet has died. The pet – say a much-loved dog that has been in the family for fifteen years – died of natural old age. No one was to blame, and no one could have done anything different, but the beautiful old dog has died. Everyone is sad, and everyone misses him. These feelings of sadness and grief are natural – no one would try to solve the problem of sadness. There are times when feelings of sadness, loss and anguish are the right and proper things to feel, painful as they are. As we feel these painful emotions, we somehow learn to work through them, and to come to terms with the sadness. In this sense, although there is a 'problem', there is no remedy. We just have to bear the sadness, until we have learned to come to terms with it.

Once you have decided there is a problem that is not just negative thinking or natural sadness, you need to think about problem-solving. There are a number of steps to follow:

1. Define the problem

Sometimes problems can seem absolutely overwhelming, and extremely complicated. Breaking them down into their component parts can be very helpful in making them seem more manageable, and in thinking about where to start.

Take Jake, for instance. Jake had finished university and was having problems finding a job. He needed to move out of his university flat, but didn't want to go home, much as he loved his family. He'd been living in his flat for two years and had accumulated a lot of stuff, which made the prospect of moving worse. He was very low and felt very despondent about his future. He knew he had to move out, and it just seemed too difficult. When he started to break the problem down into its separate parts it looked like this:

- I haven't got anywhere to go – I haven't even decided quite where I want to live.

- I can't face the prospect of moving because of all my stuff.

- The flat is filthy and I've got to clean it before I leave.

- I've got no clean clothes.

- I haven't paid all the bills – in fact I haven't even opened some of the envelopes I think they're sitting in.

Once he had written all these things out Jake at least knew what it was he had to tackle.

2. Decide the first target

Which aspect of the problem are you going to tackle? If you have written down more than one problem, decide which one to tackle first.

This can often seem a bit tricky. You could choose the problem – or the aspect of the problem – that is causing you the biggest headache. Or you could choose something much smaller, where success is more likely. In some ways it doesn't matter – now that you have started working on problems you will be able to come back to other aspects later.

In Jake's case, he decided that he would tackle the mess and untidiness in the flat first, since it was going to be almost impossible to move until he'd done this.

3. Think about solutions

We often describe this part of the process as *brainstorming*. The point of this is to write down as many solutions as you can think of, even if they seem a bit unrealistic. At this stage you don't need to think about whether the solutions will work or not – you just need to write them down. When you are thinking about solutions, there are a number of questions you can ask yourself:

- 'What would I have done before I was depressed?'

- 'Have I had to tackle this before? How did I do it then?'

- 'What would someone who wasn't depressed do in this situation?'

- 'What are my strengths? How can I use these to help?'

- 'Who else is around who might be able to help?'

- 'What resources do I have?'

- 'What resources do I need to tackle the problem?'

When you are thinking about solutions, it is very helpful to remember that there are other people around. Depending on the problem, friends or family could help, or there is a range of organizations. For example, the Citizens Advice Bureau (CAB) offers help for practical and legal problems and has offices in most reasonably sized towns. We give details of the CAB in the Other Resources section on page 541.

In Jake's case, once he'd decided to work on the clutter, he came up with these solutions:

- Move out now and leave everything I can't carry in one suitcase.

- Buy a load of black bin liners and just throw everything away.

- Invite my mates round and ask them to take anything they want.

- Get Mum to come up and help me (embarrassing but maybe necessary!).

- Get a system – put things in piles: definitely keep, definitely throw away, and ask someone else to decide for me!

4. Choose one solution

Now that you have written everything down, choose a solution! Think about the pros and cons of each solution, and consider whether you have the energy and resources to carry them out.

In Jake's case, he decided that the sensible thing to do was to start putting everything in piles.

5. Make a plan of action

It will be easier to carry out solutions if you can break the overall plan down into small and more manageable steps. Jake's plan looked like this:

1. Contact Mum. I might feel embarrassed and a little ashamed, but I know she'll help, and also she's got a big car so we can take things to the local dump.

2.   Buy vast numbers of black bin liners.

3.   Phone Matt and Jamie and ask them to come round and take away anything that was theirs, or at least tell me I can dump it. (They moved out last month, and I'm the last one left.)

4.   Start with the bedroom – it's mainly clothes and books so it will be easier to decide what I don't want.

5.   Arrange a date for a garage sale for anything that I don't want to take but might be useful for someone else. Could help with bills too.

6.   I am going to start this evening, and then I will spend an hour every morning and every evening working through the flat.

6. Put your plan into action

Now that you've made your plan, don't let anything put you off. Make your start, and remember that a journey of a thousand miles starts with a single step.

7. Evaluate the results

Once you have started to work on your solution, you need to evaluate how it's going. Is the solution helping? Do you need to do something else? In Jake's case it was very easy for him to see that he was making progress as the flat emptied out and the clutter disappeared.

Think about whether the action you have been taking has helped the problem – have things improved? Do you need to do something different? Jake could see that clearing the mess had helped a lot, but he also needed to take further steps before the problem could be solved completely.

8. Plan next step(s)

This is where you need to think about what else needs to be done. In Jake's case he could see that he needed to sort the bills out, and then think about where he wanted to go. His plan looked like this:

1. Open the bills and work out exactly what I owe. I do still have money in my bank account, and I know that Matt and Jamie will pay their share, so I don't need to be so terrified!

2. Think about where I'm going to go. I like this town, and there are a lot of opportunities here, so I am going to stop wondering about whether I should move to Australia. I can always move later if I want to.

3. Buy a local paper and look online at accommodation ads!

Key messages

- Even cognitive therapists recognize that there are sometimes real problems that are not 'all in the mind'!

- For any problem, we need to go through two steps:

  ◊ Deal with the negative thoughts that get in the way and make it worse, *and/or*

  ◊ Deal with the problem itself in a practical way.

- There are a series of steps that you can work through to help you tackle the practical side of problems.

Tips for supporters

- Sometimes it can be very hard for people who are depressed to tell the difference between a real problem and negative thinking. You can help by talking to them about how you'd feel in that situation. For example, how would you feel if you were made redundant? What would you do?

- Help the person you are supporting to tackle the negative thoughts that get in the way of problem-solving, using ideas from the Tackling NATs section (Chapter 10).

- Help them to work through the steps. Often, someone who is depressed may find it hard to come up with possibilities for solutions, and may dismiss them all as useless before they've thought of them properly.

- Help them to get ideas, and remind them that at the first stage, the ideas don't have to be perfect.

- Help them to choose a plan, and then stick to it – don't let the person you're supporting give up if it doesn't work straight away.

12 Relapse prevention: how to stop depression coming back

Hopefully by now you will have been working on your depression for a while, and you will have seen some significant changes in how you feel, and what you can do. This is brilliant! You may feel that you are pretty much better, and that the depression is a thing of the past, or you might feel that you are on the right road, and that things are starting to change for you. Whichever it is, the next step is to think about how to keep things going. It's a bit like dieting, where you don't just need to lose weight – you also need to keep the weight off. So with depression, you need to keep doing the things that are keeping you well and helping you to move forward. In Worksheet 5 (see pages 123–4) we have a list of questions that are a good way to put together all you have learned. We will illustrate how to answer the questions by talking about Tim.

Tim's story

Tim was dyslexic and didn't do well at his school, which was very academically oriented. He left with no qualifications and his family, particularly his father, were disappointed in him. He used to tell Tim that he was lazy and useless.

Tim went to work for a friend's father who had always been fond of him. As the work became more and more computerized he realized that he had a real talent for it, so he went back to college and managed to get good computing qualifications. But he could never shake the feeling that he was useless, and avoided taking on new things in case he failed at them. The crunch came when the business he was working in went bust and he was out of work. Tim thought it was all his fault and that he'd let his friend's father down.

He went through a very bad patch, during which he found it very difficult to go out and talk to anyone, and could not even think of looking for work. When things were getting very bad indeed he could not look after himself properly and stayed at home in front of the TV most of the time. Happily for Tim, his girlfriend realized what was happening and made him start thinking about his problems. She agreed to be his supporter and helped him to work through the text, while Tim made forms and drew diagrams on the computer. After a while he managed to get more active again, and started to see that the business failed because they were in the middle of a severe economic recession, and that he could not have single-handedly been responsible!

Questions to consider to help prevent relapse

How did your depression start?

In Figure 6 in Chapter 6 we showed a diagram of a simple CBT model which highlighted the role of predisposing factors and triggers in the start of depression. We also gave an example from Carol's story in Figure 13. You might have filled out a diagram like this for yourself, and if so, have another look, and just remind yourself how it started. If not, then go back to that section and think about how these ideas apply to your own depression.

Tim knew that he got depressed because when the business went bust he thought it was his fault and that it showed how useless he was.

What kept the depression going?

As we've described, very often the crucial thing in depression is what happens once you start to feel low – the maintenance factors, or the vicious circles, keep it going and make it worse. Remind yourself of the vicious circles that kept your depression going. Think of the meaning that you were placing on particular events and what you were doing to cope, which may have backfired and fed into the vicious circle.

Tim's vicious circle showed that once he lost his job he stopped doing anything. As he sat in his flat all day doing nothing, this made the belief that he was useless even worse – see Figure 20.

Figure 20: Tim's vicious circle

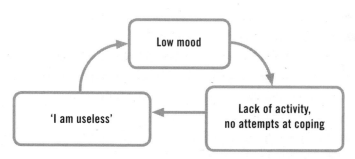

What are my most painful and unhelpful thoughts and beliefs? What alternatives did I find to them?

Remind yourself that cognitive therapy is all about the way we see things: the thoughts we have about events. Look back over the notes you've made. Very often there are particular thoughts that crop up over and over again and make you feel bad. How have you learned to cope with these? What have you learned to say to yourself as an alternative?

For instance, Tim learned to say 'I only *think* I'm useless because that's what I was told as a child. I know now that I'm actually really good at quite a few things, and people have told me that. I don't feel quite as useless now.'

What else have I learned that's useful?

We've talked about understanding the vicious circles and tackling your thoughts. What else have you learned that has helped? Go back over the chapters that were most relevant for you, and write down the ideas you found most helpful.

What situations might lead to a setback? How can I cope with them differently?

This means thinking about difficult situations that pose a risk for you. Tim realized that he was very prone to becoming depressed when bad things happened because he thought they were his fault. The biggest trigger was the business going bust, but he realized that he was vulnerable to much smaller things too – he'd get depressed if he couldn't mend the tyre on his bike quickly, or if he couldn't cook a meal well. Tim learned that he could cope much better if he stopped telling himself he was useless, and focused on the problem and how to solve it instead.

How will I know if I am becoming depressed again? What will I do differently?

Think about how you felt when you first got depressed. What were the first signs? Did you notice that you started to feel tired a lot of the time? Or did you stop enjoying things as much as you used to? If you can catch these warning signs early then you can take steps to stop the depression from taking hold. Think about the things you have tried in the sections above, and about which of them worked for you. In Tim's case, his early-warning signs were that he became less active, and started to avoid other people because he couldn't face them. Tim realized that to stop himself becoming depressed again he'd have to work on his thoughts, but would also have to keep himself active so that the idea of being useless did not have room to grow.

You might include as part of your plan the idea that you will pick the book up again and make yourself go through all the important stages.

Relapse-prevention worksheet

Fill in your answers to the questions in the relapse-prevention work-sheet below and keep a copy somewhere you can remember and find easily. Refer to the worksheet when you need to remind yourself how to tackle any future problems.

Worksheet 5: Relapse-prevention worksheet

How did my depression start?
What kept my depression going?
What are my most painful and unhelpful thoughts and beliefs? What alternatives did I find to them?

What else have I learned in this self-help book that has been useful?

What situations might lead to a setback? How can I cope with them differently?

How will I know if I am getting depressed again? What will I do differently?

Key messages

- Well done if you have made a difference and your depression is better!

- Don't think you've 'failed' if you need to use the techniques again – sometimes keeping well needs work too.

- Think about what helped you, and follow the steps above to make sure it's all summarized, so that you can look at it when you need to.

Tips for supporters

- Well done to you too if you've helped the person you are supporting and their depression is better.

- Help them to go back over what happened when they started getting depressed – if you see a lot of them you might have noticed things they haven't. Did they start getting irritable or snappy? Did they start staring into space when you spoke to them and seem very preoccupied? Were they unusually tired?

- It might be good to meet the person you are supporting once a month for a while, just to help them feel confident that you're still there. Even if this is someone you live with, you can put aside a special hour just to remind them of what they can use.

PART 2

Further strategies for tackling depression

Introduction

In Part 1 of this book we discussed the basic ideas and techniques of CBT. In Part 2 we include more detailed techniques to help you to tackle depression, all of which have been found to be very effective. Chapter 13 gives a lot more detail on how to use activity to help with your low mood – one of the most important starting places for overcoming depression. Chapter 14 talks about a very common problem – the fact that when we are depressed we go over and over things in a really unhelpful way and drag our mood down even more – and how to cope with it. Chapter 15 deals with the problem of depressing memories, and also shows us how to work with images. Chapter 16 talks about compassion: when we are depressed we often attack ourselves mercilessly, and we need to learn how to be kinder to ourselves. Finally, Chapter 17 talks about mindfulness, and how we can use this to overcome depression. Mindfulness has been shown to be helpful not just in CBT but in other aspects of life, and this chapter introduces us to the key ideas and practices involved.

The chapters are not all written in exactly the same format; some contain detailed exercises, with blank forms for you to fill in, while others contain more general advice. Some contain examples of people who have used the techniques, while others ask you to think of examples from your own experiences. Chapter 17, on mindfulness, suggests that you might join a mindfulness course, and talks about how to prepare and take part in this.

Not all these techniques are for everyone – some people find an active approach helpful, while others find being more reflective suits them better. Some people find that they work much better using images instead of words. So have a look through, and see if any of these approaches are particularly helpful for you. But remember what we said in Part 1 too – just reading through something without trying it out is like reading a book on exercise and wondering why you don't get fitter. Once you have decided that a particular chapter might be for you, then really work at it until you start to notice changes.

13 Using activity to combat depression: more about behavioural activation

David A. Richards

Introduction

The first part of this book introduced you to the CBT model and the importance of the vicious circles that keep depression and low mood going. This chapter will discuss one particular treatment, a part of the CBT 'family' that is called *behavioural activation* (BA). BA shares some but not all of the features of standard CBT, and is known to be equally effective, although the theory about why it works is rather different.

In standard CBT, we concentrate on identifying and changing the way you *think*, particularly automatic, negative and habitual thoughts. As its name suggests, BA focuses instead on your *behaviour*. We call this the 'outside-in' approach. In BA, we are of course also interested in changing the emotional, cognitive and physical symptoms of depression, but we do this by focusing the self-help exercises on behaviour. As you see changes in your behaviour, you should also see changes in your other symptoms.

What is the background to BA?

In BA we are interested in the *function* of the things you do (i.e. your behaviours). By function we mean the role that your behaviours play in keeping your depression going, even if you are not fully aware of them and their impact on your mood.

One of the reasons why depression persists is that you are experiencing fewer situations from which you might get some pleasure or good feelings. We refer to these as *positively reinforcing* situations: for example, spending some time with a friend, having a long soak in the bath, enjoying a meal, walking in the park, making something – any activity that makes you feel positive about yourself. In general, because you feel positive when doing this kind of activity, you tend to repeat it.

When you feel troubled and down, a natural response is to *avoid* things, as we have already discussed. So for example, if you believe that you will feel uncomfortable talking to someone about a difficult topic, you might avoid that person, or at least avoid the topic. You will probably then feel relieved. This is not necessarily a problem, unless your feelings of relief when avoiding this are so strong that you keep on avoiding it. This is called *negative reinforcement*, which refers to the relief we get from avoiding situations where we expect to feel bad. What happens is that the more you feel relief because you avoid, the more you continue to avoid.

You might wonder why this is a problem. Surely, if you avoid unpleasant situations you should feel less distressed, not more depressed? This can certainly be true in the short term. However, what we tend to find is that you can get into a *habit* of avoidance. It is this habit that can be the problem.

For example, maybe you feel as if you don't want to talk to a neighbour because you have a dispute with them. So you begin to avoid them. This makes you feel better and you get a sense of relief. In order to avoid the neighbour you reduce the number of times you go out of the house, in case you bump into them. Then you stop sitting in the garden as often as you used to. Both these avoidances result in you having fewer opportunities for positive experiences – meeting other people you like, having conversations with shopkeepers, seeing your flowers grow, tending to your plants.

As you can see, your avoidance – part of a cycle of negative reinforcement – has reduced your opportunity for positive experiences. Positive experiences have a good effect on your mood. Your avoidance habit is likely to make you *more* depressed in the long term, even if you started out avoiding things to make yourself feel better in the short term.

Going back to the example above, one further problem is that avoiding your neighbour does not make the dispute with the neighbour go away. It hangs over you like a black cloud. You end up thinking about it more and more, going over it in your mind. It preoccupies your waking hours and intrudes upon your sleep. Your avoidance behaviour, rather than solving the problem, actually makes it far worse.

How does BA work?

Once you understand the link between mood and behaviour, you can demonstrate to yourself that changing behaviour can change mood. When we refer to mood, we mean the emotional, cognitive and physical elements as well as the behavioural ones. In BA, you neither wait for your thoughts to change before you change your behaviours, nor do you change your thoughts directly. You also do not wait for your mood to improve before you do more things. What you do is change your behaviours directly. This is what we mean by 'outside in'.

You also need to understand the *function* of your behaviour – the role it plays in your mood. What is it doing? What are the consequences of behaving in a certain way? In addition, you want to know what *triggers* the behaviour. Is it certain situations, a thought, a feeling, a person? You need to figure out when, where, how and with whom behaviours do or do not occur.

You might notice here that BA shares many similarities with the CBT techniques described elsewhere in this book. You take a logical approach. You record examples of triggers, behaviours and the effect on your mood. You experiment. You analyse the results of your experiments. The difference is that in BA we figure out the link between mood and behaviour and then modify the triggers, or the behaviours themselves. This can change the consequences of your behaviours so that they become more positively reinforcing. Our ultimate aim is to increase the number of positive experiences in your life.

Key messages

- Behavioural activation (BA) is a treatment that focuses on changing your behaviour directly.

- In BA, we analyse the connection between your behaviour and your mood.

- BA tries to increase your chances of experiencing positively reinforcing situations in your life.

- It also tries to reduce the impact of negatively reinforcing activities such as avoidance.

Tips for supporters

- Using BA means starting to look at, and change, your behaviour even if you don't feel like it! Try to encourage the person you are supporting to think that they can start to make changes.

- Check that the person you are supporting understands what we mean by negative reinforcement and positive reinforcement – it can be tricky to understand jargon words when you're depressed.

What does a programme of BA look like?

There are three stages to BA:

1. Self-monitoring

2. Functional analysis

3. Activity scheduling

1. Self-monitoring

You have come across the principles of self-monitoring many times before in this book. This is where you write down your activities and emotions each week, using a specifically designed worksheet. Self-monitoring is so core to BA that you start it right at the beginning of your self-help programme and continue to use it all the way through to the end. The leading authors of BA treatment books (see the Further Reading section on page 542) report that there are eight main questions you can ask yourself through self-monitoring, which you can see below.

The eight main questions for self-monitoring

1. **How active am I?**
    You use self-monitoring to assess your overall level of activity.

2. **What are the connections between what I do and how I feel?**
    You can begin to see how mood and activity are linked.

3. **What sorts of emotions am I feeling?**
    You can identify the range of different emotions you experience.

4. **What did I do that made me feel positive?**
    Self-monitoring records can be used to see where you feel you have achieved something or which activity has given you pleasure.

5. **What sorts of things have I been doing this week?**
    You can examine the full range of things that you do.

6. **What should I do more of to improve my mood?**
    You can use these records to decide which activities you should do more of, because they make you feel more positive.

7. **What should I do less of to improve my mood?**

    You can also use these records to decide which activities you should do less of, because they mean you are avoiding important issues and making it harder for yourself in the long term.

8. **How am I doing now?**

    Finally, you can use these records over time to evaluate your progress towards important goals you have set yourself.

It makes a lot of sense to know what you are doing now, before you start to put in place a programme of increasing activity. If you don't carefully record a starting position, how can you know what would be a good thing to do? How do you know what would be unhelpful? You might end up biting off more than you can chew. You might even find out that what you think is a good idea is actually not helping at all. As you can imagine, this could result in a big disappointment and your giving up. We call this 'boom and bust'.

By taking a careful and planned approach to BA we can make sure you don't boom and bust. You make decisions on how to proceed by analysing the self-monitoring sheets. At first you want to know exactly what you are doing from day to day, week to week. Then you look at how what you do is related to your mood. When you are feeling depressed you may think that life is one big black cloud. Usually, however, when you look at a week or two of self-monitoring you see that your mood goes up and down and you experience a range of different emotions.

Self-monitoring exercise: activity and mood

Try the following:

Think back over the last few days. Choose a twenty-four-hour period from midnight to midnight. Try to remember everything that you did. Have a think about how you felt at each time in the day. If you cannot remember that far back, just concentrate on today so far. Write down both *what* you did and *how* you felt at the same time. To help you, we have included a worksheet below.

Worksheet 6: Monitoring activity and mood

In each box write the activities you engaged in during the hour, and how you felt. Rate your mood on a scale of 1 to 10, with 1 being the least intensity of feeling and 10 being the most.

Day and Date:

Time:		
Midnight–1 a.m.	Activity	
	Mood	
1–2 a.m.	Activity	
	Mood	
2–3 a.m.	Activity	
	Mood	
3–4 a.m.	Activity	
	Mood	
4–5 a.m.	Activity	
	Mood	

5–6 a.m.	Activity	
	Mood	
6–7 a.m.	Activity	
	Mood	
7–8 a.m.	Activity	
	Mood	
8–9 a.m.	Activity	
	Mood	
9–10 a.m.	Activity	
	Mood	
10–11 a.m.	Activity	
	Mood	
11 a.m.–noon	Activity	
	Mood	

Noon–1 p.m.	Activity	
	Mood	
1–2 p.m.	Activity	
	Mood	
2–3 p.m.	Activity	
	Mood	
3–4 p.m.	Activity	
	Mood	
4–5 p.m.	Activity	
	Mood	
5–6 p.m.	Activity	
	Mood	
6–7 p.m.	Activity	
	Mood	

7–8 p.m.	Activity	
	Mood	
8–9 p.m.	Activity	
	Mood	
9–10 p.m.	Activity	
	Mood	
10–11 p.m.	Activity	
	Mood	
11 p.m.–midnight	Activity	
	Mood	

Take a look at what you have written. Ask yourself the following question: *is there a connection between what I have done and my mood?*

- From your self-monitoring record it may be possible to identify activities that are associated with a better mood. Can you also spot things you were doing that were connected with a worse mood? As you identify these changes in your mood, have a think about the activities that occurred before, during and after them. Write these down on another sheet of paper.

- Next, look at the overall worksheet. Do you notice any patterns in the relationship between what you did and how you felt? Were there some regular times where your mood was low? Was your mood always low when you were doing (or not doing) certain things? Are there similar relationships where your mood was better? Make a note of these observations.

- Finally, do you notice things that are missing? Maybe there are behaviours that you might have done in the past that would have had a positive effect on mood. We call these antidepressant activities (lots of things are antidepressant – not just medication!). Does your record show that you are not doing these things as often as you used to do them? Have your usual routines been disrupted? Once again, write these things down.

The point of this is to help you become very aware of the way your behaviours and your mood are linked. The above exercise should give you an idea of how to start. We suggest that you do this over a period of several days, even a couple of weeks. Although this example required you to think backwards and remember what you did and how you felt, our experience is that it is far better to fill in the self-monitoring forms frequently as you go along, hour by hour through the day.

Some people feel that writing a detailed record can be a negative experience in itself. They feel that it highlights just how bad things have become. They think that recording this might make the problem worse, and avoid filling in the recording sheet.

This is a classic example of negative reinforcement – how avoidance of an immediately uncomfortable emotion leads to more problems in the long term. Even though it is difficult, remember that the first step towards changing depression is to know where you stand with it. If you avoid this, you will find it very difficult to make a start with tackling your low mood. The consequence of not completing the record is that you then cannot move to the next step of solving the problem. So, although it might feel uncomfortable, we advise you to continue and we hope you will feel a sense of achievement at making the first step towards your recovery.

When you have got a good record of what you do and have seen how these different behaviours are associated with different emotions, you can start to plan activities that you think will improve your mood. But how can you decide what to do? To help yourself, you need to act like a scientist by examining the details of your activities and your moods. Most importantly, you need to understand the function of your behaviours. We call this a *functional analysis*. It is the second stage of BA, which we will discuss in the next section.

Key messages

- The first step of BA is to record both your activities and your mood (Worksheet 6 on page 135).

- When you have recorded these, you can ask yourself eight important questions to find out what you are doing and how you are feeling.

- Your worksheets can help you notice the connection between your behaviours and your mood.

- The records can help you notice patterns in your life.

- They can also help you think about things you are *not* doing.

Tips for supporters

- Help the person you are supporting to understand that BA is about working from the outside in, changing behaviour before your partner feels less depressed.

- Help the person you are supporting complete their self-monitoring sheets, recording both activity levels *and* mood. Try to help them see the connection between the two.

- It can be hard for people to motivate themselves to behave differently. Give them plenty of encouragement and remind them that BA works. Look at the monitoring sheets and show them times when they have felt a bit better after being more active.

2. Functional analysis

The term *functional analysis* may seem a bit technical, but it really just means the study of our patterns of behaviour. In particular, we are interested in the way behaviours vary, what triggers them and what the consequences of these behaviours are. The point of a functional analysis is to figure out if anything triggers a behaviour, and what rewards we get from it.

For example, if you go to a café and the food is good, you will probably go back. If it is bad, you will not return. If you go back to the good café, you will be rewarded by good food and an enjoyable experience. In this case your visits to the café will be positively reinforced. If you avoid the bad café, you will not have to experience poor food and your avoidance will be negatively reinforced. In both cases, the consequences of your behaviour make it more likely that you will repeat the same behaviour: in the case of the good café, you go more often; in the case of the bad café, you avoid it.

In the above example, the *function* of the behaviour is either to increase the chances of having a positive experience or to decrease the chances of a negative one. Although the example of the café is an obvious one, many of the reasons we do or do not do things will be far less obvious. Reinforcement happens all around us, all of the time. Most of the time we are not even aware of it. When you are depressed, you may find yourself repeating the same behaviours over and over again without realizing how those behaviours are affecting your mood. You may not realize what triggers the behaviours, either, or what reinforces them. They become habits. We can see this in Jane's story.

Jane's story

Jane is a mother with two children. She lost her job four months ago. Her children get themselves ready for school and walk there with friends. She gets up after they have left and spends her mornings sitting watching the TV. She feels bad about this but it has become a habit.

Jane recorded the above facts in her self-monitoring worksheets. It was the same pattern every weekday. When she discussed this with her supporter, it was obvious they needed more information. Between them, Jane and her supporter analysed what happened in more detail. Jane discovered that the trigger for sitting watching the TV was going into the kitchen and seeing the dirty dishes from the previous night and her children's breakfast things. When she saw these she felt disappointed and went to the living room to avoid looking at the mess or washing the pots up.

As she sat on the sofa, Jane initially felt better, having avoided looking at the mess. Over time, however, she kept thinking about the washing up and felt guilty about it. She also thought the TV programmes were rubbish and that she was wasting her time. Her mood was worse the longer she stayed in the living room. As the day moved on, although she felt hungry she would avoid going into the kitchen because of the mess. Eventually she would raid the biscuit tin.

As we can see from this story, the function of Jane's behaviour (avoiding the kitchen) was to escape from her feelings of disappointment. She achieved this escape by sitting in the living room, but her behaviour also had other consequences. She felt guilty and her diet was adversely affected. She had developed an avoidance pattern that temporarily reduced her distress but had other long-term negative consequences.

The important lesson from this story is that Jane did not know why she sat and watched TV every morning. She knew she did not particularly enjoy it but found herself habitually on the sofa in front of the TV every day. Her functional analysis identified the *trigger* (unwashed pots); the *emotional response* (her disappointment); the *behaviour* (avoidance); and the *consequences* (short-term relief or escape from disappointment but long-term guilty feelings, worsening mood and a poor diet).

Most of us are in the same boat. We engage in all sorts of behaviours for a purpose – it is just that we often don't realize this; we are on auto-pilot a lot of the time.

Now have a go at doing your own functional analysis. Try the next exercise. We have provided a simple worksheet for you do this (Worksheet 7 on page 145).

Self-monitoring exercise: triggers, behaviours and consequences

1. Examine the previous self-monitoring sheet you filled in (Worksheet 6).
2. Try to identify instances where it looks as if your low mood and behaviour are associated with each other. If you cannot find a link, look for examples where low mood is associated with *not* doing something (i.e. avoidance). Write the behaviours down on the following sheet (Worksheet 7 on page 145).
3. Alternatively, you could look for times when your mood has improved and see if this is associated with your doing something specific. Write these down.

4.   Did you record triggers for these behaviours? If you did not record them, think about what was happening immediately beforehand. In your mind, put yourself back into the situation. Try to recollect what was happening, where you were, whether you were with anyone, how you felt at the time. Write these things down.

5.   Try to work out the consequences of the behaviours or avoidances you have identified. What was the immediate impact of your behaviour? What did you feel? Did these feelings change over time? Once again, record these on the sheet.

This exercise should help you to uncover the triggers and consequences of your selected behaviours. In the triggers section, do not forget to include information about the environment these behaviours occur in – where, when and with whom.

Hopefully, when you break this information down in such detail using functional analysis you will begin to uncover the reason why you do, or do not do, certain things. You will see how the results of your behaviours – the consequences – reinforce them. And guess what? All behaviours are fair game. For example, if you have avoided doing this exercise itself, you can even do a functional analysis on why you avoided it! You might find out what is driving your reluctance to complete exercises that we think might help you. You could then take this into account in future planning. It is not such a daft idea.

At this stage you might question why you need to do all this preparation and investigation. Many people want to get on and 'just do it'. We agree that this can be tempting. However, we want you to have the best chance of success. We definitely want to make sure you don't get into a boom-and-bust cycle. Our experience is that the better the preparation, the better the chances of a successful BA programme. If you understand the circumstances behind a particular behaviour or set of behaviours, and if you understand the reasons why these occur, particularly if they are habitual, then you can really get to grips with the next stage. We call this next step 'activity scheduling'.

Worksheet 7: Triggers, behaviours and consequences

Triggers	
Behaviours	
Consequences	

Key messages

- By doing a functional analysis you can find out why you are doing something.

- A functional analysis helps you identify the immediate triggers for your behaviours.

- It can also identify the short- and long-term consequences of them.

- Once you know what is triggering and reinforcing your behaviours you have a firm basis to start making changes in your life.

Tips for supporters

- When the person you are supporting tries the functional analysis stage of BA, you might need to help them think through all the elements of the 'trigger–behaviour–consequence' cycle.

- Try to help them analyse what the function of their behaviour really is.

- It could be very hard for the person you are supporting to motivate themselves to behave differently. Be patient, and just keep gently encouraging them – point out times when things have gone a bit better to reinforce the message.

3. Activity scheduling

We have already come across activity scheduling in earlier chapters. The difference here for BA is that you do not just select activities to try out from your self-monitoring records. Rather, you pay particular attention to your functional analysis. In BA you select activities that you think will do one of two things: reverse the cycle of avoidance (caused by negative reinforcement), or set up situations that you find rewarding (increase positive reinforcement).

Like most other CBT and related techniques, we adopt a scientific approach. This just means being systematic about your choices and curious about the results of your plans. You analyse your situation carefully. You predict what will happen if you change something. You then try out the changes systematically. Finally, you review what happened and decide whether to press on or to change your strategy. This experimental attitude helps you make further decisions.

The great thing about activity scheduling is that you have a lot of choice. If one thing does not have the desired effect, you can try something else. Activity scheduling is not just about doing more of the things you have stopped doing. Nor is it a test of endurance. Activity scheduling can of course re-introduce things you have stopped doing. It can also introduce new things that are consistent with your personal values. It can be aimed at breaking the 'trigger–behaviour–consequence' pattern. Sometimes you can plan activity into a regular schedule. Other times you can set up a plan to respond in a different way from usual when a specific trigger occurs. Activity scheduling can be used to break habits, introduce new behaviours and prevent avoidance. It can even help stop you *ruminating* about your problems (see Chapter 14 for more on rumination). Let us examine these choices one by one.

Reducing avoidance

When you first start using BA to overcome depression, you may want to concentrate on basic activities that are just not happening for you at the moment. You can reduce avoidance directly by increasing your daily routines. Although these will not necessarily be pleasurable, routines do provide you with a safe emotional anchor. Simple things such as a regular walk, doing some tidying and clearing up the dishes may not be the most pleasurable of activities but they can begin the process of activation. In fact it is very important that you do not *wait* to feel ready to do these things. You do them *now* to help you feel better over time. This is the outside-in principle working. Nonetheless, it is still important to identify activities that make sense to you, and that you also find desirable or useful.

One opportunity to reduce avoidance is when you have identified something absolutely essential that you need to do. An example might be getting a roadworthiness certificate for a car (in the UK, an MOT). Although you might be finding it really difficult to motivate yourself to do this, if you do not do it the consequences could be even more serious and could include a fine or having penalty points put on your driving licence. In this case, you need to break out of your pattern of avoidance immediately to address this one specific issue.

Introducing alternative behaviours

If you have identified that some behaviours are not helpful, you can decide to substitute them with different ones. There are three types of these *alternative behaviours*.

1. You can choose activities that you know are more likely to be positively reinforcing. These are things that you can predict will make you feel better. In general, at least initially, these should be things that you already know you like to do. Walking, talking to friends, cooking a meal, making something, reading a newspaper – there are almost as many things on such a list as there are people in the world. We are all different and your activities should be the ones *you* like to do.

2. You might choose an alternative behaviour that *disrupts* a situation where you get depressed. Here we are less concerned about doing a positive action. We are more interested in *not* doing something that

makes your mood worse. So, for example, if you know that sitting down alone in the morning causes you to feel low, you can decide to put the radio on, go for a walk or do some jobs around the house. The point is that doing one of these things disrupts the vicious circle of sitting down and low mood. These disrupting behaviours do not have to be in themselves rewarding. The objective is to interrupt the trigger–behaviour–consequence sequence.

3. Finally, you might choose a behaviour that is the direct opposite of something that causes your mood to be lower. Suppose you are avoiding some paperwork at home or at work and this is making you feel worse about yourself. You could choose to do the paperwork – maybe not all at once, but at least you could make a start. Another example would be if you find listening to music makes you feel sad. You could turn the radio off, retune to a different channel or get up and leave the room where the radio is on. Here, the alternative behaviour is the exact opposite of what makes you feel down.

How do you identify alternative behaviours?

When you are depressed it can be very difficult to see the wood for the trees. You simply cannot see any alternatives. Although the self-monitoring stages and functional analysis should help, it can still seem hard to decide what to do. Being depressed tends to slow your thinking down and make you feel helpless. However, there are a number of useful questions you can ask yourself to help with this.

*   *Think of all the possible alternative approaches to this – anything at all.*

    You can write all of the ideas down, no matter how unlikely they seem at first. Later, you can choose which behaviours might work well and pick the most likely one.

*   *Have I had similar situations in the past when I was not depressed? Did I deal with this in a more helpful way? What did I do?*

These are great questions to ask yourself. You can use them to remember a time when you faced a similar situation. You can then compare and contrast how you responded.

• *If I knew someone else with a problem like this, what would I recommend they should do?*

Standing outside of yourself like this can help you to be more objective. What would you say to a friend in this situation?

Making a plan

Once you have identified alternative behaviours you must make a plan. If there is one message about self-help BA that is absolutely vital, it is the importance of planning. Quite simply, waiting for things to happen by chance will not be very effective. You cannot just hang around in the hope that a trigger will show up. You cannot hope that you will come across an ideal situation in which to practise your new alternative behaviours by accident. No, you have to *plan to act*.

You can think about activity scheduling in seven steps, summarized below.

1. First of all, as described earlier in this chapter, you should identify situations and behaviours from the self-monitoring record forms that are associated with your low mood.

2. Next consider alternative behaviours, just as we described in the previous section.

3. Select one or more of these alternative behaviours and schedule them into a weekly plan, as small steps, not giant leaps. We have included an example of such a planning sheet on page 152. Once again, we can only stress that writing things down is the very best way to give yourself a fighting chance of making your plans really happen.

4. When you select an alternative behaviour, adopt an 'experimental' attitude to your activity scheduling. Be curious about the results of trying this new behaviour. *Experiment* with it. Putting the new behaviour into effect is not supposed to be a test of perseverance. It is a test of the effect of this alternative behaviour on your mood.

5. The acid test of course is what you do next. Put your new behaviours into action, using your weekly schedule to guide you. It is better if this plan includes trying the behaviours more than once if possible. Try one new behaviour several times rather than many different behaviours only occasionally. Repeated practice is the key here.

6. In line with your experimental attitude, you should evaluate the results of trying out these new behaviours. You are interested in the effect they have on your mood. Just like when you make a plan, you should write these effects down. Using a system like the self-monitoring records (in fact you can use either these sheets or the activity-planning sheet – whatever feels easiest), record your mood and its strength alongside your activity records. So, records kept in activity scheduling should include a rating of activity *and* mood.

7. The final stage is to review, adjust, and repeat. Continue with your experimental attitude. You should not expect quick fixes. You need to try the same activities repeatedly until you are sure they do or do not work for you. If they do not work, this is not a disaster. Rather, you have learned something. Adjust your activities and try something else instead. You have to be careful not to give in too early, but equally there is no point in persevering for no reason. This is how the experimental attitude can help you. Ask yourself, 'Is this working? Am I sure it is not working? Do I need to practise some more? Is there anything else that might be better?'

Worksheet 8: Activity planning

Time	Monday	Tuesday	Wednesday	Thursday	Friday	Saturday	Sunday
Midnight–1 a.m.							
1–2 a.m.							
2–3 a.m.							
3–4 a.m.							
4–5 a.m.							
5–6 a.m.							

6–7 a.m.	7–8 a.m.	8–9 a.m.	9–10 a.m.	10–11 a.m.	11–noon

Time	Monday	Tuesday	Wednesday	Thursday	Friday	Saturday	Sunday
Noon–1 p.m.							
1–2 p.m.							
2–3 p.m.							
3–4 p.m.							
4–5 p.m.							
5–6 p.m.							

6–7 p.m.	7–8 p.m.	8–9 p.m.	9–10 p.m.	10–11 p.m.	11 p.m.–midnight

Although we have emphasized that regular planning is the cornerstone of activity scheduling, you do also have to prepare yourself to take advantage of less predictable situations that lower your mood. When these occur you want to be ready to react. We call these 'What if . . . then what?' plans (the next chapter, on rumination, suggests something similar – 'If . . . then' plans). Prepare yourself so that *if* some specific trigger occurs *then* you know what to do next.

Setting up a 'What if . . . then what?' plan

The best thing about having identified triggers for certain behaviours is that you know the warning signs that are connected with your low mood. You can be on the lookout for them. Every time you come across the trigger you can recognize it and put in place your selected alternative behaviour.

For example, if you know you avoid certain things when you come across them – talking to a manager at work, for example – you can practise doing an alternative behaviour. This might be saying 'Hello', making eye contact, or offering a few pleasantries. The points to remember here are that: a) you are selecting an alternative behaviour to replace something you do that is not very helpful; and b) the alternative behaviour is your new response when the trigger occurs.

Another example might be if you tend to avoid confrontation when someone expresses a view you do not agree with. Although this reduces anxiety about putting your point of view across, it makes you feel inadequate afterwards. In this case the 'What if . . . ' element is 'What if I don't agree with what someone says and I can't express it?' The ' . . . then what' could be: 'If I notice that I disagree with someone, then I will practise expressing my point of view.'

Key messages

- Tackling depression using BA is easier if you have a regular plan.

- You use activity scheduling to decrease your avoided activities, increase your positive experiences and replace unhelpful behaviours with alternative ones.

- There are many different choices you can make in identifying alternative behaviours, but these choices should always be guided by your functional analysis.

- When you select alternative behaviours you can choose some that are positively reinforcing, some that disrupt your usual depressed pattern or some that are the opposite of what you do now.

- You should follow a seven-step plan when doing the activity-scheduling part of BA.

- Throughout, adopt an experimental and curious attitude to your plans.

- Where you cannot predict when something will happen you can have a 'What if . . . then what? plan.

- You will be more successful if you keep a record of activities and mood and review these records regularly.

Tips for supporters

- Help the person you are supporting to take an experimental approach. In BA, there is no right or wrong thing to do. Try out different things to see what works best.

- Sit down with them regularly and look at the self-monitoring or activity-planning sheets, offering support and encouragement.

- When your partner, relative or friend tries to think of alternative behaviours, help them use the functional analysis to come to a decision. Be as creative as you can.

The special case of rumination

Almost everyone who has ever experienced low mood, anxiety or depression will know what we mean by 'rumination'. For the record, this is when we find ourselves repeating the same types of thoughts over and over again. When we ruminate, we are more likely to think quite negatively about ourselves, our behaviours, the world around us and so on. We tend to judge ourselves negatively. We might compare our actions or ourselves with other people. We might even worry in a general way about why bad things always seem to happen to us.

You might wonder why part of a chapter on changing behaviour in depression should concern itself with a type of thinking. Some other chapters in this book have spent a lot of time explaining how we can change the content of our thoughts. However, researchers have recently started to understand rumination differently. One way to look at rumination is to see it in the same way as any other behaviour. It is triggered by circumstances, it has a function and it has consequences. Let us consider an example.

Simon's story

Simon always prided himself on being a logical sort of guy. He worked as an accountant and was used to working on detailed sheets of figures. When he could not make his figures add up, he would be very meticulous in finding out where things were not correct. He used to do this systematically and always found where the problem was and then worked out how to fix it.

When he became depressed Simon started to spend hours going over and over in his mind things that had not gone well. When he got home each evening he would sit and replay the day's events time and time again. He kept trying to work out what had gone wrong. For example, he had started to argue with his colleagues over trivial things – unwashed coffee cups, colleagues being a few minutes late, people making minor mistakes in their work. He would go over these events throughout the evening, and would spend several hours sitting or even pacing up and down unable to get these thoughts out of his head. He would imagine many different situations and how they might go differently. He also started to ask himself, 'Why me?' 'Why am I feeling like this?'

After all this he found himself exhausted but also unable to sleep, his mind in turmoil. This meant that when he went to work the next day he was more tired than usual. He found himself getting to work late and making mistakes.

As we can see from Simon's story, the trigger for his rumination was not necessarily the events that initially bothered him, but getting home and sitting quietly. His thinking and pacing the room did not relieve his feelings, but he was unable to stop himself thinking in this way. Ironically, the consequence of trying to sort out his thoughts was that he himself started making the same mistakes that so irritated him about others.

A behavioural-activation approach to rumination is to ignore the content of people's thoughts. The important thing to discover is the *function* of the rumination thoughts. Simon was using an analytical approach that he had learned previously, and which he had found very useful indeed in his daily work. So he used it for this situation, since it had worked for him before. Unfortunately, when he used it for less logical situations like this, it was only making things worse. Unlike an accountancy problem, where he usually came to a satisfactory solution, these work situations could not be resolved through thinking. They just carried on and on in his mind.

Tackling rumination is no different from tackling other triggered behaviours. We can interrupt the trigger–behaviour–consequence cycle; we can replace rumination with another behaviour; we can stop avoiding the thing we are worrying about. These are just the same types of strategies we have become familiar with earlier in this chapter. We use self-monitoring, functional analysis and activity planning in just the same way. The seven-step approach to activity scheduling ('Making a plan', page 150) is all-important for tackling rumination.

The following chapter talks about understanding and dealing with rumination in much more detail, with more tips for finding and putting in place alternative behaviours.

Key messages

- Ruminations (or repetitive thoughts) are triggered by circumstances, have a function and have consequences.

- A BA approach to rumination is to see it in the same way as any other behaviour by trying to work out what its function is. In BA we do not address the content of the thoughts directly.

- Try to identify the triggers, and substitute the ruminations for alternative behaviours.

- We can use the same behavioural strategies for ruminations as we did for other behaviours.

Tips for supporters

- Although rumination is a way of thinking, we can also see it as a form of behaviour. So instead of concentrating on the content of the rumination, BA tackles it by looking at its function. If the person you are supporting finds it difficult to accept this, and argues that they need to keep ruminating, then make sure they read Chapter 14, which will explain in more detail. In the meantime, encourage them to experiment – do they feel better when they ruminate or when they don't? Use the functional analysis to show that rumination almost always makes them feel worse!

- Give the person you are supporting plenty of encouragement, particularly in the early stages of BA or if their progress flags a bit. Help them to see how things have changed, compared to when they first started.

14 Thinking too much: dealing with rumination in depression

Edward Watkins

What is rumination?

Sadie's story

Sadie is a thirty-two-year-old technician working in a science lab. She works hard and wants to do well at her job, but feels that her colleagues don't value her, and that her boss sometimes overlooks her contributions. Sadie was very bright at school, but always felt that other girls, who were more attractive and extrovert, got more attention than her and seemed to get more praise for what they did – so this is a familiar story for her. Sadie spends an awful lot of time dwelling on why this always happens to her. She has a long drive home after work, and as she drives, she thinks, 'It's so unfair. I've never been valued; what's the matter with me? Why does everyone always ignore me? What am I doing wrong?' She replays scenes in her head when she thinks someone has been unfair, and has imaginary arguments with people. In reality she never brings this up. Often by the time she gets home she feels extremely low and desperate.

Do you ever find yourself constantly dwelling on a problem without getting anywhere? Do you get stuck thinking about why you feel down or going over your mistakes and failures in your head?

These are examples of what we call rumination – repetitive thinking about problems, difficulties and feelings. In depression, rumination is characterized by thinking about the symptoms of depression, their causes, consequences and implications. Rumination often includes 'Why?' questions such as 'Why do I feel so bad?', 'Why are things much harder than they used to be?', 'Why did this happen?', 'Why did he treat me like that?'

Rumination can involve dwelling on an upsetting event, such as the death of a loved one, losing a job or the end of a relationship. It can also focus on current concerns and problems, on your sense of self, and especially on those aspects of yourself that you don't like.

It is a common problem, particularly for people who experience prolonged or repeated depression. Research conducted over the last twenty years has shown that people who ruminate are much more likely to get depressed, and to stay depressed. Individuals who report high levels of rumination at one time are more likely to have become clinically depressed when they are followed up later.

Experimental studies have also shown that rumination tends to make feelings worse. So if you are already feeling down and sad, and begin to ruminate, those sad feelings are likely to get stronger. The same applies for feelings of anxiety and anger. It is like a supercharger that boosts the effects of negative thinking on your mood.

You may already have realized that rumination involves Negative Automatic Thoughts, as described in Chapter 9. However, rather than being a single isolated negative thought, rumination is an automatic *chain* of negative thoughts, which makes it much harder to stop. Rumination is the habit of going back over and over the same concerns. So successfully challenging one negative thought may have little benefit, because it is shortly followed by another negative thought on a similar topic. When you have a whole waterfall of negative thinking cascading down, it may not be helpful to try to stop each single drop! Rather, it may work better to divert the whole flow. That is what this chapter will teach you to do.

The consequences of rumination

Let's try and get a sense of how much rumination may be a problem for you. Think about the last time you spent a lot of time ruminating, or make a mental note to yourself to notice the next time you start. Write down how you felt before you started, and how long you spent ruminating. How did you feel afterwards?

- Do you find yourself spending a lot of time thinking over problems, without making much progress? Is this something that you find yourself doing often when you feel sad or down? Does it occur nearly every day, every week or every month?

- How long do these periods of rumination tend to last? Is it minutes, hours or days?

- What effect does it have on you when you worry or dwell on things? Does it make you feel better or worse?

- Does it increase or decrease your energy?

- Does it increase or decrease the chance that you will go through with plans or activities?

You probably now have a sense of whether rumination may be a problem that contributes to your depression.

You probably found that when you ruminate, it makes your depression and anxiety worse. This is typical. The most common negative consequences reported for rumination are that it increases anxiety, sadness and anger; reduces motivation; makes it hard to sleep; interferes with concentration; prevents problem-solving; and makes it hard to enjoy normally pleasurable activities.

Repeated thinking can be normal and helpful

It is important to recognize that dwelling on problems and losses is a normal and universal process. We all do it. When something does not go to plan or we experience an unexpected loss or setback, it is typical to think about it. We need to spend time dwelling on upsetting events in order to come to terms with them. Following bereavement, for example, we need to spend time thinking about the person we have lost, and feeling sad about them. If we have been rejected by a partner, or lost a job, it is natural to spend time dwelling on what has gone wrong and on how we feel.

Part of how our minds work is that our attention is focused on unresolved goals. This focus is valuable in helping us to be aware of problems, and it can drive successful planning and problem-solving.

So what is the difference between this helpful process of repetitive thought, and what we call rumination? The normal process seems to become a problem when we use it too much, when we find it difficult to control how much we are ruminating, or if we are using it in ways that don't help us. The trick, as with many things, is knowing *when and how to keep thinking about difficulties, and when not to*. This chapter will explain some of the ways that repeated thinking about difficulties can become unhelpful rumination, and will show you ways to overcome this.

Key messages

- Rumination is repetitive negative thinking about problems, upsetting events, and sad feelings.

- It is a normal and universal response to difficult events.

- Sometimes thinking things over can be helpful. However, it can become problematic if it becomes a habit, occurring automatically and without control across many different situations.

- Excessive rumination is a major contributor to the onset and maintenance of depression.

Tips for supporters

- Remember, we all ruminate. Often when people are ruminating, it is because they are trying to resolve something that is important to them. Thus, it is not surprising that the person you are supporting may be constantly thinking over the same thing.

- Because of this, it does not help to suggest that they just stop ruminating or put it out of their mind. How easy would you find that if you were thinking about something important to you?

- We don't want to be telling people not to think about genuine problems they may have because this would minimize and invalidate their experience, and probably make them feel worse and less willing to engage with your support.

- Rather, it can help to discuss how it makes sense that the person is ruminating, and then explore together if there is a more effective and constructive way to think through the problem or loss.

Rumination as a habit

Repetitive thinking about problems is unhelpful if it becomes an automatic habit that is triggered in lots of different situations. As a habit, it can be set off and start running out of control before you even realize it.

The pioneering work on rumination in depression was conducted by Professor Susan Nolen-Hoeksema at Yale University. Her research indicates that rumination is a learned, habitual way of thinking that people adopt when they feel sad or down.

At its simplest, a habit is a way of responding that has repeatedly occurred in particular circumstances, so that those circumstances then become a cue for the response to occur automatically. For example, an individual may have regularly smoked when in the pub with his friends (before the change in the law), so that going to the pub and having a drink could act as a cue to lighting up a cigarette without realizing. This is one reason why giving up smoking can be difficult, unless the routines and places associated with smoking are replaced. Likewise, to build up a positive habit like exercising, it helps to have a regular routine, where you go for a run at the same time each day. As such, rumination can be considered a mental habit, triggered by feeling low.

Like all habits, rumination can be changed, but such change requires two things. First, becoming more aware of the habit, and second, repeatedly practising a different response in those circumstances. For example, someone who is trying to break out of the smoking habit needs to notice their cues to light a cigarette (feeling stressed, internal craving) and then practise an alternative response that is not smoking (such as exercising to reduce stress, or chewing nicotine gum to reduce craving).

Habits occur frequently and automatically, without effort, and are hard to control. So, if you notice that your rumination has any of these qualities – that you do it without thinking about it, that you start doing it before you realize you are doing it, or that you find it hard to stop – then it may well be a habit for you.

Habits can be learned in two ways:

1. They can be learned from another person – if your mother or father was a worrier, you might have copied their tendency to ruminate when you were younger.

2. Habits can develop through repeated practice of an action in the same circumstances, especially when the action has some reward (for example, when it makes you feel better or avoids something upsetting).

Why is it so hard to stop ruminating?

Rumination as avoidance

There is a growing view that rumination may become more frequent and habitual because it sometimes acts as a form of avoidance. When we avoid situations that are difficult for us we get an immediate relief from anxiety and distress, but in the long run this makes the depression much worse. These ideas are discussed in more detail in Chapter 13 on behavioural activation. The same argument is now made about rumination. Rumination allows us to avoid things because we are thinking about them. We might tell ourselves that we can't do anything until we have thought about it properly. This means that we can put off taking any action or really tackling a difficult or frightening situation 'until we have sorted it out' in our heads.

The problem is that this means we never do tackle the real problems, which remain unsolved, and our confidence in ourselves diminishes even further. As many other chapters of this book have pointed out, avoidance works in the short term, but in the long term it almost always makes things worse, and needs to be tackled straight away!

Positive beliefs about rumination

Another reason why it may be hard to stop ruminating is that you might think it is helpful or that something bad will happen if you do not do it. These are just some of the beliefs that people hold:

- Rumination helps me to work through my problems.

- Rumination helps me to cope with my feelings.

- If I can just keep thinking about this for long enough, I will eventually come up with an answer.

- Rumination shows that I care.

- If I stop ruminating I might miss an opportunity to find the answer that will make everything okay.

- If I stop ruminating I might never sort my feelings out.

- If I don't ruminate about what I did wrong or what I could do better, I will become selfish and arrogant.

In fact, what we know about rumination shows that these beliefs *are more or less opposite to the facts*. We know that when people ruminate their ability to solve problems in a constructive way gets worse, and their negative feelings get stronger. We also know that to show you care about something, it's usually better to do something constructive than just to think about it.

Even though rumination may be causing problems for you, it will be very difficult for you to make changes unless you believe that it's a good thing to stop. Before reading on, go over the arguments against avoidance and against the positive beliefs. Make up your mind that you will try to stop ruminating, and see what happens!

Awareness as a first step to changing the habit

The first step to changing a habit is to become more aware of it – to notice when it is happening and to try and spot its warning signs. This involves acting like a detective to spot what is happening just before you ruminate.

One way to do this is by keeping a record of when you are ruminating. We recommend completing a diary similar to those described earlier in this book, but focused on your rumination. The key things to record are what was happening just before you started to ruminate (where you were, what you were doing, what happened, how you felt), the content of your ruminative thinking, and then what happened next – for example, how you felt after the rumination. This record could be on a form like the example on page 170, or could simply be noted down on paper, or into an electronic device. Use whichever approach suits you better.

Table 21: Rumination monitoring sheet

Date and Time	Situation – where was I, what was I doing, who was I with, what was I attending to, when rumination started?	How did I feel when I started to ruminate? What physical sensations did I notice?	What did I ruminate about?	How long did I ruminate for?	Consequences of rumination: How did I feel afterwards? Have I achieved anything?
Monday 6 p.m.	Driving home from work, remembering staff feedback earlier, asking myself why I did not get any praise, attention turning inward.	Upset about not getting the credit for my report, feeling tense in my shoulders.	How unfair Sue was to me at work – she ignored me and praised everyone else instead. What did I do wrong?	About half an hour of driving, then carried on for another hour at home.	Feel more upset, and furious with people at work, want to go and write angry emails. Didn't take enough notice of Michael when I got in.

It is a good idea to try to complete the form every day; this will make it easier to remember the events accurately. You may find it helpful to do it at a fixed time, for example at the end of the day, so that you won't forget to do it.

By doing this, you will start to pay more attention to how you are feeling and what you are doing. It will help you to notice how much you are ruminating so that you will become more aware of the habit, and will be able to respond in a less automatic way. This will put you more in control.

Warning signs

You are looking for the warning signs that tend to trigger off your episodes of rumination. Most people have their own particular cues. A common warning sign is beginning to feel stressed, with the associated physical response of increased tension, increased heart rate, a sinking feeling in the stomach and attention narrowing, but yours may be different.

Once you spot those warning signs, you have the chance to 'nip rumination in the bud' by doing something else instead before it gets going. This is how you change the habit: by doing something different from rumination when you notice the warning signs. Repeated practice of your new alternative response will eventually build up a more helpful habit.

When trying to spot warning signs, it is helpful to look at the situations in which rumination occurs in as much detail as possible, so that you don't miss any important clues. It is helpful to pay close attention to the sensory details of the situation – the sights, sounds, feelings – and notice their details, for example how people are speaking or standing. It might be that there is something quite small, such as a smell, or a tone of voice, which reminds you of difficult times in the past and thus triggers rumination.

Try to figure out what your warning signs for rumination might be by looking closely at your diaries. Because some warning signs come up fairly frequently, it may be helpful to review the checklist below to see if any of these apply to you.

Once you have identified your warning signs, you can look out for them and then try to react differently.

Common triggers for rumination

- When I'm under pressure
- When I'm judged, compared, evaluated
- When I feel alone, isolated
- When I'm bored, don't have anything to do
- When I'm hurried, rushed
- When I'm being criticized, punished
- When I'm reminded of a particular event
- Anniversaries of past difficulties or losses

Bodily responses:
- Tension in the shoulders, neck, back
- Feeling wound up
- Feeling anxious
- Feeling irritated and frustrated
- Becoming hot/flushed
- Increased heart rate
- Butterflies in my stomach, sinking feeling
- Heavy feeling, like I need to lie down

Key messages

- Unhelpful rumination tends to be a habit that is automatically triggered by particular cues, such as sad mood or anxiety.

- Habits can be changed – although this will take some time and regular practice at responding differently to your warning cues.

- The first step towards reducing rumination is becoming more aware of when it happens and of its warning signs.

Tips for supporters

- Help the person you are supporting to understand that rumination is unhelpful to them, and to be willing to try to stop.

- Work with them to help them spot common patterns in their diaries that may indicate warning signs for their rumination. There are often particular cues that precede it.

- Encourage them to be as specific and concrete as possible when describing events and reviewing when they ruminated. As much detail as possible will be helpful in working out warning signs. Ask 'when, where, who, how and what' questions to get more information.

- Looking together at the consequences that follow rumination might help to identify whether it has any effects or benefits that contribute to its maintenance. You may discuss what is helpful about the rumination, what it avoids, or what would happen if the person stopped.

What to do when I spot the warning signs: 'If . . . then' plans

The way to change the habit is to do something else more positive in response to the warning signs. This will interrupt the rumination and stop it developing. It is important to nip it in the bud as early as possible, because once it gets going, it can be difficult to stop. With enough practice, the alternative action will become a new habit that replaces the tendency to ruminate.

This is very achievable and doable. Most of us can recall times when we have developed new habits (our routine before going to work or to bed) or got into healthy habits (regular exercise, stopping smoking). It can be a lot of work and can take quite a lot of practice and repetition, but if you keep at it, a new habit does form. This is why we recommend you practise regularly and continue to do so when you put new plans into place.

Most importantly, do not be discouraged if the new plan has not made much difference after a few weeks: we expect it to take many repetitions to change a well-established habit. Try to be aware of small changes in what you are doing – there may be little things that are better. It's important to *remind* yourself that habits can take time to change, so that you keep yourself motivated, rather than blaming yourself if things don't seem to be improving as much as you'd like. Also, old habits tend to come back when we are tired or stressed, so be prepared for there to be times when the rumination comes back. You won't be able to successfully perform the new alternative to the warning signs every single time – however, if you are doing it more than 50 per cent of the time, gradually the rumination will come down.

The plans we recommend are simple plans in the following form: *if* I notice this sign of stress/warning sign/trigger, *then* I can do this more effective alternative. We call these 'If . . . then' plans, similar to the 'What if . . . then what?' plans we saw in the previous chapter.

For example, if feeling tense in your shoulders is a warning sign that you are about to worry, then you could have a plan like 'If I notice that I am getting tense in my shoulders, then I will practise my relaxation exercises to stop myself getting more wound up.'

The 'If . . . then' plan explicitly and consciously makes a link between the warning sign for rumination and starting the alternative action, and makes it easier to change.

For all of your 'If . . . then' plans, it is helpful to clearly specify when, where, how, what and with whom you will be implementing the plan. The greater the detail in planning the easier it will be to implement.

For instance, in Sadie's example, she realized that ruminating about what happened at work made her feel worse by the end of the journey. Although she wanted to solve the problem, she recognized that the way she was thinking about it didn't achieve this. So she decided to put an 'If . . . then' plan in place. She decided that she would keep a close eye on what she was thinking when she got into the car at the end of the day. If she was feeling tense and noticing that she was beginning to ask herself 'Why?' questions and think about past events, she would instead focus her attention outwards by listening in the car to an interesting audio-book she had chosen for herself.

Alternatives to rumination

There are many different possible alternative responses and strategies to use instead of rumination. Here are some of the ones that our patients have found to be most useful, and which are relatively easy and simple to put into action. Of course, this is not an exhaustive list and you may be able to come up with your own as you get more practice. Different strategies will work for different people so it is worth trying a few out to see what fits for you.

Slowing things down

Let's imagine that you've got too much to do, you are at home, you are feeling anxious and your heart is pounding; you are very hurried, trying to do everything at once, and your thinking is jumping from one thought to another. This looks a likely situation to get stuck in ruminating.

What 'If . . . then' plan could you develop?

When stress is linked to feeling under pressure and rumination occurs when you are trying to do too many things at once, it is helpful to slow things down, to pace yourself and to prioritize what you are doing. For example, it can be helpful to say to yourself 'I am going to do one thing at a time' and to focus only on the task in hand.

Becoming more active

Let's imagine that you are bored and don't have anything to do. You are at home listening to sad music, feeling tired; you are inactive, just lying around, and you are having all sorts of negative thoughts. Moreover, this combination is a warning sign for rumination for you.

What 'If . . . then' plan could you develop?

In this situation, it might be a good idea to plan to do something interesting or enjoyable at those times – to be more active. You could call a friend, play a game, listen to positive music and so on. It might also be useful to identify your schedule and sequence of activities over the week. Are there particular periods that tend to have more dead time? Perhaps it would help to plan to be more active at those times.

This is where Chapter 13 in this book on behavioural activation will be relevant. The strategies described there (and indeed in other chapters throughout the book) could be applied here and practised as an alternative to rumination.

You may notice particular places or times where you are more likely to ruminate, such as lying in bed before you get up or go to sleep, or when you sit down for a coffee after work. When you notice regular places or routines associated with rumination, it can be helpful to change those routines.

For example:

> **If I notice** that I start to worry in the morning when I am still in bed and cannot sleep . . .

> **Then I will** get out of bed and do some yoga stretches to focus my attention on my body and wake up.

Breaking tasks down into smaller steps

Let's imagine that you have a big task or assignment ahead of you. You are feeling anxious and wound up, but you are putting off starting the assignment, and you are having doubts about whether you will finish it at all. You know from past experience that this is the kind of situation that typically triggers your rumination.

What 'If . . . then' plan could you develop?

If something seems too big or impossible to do, and you feel overwhelmed and stressed, it can help to break the task down into smaller steps. Ask 'What is the first and smallest step necessary to start moving forwards on the task?' and start on that. Try to break the task down into the smallest steps possible.

Opposite action

If rumination is linked to a particular emotion, it can be helpful to have an 'If . . . then' plan that focuses on generating a counter-emotion. For example, if you are feeling tense or irritable, focus on doing something that calms you; if you are feeling low and lacking in energy, do something positive and energizing. This is the idea of *opposite action.*

Before people ruminate, they often feel wound up and tense. You may find that your mind jumps from one thing to another. This stress can also be felt in your body. For example, you may be tired, have a headache, or tensed shoulders and a tensed back. In this circumstance, relaxation would be a good example of opposite action that could help to break up the rumination.

Rumination can often consist of dwelling on the way someone else is treating us. It is easy to turn in on ourselves and focus on what is bothering us, without communicating with others. In these circumstances, a useful opposite action can be to assert yourself with the other person, clearly and calmly expressing your point of view and seeking their perspective, without getting stuck in your thoughts.

Similarly, rumination often has a self-critical and self-blaming quality. However, some people report that this aspect of it acts to spur them on, motivating them in the short term and keeping pressure on them to do things; it stops them slipping into complacency or other unwanted traits. This is another way that rumination may be reinforced to become a habit. We agree that keeping yourself motivated is a good thing, but there are other ways of doing it. You could try being encouraging and supportive of yourself instead. The chapter on compassion (Chapter 16) will explain how you can do this.

Becoming specific and concrete

One thing we find important to reduce rumination is to be *concrete* and *specific*. Rumination has a tendency to involve abstract thinking about the meanings and implications of what has happened, including asking 'Why me?' This abstract thinking tends to move away from the specifics of any particular situation, leading to over-generalizing: all situations get tarred with the same brush.

For example, a thought may have started because you overheard your name in a conversation and thought that people were talking about you. Pretty soon your thoughts may turn to many more negative ideas: what these people must have said, negative things people have said about you before, all the people who don't like you, all the things you don't like about yourself. Sadie would start to think 'Why me?' if she felt that she was being passed over in favour of someone else.

It can be hard to stop this flow of negative thoughts once it has started, but getting *specific* and *concrete* is an important step, because it helps to ground you in the detail of the here-and-now. This helps to keep difficulties in perspective, improves problem-solving and moves you towards actions. To do this, you have to focus on the specific details of what is going on *now* – to notice the circumstances and what led up to the situation.

Let's try a quick experiment to compare the effects of two different ways of responding to the same situation.

1. As vividly as you can, imagine that you are in a hurry to get to an important meeting. Make the meeting important for whatever reason works best for you, whether it is professional, family-related or romantic. Imagine getting into your car and turning the key in the ignition . . . but the car does not start! Imagine this situation as vividly as you can, as if you are there right now. Notice how you feel and what thoughts you have as this happens. Continue to imagine this situation, and ask yourself the following questions:

- *Why did this happen?*

- *What will the others think of me?*

- *What does this mean about me?*

- *What will the implications of this be?*

- *Why did this happen to me today?*

- *Why me?*

- *Why does this keep happening to me?*

Notice what you are experiencing after spending a few minutes imagining this event whilst asking these questions. Briefly note down your thoughts, feelings and other experiences.

2. Now imagine the same situation again, as if you are there right now looking out from your eyes. You are in a hurry to get to an important meeting. You go to your car, get in and turn the key in the ignition. But the car does not start. Imagine this as vividly as you can. Notice how you feel and what thoughts you have as this happens. Continue to imagine this situation, and ask yourself the following questions:

- *How did this happen?*
- *What did I notice when the car did not start?*
- *What was the sequence of events leading up to the car not starting?*
- *What happened next?*
- *How can I start to move forward from this situation?*
- *How can I resolve this problem?*
- *What is the first step I can take?*
- *How can I decide what to do next?*
- *What is the next step?*

Notice what you are experiencing after spending a few minutes imagining this event whilst asking these questions. Briefly note down your thoughts, feelings and other experiences.

Now compare your two experiences of imagining the same situation. Many people find that the first way of responding doesn't help with finding a solution. Instead it makes you feel worse – sadder, more anxious and frustrated – leading to more negative thinking, and a loss of energy and motivation. This is a good example of the *abstract* style typical of depressive rumination – by which we mean thinking focused on the meanings and implications of events: asking 'Why did this happen? Why me? What does this mean about me?'

In contrast, most people report that they handled the situation much better the second time. It is easier to make plans to solve the problem. People usually report feeling more positive, calmer and more empowered the second time. Questions focused on asking 'How?' and 'What?' move you to *concrete* thinking that takes into account the specific details, circumstances and context. Being specific gives more options to fix a problem, because it gives you clues as to what you could do differently in the future. It focuses you on the environment and your behaviour, which you can change, rather than on more abstract concepts like your personality and characteristics, which are harder to change.

So being concrete and asking 'How?' is another alternative response to consider in your 'If . . . then' plans:

> **If I notice** my warning sign of asking 'Why?' questions . . .
>
> **Then I will** ask myself helpful 'How?' questions about what happened and what I can do next, e.g. 'How can I start to tackle this?' and 'How did it happen?'

In the example above, for instance, asking 'Why?' questions will only lead to rather unhelpful answers, such as 'because I am useless', or 'because the fates are against me'. On the other hand, asking 'How?' and 'What?' questions can lead to more specific answers, such as 'because it's very cold and the engine is old', and plans what to do next, such as 'I could call for a taxi. I could call the AA.'

Here is a prompt to the main steps of concrete thinking:

1. *Focus on sensory experience and notice what is specific and distinctive.*

    Ask yourself: 'What is happening? How? Where? When? With whom? How is it unique, and different from other events?'

2. *Notice the process by which events and behaviours unfold.*

    Be aware of the sequence of events, what comes before, and what follows each action and event.

    Ask yourself 'How did this come about? What are the warning signs? What might change the outcome?'

3.   *Focus on how you can move forwards*

   Plan. Ask yourself how you can break things down into manageable steps which you can take to move forwards into helpful action.

   Act. Take the first step in the chain of actions (whether mental or physical) that you can do to deal with a given difficulty. Then follow the sequence, step by step, dealing with new difficulties as they arise and acknowledging your own progress when things go well!

   Ask. 'How can I move forwards? How can I break this down into smaller steps? What is the first step I can take?'

We have good evidence from clinical trials that daily practice for just four to six weeks of being more concrete in response to warning signs reduces both rumination and depression. You can see that this is an effective way to improve problem-solving. It can also be useful to look at a more structured problem-solving approach, involving a number of steps, such as those spelled out in Chapter 11 in Part 1.

Discriminating between helpful and unhelpful thinking about problems

It is also helpful to discriminate between thinking that is useful problem-solving versus unhelpful rumination that goes around and around without making progress. Spotting the difference can help you to step out of rumination earlier and avoid getting stuck. Moreover, comparing helpful versus unhelpful thinking about a personal difficulty can give you clues as to what you can do to address problems more constructively.

Perhaps when you are thinking more helpfully, or being more considerate and encouraging to yourself, you might be asking yourself different questions (such as 'How' questions). It would then be a good idea to build those approaches into your thinking more often as part of an 'If . . . then' plan. That is, you are learning from your own experience to make your thinking more effective. For example, Sadie could learn that asking

'Why do I not get recognition at work?' is not very helpful, and that it is more fruitful to ask 'What can I do to get recognition?'

There are three rules of thumb that can help you decide whether repeated thinking about something negative is helpful or not.

- *First rule of thumb: is this an unanswerable question?*

  Are you focusing on a question to which most people would find it hard to give a definitive answer? Is it the kind of question where the possible answer keeps changing, or is too open-ended? If it is, then it may not be helpful to keep thinking about it. This is particularly the case when it comes to understanding people or emotions, and when asking existential and philosophical questions (for example, 'Why me?'). Rather than spending time wondering about the reaction of the other person before a difficult conversation, it may be easier to think about what you really want to say.

- *Second rule of thumb: stop thinking if it leads nowhere after a period of time.*

  Keep in mind how long you have been ruminating. How long does it normally take to come up with a useful answer or make a decision? People report that effective thinking mostly leads to an answer within about half an hour of concentration, whilst unhelpful rumination can go on for hours without leading to a solution.

- *Third rule of thumb: ask yourself 'Are these thoughts leading to a decision or action?' If not, your thoughts are probably too abstract and unhelpful.*

  If your thoughts about a problem just lead to more thoughts, then you are probably being too abstract and you are likely to end up in a spiral of rumination and inactivity. However, when your thoughts lead to a response, whether that it is a plan or a decision or some kind of action, then it is much more likely to be helpful thinking rather than unhelpful rumination.

Preparing your 'If . . . then' plans

Write out your own 'If . . . then' plan based on the warning signs you have identified and the strategies you have read about above. Think of a couple of different alternatives to rumination, so that you can use the one that best fits the situation you find yourself in.

In the 'If I notice' column write a trigger or warning sign for rumination. In the 'Then I will' column write what you will do – be clear about when, where, with whom, how and what.

Table 22: Example 'If . . . then' plan

If I notice	Then I will
I'm ruminating on the way home	I will put my French tape on and learn four new phrases by the time I'm home

Key messages

- Make an 'If . . . then' plan to use an alternative strategy in response to the warning signs for rumination.

- Habits can be changed – although this will take some repetition and regular practice at responding differently to your warning cues.

- Try out different responses and stay with the one that works best for you.

- Don't be discouraged – you won't be able to use the new strategy every time you notice the warning signs, but keep practising whenever you can.

Tips for supporters

- Work with the person you are supporting to help them choose what looks like a sensible alternative strategy to practise instead of rumination. A good alternative will be something already in their repertoire, which naturally links to the warning sign, and which potentially serves a similar function to the rumination. For example, if rumination is used to control anger, relaxation would be a good alternative.

- Help them to make specific and concrete 'If ... then' plans, including the *when, where, how, what* and *with whom* of how the plans will be implemented.

- Encourage the person you are supporting to keep working at the new 'If ... then' plans frequently and for a good month to give it a chance to become a new habit.

- Model being specific and concrete when you talk with the person you are supporting.

- To support progress, identify and point out any changes, however small.

- Changes in habit take some persistence and some time. It is essential to support and motivate the person you are working with. It is helpful to remind them that habits do take time to change, and that it may take several weeks of repeated practice before any benefit is seen.

15 Using images to help with depressing memories

Jon Wheatley and Ann Hackmann

'Memory is the diary that we all carry about with us.'
Oscar Wilde

Introduction

In CBT we assume that the beliefs that we hold about ourselves and the world are shaped by our past experience, and much of this is stored in our memories. A large part of our identity, our sense of who we are, is based on these memories. Furthermore, our memories of past events can influence how we react to things now, even if we aren't always aware of it, and even if the events on which those memories are based took place a long time ago. In this chapter, we look at the way distressing memories can play a part in maintaining depression.

We will then consider how we can use our imagination to examine the meanings we have given to certain events earlier in our lives, and how to work with bad memories so that they no longer upset us so much.

Section 1: How our memories influence the way we see ourselves and the world

Memory and depression

Part 1 of this book looked at the way we think when we are depressed. Our thoughts and beliefs tend to be negative, as if we are seeing everything through dark glasses. The themes in our thinking typically involve loss, failure and defeat. We also looked at the part played by negative thinking in maintaining low mood. We saw that there is a vicious circle involving negative thinking and low mood, and that both make the other worse. We also saw that when we are depressed we believe our negative thoughts and don't question them, and that we can become very withdrawn and hopeless as a result.

When we talk about 'thinking', we mean a combination of a lot of mental activity. Sometimes thinking means thoughts in words, but sometimes it can mean mental images – pictures in your mind. These images can be of events that we think might take place in the future, and also of things that have happened in the past – our memories. Your images and memories may carry important meanings, and may influence the way that you feel about yourself, the world and other people. If these meanings are overly negative or distorted they too can play a part in maintaining depression.

Many people who suffer from depression frequently recall memories of perceived failures, losses and other tragedies. Often our most painful memories concern our families, our work and romantic relationships. Sigmund Freud once said that 'Love and work are the cornerstones of our humanness' and difficulties in our working life or in intimate relationships can sometimes result in stress and depression. Memories of difficult times can come back to haunt us when our mood gets low. However, it is not just the memories that are important in depression, but the meaning that we give to them. For example, Maggie had experienced many illnesses and losses throughout her life (including severe illness in childhood, and the death of her sister in a car accident). Maggie felt that the losses in her life meant she was cursed, and that there was no point trying to make life better, or to overcome her depression, because she was likely to attract more disasters in the future. It is clear that thinking in this way made her depression much worse than if she had believed that these events were terrible things that might have happened to anyone, and that there was nothing unusual about her that meant they would happen again.

Are memories facts?

So the ideas that we have about ourselves are often based on our memory. However, memories are not always an accurate record of events. Several people who witness the same event are likely to give different accounts of what they think happened. Often we can't be sure whether we can remember an actual event itself or the way that this event has been told and retold.

Our recall of the past is never perfect, partly because what we remember is based on what we understood was happening at the time. This is particularly true of events in early childhood, when our memories were stored with the limited understanding that we had of the world then. Furthermore, as we learned in Part 1, the mood we are in also influences the way that we see things. If we are depressed, then we interpret a situation very negatively, and it is the negative interpretation of events that we will remember. So our memories are always partly a reconstruction of the past rather than being a completely accurate record of events. For example, Jill was involved in an unavoidable car crash. When the car came to rest she felt that this accident was a punishment from God, because she was a bad person. She believed this very strongly, despite the fact that the police had assured her that she was completely blameless. Her memory of the crash had been coloured by messages she had received about herself as a child, from her mentally ill mother who had been very critical of her.

Another reason why memory recall is never a straightforward process is that our current mood state influences what we remember and the meaning that we give to these memories. When we are depressed we find it much easier to recall unhappy memories than happy ones. In one famous psychology experiment a group of patients suffering from severe depression were interviewed twice – once in the morning when they were feeling at their most depressed and once in the evening when they were feeling less depressed. When they were interviewed in the morning, the people in the experiment recalled many more negative experiences than they did later on in the day. Not only that, but they rated the memories as being more upsetting. This is a process called *mood-congruent memory* which simply means that we find it easier to recall memories that fit with our current mood state. So when you are in a depressed mood you are more likely to remember negative times from the past, and more likely to remember those times as being worse than they might really have been.

This also means that we don't remember good times if they are not consistent with our mood now. For example you may believe that you are worthless because you can't ever remember being treated with kindness. There may in fact have been some times when other people (a grandparent perhaps, or a kindly teacher) did something to help or nurture you, but the strength of your negative mood makes it almost impossible for you to remember these times.

As Albert Einstein once said, 'Memory is deceptive because it is coloured by today's events.' As we shall see later in this chapter, he should perhaps have also added 'and by past experience'.

Memories as 'ghosts from the past'

When you are feeling depressed you may have very distressing memories from key times in your life which seem to provide strong evidence for your negative beliefs. These are likely to be times when you felt intense emotions such as sadness, shame or anger. Such moments may become 'negative self-defining memories' that, when viewed through the dark lens of depression, seem to prove or reinforce your negative views of yourself. For instance, Michael had a very strong memory of pushing a frail old lady when he was working as a cleaner in a hospital. He felt terrible shame about this memory and believed himself to be a very nasty person because of it. He did not remember that the lady had been angry and confused at the time, that she had been pulling at his clothes and his hair for many minutes, and that he had been trying to get away from her because she was out of control, and causing him a lot of pain. In that context his actions seemed understandable and not at all cruel.

It seems that memory sharpens at times of great stress and difficulty, which means that we may recall specific details of these distressing events long after they have passed. The sort of events that seem to haunt us, almost like ghosts from the past, are times when we have felt threatened or humiliated in some way, or when we have experienced failure or loss. For example, you may have felt intimidated, bullied or abused in a close relationship or in the workplace. You may carry around a mental image of someone from this time shouting at you, perhaps 'hearing' their voice almost as if they were still present. Memories of such experiences may then return to you at times when you feel stressed or uncertain – when starting a new relationship you may be troubled by memories of difficulties in past relationships. When you start a new job you may recall times when you struggled or were unfairly criticized in a previous job. If your new partner is a bit short with you, or if your new boss asks you to change a piece of work, the old memories surface. The current event can then be seen as providing confirmation of previous negative or critical beliefs about yourself, the world and/or other people, and the feelings you had at the time that the bad memories were formed may come flooding back.

We may also respond to cues that match aspects of our earlier experience: for example you may feel an instant aversion to someone who looks or talks like someone who hurt you in the past, simply because they remind you of that particular bad experience. For example, Bill was being bullied by a new manager in his department at work. One day he was on a train, feeling quite relaxed, when he suddenly felt very sick and then angry with a pounding heart – all for no apparent reason. He realized that a man in front of him on the train had an identical haircut and very similar colouring to the bully at work, and his body and his brain were responding emotionally as if the boss was really there.

Memories can be triggered by all sorts of cues in the world around us; smell and taste are particularly powerful triggers for memories. Sarah, who had been abused by a carer as a teenager, experienced intrusive memories and felt disgusted whenever she smelt a fried breakfast, because this smell had always preceded acts of abuse. This may be one way that our brains try to protect us, triggering an 'early-warning system' that something bad is about to happen so that we can take action. However, although this is designed to protect us, our memory and sense of threat may be triggered when there is no actual danger present, like a smoke alarm that goes off when we burn the toast.

Small reminders of bad memories can be enough to trigger very powerful thoughts and feelings. A fleeting image or sensation can be enough to bring the entire memory back. This is a bit like clicking on an icon on a computer screen; there may be a large memory file that suddenly opens up in an instant. Another woman, Becky, experienced very upsetting memories of her parents fighting whenever she heard someone raise their voice. Like clicking on the icon on the computer screen, raised voices made her remember all the times when she had hidden in her bedroom, hearing her parents shouting and screaming at each other. When this happened she would feel like a small, anxious child again, even if the person raising their voice wasn't angry with her.

Recurrent intrusive memories in depression

If we are currently facing difficulties in our lives then we might experience spontaneous intrusive memories. These are memories of past events that match the current difficulties in some way, which appear in our minds automatically, and are often very unwelcome. The same memories can come up over and over again. It is worth paying attention to these because they can be one of the factors that maintain depression – that is, when you are depressed you are more likely to remember very negative events in your past, and in turn these memories may make you feel much more depressed.

You might be depressed because you think that no one likes you or wants to be with you. When you remember the past, all you can remember are times when people rejected or ignored you. So you believe ever more strongly that no one likes you, because you simply can't remember the good times when other people have accepted you. For example, Tim moved to a new town for work in a very small firm, and was having trouble making new friends. He had been bullied at school, and had a horrible memory of a group of children standing round him saying, 'Nobody likes you, you're such a freak.' When he thought about trying to make friends this memory would come back to him in vivid detail, and in his mind proved that there was something wrong with him, and that no one would be friends with him.

If you don't deal with these memories then you may find that they come back to trouble you whenever you feel low in mood, even after your depression has lifted. The good news is that there are powerful techniques for dealing with upsetting memories like these, which we will discuss later in this chapter.

General versus specific memories

Another way in which depression affects memory is that when we are depressed we may tend to generalize. For example you might say, 'My parents were never there for me,' rather than remembering some times when they were there and other times when they weren't. This can be a problem in two ways. First, being able to access specific memories can help you to weigh them up in a new way, and question whether the lessons that you learned from the memories really are true. You may have reached very distorted conclusions – that your parents didn't care for you, for instance – as a result of this lack of specificity. Second, if your memories are generalized you might find it harder to solve current problems, because you don't remember how you have tackled things in the past.

CBT techniques can help you begin to bring specific memories to mind, to examine the accuracy of any distorted, negative conclusions that you may have drawn about them at the time, and also to remind you of more positive events in the wider context of your life. By doing this you may be able to get a sense of yourself as much stronger and more resilient than you currently think you are.

Key messages

- Our sense of identity is coloured by past experiences stored in memory.

- Memories of distressing events can appear to have important meanings about yourself, the world and other people, and seem to confirm negative views. However such memories are often negatively biased.

- When you are depressed distressing memories can be easily triggered. These can maintain depression because they trigger thoughts and feelings that you experienced at the time you were distressed. The impact of depression makes it difficult to retrieve memories that might contradict these.

- Overall, it seems that our negative memories play a very important part in maintaining depression. We will go on to discuss techniques to redress the balance.

Tips for supporters

- Thinking about memory, and understanding how it affects you, can be quite a complicated business, especially when you are depressed. Help the person you are supporting to talk through this section, and to understand the points below.

  ◊ Has the person suffering from depression been able to identify any recent events that evoked strong negative emotions?

  ◊ Were any of these experiences accompanied by a mental picture of something bad that they felt was happening, or that might happen in the future?

  ◊ What emotions came up for them, and how did they feel in their body?

  ◊ Do they experience recurrent memories of particularly upsetting events that trigger powerful thoughts and feelings?

Section 2: Working with troubling memories

Memory as images

This section of the chapter will teach you some helpful ways to respond when you become aware of having a distressing memory. In particular we will describe how using your capacity for creative imagery can be a powerful tool to help you reduce your distress.

Often when we say that we have a memory what we mean is that we have a visual image – we can see what happened in our mind's eye. This is important because images are more closely linked to emotion than verbal thoughts. It is often said that 'a picture is worth a thousand words' and this applies to mental pictures too. For example, if you form a vivid mental image of your favourite meal, this is more likely to make you feel hungry than if you are just thinking about what you are going to have for dinner. Similarly, Tim (in the section earlier) could describe his experience in words – 'I was bullied' – but the real emotional pain for him came from the image of being surrounded by people shouting and laughing at him. The picture is much more emotional than the words.

Images may not just be visual. Bill was troubled by a recurrent memory of his boss bullying him, but instead of mentally picturing his boss he would 'hear' his voice and feel the sensation as if his boss were standing behind him, looking over his shoulder and criticizing him. Bill was therefore 'hearing' his boss's voice in his head and feeling the stress and tension in his body that he had felt at the time. This shows that whilst sometimes experiences are stored in our minds as mental pictures, we can also be left with sounds and bodily sensations that we experienced at the time of the event.

Another reason images are important is that they may be linked to particular emotional memories. Fragments of past memories may be stored as mental images in our minds, even if we cannot recall the memory in its entirety. These fragments of memory often represent the worst moments of a traumatic event. For example one woman imagined herself to be shrinking down in size whenever she felt anxious in social situations. She had a vivid image of herself as a small child cowering in a corner with much bigger people standing over her, but she could not remember what the whole story was, or why she had been in this position.

Sometimes there can be a whole host of meaning contained in a single picture. For instance, Rob was about to take an important exam, which he was very worried about. He had a vivid image of himself coming out of the exam room on his own looking exhausted and despondent, while everyone else was chatting and laughing. He realized that this image had a very clear meaning for him – 'you are going to fail and everyone else will pass' – which was having a very negative effect on him. Once he was aware of this, and realized that it meant he was predicting that he would fail, he was able to put it out of his mind and concentrate more on his studies.

Key messages

- Distressing memories are often stored as images, sounds and bodily sensations rather than as words.

- The images have a lot of emotional power, and carry important meanings that we are not always aware of.

Tips for supporters

- Because we are talking about memories, it is possible that some very distressing memories will come into the mind of the person that you are supporting, perhaps memories of some events that they have not thought about for many years. Upsetting though this may be, it could present a very good opportunity to work through them using the techniques we are going to discuss below.

> • Make sure that the person you are supporting is approaching memories in a different way – not just replaying them, but really thinking them through and trying out the strategies that we suggest.

Using imagery to help us work with memories

Next, we will show you how to deal with memories using the power of imagery to help you. Before we go on, it is important to point out that there is a difference between 'thinking about' an upsetting memory and 'thinking it through'. If you just think *about* a distressing event from the past, then you may not learn anything new about it; you may just re-experience the emotional pain associated with that time. Thinking *through* a past experience means that you reflect on it in a different way – you will be trying to bring the knowledge from this chapter into the way that you think, so that you can arrive at a different understanding of the memory. This is not an easy thing to do, but with patience and kindness towards yourself you can begin to think and feel differently about events that may have troubled you for many years.

Step 1: Identifying 'ghosts from the past'

As mentioned earlier in this chapter, distressing past experiences can colour your experience of the present. So the first step is to try and bring the past experiences to the foreground so that we can work on them in a different way.

If particular situations reliably make you feel anxious, miserable or unconfident then it can be helpful to think about whether there are particular memories that come back when you are in those situations. Try asking yourself the following questions:

• Are there some bad memories being brought to mind when I find myself in this situation?

- Is the way I respond to current stress based on my understanding of the current situation, or am I being influenced by memories of the past?

A good way to identify problematic memories from the past is by using a technique called 'the emotional bridge'. This simply involves exploring links between things that distress you today and your past experiences. The process is described below:

The emotional bridge technique

If you discover that a particularly distressing emotion keeps on returning to you, then ask yourself the following questions:

- *How do I actually feel right now? How would I describe this feeling to someone else?*

- *How do I feel in my body when I feel this way?*

- *What thoughts am I having when I feel this way?*

- *Do I have any mental pictures in my mind?*

- *What am I afraid might happen next? What is the worst thing that could happen?*

Once you've identified the feeling then ask yourself the following questions:

- *When in my life do I first remember feeling this way?*

- *Were there key times in my life when I felt like this?*

Try to be aware of the memories that come into your mind when you get this feeling. Reflect on whether it is possible that what you are feeling now is coloured by input from events much longer ago.

If you find that you recall a number of different events from the past then choose to work on *a memory of the time when you had this feeling most strongly*. We will show you how to do this in the section below.

You may not be able to answer these questions straight away so don't worry if nothing comes to mind to begin with. Simply allow yourself to become curious about the question, perhaps returning to it from time to time, and see what comes to mind. With a bit of gentle enquiry like this we can often make links between how we are feeling now and how we might have felt in the past.

Remember that your memories often take the form of images, so try to tune in to what you see in your mind when you ask yourself the questions, and see if any pictures come. If it would help, use the blank worksheet below to help you think it through.

Worksheet 9: The emotional bridge technique

How do I actually feel right now?

How do I feel in my body when I feel this way?

What thoughts am I having when I feel this way?

Do I have any mental pictures in my mind?

What am I afraid might happen next? What is the worst thing that could happen?

When in my life do I first remember feeling this way?

Were there key times in my life when I felt like this?

Peter's story: making links between past and present experiences

Peter's depression started when a complaint was made about him at work. The complaint was totally unsubstantiated and it was eventually proven that he had done nothing wrong. Nevertheless Peter believed that he had done something awful and that he would soon be found out as being a terrible person. This fear drove him to work long hours to ensure that he didn't make even a small mistake. He worked so hard that he became exhausted and was eventually signed off work with clinical depression.

Peter was vulnerable to developing depression because he had always believed that he was a bad person and he had tried to compensate for this by striving to be the perfect worker and family man. Having a complaint made about him at work seemed (to him) to confirm his worst fears about himself: that he was wicked and lazy. When he became depressed he had intrusive emotional memories of his mother calling him a wicked child and being told to wait until his father got home, when he would be shouted at and criticized .

He realized that his reaction to the complaint – which would have been undoubtedly difficult for anyone – was so strong because it was being influenced by his past memories. He was able to see the whole situation in a new way, and to think about how he might react differently. He was also able to reappraise his experiences and conclude that he had not really been a bad child and that his parents' criticism of him had been excessively harsh. This new understanding helped him begin to be kinder to himself; he was able to return to work and no longer felt the need to drive himself quite so hard.

Table 23: Peter's completed emotional bridge form

How do I actually feel right now?   *I feel sad and afraid.*
How do I feel in my body when I feel this way?   *Tense and hunched up.*
What thoughts am I having when I feel this way?   *I am really in trouble here – other people are going to give me a hard time and be very critical of me.*
Do I have any mental pictures in my mind?   *I can see my mother's face, looking cross and disapproving.*
What am I afraid might happen next? What is the worst thing that could happen?   *I might get told off and severely criticized for making a mistake.*
When in my life do I first remember feeling this way?   *Hiding as a small child, waiting for my father to get home and expecting him to tell me off.*
Were there key times in my life when I felt like this?   *There were a lot of times as a child when my school report wasn't good enough for my parents and they would get angry and tell me I was stupid and lazy.*

Step 2: Changing the meaning of distressing memories using cognitive therapy

Once you have identified a recurrent, distressing memory you can try completing the worksheet below to help you explore the meanings of the remembered event, update the meaning of the memory and start putting it into perspective. Peter's completed version follows the blank form.

Worksheet 10: Changing unhelpful beliefs

What conclusions might I have drawn (as a child, or at the time of the event) based on my experience?
What sense did I make of the experience at the time?
Are these beliefs still around with me today?
How would I rate the strength of these beliefs?
What do I think about this event now, from my current perspective?
What would a compassionate friend say?
How could I update my old beliefs based on my adult perspective and the views of people who care about me?
How would that change my unhelpful beliefs?

Table 24: Peter's completed cognitive therapy form

What conclusions might I have drawn (as a child, or at the time of the event) based on my experience?
That I am a bad person who deserves criticism.
What sense did I make of the experience at the time?
That my parents' criticisms were fair and that I must have done something wrong.
Are these beliefs still around with me today?
Yes, I still feel as if I have done something wrong and that I am going to be criticized.
How would I rate the strength of these beliefs?
I believe that I am a bad person (95 per cent) and that I am going to be criticized (80 per cent).
What do I think about this event now, from my current perspective?
I really wasn't that bad or naughty as a child. Now that I have my own children I can see that my parents were really very harsh and that their criticism was too severe.
What would a compassionate friend say?
They would say that I am being too hard on myself, that I am a good and conscientious person.
How could I update my old beliefs based on my adult perspective and the views of people who care about me?
Maybe I've been pushing myself too hard because I've been afraid that people will find out 'the truth' that I am bad and lazy. However perhaps that isn't the truth after all – perhaps I am actually a good person who is doing the best that they can.
How would that change my unhelpful beliefs?
I am less sure that I am a bad person now so that belief is 60 per cent. Perhaps I believe that I am a good person (40 per cent), although that idea is going to take some getting used to. I still worry that I might be criticized if I make a mistake, but that has reduced to 40 per cent.

You can see that following this process Peter has started to question some of the unhelpful beliefs that he had about himself. The strength of his old, negative belief system is reducing and he is starting to build up new, more helpful beliefs about himself. For another example of how this might work in practice see Linda's story below.

Linda's story: identifying and changing the meaning of upsetting memories

Linda found that she often felt unconfident and helpless during meetings with her boss. At such times she had the sense that she might get told off, even though she knew that she had not made any mistakes at work. She was able to link this feeling back to her experience of being punished as a child by a strict, authoritarian father who would often discipline her, seemingly without reason. As a result of these experiences she had grown up with a terrible anxiety that she might be suddenly 'found out' and punished for some wrong that she did not know she had done. The beliefs that were still around when she encountered an authority figure were:

- I am no good, and I will make mistakes. I believe this at least 90 per cent.

- I will be 'found out'. I believe this 100 per cent.

- Others are cruel, and I will be punished. I believe this 95 per cent.

Whenever she encountered authority figures Linda felt like a frightened child whom she came to know and identify as 'Little Linda'. She found it helpful to remind herself that Little Linda may have had good reason to feel frightened in the past but that she didn't need to worry so much now, as a mature and capable adult. This also helped Linda to become kinder to herself, because she felt some compassion for Little Linda, the frightened girl who had not done anything wrong. Deliberately bringing the memories to mind had made her realize that her father had been unusually punitive, and that in reality she was as capable as anyone else, and was no longer scrutinized by anyone in such a hostile way.

Linda had always believed that her parents had been rather strict and her memories of them were quite general: that they were cold and distant, and that they valued discipline. However when she started to recall specific times when she had been punished (using the emotional bridge technique described above), she came to realize that her parents had been more than strict – they had actually been cruel at times. She changed her perspective on these experiences, reflecting that she had a child of her own now, whom she would never treat in such a cruel way. This reappraisal of her past had a big effect on her current emotional state. Linda initially became angry with her parents for having treated her so cruelly in the past, then she started to feel sad because she hadn't received the care, warmth and encouragement that she had needed as a child. It seemed as if her depression had been masking these deeper emotions, which she was only able to access when she started to remember more specific details about her childhood and to reflect on them as an adult. Once she had put these childhood events into perspective she stopped thinking of herself as so worthless and her symptoms of depression started to lift. She was able to form the following alternative beliefs about herself:

- I am a good person, and I have high standards for myself, but I am only human and I will sometimes make mistakes (80 per cent).

- Other people are not trying to 'find me out' but they are quite happy for me to work very hard for long hours (65 per cent).

- I have lived my life trying to please other people, but this has sometimes made me unwell. If I want to look after myself then I will need to worry less about what other people think and start caring for myself more (90 per cent).

Key messages

- Thinking about an upsetting memory is not helpful if all we do is replay it and re-experience the negative emotions. We need to try to think about the memories in a different way.

- It is important to identify the meaning of an upsetting memory and then reflect on whether or not our thinking about the original event may be biased in some way.

Tips for supporters

- You may have helped the depressed person work through Steps 1 and 2, as listed above, or they may have worked through them alone. At this stage they may say that this new perspective makes sense intellectually, but does not really change the way they feel. In this case it is useful to help them consider moving on to Step 3.

Step 3: Using imagery to help change negative beliefs and to lift depressed mood

Sometimes thinking things through and verbally challenging the meaning of an upsetting memory works very well, but this doesn't always change the way we feel about a past event. This is what we call the 'head-heart' lag: you may be able to see that rationally the past event wasn't your fault, but you still *feel* that it was, and so you still feel bad about it. This is where creative imagery techniques can be particularly helpful. Imagination is a powerful psychological tool. As human beings we are able to conjure up all sorts of weird and wonderful scenarios in our minds. It seems from scientific research that our brains don't distinguish very well between reality and fantasy. We tend to respond to vividly imagined scenarios almost as if they were really happening. This is why pleasant fantasies and daydreams can be so delightful; it's also why it can be difficult for us to get to sleep after we have watched a scary movie. Our capacity for imagination can be a double-edged sword: it can plague us with frightening images of future threat, or motivate us if we picture ourselves reaching a valued goal. The therapeutic power of imagery is something that sports psychologists have been using for many years; cognitive therapists have only recently started to research and make use of it, with very good results so far.

Using imagery in this way can enhance both motivation and performance, as well as belief in the possibility of success. 'Visualize to energize' is a popular mantra amongst sports psychology coaches. What this means is that the more vividly we can imagine something, the more likely we are to act according to the image we have in mind. In order to be effective, creative imagery has to be detailed enough so that it feels convincing. Use all five senses to help you: what you see, hear, smell, touch and taste, so that you can really get a sense of the experience. Smell can be a particularly powerful trigger for imagery. Have you ever smelt a certain perfume or aftershave that immediately reminds you of someone in particular? One man described how the scent of roses always made him feel sad and guilty because it reminded him of being told off for accidentally stepping on one of his father's prized rose bushes as a small boy. Whenever he smelt roses he was mentally transported back in time to that particular summer's day and he recalled the emotions he had felt at that time.

If you don't think that you use much imagery in your daily life then ask yourself the following simple question: what does a bicycle look like? How do you know? Usually in response to this question we form a mental picture of a bicycle. Let's try another question: what did you have for breakfast this morning? How do you know? Often we remember the sensation of eating breakfast, such as buttering the toast, or the taste of the cereal and the smell of the coffee, or we picture the place where we usually sit each morning. So we all have a capacity for imagination that can be used to our advantage when struggling with low mood or anxiety. This means you can put it to use when exploring memories that have negative meanings, to arrive at a new perspective on situations that may have haunted you for years.

Wendy's story

Wendy described her depression as feeling like she was stuck down a very deep well. On the days when her mood was lowest she had an image of herself stuck at the bottom of the well in the dark; in the image she could not see the top, and other people could not see or hear her because she was so far down. A friend in whom she could confide asked her what she needed, and Wendy realized that she could see her friend passing her down a very long ladder to help her climb back to the outside world. She began to think of things that she could do to start her journey back to the 'surface' and to see each of these positive actions as being like rungs of her recovery ladder. She found that simple steps such as taking some exercise, eating well, making the effort to contact friends and answering the telephone when it rang all helped her to move her mood further out of the well of her depression.

Reducing the sense of threat associated with a particular memory

Negative memories and images can make you feel more threatened than you are in reality. Creative imagery techniques can help to reduce this sense of current threat. Has anyone ever advised you that if someone makes you feel intimidated then you should imagine them sitting on the toilet? This can work because it changes the meaning of the image, from 'this is someone powerful and threatening' to 'this is just another human being'. If you are being troubled by a 'memory ghost' of someone who has hurt you in the past but who is in reality no longer a threat, you can use imagery in all sorts of ways to tackle the impact of it. Remember that you are using the creative power of your imagination here, so you have full artistic licence to create any scenario you like that changes the way you feel about an event. Working with distressing images in this way can help restore a sense of control; it can also bring lightness and humour to some of the darkest moments of our lives.

Changing the image

Just because the image in your mind has taken one particular form, it doesn't mean it has to stay that way. For instance, Jessica remembered her abuser shouting terrible insults at her and imagined him shrinking down in size until he became a tiny cartoon-like character with a quiet, squeaky voice, who could no longer threaten her. Experiment with what you can do with the image.

Changing the perspective

Some people find that troubling images can be made easier to bear by changing the perspective, or the form, of the image. For instance, your image might be of a time when you were bullied. See if you can draw back from it and see a television around it. Instead of being 'in' the image, imagine you are watching it on TV. See if you can switch channel, or turn it off. Or turn the image into a cartoon and make it ridiculous, as in the example of Jessica above.

Talking to the image

Another thing you could try to do is talk to the people in the memory. Emma had been in a difficult marriage with a very critical man, and when she was in any kind of conflict she remembered all his critical remarks. She found it helpful to imagine herself telling him (in her mind's eye) that she had moved on in her life and now had the support of her adult children, who wished her well. She then imagined sending her previous partner backwards down a 'time tunnel' into the past.

Using imagery to 'travel back in time'

Using imagery techniques can be a bit like mental time travel, in which you choose to revisit those parts of your past that are still causing you distress. You might find it helpful to imagine yourself as you are today, travelling back in time to give your past self a message from the future. For example, one woman sent her adult 'survivor self' back to give her younger self a message of hope at a time when she had been feeling suicidal.

Lucy's story

Lucy was troubled by memories of being bullied by a group of older girls when she was young. She believed that this meant she was weak and powerless. However she also remembered that as a teenager she had been able to stand up for herself when another girl had tried to bully her. This later memory challenged her belief that she was fundamentally weak. She imagined her teenage self travelling back in time to protect her child self. She realized that she may have been powerless as a child, but that this wasn't her fault and she was a much stronger person now. She started to behave more assertively with people around her and her depression began to lift.

Taking action to reduce the sense of suffering in the memory

Another way to directly change the distressing memory itself is to ask yourself a series of questions:

- How were you suffering at the time of the original event? Were you feeling frightened? Unsafe? Unloved? Ashamed?

- Then, once you have identified your emotions, ask yourself how your past self (in your distressing memory/image) needs to feel. Safe? Loved?

- Then ask yourself what needs to happen (in the image) in order for your past self to feel that way?

- Then try to imagine that happening.

For example, Pauline was left feeling dirty following an experience of sexual abuse as a child. She imagined her adult self travelling back in time to prevent the abuse from happening. She then imagined giving her child self a warm bath with bubbles and fluffy towels, just as she had enjoyed doing when caring for her own children.

If you can't easily imagine yourself intervening in this way then you could try imagining someone else taking action on your behalf – either someone you know (like a trusted friend) or someone whose values you admire. It need not even be a human being who intervenes on your behalf. One man who had experienced mistreatment in a care home as a child imagined his beloved dog travelling back in time to chase off his childhood tormenters and sleep under his bed, protecting him at night.

Changing the ending of a bad memory

Another way to transform the meaning of bad memories is to give them a different ending. It doesn't matter that this alternative ending didn't actually happen. As we said earlier, the brain doesn't distinguish so well between imagery and reality, so if you are able to vividly imagine something good happening at the time that you most needed it (such as being rescued and/or soothed when you were distressed) then you will be creating a new representation of that experience in your mind. It doesn't even matter if what you imagine is so fantastical that it could never have really happened. What matters is that you are actively changing the mental pictures that are held in your mind. Remember that these distressing memories will have been stored with the negative meaning that they had at the time of the original event. What we are doing here is using your imagination to update these images so that they become more consistent with the way that you see things now.

Becky's story

Becky had always believed that she was a bad person because her parents had fought each other so much when she was younger. As a child she had felt as if she was to blame for their rows, but as an adult she could see that her parents' unhappiness wasn't her fault. She mentally revisited memories of specific times when her parents had been fighting and imagined herself asking them to stop and think about the harmful impact of their behaviour on their child. She also found it helpful to imagine a kindly schoolteacher she had known in her childhood sitting both her parents down and giving them a bad report on their parenting skills. She said at the end of this process: 'I know that the way I changed the memory in my imagination didn't actually happen, but it feels in a way like it did. I feel as if a weight has been lifted from my mind. I feel more grown up.'

Using imagery to place a distressing memory in a wider context

---

Deidre's story

Deidre was haunted by distressing images of her father, who had died of cancer some years ago. She pictured him collapsing on the floor, or looking very thin and unwell. These images were associated with the thought that she was now on her own, without an ally. Her father had been the only member of her family who had shared her values and sense of compassion. She also found that her memories of him becoming thinner and more fragile were very hard to bear. With the help of her therapist she began to remember other, happier times when he was stronger, finally picturing him at his workbench in his shed, advising her on her current problems. She began to picture her father as he had been when he was healthy, smiling at her and wishing her well. When she pictured him this way she felt a sense of warmth that soothed her because it reminded her of how her father had made her feel safe, protected and loved. Deidre began to bring this soothing image to her mind whenever she was feeling low, stressed or lonely.

Working with images is a skill, and takes practice

Don't be disheartened if you find it difficult to transform a distressing memory or image. This can be a complicated process, partly because the original representation of the upsetting events in your memory will probably have been well-rehearsed over time. Most people find that it takes time and practice before they are able to transform an upsetting image into something that they find more soothing and / or less threatening. You might want to practise your imagination on neutral material before working with more emotionally 'hot' images. For example, spend a moment imagining a kettle boiling to make a cup of tea. Imagine the sound of the water heating up, the whistle blowing and the steam escaping. Now imagine the whole process again, but this time in reverse, with the steam disappearing into the kettle. Now imagine flowers growing up out of the kettle. With simple practice like this you might find yourself, like the White Queen in *Alice in Wonderland*, able to imagine six impossible things before breakfast!

Key messages

- Memories and mental pictures can have a big impact on the way that we think, feel and behave. This impact can sometimes be negative (when painful past memories come back to haunt us) but we can also use imagery to transform our thoughts and feelings in a positive direction.

- It may sometimes be necessary to revisit the past in order to make sense of our emotions and actions in the 'here and now'. We can use the power of creative imagery to help us change the meaning of distressing events and to create new perspectives on the past.

- Distressing memories are often stored with the meaning that they had at the time of the original event and may not be accurate. Childhood memories may be based on a child's way of understanding the world and the meaning of these memories may need to be updated to represent a more adult view. It can be useful to see events from our current perspective, or from the perspective of a close friend. This can help us to move towards a more realistic and compassionate view of things, which serves us well in overcoming depression.

- In particular we may need to develop compassion for ourselves as we revisit some of the most distressing moments of our lives. Imagery can help us to reflect on the past so that we no longer view it through the dark glasses of depression.

Tips for supporters

- Depressed mood can make it much easier to recall over-generalized, negative memories than positive ones. This processing bias is part of the experience of depression. It doesn't mean that the sufferer is purposely choosing to dwell on the negative.

- Memory images are more closely tied to emotion than verbal thoughts are, so don't dismiss them as being unimportant or try to push them out of your mind. Instead, ask yourself what the memory means and why it might be so upsetting. Then see if you can transform the image into something less threatening and/or more soothing. Use your imagination to give the event a different ending. You might be surprised at how effective this can be.

16 Compassion–focused therapy for depression

Paul Gilbert

Introduction

So far this book has offered you many ways of thinking about your depression and things that you can do to help yourself. Compassion-focused therapy (CFT) is a way of *focusing* these efforts so that you create the conditions within your mind for them to work for you. This chapter spells out why we need compassion and how we can develop it for ourselves, dispels a lot of the myths of compassion – that it's a weakness or soft in some way – and explains how cultivating it will help us in whatever efforts we put into working on our depressed minds.

We begin first by recognizing that, in the human condition, depression is very common. The World Health Organization suggests that there are well over 120 million depressed people in the world today. One thing you can guarantee is that, sadly, you are far from alone in your suffering. Even animals can suffer severe depression. So we have to think about how it is that our brains can be so easily tipped into depressed states and what that means about how we can help ourselves.

When we get depressed, a very common experience is that of shame, the feeling of being inadequate, weak, inferior, worthless, useless, unlovable – that there is something bad or just not right about us. When depressed, we can be notoriously self-critical and at times even self-hating. So the first compassionate thing we do is to stand back from all this personal focusing and do (what we call in compassion-focused therapy), a reality check. This can help us reduce our shame and self-criticism.

Reality check

The first reality check is that all of us are part of the flow of life; that is to say we are an evolved species. So like any other species on this planet our brains and bodies have been built *for us* by the genes we've inherited from our parents, and they from theirs and they from theirs, back and back into the distant past. Because we are an evolved species it means that our brains and bodies are designed to feel and think in certain ways. We, like many other animals, are oriented to seek out food and avoid becoming food! We wish to have some position in our social groups, to be liked rather than rejected. We respond well to affection but become distressed by rejection. Your brain, with its capacity for anxiety, anger, envy, lust and of course depression, *was not built by you* but by your genes. So your brain has a built-in capacity for a whole range of emotions and desires, but also depression – and that is *absolutely not your fault* – this is something we will come back to time and again.

The second reality check is the fact that we all just find ourselves here, being born, growing for a while, and then, I am afraid, declining. We are all subject to many ups and downs of life, and many of the major things that happen to us are completely out of our control. For example, sometimes people lose their jobs because of problems in the economy; sometimes we can be confronted with illness, or are involved in a car accident, or somebody we love dies. Things can hit us out of the blue – again that's not our fault.

The third reality check is that we are partly constructed by our environment. Consider that if I had been kidnapped as a three-day-old baby and brought up by a violent drug gang, this version of me, which was lucky enough to be educated and become a psychologist, would not exist. It's likely I would now be quite violent, only interested in myself and my gang and making money. Maybe I would be in prison or even dead. Also because I would not know anything about this other possible version of myself (the psychologist version) I might even want to hold on to my identity as a drug baron. I didn't ask to be kidnapped any more than I asked for the background I actually had; and you didn't ask for the background that shaped you. We also know that even our genes are expressed in different ways according to the kind of background we come from.

The fourth reality check is that we are the most social and interdependent species that has ever lived on this planet. Every aspect of our lives depends upon the actions of others. The houses we live in, the food that turns up in the supermarkets, the cars we drive, the medicines we get from our doctor – everything comes because of the actions of others. In fact, even our brains' ability to generate speech comes because we have evolved to be a highly social and interdependent species. Now when we become depressed we often forget this and want to withdraw from those around us or reduce our activities – once again that's not our fault, but it can have unfortunate consequences.

So we can see then that our tendencies to depression are absolutely not our fault – no one chooses to be depressed, no matter what you think about it. This can be quite a humbling insight in some ways, but also quite liberating because we then begin to think about giving up blaming and shaming ourselves for being depressed, or focusing on the negative within us. We are then in a better position to start to stimulate our minds to feel better.

Responsibility

So here's the other side of the coin! Even though it's absolutely not our fault that we have a brain that is capable of depression, that we have to face tragedies in life, and that we have a 'self' shaped for us rather than by us – it is our responsibility to do something about it if we are suffering. This may seem unfair to you but unfortunately that is the way it is. It may not be fair that we have genes that make us put on weight, and it is certainly not fair that we live in a world where the food industry, in the pursuit of profits, has given us exceptionally fattening foods. However, carrying too much weight puts us at risk of a whole range of health problems such as diabetes, cardiovascular diseases and cancer. So although it might not be our fault that we put on weight, we still need to do something about it. Similarly it's not our fault that we are vulnerable to depression, and there is no law that says we must change our behaviour. However, if we don't try to take responsibility and start to work with our minds and our brains as they are, we may stay depressed, or remain vulnerable to relapses into depression.

So, many of the chapters in this book provide you with ideas of how you can 'look in' on your depressed mind, see what it is up to and then make deliberate efforts to change what goes on there. The compassion-focused approach very much takes this view, as we will see.

Key messages

- We all just find ourselves here in life, shaped by a biologically built brain that we didn't choose and early life experiences that we didn't choose either.

- Regulating our emotions, and our sense of self, can be very difficult for us because of the way our brains evolved.

- This means that a susceptibility to anxiety, depression and other difficulties is absolutely not our fault.

- However, we can learn about how our minds work and how to take steps to try to create the states of mind we want.

Tips for supporters

- Remind the person you are supporting not to blame themselves for how they feel.

- Recognize that well over 120,000,000 people suffer from depression, so it's a common human condition.

- Help them to stand back and see it this way, so that it becomes easier to take steps to change.

Emotions and depression

It is pretty obvious that it is our emotions that cause us most pain and suffering when we are depressed. Emotions associated with joy and pleasure are reduced, while those associated with sadness, threats, anxiety and anger are increased. So let's take a closer look at how the brain is designed, because this will help us 'look in' on our minds. We will then be more able to move between different emotional systems, from those which are less helpful to those which are more helpful.

Basically, we have different types of emotion systems in our brain and these are designed by evolution to do different things. We sometimes call these emotion systems 'Affect Regulation Systems'.

The three systems we are going to consider here are:

- Those that evolved to deal with threats, and are designed to help protect and defend us (threat system).

- Those that evolved to excite and inspire us to go out and achieve things (incentive/resource system).

- Those that evolved to help us feel contentment and wellbeing, when we are not under any threat and not trying to achieve anything

They are shown in Figure 25 below.

Let's look at each of these in turn. We can represent them as three interacting systems. Now although I'm going to present them as different systems, in reality they are more blends of different patterns in the mind.

Figure 25: Three types of affect regulation system

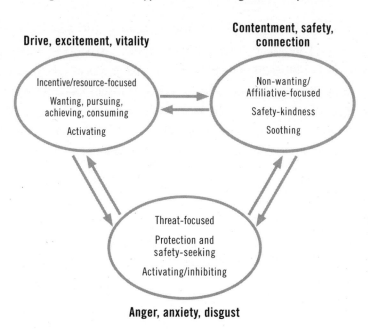

From Gilbert, *The Compassionate Mind* (2009), reprinted with permission from Constable & Robinson Ltd.

Threat system

This could also be called the 'threat and protection system'. You and I, like all other animals, need systems in our brains to alert us to dangers and stimulate our bodies to take defensive actions. So if we were walking in the jungle and saw a lion we would need to immediately become anxious and run. Anger, too, is a built-in emotion that we need to cope with. If we are doing something important and then get thwarted, we need to put more energy into it, and this is called frustration and anger. It doesn't really matter whether it's something or someone in the way, thwarting our needs – how we learn to recognize this automatic system, and deal with it, can be important in depression.

Incentive/resource system

This could also be described as the 'activating and seeking system'. Life isn't just about avoiding threats or dealing with blockages; we are also going out and achieving things. When we are not depressed we get pleasure from achieving things, and become energized by the possibility of doing so. Think of all the activities people do because they want to achieve something and/or because it gives them a sense of pleasure. Going out with friends, going for a walk in the spring air, cooking a meal, watching a favourite TV programme, playing football, abseiling down a cliff – they give us some kind of positive feeling.

Non-wanting/affiliative system

This could also be described as the 'contentment and soothing system'. There are times when we are not under any threat and nor do we want to achieve or do something; we are content with the way things are and simply chilled out. Our minds slow down, and this feeling of slowing can help us learn to be *present in the moment* (to see why this is important look at the mindfulness chapter). It turns out that the brain systems involved in helping us feel content, calm, not threatened or rushing around doing thing, are also very importantly linked to kindness and affection. How does that work? Well, consider the baby who is distressed. What will calm the baby? Sometimes stimulating and distracting him or her can help, but mostly it is receiving a cuddle and the soothing tones of the mother's voice. Indeed, when we are distressed we often like to turn to other people who (we hope) will be understanding, supportive and kind – and these qualities often calm us down. It doesn't necessarily reduce the problem as such, but to feel understood and valued is very important.

If you are depressed, you may say, 'Yes, but I don't have anybody who really understands me.' If this is true it does at least highlight the fact that you intuitively understand that the quality of your relationships is very important to your wellbeing. Sometimes we need to work to build relationships, and of course that's a two-way process. If you want other people to take an interest in you, it helps to place yourself in situations where there are people you can relate to – for example, working for a charity or joining a club. Taking an interest in other people helps, too. There is now good evidence that the more interest we take in others the happier we are, whereas the more we get focused on our own problems the less happy we are.

However, there is one type of relationship that is essential to you and does not depend on other people – this is the relationship you have with yourself. We know that signals of kindness are very powerful to our brains, so it makes sense that if we learn to be kind, valuing and supportive of ourselves this will stimulate the brain systems that create positive feelings in us. In turn, this will help us to lift out of depression. In contrast, if we are critical and constantly putting ourselves down with an angry voice then we will be stimulating the threat system. When we do that we are stimulating all kinds of processes in our brains and bodies that can make us feel bad – and if we do that day in, day out then you can see how this can only increase or maintain depression, not lift us out of it.

The depressed mind

If we use the three-circle model, we can see that what happens when we get depressed – our emotions can become severely out of balance. Figure 26 shows this.

Figure 26: Depressed states

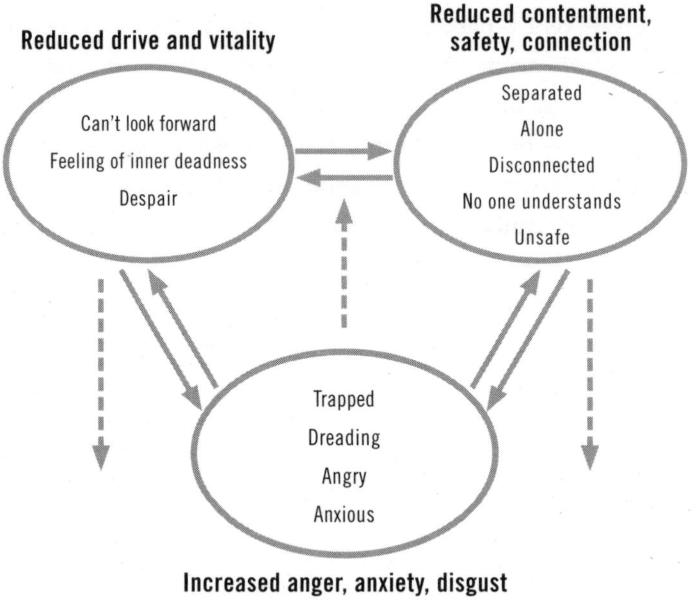

Reduced drive and vitality

Can't look forward

Feeling of inner deadness

Despair

Reduced contentment, safety, connection

Separated

Alone

Disconnected

No one understands

Unsafe

Trapped

Dreading

Angry

Anxious

Increased anger, anxiety, disgust

First, we can see that the threat system has become overstimulated so the dominant feelings are increases in anxiety, tension, frustration, irritability and anger. Second, many of the things that give us pleasure don't seem to any more. So it is as if our capacity to experience pleasure and excitement and look forward to things has taken a dive. When this happens, life can feel flat and we can feel hopeless or even despairing. Third, we often have a feeling of disconnectedness from others, which can be associated with intense loneliness. Sometimes we feel as if there is a barrier between us and other people; we are emotionally cut off from them. It may be difficult to feel affection for others, even if we want to or they are showing affection to us. We might then feel sad or guilty about that, but again that's not our fault – it's how the system is working in this moment. We can still try to behave in caring ways though (assuming we want to), even if we don't feel it. So this is the connectedness and soothing system taking a bit of a dive. Once again *this is not your fault*, but is to do with the way in which our emotion systems have got out of balance.

Looking at it this way helps us to stand back and see that there are certain patterns in our emotions that are related to depression. Of course, there are different types of depression with slightly different patterns. For example, some depressed people are more focused on the loneliness and sadness, and can be tearful and yearn for connection. Others feel a deep sense of inner deadness. Yet others are more dominated by feelings of anxiety or anger. Indeed increasing irritability and 'scratchiness' can be an indicator that we are beginning to become stressed or even depressed. Sometimes that anger has been around a long time. But whatever pattern seems true for you, the key thing is to *see it as a pattern* in your brain and then think about what you can do to change this pattern.

Key messages

- When we are depressed we can experience an increase in the threat emotions of anxiety, anger and irritability.

- We can also experience a reduction in two types of positive emotion: a loss of feelings of enjoyment, fun or pleasure; and a loss of feelings of connectedness with others.

Tips for supporters

- Help the person you are supporting to recognize that sometimes we need to work on all the emotion systems.

- What could you do that would help them become more active?

- What could you do that would help them take an interest in other people, becoming more connected to those around them? Help them to see that sometimes focusing on others rather than yourself can be really helpful when you are depressed.

Understanding how our thoughts and imaginations can push our emotions out of balance

Your brain can get out of balance for all kinds of reasons: maybe you are under a lot of stress, or something physical, such as a virus, is affecting your immune system and changing your mood. But as we saw in Part 1, a common reason that our brains get out of balance is that we get locked into spirals between types of thinking and feeling.

This happens partly because humans have evolved to be able to think, reason, plan, imagine, anticipate and ruminate more than any other animal. This is good in that it allows us to solve complex problems, anticipate future difficulties and create wonderful things, too – it gives rise to science, medicine and mobile phones. But these human abilities can also cause us all kinds of difficulties. Here's an example to show how. Consider a zebra running away from a lion. After ten minutes or so the lion gets exhausted and wanders off. The zebra will very quickly calm down, return to the herd and start eating again. However, in con- trast, if this were to happen to a human, relief would be associated with beginning to anticipate, imagine and ruminate: 'Oh gosh [or some other four letter word], can you imagine what would have happened if I had been caught by the lion? I can just picture myself now being choked to death and eaten alive in agony . . . ' Intrusive images might come into their mind over and over. They might wake up in the middle of the night and start thinking, 'What will happen tomorrow if the lions are still about? And what about my children? And what about . . . ' Unlike the zebra, they would be going into a state of shock partly because of the constant *holding it in mind*. Robert Sapolsky wrote a very famous book on exactly this issue, called *Why Zebras Don't Get Ulcers*; they don't hold things in mind that constantly stimulate the threat system.

Now, in one way this is our threat system trying to forewarn us, but in another way it is going to trap us into constantly worrying about the lions, holding our body in a state of high tension and anxiety. Our zebra does not have any of these problems! So humans are constantly thinking, quite naturally, 'What if . . . ?' and 'Suppose . . . ?' And because we are creative we often come up with the worst scenarios. We can also look back on things and think, 'If only I had . . . ' or 'If only I hadn't . . . '. These are all perfectly natural and normal ways of thinking, but they can also be very troublesome indeed if we don't take steps to notice them and get out of the loops.

Here's another reason why paying attention to what goes on in your mind is so important – it is to do with how our imaginations and our thoughts *cause our bodies to change*. Imagine that you are hungry and you see a meal; this will make your saliva and stomach acids flow. But if it is late at night and you just fantasize about a meal, the same thing will happen. In other words, the image you create in your mind stimulates a particular part of your brain and body. Lying in bed and having erotic thoughts can also do things to your body. This is because your imagination is stimulating an area of your brain called the pituitary, which releases hormones. So, make no mistake, your thoughts and imagination can literally act as *a probe into your brain*, stimulating hormones and brain chemicals. Clearly you don't want your repetitive ruminative thinking and fantasies to be stimulating the threat/stress system, because if you do that you will end up pushing stress hormones into your body.

When you think about it this way it's not surprising that thoughts and imagination can be so powerful. But it has important implications for all of us. If we don't pay attention to what's going on in our minds, we can get locked into thoughts that set off an unhelpful system. A classic threat-system stimulator is self-criticism: it puts your body into a constant state of tension, until eventually you feel exhausted and terrible. Now, once again that's not our fault. But what if we notice this and make a deliberate decision to switch our attention to stimulate a part of our brain that is more conducive to our wellbeing? We can certainly stay in the threat system if we want to – there is no law against it, as they say – and it can have a very strong pull: it doesn't mean that there is anything 'wrong' with us. It's how our brains and body naturally work.

And if you have had unpleasant things happen to you in the past, the threat system will more easily claim your attention. The question is, do we want it to do that? Or would we rather train our minds, as best we can, to shift out of the threat system into the doing or soothing system?

The importance of attention and how to switch it

So we recognize that a lot of what goes on in our heads, and the reasons for feeling depressed, are not our fault at all, but at the same time we want to take more control over our minds, and where our attention settles. Think of it this way: your attention is like a spotlight, and what it settles on becomes bigger in your mind. If I ask you to focus your attention on your left foot, and then rub your thumbs over your fingers, you will notice that while your attention is on your foot you become more aware of the sensations in it. But notice that the spotlight of attention *puts things into the shadows, too*. When you are focusing on your left foot you are not aware of your fingers. Notice too that your attention is movable – from your foot to your hands.

It's the same with emotion and attention. Because your threat system keeps hold of your attention it puts potentially positive awareness into the shadows – you literally don't notice these things. When we are depressed we don't notice the colour of the sky, the fact that we can breathe, or that we can see colours and hear sounds (some people can't). We do not notice the sensory experiences we are having *right now*.

Here is another important example. Imagine you go Christmas shopping in ten shops and in nine of them the assistant is helpful to you and you are very pleased with the present you buy. But in one shop, the assistant is rather rude, keeps you waiting and gives you the wrong change. Who do you think about when you go home? Well, many of us will be dwelling on whether to write to the manager about the rude assistant, and thinking 'How do these people keep their jobs?' and so on. We stay ruminating about how angry we are with the rude assistant

– that's because our brain is designed to focus on threats. Yet this will do our bodies no good at all, because we will be pumping stress hormones into them. And the fact is that 90 per cent of people were kind! What would happen if we deliberately started to notice how our attention gets so easily grabbed by the threat system and then, on purpose, we focus on more helpful ways of paying attention?

In the next sections I will offer some ideas of how to do that.

Key messages

- What we pay attention to influences our bodies. Be aware of where your attention goes to, and how it affects your body and moods.

- If we can start to notice where our attention is, then we can start to make changes to what we focus on.

- Our attention is very easily taken over by our threat and drive systems. We can consider how to refocus it (see below).

- Rumination is where our attention gets stuck – often in the threat system.

Tips for supporters

- When you are with the person you are supporting you may be able to see when they are tense and unhappy. Ask them what their attention is focused on, and help them to see the connection between the focus and how they are feeling.

- Gently try to encourage them to focus their attention onto something more soothing or enjoyable, even if it is difficult for them to do so.

Working with your body

There are many ways we can work with the body to balance our emotions, but one way is to try and deliberately stimulate more positive emotion systems. We notice that lying in bed and thinking erotic thoughts will stimulate an activating system – sometimes that is helpful too, but for now let's focus on the soothing system, which will also help you develop feelings of connectedness.

Practising breathing is a good way to do this, because slowing and deepening the breath helps to stimulate the soothing system (well, actually it stimulates a part of us called the *myelinated parasympathetic system*, but we don't need to know that in any detail). Here's what you do. First, stand up straight with your feet close together. Imagine what would happen if somebody pushed you from the side. You would topple over. This is because this standing position is *unstable*. So now stand with your feet slightly apart and really feel your weight going through your hips, with your knees very slightly bent (not locked); get a sense of being *grounded and stable*. Imagine now that somebody pushes you from the side – you will be secure. So finding the point of inner stability in the body is important. We're going to focus on that now; don't worry if it takes time.

Sit down on a chair with your back straight, feet flat on the floor. Breathing in and out through your nose, begin to deepen the breath, letting it sink deeper into your diaphragm. You're going to be aiming for about five or six breaths per minute. The out-breath is especially important to focus on. Try not to force it out, just let it out by itself like a balloon collapsing when you're not putting air into it. So try counting into it: in, two, three, and out, two, three, and then in, two, three, four, and out, two, three, four; and then next in, two, three, four, five and out, two, three, four, five. The key is to find a comfortable pattern of breathing that is relatively easy for you but also gives you the feeling of slowing down. So when you are in flow, just focus on that feeling of slowing as you deliberately slow the breath. Sometimes people can deepen the movement of the diaphragm by deliberately pushing out the belly and then pulling it back in. Don't be over-focused on the diaphragm, though; try to get air into all of your lungs, but don't force anything.

Next, when you feel you have this rhythm (the in-breath and out-breath should be nice and even) notice how you may feel slightly heavier sitting on your chair. The idea is to now sense a point of inner (relative) stillness. It is a form of relaxation, not with floppy muscles but more a sense of inner calmness. The point of inner calming and stilling can sometimes seem to lie somewhere in your solar plexus (tummy) area. This can also be experienced as a point of inner strength, linked to feeling slightly heavier and slightly more grounded and solid. This feeling comes because we slow the breath. When you have a sense of that, you might also want to imagine a still scene such as a lake at dusk or a beautiful tree with no wind, or a mountain. Create images of stillness.

Mindful attention

Given that your attention is such a powerful source for activating your body, learning to recognize how your attention moves in your mind is very important. In Chapter 17 by Willem Kuyken and Halley Cohen you will discover much about mindfulness and how to practise it. The important thing is that although our attention is physiologically very powerful, we often don't have much control over it, as Willem and Halley help you to discover. But we can train our minds to notice and gain more control.

Recognition and acceptance

When feelings and thoughts arise, we sometimes try to push them away and avoid them, or we might ruminate about how to get rid of them. This inevitably causes more upset. So it is important that we compassionately recognize that much of what goes on in our brains is to do with the way they have been constructed by evolution and life's circumstances. Really what you are observing is 'nature's mind'.

Supposing you have the thought, 'I really hate that person because they were so unkind to me.' Well, you could get caught up in the feelings of hatred (which will then play out in your body and make you feel bad) or you could tell yourself you shouldn't be feeling that and feel ashamed of your thoughts. But supposing you look at this and think to yourself, 'Oh, this is how nature's mind is when it confronts something it doesn't like.' From there you can recognize your common humanity, knowing that for thousands of years, all over the world, people have been having exactly that kind of thought and exactly that kind of feeling when they get upset: you're absolutely no different!

There might be a whole range of these types of thoughts and feelings, such as feeling worthless or ashamed or unlovable. The trick is not to get too caught up with them or personalize them but see them for what they are – nature's mind at work when dealing with difficult things. The more you link to what we call common humanity, and recognize that throughout the world depressed people have these kinds of thoughts, the less you will see them as personal and unique to you. Of course we still have the issue of dealing with them, but it's often the feeling of 'it's only me' that causes us so much pain.

By being mindful we can become observant and aware of all the mind's tricks and shadows. The most important thing is to not take this too personally because there is nothing in your mind – no matter what it is – that has not been in the mind of somebody else some time in history. For example, people are often amazed when they see research showing what other people think about, be it aggressive fantasies or sexual fantasies with just about anything and everyone – the human mind is capable of all this and it is not a symptom of badness. There is a very good book called *The Imp of the Mind* by Lee Baer which goes into this – it is mostly for people with obsessional disorders who worry about what goes on in their mind, but it can be quite useful for depression as well, because depressed people can have all kinds of fantasies and thoughts that frighten them. We can learn to be compassionate towards ourselves for having these thoughts, and just accept them without being frightened or repulsed by them, rather than blaming ourselves for having them and thinking we are bad and horrible because we do.

Imagery

A good way of stimulating our brains is with imagery – and so it could be very useful to you to look at Chapter 15 on memory, which discusses imagery. We are going to do compassionate imagery mindfully, which means that should your mind ever wander from the task this really doesn't matter at all – you simply know this and bring it back.

People often say that they are no good at imagery. This is because they don't really understand what we mean by it. For example, if I say to you 'What's a biscuit?' or 'Where did you go on your last holiday?' you would probably be able to answer. You can because you have images flashing in and out of your mind. They may be very vague, fleeting and shadowy but they are there.

The most important thing about imagery is that it often comes with a 'felt sense'. As we discussed earlier, if you lie in bed and create an erotic image you might get aroused because the image you are producing simulates the pituitary area of your brain, which then releases hormones into your body. No surprise, really. And of course if you bring to mind memories or images of a recent argument then a totally different set of bodily processes will be stimulated. Your attention and the images are powerful influences on your body.

However, these images may not be clear, vivid ones but hazy and impressionistic. So when we deliberately use images to stimulate the body, you do not need to create clear visual images – in fact at times you may see very little. It is more the feeling that goes with your focus of attention that is important.

This is different from the previous chapter, where we needed to get very clear images in order to cast ourselves into the scene and make changes to it. In this case it is the feeling, not the image itself, which we are interested in.

Compassionate self

The following exercises use imagery but also other techniques to stimulate different brain systems within us. Earlier, we learned that we can stimulate different parts of our brain and body systems by deliberately generating images and thoughts. Remember we used the example that we can get ourselves aroused by deliberately creating erotic thoughts. What about if we use exactly the same idea, but with a focus on compassion and balancing our minds?

Now it turns out that actors can deliberately stimulate things in their minds and bodies so that they can really get into a role. In fact, if we put good actors into brain scanners and ask them to get into an emotional role, we see that the areas of their brain linked to those emotions light up. If they're trying to become an angry, sad, anxious or happy character, they can stimulate those parts of their brain.

So it is the same with imagining ourselves becoming a compassionate self: we can stimulate parts of our brain that can help us to rebalance and come out of depression. In this next exercise we're going to imagine that we are a compassionate character, like an actor playing a role. It is by far best to do it this way because if you try to imagine yourself genuinely being a compassionate person, the self-critical self can kick up and say, 'Oh no, you're not compassionate.' Just begin to imagine what it might be like to have certain qualities – to become a certain character for a role. And then carry this role into your life so that you start acting in compassionate ways.

First, think about (and, if you like, write down) the key qualities you would have if you were the most compassionate person – your absolute ideal of compassion, no matter how unrealistic it might seem to you. Think about why those are compassionate qualities. Clarify in your mind the strengths; notice that compassion is not about being submissive or a pushover. Now, sitting in your chair, engage in your soothing rhythm breathing, and, when settled, imagine having those qualities. It helps if we start to do this playfully, even though the intent is serious.

Don't worry, and don't criticize, if it doesn't come easily. The idea is to be curious, and explore what happens, as opposed to trying to make something happen and then being critical if it doesn't. What's important here is your *intention* to be compassionate.

Next, explore your facial expressions: starting from a neutral expression, create a friendly smile on your face for around fifteen seconds and then go back to neutral. Then once again fifteen seconds of friendly face and fifteen seconds of neutral face. Cycle through and end on friendly face. Did you notice any slight difference in how your body felt, no matter how subtle? Well, you might have noticed that a friendly face gives you a slightly warmer feeling. That is because you are deliberately working the muscles in your face which have connections to your brain.

Next, we are going to focus on friendly voice tones. So now, in a very neutral tone say, 'Hello . . . ' and name yourself. So for me it would be, 'Hello Paul.' Okay, so on each out-breath say 'Hello . . . ', doing this for fifteen seconds with the neutral voice and then creating as friendly and supportive a voice as you can for fifteen seconds. Do that twice (more if you like). Once again, notice the difference when you deliberately change your voice tone. As you do this, you start to generate a friendly and supportive inner voice too. You have probably already guessed that when you get familiar with that kind, supportive and encouraging inner voice it will help you in various ways and certainly be a counterweight to the hostile voice of the inner critic. Learning how to generate a kind voice will be helpful. If you are using any of the techniques or strategies from other chapters, try to talk to yourself in this kind voice while you are doing them.

The reason for deliberately trying to create a friendly voice tone is because when we get depressed, self-criticism is so pervasive that we don't even notice it at times; we don't notice that our emotional tone to ourselves is frustrated and angry or even contemptuous. This inner emotional tone of our thoughts can be quite damaging. Just imagine what's happening in your brain if, day in and day out, you say negative things to yourself in a slightly angry or contemptuous tone. And think about which brain systems you are stimulating. Not good. But you can, on purpose, start to change this by practising *how* you talk to yourself as well as what you say to yourself.

Now – with our slowing of the breath, focusing on inner stillness and strength somewhere in your solar plexus, and with your intent to become the compassionate self – we are going to focus on three core qualities. These are wisdom, strength and commitment – all with feelings of friendliness and kindness.

The wisdom you have comes partly from reading this book and partly from recognizing that we all find ourselves here on this planet, with this brain, for just a short time, doing the best we can. There are many millions of us who get depressed because we have a brain that is easily tipped into depression, so it is not our fault. We also know that when we get depressed we automatically begin to feel and think negative things that spiral us further down. So even if very unfortunate things are happening in our lives at least we can recognize we didn't choose any of this, it's not our fault, and therefore we begin to treat ourselves with more support and kindness. We also have the wisdom that kindness has very powerful effects on our brain and, even if we resist it, learning how to overcome our resistance and be kinder to ourselves is good for our brains. So we can reduce shame and blame, and move towards taking responsibility and change.

The strength element comes from feeling more grounded in our body, with a sense of slowing down. It helps if we walk around practising centring on the body, keeping an upright posture, breathing slowly and practising our facial expressions and voice tones so that we begin to experience the strength and calm that come with these. Also our sense of strength comes from our wisdom, from a deep insight into the nature of the difficulties of depression.

Last, and crucially, consider your commitment to try to be as supportive and helpful and encouraging as you can to yourself and others. We know that when we get depressed we won't have any trouble at all being angry and undermining to ourselves, and to others too sometimes, but the challenge is: can we turn this around? It may take quite a lot of courage to develop this, but if you do not make the effort you will never know. In your mind try as best you can to make a commitment:

- *I will do my best to treat whatever arises in me with kindness and understanding.*

- *I will do my best to treat whomever I meet with kindness and understanding.*

Keep in mind though that compassion, kindness and understanding are not about being submissive. Sometimes they are about being assertive. If your child wants a second hamburger and you know that's bad for them, you say no. Saying no here is the compassionate thing to do even if they complain! Compassion certainly involves honesty and, at times, courage. The kindness really comes from our insight into the real nature of our brains.

Now, whenever you are confronted with something difficult, spend a moment slowing your breathing, feel rooted in your body, and imagine approaching that difficulty from the compassionate self. Think of the alternative ways in which you can look at your thinking, or work with your attention. Each time you engage with trying to make a change, take a few breaths, bring the compassionate voice tone to mind and then engage with the task.

When to stimulate

Keep in mind that it's all about balance. So the above – slowing down – is very important, but so is stimulation. We know for example that when we get depressed our metabolism slows down. So sometimes we need to speed things up a bit. One way of doing this is by exercise, and there is good evidence now that exercise helps people who are depressed. Have a look at the NHS site (See Appendix 1). We have to increase our activity level, as we saw in Chapter 13, and try to do more pleasurable things, because our brain systems don't just function by themselves; they need stimulating. But even here, learning how to activate ourselves in an atmosphere of support, encouragement and understanding will be more helpful than trying to bully ourselves into activity. So finding out how to encourage yourself, especially when things are difficult, is a key to success.

Compassionate image

Another way in which we can stimulate and balance our minds is by being open to the compassion of others. Remember the example above of Christmas shopping – how it's so easy for us to focus on the one person who was unhelpful and completely put out of our minds the other nine who were helpful? So training our attention to be compassionate means each day trying to notice and remember people who are kind to you. It may only be somebody on the bus who smiles, but even little things can make a big difference. Your brain will be very good at picking out threats and negatives, so it can take effort to balance and learn to look at the good things. Depression becomes more stuck when we focus on the things we don't like, rather than trying to build on the things we do. Keep in mind that this is not your fault, because your brain is naturally oriented towards threat, but once you know this you can make a decision to retrain it.

Learning to stimulate compassionate feelings can also be done through imagery. Once again this works the same way as your erotic fantasies – using imagery on purpose to shift our mental state. In this situation, consider *your ideal compassionate other*. If you could encounter the most compassionate person in the world, what qualities would they have? Because they are ideal they will be beyond human frailties such as having off days, and getting irritable or sick! Sometimes, people bring to mind a loved parent or grandparent, which is okay to start with, but if it's someone who has died there can be grief associated with it, which is less helpful. So ideally, create your own *unique image*. This image will have the great wisdom and understanding we mentioned before. It will convey a profound sense of strength and capacities for endurance, a sense of complete commitment to you, and a deep wish for you to be able to work on your depression. Your compassionate other has the same qualities we saw developed in the compassionate self above. Remember, you don't need to create clear visual images because fleeting impressions are fine – it's the 'sensed feeling' that comes with this practice, and the focusing of attention, not the clarity of the image that is important. One of my clients had the impression of a female Buddha but never really saw anything clear, just sensed a compassionate being.

So when you imagine your compassionate image, you can consider whether they are male or female or sort of neutral, older or younger than you, and whether they are human. Some depressed people prefer to have animals as their compassionate image. But whatever image you have, focus on the qualities of wisdom, strength and commitment to you. And of course these are offered in a warm way. Once you have created this in your mind then imagine them wishing for your recovery from depression with a deeply heartfelt sense of concern for your well-being. This image will never criticize you because it has the wisdom to understand that no one chooses depression. Consider the warmth and strength of their tone of voice and any other characteristics that would be helpful to you.

Sometimes it helps to dialogue literally with these images, understanding that they are imaginary. Maybe you will recognize that this is what happens in religions, such as with prayer. And, indeed, many people draw comfort and strength from these imaginary conversations with gods. In the CFT approach though, we are not giving these practices any spiritual meaning, but simply offering them as ways to stimulate our minds. Our brains are very sensitive to social signals and therefore creating these in our minds can be helpful. After all, if you sat and imagined people being critical and hostile to you, you can see that it would be upsetting. So in this exercise we are learning to focus and create compassionate interactions in our imagination.

We can also use compassionate imagery when we remember people being kind to us. Sometimes it's useful to spend some time sitting quietly and really focusing on what we call 'gratitude and appreciation'. Bring to mind people who have helped you, encouraged or supported you. Imagine what their intent was while they were engaging in this way with you. Try to recall how you felt when you received that kindness from them. Once again, the idea is not to make us feel guilty and obligated but just to open ourselves up to feelings that will help us to combat depression. When you are thinking of a compassionate person, though, there is a danger that your depressed mind will kick in. You might remember someone who has died and become very sad; you might start to think that there is no one like that in your life. For example, one client remembered her mother, now dead. This brought up grief. So when you are doing this exercise keep in mind that if the image makes you sad it might be better not to use it. Try to think of another image, or see if you can concentrate on the good aspects. Always remember that our depressed mind can control our attention, feeling and thinking unless we take deliberate steps to refocus.

Compassionate writing

Sometimes, if we have a particular difficulty it can help us to write about it. In your writing, don't collapse into distress but take a compassionate position. Imagine you are writing to yourself from your compassionate self, or possibly hearing the voice of your compassionate other. Don't forget to do your soothing rhythm breathing and body-focusing first as well. It's quite interesting that when we write we get a different perspective, so writing letters to and about ourselves can be very helpful. Indeed, there is now good evidence that compassionate letter-writing can help us cope with difficulties.

There are two types of letter. One that you would keep private, possibly even destroy after you have read it. Another could be shown to your best friend or partner. Sometimes explaining things in letters is easier. Although you can use letters to convey a message of assertiveness or something you are unhappy with to your partner, this is not really the idea; compassionate letter-writing focuses on bringing the wisdom and strength and kindness of compassion to whatever we are writing about. Sometimes people find it difficult to get started, but just write anything to begin with to get you in the flow. When you read your letter consider if it is a letter that you would be happy to give to a friend – that is, would you write to a friend like that about their difficulties. Does it convey real understanding and support (not just giving advice)? In her book, *The Compassionate-Mind Guide to Recovering from Trauma and PTSD*, Deborah Lee offers a whole chapter on how to write compassionate letters.

Compassionate behaviour

There is increasing evidence that when people feel meaningfully engaged with activities in their life, and that they can make a difference to somebody else, this helps with depression. If you take a genuine interest in the welfare of others, it can help you, too. Depression tends to be a very self-focused problem. Some people have found that taking up charity work or doing random acts of kindness is helpful.

Helping others can put meaning into our lives – but this is not a submissive sort of helping others, so that they'll like you; then you can get disappointed if they don't. This is cultivating a genuine understanding that all of us are vulnerable to the ups and downs of life, all of us are on the same journey, and therefore generally reaching out to each other and helping each other is a way we can cope better.

Compassionate behaviour is often also about courage. For example, if you suffer from a fear of going out (*agoraphobia*), then compassion is about encouraging yourself with kindness and understanding to go out a little further each day if you can; if it gets too difficult for you, be supportive and tell yourself to have a go maybe tomorrow. Compassion is *not* sitting at home eating chocolates because it is soothing! Kindness in this context is not avoidance, or just having a nice warm bath with candles. Compassion is about approaching problems with support, encouragement and an understanding of the difficulties. In fact you already have the compassion and wisdom to know this. Imagine you have a child or somebody you really care about, who has to do something frightening, or that they find difficult – what attitude would you take? How would you support and encourage them? Why would you *want* to encourage and support them? The answer is, of course, because you intuitively have wisdom that tells you that kindness, encouragement and support will help them, whereas criticism and bullying won't. So you have the knowledge already that compassionate behaviour is the way to engage with our problems and those of others.

Another key aspect of compassionate behaviour is turning to others. When we are depressed we can have a sense of shame and often hide away; we don't share our problems, and we don't seek help. Indeed, one of the problems with depression today is that many people suffer in silence because they are too ashamed to see their general practitioner (GP). But compassionate behaviour means opening ourselves to the potential helpfulness of others. This doesn't mean we go around burdening everybody we meet with our problems. It means that we genuinely seek sharing, support and help from people. Some innovative approaches to depression in men, for example, have involved setting up groups and small football teams to encourage depressed males to socialize more – and this has proved very effective. Try to make more effort with your friends.

Body compassion

It's not just about how we nurture and are compassionate to our minds that's important in this approach. We need to be compassionate and nurturing to our bodies, too, treating them with respect and kindness. The compassionate-mind approach is concerned with understanding the interactions between mind and body. We are *embodied* beings and what goes on in our bodies can affect our minds in a two-way manner – that's why we've been talking a lot about using imagery and other practices to deliberately stimulate both your brain and your body.

There is increasing evidence that poor diets are not only bad for our physical health, but can be bad for our emotional health, too. The reason for this is that they impact on the immune system and cardiovascular systems, both of which affect brain systems. So looking after your body with a good diet is of immense importance – particularly because some people are very vulnerable to diet-induced mood change. Reducing caffeine intake can help some people, as can reducing alcohol. As previously mentioned, taking regular exercise is known to be very good for depression too. When we get depressed our metabolism starts to slow down and we do less, and then we feel more tired and so do even less. So exercise that gets us moving a bit can be good. It can also help with sleep. So while slowing the breath can be helpful when you are very keyed up, if we are sluggish we may need invigorating exercise that gets our systems moving. (We should just say here that if you haven't done exercise for a while, or if you are worried about your fitness, it might be sensible to check with your GP before starting an exercise programme. Some GPs have access to exercise schemes, where someone can advise you what is best for you.)

The key here is to experiment to get an idea of what works for you. For example, some people find that yoga can be extremely helpful for both their minds and their bodies, but others don't really relate to it at all. The point is that compassion-focused therapies do not ignore the body, but recognize how important physical wellbeing is to our mental wellbeing.

Practising compassion

Some people often say, 'I don't deserve compassion,' or 'I'm too angry inside to be bothered with compassion,' or 'It's too difficult,' or 'It's a weakness.' First, I hope I've shown you that it's not a weakness. It's really about how we stimulate our brains and create certain types of relationships, not just with other people but also within our own heads – with ourselves. And if you think about our basic description of compassion (page 241) then what is weak about that? If you think you don't deserve compassion it is like saying you don't deserve to be fit or have a healthy diet. In fact, if you are depressed, you are the person who deserves most compassion. Think about just how much easier it would be for you if you did get on with other people; and if you felt better, how much energy you might have to be able to help other people in this tricky life.

It's also important to *remember to practise* and there are various ways to do this. One is to remember your commitment to become compassionate each day – saying your mantra before you get up, and running through a short breathing exercise and compassion focus (in my book *The Compassionate Mind* (see page 545) I call it 'two minutes under the duvet'). Write on the back of your hand 'pay attention to kindness'; hold a stone or something else small in your pocket so that every time you put your hand in there you can feel that and remind yourself of your intention to become the kind of person you want to be in this world while you are here. Place a 'compassion candle' at the end of your bath so that while you are in it you can practise your compassionate imagery work. Find a smell you really like and then when you do your soothing rhythm breathing, put this onto a handkerchief and smell it. Then during the day, stop for a moment, take out the handkerchief, slow the breath, have a smell and recreate the friendly facial expression and voice tone.

If you can put aside a regular time to practise mindfulness and compassion focusing, that is the ideal, but if you can only take snatches of time during the day that will be helpful too. One of the key things is *not* to make it into a chore or a duty or something you're *supposed* to do. Depressed people do not do very well under those conditions. If you do that, you may find you have less motivation to keep going. So try to make practice fun – for example, put a smiling face on the back of your toilet door so that every time you close the door it reminds you of the kind of self you are trying to train yourself to become. (If you find that just annoys you then obviously don't do it, but also reflect on why it would annoy you.) Try to be innovative in the ways you 'wake yourself up to the present moment' and commit yourself to the compassionate path. Always notice the breath. The more playful you can be with ways to stay in the present moment, the easier it will get. And remember: it's very important to notice the emotional tone of the thoughts that run through your head. Notice if the tones are aggressive, hostile or critical, and make a real and deliberate effort to create a voice tone in your mind that is kind, supportive and understanding. Even when you make mistakes or do silly things try to remember that on the whole we don't cause ourselves suffering on purpose.

Key messages

- We are vulnerable to depression because of the way our brains are, our backgrounds, current life circumstances and how we feel we are coping.

- When we see how common depression is, and that most depressed people tend to think and feel the same way, we can see that it is not our fault – but there are things we can do to help ourselves, even so.

- It can help to understand that there are three basic emotion systems involved in depression. We can feel increased threat, reduced drive and enjoyment, and a sense of being cut off from others.

- Our attention has the power to affect our bodies, and we can use this by learning to focus it.

- If we learn to treat ourselves in supportive, kind and compassionate ways, this can influence our brain to bring us out of depression.

Tips for readers and supporters

- So, if we learn to understand how our minds work, how easy it is to get trapped in our threat system, how easy it is for our attention, thoughts, feelings and behaviours to be guided by it, then we can begin to become mindful and aware of that. Once we are more aware of what's going on in our minds then, on purpose, we can practise shifting our attention, thinking and behaviour to a more balanced approach supported by encouragement, understanding and kindness. This is not avoidance of the negative, but just learning how to balance things. In addition, we can use many of the other suggestions outlined in this book – always doing so with a compassionate focus. Practising these things on a regular basis may well be helpful to you.

- Many compassionate wishes to you.

17 Mindfulness: befriending depression

Willem Kuyken and Halley Cohen

Dawn's story

Dawn was a woman for whom mindfulness became key to her recovery from recurring depression. Her depression started when she was in her late teens. For Dawn her struggle had been characterized by each episode seeming to take on a life of its own. She described the experience as 'like being dragged towards and then over Niagara Falls', capturing her feelings of helplessness, fear and horror. It was as though depression 'came out of nowhere'. Her symptoms and negative thinking would spiral quickly, with a sickly sense that the escalation was beyond her control.

In her recovery from depression, following mindfulness-based cognitive therapy (MBCT), Dawn described how, through being in the moment, she learned to spot the subtle changes in her thinking and behaviour that marked the early-warning signs of depression. She learned to see herself and her situation with a newfound compassion, patience and acceptance. She could respond in more nourishing and helpful ways. This experience was empowering, spurring her to make positive changes in her life.

What is mindfulness?

'Mindfulness is the awareness that emerges through paying attention:

On purpose,
in the present moment, and
nonjudgmentally to things as they are.'

Jon Kabat-Zinn, *Coming to Our Senses*

We hear the word 'mindfulness' a lot in conversation and in the media. Put simply, mindfulness is about developing our awareness. It uses mind-body-based trainings, called mindfulness practices, to enable us to bring our attention, deliberately, to everyday activities so that we can tune into our thoughts, emotions, moods, senses and bodily sensations as they are right here, right now. This focus on the pesent moment is a key aspect of mindfulness, for it is only in the *present* that we can pause and give ourselves the space to respond to thoughts, feelings and events in our lives.

For example, very often we eat without much awareness. Eating mindfully involves deliberately slowing down to savour the taste, smell and texture of food. You can try for yourself some of the practices that we describe later, incorporating them into your daily life.

In this chapter, we will look at how mindfulness and, in particular, mindfulness-based cognitive therapy (MBCT) can help break the cycle of recurrent depression. MBCT is an intervention that integrates the ideas and practices of mindfulness with techniques and understanding from cognitive behavioural therapy, to help people who have experienced recurrent depression to stay well in the long term. As you learn more about mindfulness, perhaps even choosing to participate in an eight-week MBCT course, you may acquire some of the same newfound skills and attitudes as Dawn.

More information on how to find courses is given on page 275.

It is often said that it is difficult to describe mindfulness in words, and a better way to understand it is to experience it. The brief exercise below is a good taster of mindfulness – read it first before trying it for yourself.

A brief mindfulness practice – 'mindfulness of the breath'

If possible, find a quiet place where you can sit or lie down. After getting yourself comfortable, place your hand on your belly. Let go of passing thoughts as best you can. Deliberately, intentionally focus on how your hand feels and on the place where it makes contact with your belly. Sense the movements of the belly as the breath moves into and out of the body. In each moment, allow yourself to experience the sensations in your hand and on your belly exactly as they are. You have no place to be, nothing to achieve; there is just the simple awareness of your hand and your belly in this moment. Dwell in these sensations for a few minutes. Each time the mind wonders off, that's okay – that's what minds do – so gently, kindly, but firmly escort your attention back to your belly. Continue for a few minutes, observing what you experience.

What are mindfulness-based approaches?

There are a number of different mindfulness-based approaches that are based on contemplative traditions and meditative practices that are thousands of years old and that many millions of people around the world have found helpful. Mindfulness-Based Stress Reduction (MBSR) was originally developed in the 1970s by Jon Kabat-Zinn as a 'training vehicle for the relief of suffering'. He wondered if people with long-standing and serious health problems such as chronic pain, psoriasis, cancer and heart disease might benefit from learning mindfulness, and distilled the contemplative traditions and practices into a secular eight-week training programme. The MBSR programme introduces several core mindfulness practices for people with chronic physical health problems, to help them live with these conditions with less stress and a greater sense of wellbeing. Those who do the course learn to recognize patterns of thinking and feeling that cause suffering; to bring awareness and compassion to these moments; and to learn more 'choiceful' ways of responding to situations. Over time and with practice people learn the willingness and capacity to be present in their experiences with discernment, curiosity and kindness. After the course they typically report feeling better able to cope, not only with their chronic health problems, but also with their lives more generally.

Recently, the psychologists Zindel Segal, Mark Williams and John Teasdale reasoned that people who suffer repeated bouts of depression might also be helped by mindfulness training. Building from the work of Jon Kabat-Zinn they developed mindfulness-based cognitive therapy (MBCT). MBCT encourages participants to change their relationship to thoughts, feelings and body sensations. This provides an opportunity to discover that these are fleeting events that they can choose to engage with – or not. That is, repeated practice in noticing and observing, with curiosity and compassion and shifting perspective, helps participants realize that their thoughts, emotions and sensations are just thoughts, emotions and sensations, rather than 'truth' or 'me'.

Those who practise MBCT learn to see more clearly how their minds work and to recognize when their mood is beginning to dip, without adding to the problem by getting caught up in analysis and rumination – to stand on the edge of the whirlpool and watch it go round, rather than disappearing into it. This helps break the old association between negative mood and the negative thinking it would normally trigger.

So if you practise MBCT, you develop the capacity to allow distressing emotions, thoughts and sensations to come and go, without feeling that you have to suppress them, run away from or fight them. You learn to stay in touch with the present moment, without being driven to ruminate about the past or worry about the future.

How can mindfulness help people with depression?

All of us go through times of stress, sadness and irritability. For those who have been affected by depression, though, the downward spiral of anxiety, exhaustion and despair will be all too familiar. As we described in Dawn's story above, what can begin as an ordinary bout of low mood can quickly tailspin into a full-blown depressive episode.

One of the most common strategies we use to make ourselves feel better is to try to think our way out of our problem or mood. When it doesn't work, this can become an endlessly looping tape and we start asking ourselves questions such as, 'Why can't I just get on with it? What is wrong with me? Why am I such a failure?'

This looping rumination is the mind's understandable attempt to solve our emotional problems and feel better, but it usually has the effect of making us feel worse. No matter how hard we try to use thinking to fix things, no matter what we tell ourselves, nothing seems to work, at least not for long. Indeed, our attempts to find a cure for our depression often drag us further away from the happiness that we want – and that other people seem to grasp so easily. Cognitive therapy and mindfulness can both help us use our minds in a constructive way, to respond to negative thinking.

Research has shown that at least 50 per cent of those who have experienced depression find it comes back. After a second or third episode, the risk of further episodes rises to between 80 and 90 per cent. Why is this the case? Simply put, depression creates a pathway in the brain between sad mood and negative thoughts to the point where even normal 'everyday' sadness can trigger major negative thoughts that spiral into depression. For people with a history of depression, this can happen extremely quickly, and lead them to feel quite helpless. Mindfulness provides a way of becoming aware of, and stepping out of, these patterns.

Do mindfulness-based interventions work?

Over several decades, numerous studies have shown that MBSR does enable change in people with a broad range of stress-related health problems. Data from trials indicate that when MBCT is compared with the treatment that people usually get, such as medication and support from their GP or mental health team, it is associated with a 44 per cent reduction in how likely they are to get depressed again – although this is only true for people who have been depressed at least three times. When compared with antidepressants, MBCT is as good. Even though the course involves learning skills that have not historically been part of mainstream Western society, following the trials people reported finding mindfulness-based approaches extremely accessible and acceptable. As a result of these studies, the National Institute for Health and Care Excellence (NICE), the national body in the UK that advises healthcare professionals on treatments for physical and mental-health problems, recommends MBCT as one of its preferred treatments for depression.

Interestingly, studies have shown that mindfulness can not only prevent depression, but also has a positive effect on the way the brain deals with underlying day-to-day anxiety, stress, depression and irritability. Although you will still experience these from time to time (because they are part of the human condition), you will be able to recognize and respond to them more readily.

Key messages

- Mindfulness-based approaches are based on contemplative traditions and meditative practices that are thousands of years old. Many millions of people around the world have found these practices helpful.

- Mindfulness-based cognitive therapy (MBCT) is used to help people with recurrent depression. It is one of the preferred treatments recommended by the UK's National Institute for Health and Clinical Excellence (NICE).

- Studies show that when people use MBCT, there is a significantly reduced chance of becoming depressed again, compared with usual care. MBCT is as effective as staying on a maintenance dose of antidepressants, but without the side effects medication can have.

Tips for supporters

- The person you are supporting may think that mindfulness or meditation is not for them. Later in the chapter (page 262) we talk about some of the myths about mindfulness. Have a look and see if you can use the myths to explore what the blocks to trying mindfulness might be.

Autopilot mode and mindfulness

We spend much of our lives in automatic pilot mode, not really paying attention to what is going on around us, much less to what is going on within ourselves. We can eat an entire meal, for example, without truly tasting a single bite, because we are eating and talking, or eating and watching television, or trying to get it down as quickly as possible so we can get on to the next thing. There are many other examples where we operate on autopilot, including driving our daily commute without remembering any part of it. We can conduct entire conversations, even important ones, while we work at the computer, or answer a text, or attend to any number of tasks that seemingly *just can't wait*.

Autopilot mode helps us get through the day-to-day reality of having busy lives. While we attend to something in the foreground (for example, talking to a friend), automatic pilot enables us to take care of all the other things we need to do in that moment (such as driving). A certain degree of autopilot, where we do everyday tasks that we have done many times, can be highly functional and enable us to achieve a lot in the face of competing demands for our time, energy and attention.

For those who suffer from depression, though, autopilot mode can sometimes pose a problem. While we are in this mode, we can miss the subtle early-warning signs in our thoughts, feelings, senses and body that may signal a downward slide into depression. Interestingly, we may *believe* we are aware because we spend a large amount of time focusing on our thoughts and feelings, but in reality we are going over old ground, trapped in the same patterns of thinking that have got us stuck over and over in the past. This ruminative thinking starts on automatic pilot!

As Dawn described it, 'I would lie awake at 4 a.m. trying to problem-solve why I felt so bad, what made me feel this way, why I couldn't step out of these destructive habits. I'd end up tired, confused and my mood would be worse.' For Dawn, this familiar 'perfect storm' of physical fatigue, low energy, negative thinking and trying to think her way out almost inevitably led into a downward spiral of depression.

Mindfulness is about awareness

When we are mindful, we pay deliberate attention, in the present moment, to things as they *are* rather than to how we wish them to be. We broaden our focus beyond our thoughts, to all of our senses (hearing, seeing, tasting, touching, smelling), our emotions and our bodily sensations. Instead of ruminating on the past – which we can't change, or worrying about the future – things that may or may not ever happen, mindfulness can help keep us grounded in the full experience of the here and now. This is invaluable: it is only in the *present moment* that we have an immediate choice about how we are going to respond to whatever situation we are in, or to how we are thinking or feeling.

> *'Between stimulus and response there is a space. In that space lies our freedom and power to choose our response. In our response lies our growth and freedom.'*

Viktor Frankl

Mindfulness enables us to pause, instead of falling victim to the endlessly looping tape of our thoughts and feelings. When we pause, we give ourselves the space and time to see that there may be other ways to respond to situations, freeing us from the tyranny of the old thought and behaviour patterns that automatically pop up. Most importantly, we may eventually come to realize, on a deep level, that thoughts are just thoughts. They are not necessarily reality and we don't have to give them power. For example, you may wake up in the morning with the thought that you *absolutely must* get a certain number of things done that day, and that it's going to be busy and hectic. With that waking thought, you may immediately feel stressed, tense and overwhelmed, feelings that you then carry with you throughout the day as you struggle, feeling more and more drained, to complete everything. You might have had a very different, less stressful kind of day, however, if you had paused for a moment when you first had your waking thought about your busy day. If you had paused, you might have been able to make a more sensible decision about what really needed doing, so that your day would be more manageable.

In the popular book *Wherever You Go, There You Are: Mindfulness Meditation for Everyday Life* (see page 548), Jon Kabat-Zinn writes, 'Awareness is not the same as thought. It lies beyond thinking, although it makes use of thinking, honouring its value and its power. Awareness is more like a vessel which can hold and contain our thinking, helping us to see and know our thoughts as thoughts rather than getting caught up in them as reality.' If we extend this further, we come to realize that this 'vessel' of awareness contains not only thoughts, but also feelings, moods, senses and bodily sensations. For depression, this awareness can empower someone to develop a radically different relationship with these things.

Practising the pause

This practice will help you experience the power of the pause. Read it first, then try it for yourself.

Choose a time when you are involved in a goal-oriented activity such as reading, working, cleaning, eating – and explore pausing for a moment. First, stop what you are doing, sit comfortably and allow your eyes to close. Take a few deep breaths and with each out-breath, let go of any worries or thoughts about what you are going to do next. Release any tightness in the body as best you can.

Now, notice what you experience as you inhabit the pause. What sensations are you aware of in your body? Do you feel anxious or restless as you try to step out of your mental stories? Do you feel compelled to get back to whatever you were doing before? Can you simply allow yourself, for this moment, to sit and be aware of whatever is happening inside you?

Key messages

- *Thoughts are not facts* and we have a choice, in the present moment, about whether to give them power over our minds and hearts. In the same way, we also have a choice about whether, in any given moment, to react to our moods, bodily sensations and emotions. Instead of reacting, we can choose to observe the difficult sensations and feelings without doing anything to change things, to let them drift by. This can be a powerful lifeline for people prone to depression.

Tips for supporters

- Help the person you are supporting to look back on their day/week to see when they were in autopilot mode. It can be useful to do this yourself, too. The amount of time we spend *not* paying attention can be very surprising.

- Supporters can also benefit from doing the above mindfulness practice, either on your own or with the person you are supporting. Afterwards, think about or discuss with someone else how it felt to pause and to pay deliberate, mindful attention to the sensations and feelings within yourself.

Being compassionate and non-judgemental

When Dawn first did the exercise above her mind was very judgemental. She had a sense of wanting to resist being in the present moment and, when she did focus momentarily on her hand on her belly, she was taken aback by how critical her thoughts were: 'I am overweight, gross; I need to lose weight. I'm not getting this. Everyone else can do this, but I can't – I keep being distracted.'

When we are being mindful we open ourselves up to the present moment as it really is, without getting sidetracked by our usual pattern of negative thinking or self-recrimination, or by our tendency to dwell on the past or future. This is not to say that thinking will stop – it won't, because thinking is what our minds do. Instead, mindfulness means that when we do have judgemental thoughts about ourselves or anything else, we learn to recognize these as *just* thoughts that, if left alone, will pass by without our needing to react to them, in the same way that we can sit and watch waves roll in and out at the seaside. This new mode involves observing how thoughts arise in the mind. With kindness and acceptance, we begin to avoid getting caught up in negative spirals and to steer ourselves back into the present moment. With practice, it becomes easier to understand these negative thoughts for what they are: they are simply thoughts. They are not reality and we do not have to respond to them.

We are our own worst critics and probably far harsher with ourselves than we ever would be towards someone else. We even berate ourselves for not being able to 'fix' our depression, despite numerous and courageous attempts. Through practising mindfulness, we learn to be more compassionate and less judgemental, opening ourselves up to the concept that it is okay to *stop* seeing depression as a problem to be solved. In fact, it can be helpful to stop trying to 'fix' our depression, because our usual ways of fixing our problems often make depression worse. As we pause, we give ourselves the time and space to choose what is best to do for ourselves. Sometimes, this means finding a solution that feels right in our minds and hearts. Alternatively, choosing to leave matters alone, for now, can be the best solution.

The thirteenth-century poet Rumi, in his poem 'The Guest House', illustrates how important it is for us to accept and honour our thoughts and emotions as an inevitable part of being human, that both the good and bad have something to teach us.

> This being human is a guest house.
>
> Every morning a new arrival.
>
> A joy, a depression, a meanness,
>
> some momentary awareness comes
>
> as an unexpected visitor.
>
> Welcome and entertain them all!
>
> Even if they're a crowd of sorrows, who violently sweep your house
>
> empty of its furniture,

still, treat each guest honourably.

He may be clearing you out

for some new delight.

The dark thought, the shame, the malice.

Meet them at the door laughing,

and invite them in.

Be grateful for whoever comes,

because each has been sent

as a guide.

People's minds in the thirteenth century were in many ways no different from ours, when we stop with awareness to see how they work.

When Dawn was invited to see her thoughts about being overweight and 'no good' with a kindly, non-judgemental awareness, she could see how punitive and damaging they were. They led to a sort of inner collapse and tended to trigger all sorts of other negative thoughts and memories. She used the Rumi poem above and joked, 'I can see those thoughts as dark guests and just about welcome them, but I don't need to offer them a seat or a drink.'

Importantly, mindfulness teaches us that we don't have to be perfect. We particularly don't have to be perfect at being mindful! Our minds are naturally prone to wandering, particularly down well-trodden paths, and it takes practice to be more in the present moment. All minds wander; even people who have been meditating for years experience negative thoughts, feelings, physical sensations and the pull of familiar ways of reacting. What changes is that we can see these experiences are transient (passing), and change our habitual ways of reacting. Developing mindfulness skills, with patience, composure and discipline is both an act of kindness towards ourselves and an important part of healing. It counters the all-too-familiar thoughts of not being good enough or not deserving happiness.

Key messages

- Mindfulness is about being more aware of not only our thoughts, but also our feelings, moods, senses and bodily sensations as they are *in the present moment.*

- By learning to focus on the present moment, we become better equipped to spot the early-warning signs of depression, so that we can deal with them more effectively.

- Being in autopilot mode can help us get a lot done. However, it can be problematic for people with depression because when we stop paying attention to what is happening, we risk missing the early-warning signs of depression.

- Thoughts are not facts and we have a choice about whether to give them power over us.

- Mindfulness allows us the space to pause so that we can choose to respond instead of reacting automatically.

Tips for supporters

- Mindfulness can be helpful to supporters as well, and we encourage family members, partners and friends to try out the practices described here so that you are able to offer the best possible support. Many supporters are likely to find that they also derive benefits from doing these.

- Mindfulness is not a quick fix. It requires discipline, time and patience to cultivate attentional control and some of the qualities we have outlined above. Supporters can help people learning mindfulness by providing support and, more practically, the space and time to commit to a daily mindfulness practice.

- Some people require the discipline of having a set place and time to do their mindfulness practice, while others prefer to do it in different places at varying times of the day. It's not always easy to earmark some time, or to find a quiet place, but do the best you can with whatever time and location you have available. The important thing is to just do it!

- There is an excellent book, *Living with a Black Dog: How to Take Care of Someone with Depression While Looking After Yourself*, written by Ainsley Johnstone, a supporter of Matthew Johnstone, who suffers from depression. It provides an animated perspective on both the experience of being a supporter and seeing someone recover with the help of mindfulness. See the Further Reading section on page 547 for this chapter.

What are mindfulness practices?

Mindfulness practices include focusing on the breath and body through meditation, movement and the development of a more mindful attention to everyday activities. All of these approaches help us learn to recognize the feelings and patterns of thinking that cause suffering, so that we can respond in ways that cultivate wellbeing and happiness. Many people find they need the support of a guided CD when starting out (see page 548 for details of some audio recordings that we recommend for guided mindfulness practice).

Mindfulness practices are deceptively simple, but the clue is in the word 'practice'. Though the techniques are easy to learn and can be done anywhere, long-term positive benefits require gentle patience, perseverance and regular practice.

Although we've all heard of meditation, many don't really know what it is and are a little bit hesitant to try it ourselves. Before we describe the practices, we would like to take this opportunity to dispel a few myths:

- Although meditation is rooted in the Buddhist tradition, it is not a religion. In fact, the practices can be traced back to many different contemplative traditions. It is a form of mental training that can be done by anyone, regardless of whether they follow a religion, or are atheist or agnostic. It is beneficial to people of any age and background.

- You don't have to sit in the lotus position on the floor (unless you really want to).

- Meditation is not complicated. It is also not about 'success' or 'failure'. Even when it feels hard, such as if you become sleepy, you can still learn something important about how your mind, senses and body work that will benefit you psychologically. In fact, some of the best learning may come from these struggles if we can stay open and present to what happens within us.

- Meditation does not have to take a lot of time, although persistence, patience and practice are needed. In fact, some of the practices we will suggest only take three minutes!

- Meditation will not deaden your mind, nor turn you into a zombie who has cut off from your thoughts and feelings. Instead, it gives you a way to pay attention to your senses, mind and heart as they are in this present moment, so that you can make wiser choices based on a deep understanding about what is right for you.

- Mindfulness is not 'new-age' or alternative. It is quite ordinary, simply learning about how we think, what we feel and what happens in our bodies, to help us respond more skilfully to stress, enjoy greater wellbeing and maybe even lead better lives.

Mindfulness practices

We will now describe a series of practices that are taught in most mindfulness-based approaches, including MBCT and MBSR, and which you can learn at home. When trying these at home, perhaps with the help of a CD, be guided by what feels right, paying attention to any physical limitations and by what your experience tells you is helpful. If you have any questions or concerns, seek out an experienced mindfulness teacher for guidance. If you have a sense that something is not right for you, for whatever reason, trust your judgement and proceed only with what feels right, perhaps starting with some of the shorter practices and/or seeking out a teacher or mindfulness course local to you. Many people who join a course find that they benefit not only from the experience of the mindfulness teacher, but also from the support and insights of their fellow participants.

Mindfulness practice 1: Body Scan

The Body Scan can be done on your own or with the guidance of a mindfulness teacher, either by listening to an audio recording of a guided practice (see page 548 for details) or by attending a local mindfulness class. It doesn't matter where you are when you do this practice, as long as you are comfortable, sitting or lying down, and have enough uninterrupted time and space to give to this practice. The Body Scan can be as short as ten minutes or as long as you wish to make it. Many people find twenty to forty minutes works well for them.

The Body Scan involves moving your attention around your body, focusing your attention on each region in turn in a non-judgemental way, before disengaging and moving onto another region. For example, you could start by focusing your attention on your left big toe, and then move your focus to each toe in turn before moving on to the rest of your left foot, the ankle, calf, knee, thigh. You could then apply this same awareness to your other leg, the different parts of your torso, each arm, before ending at the top of your head. Be aware of how and where your body makes contact with any surfaces, your clothes and any sensations on your skin. If you find that you don't feel anything at various points, acknowledge that that is the way it is at that moment and continue with the Body Scan.

Regardless of what happens (whether you fall asleep, become distracted, feel bored or anxious, or forget which part of the body you were focusing on), don't worry; this is part of the practice. Just note the experience (for example, 'sleepiness') before coming back to the practice. It's not a test – there is no right or wrong. The important thing is to do it. As best you can, let go of any expectations, allowing yourself to be open and curious to whatever is going on inside you. This is an opportunity to experience your thoughts, feelings and bodily sensations in the present moment, with kindness and without judgement.

If your mind wanders, note that this is happening before gently bringing your mind back to your body. Trying to block unpleasant thoughts, feelings or body sensations will only create upsetting feelings and take you away from your experience in this moment. If possible, note how your mind reacts, and if you notice your mind is saying things aren't as they should be, as best you can, view your experience in each moment with an accepting attitude.

You will feel the benefits if you are able to do this practice every day. There will, of course, be days when you really don't want to do a Body Scan. Sometimes these are the days when it is most important to do the practice. On these days, observe your resistance and the thoughts and feelings behind it. This is an opportunity for you to experience the workings of your mind and heart without reacting. By persevering with the Body Scan over days and weeks, you are likely to discover a new freedom from the tyranny of unhelpful thoughts and negative thinking, and to develop a new intimacy with your body and the teaching it can offer us.

Mindfulness practice 2: Breath Practice

Everywhere we go, we are breathing. No matter what we are doing or feeling, we always have our breath to connect us to the present moment. Although breathing itself is one of the most natural, automatic things that we do, it is not always easy to focus our attention on it as our minds tend to get distracted with other things. As you do the following Breath Practice, try to greet the comings and goings of your mind as both natural and inevitable. The important thing is to recognize when your attention has wandered and to gently bring it back to the breath.

If possible, allow yourself fifteen minutes or longer for this practice. You can choose to sit on a chair or cushion on the ground. If you choose a chair, place your feet flat on the floor with your legs uncrossed. Sit up straight but not rigidly, ensuring that your spine is self-supporting and not slouching against the back of the chair. If you choose a cushion, sit cross-legged with your buttocks raised by the cushion and your knees at a lower level touching the floor. This will reduce the strain on your back. This posture will feel open, upright and dignified, supportive of mindfulness practice.

Once you have found an upright, comfortable position, gently close your eyes and begin. For the first minute or two, direct your attention, with kindness and curiosity, to the sensations of your body. This can include focusing on where your body meets with the floor and/or chair and any other sensations of contact that you are experiencing.

Gradually, shift your awareness to your lower abdomen as it rises and falls with each breath. At the beginning, it may help to place your hand on your abdomen until you are tuned into the physical sensations in this area. You can remove your hand as your focus deepens. If your mind wanders, or even if you fall asleep momentarily, bring your focus back, with kindness, to your lower abdomen and the steady flow of your breath.

You do not have to change your breathing in any way. Allow your body to breathe as it would naturally, in and out, your abdomen expanding and contracting. As best you can, bring an attitude of acceptance to the experience, surrendering to the moment. There is no need to change or fix anything. Even the slight pauses and hitches in your breathing are natural, each breath unique and complete.

This awareness of the breath is central to all mindfulness practices. It is an invaluable tool that helps anchor us in the present moment so that we can be aware of what is really happening within ourselves as we go about our day. As you gain experience with the Breath Practice, you will notice in particular that your breathing changes with your moods, thoughts and body movements. You then can use your breathing to help deal with the pain, anger, relationships or stresses of daily life.

Mindfulness practice 3: Mindful Movement

Mindful Movement is simply a meditation practice that uses physical movement to help us become more aware of what is going on in our minds and bodies. Many people find that it is a very natural way to release the day's tension from the body and mind, through slow, gentle stretching and the realignment of muscles and joints.

It can be useful to follow some sort of guidance for this practice, either recorded or with a mindfulness teacher, since some of the exercises require quite precise movements, but you can get a taste of what is involved by following the instructions below. If you have any health concerns, such as back problems, it might be a good idea to consult your GP, or specialist practitioner if you have one, before trying Mindful Movement.

While carrying out the movements, keep in mind that the aim is not to feel pain or to challenge the limits of your body. It is important to look after yourself and be guided by any signals from your body telling you how far to stretch and how long to hold any position. Sometimes, your body may tell you to back off from a stretch. You will then need to ask yourself if you are pushing yourself too much. If you find yourself doing this, make a mental note of it while making a skilful choice about whether to keep pushing or to withdraw totally or partially.

As you learn to pay attention to your bodily sensations, good and bad, and the thoughts they trigger, you will find a new interconnectedness between your mind and body. Many people, particularly those with chronic pain, find that instead of fighting their bodies, the Mindfulness Movement practice teaches them a new relationship with it.

How to do the Mindful Movement meditation

It can be beneficial to do this exercise in bare feet or socks so that you have more contact with the ground. First, stand with your feet hip-width apart, your knees slightly bent. The four stages of this practice can be done in the following order:

1. **Raising both arms.** On the in-breath, slowly raise your arms out to the sides, parallel with the floor. After breathing out, raise your arms as you breathe in, slowly and mindfully, until your hands are raised above your head. As your arms move and then you hold the position, try as best you can to be aware of the workings and stretching of not only your arm muscles, but also the muscles and joints of different parts of your body, with care and patience. Continue breathing, allowing the breath to flow in and out, as you continue to stretch upwards. Remain open to any changes in your breathing and to the sensations and feelings within your body as you maintain this stretch for as long or as short as you wish.

    When you are ready, lower your arms slowly on the out-breath. Feel the different sensations as they come down and as they rest loosely by your sides. You may find that closing your eyes for this part of the exercise helps you connect with the various sensations and with your breath.

2. **Picking fruit.** Open your eyes if they were closed. Gently raise one arm, stretching upwards with your hand as though you were

picking fruit from a tree that is just out of reach. Turn your face upwards and allow your eyes to look past the tips of your fingers. Be aware of the sensations within your body and your breathing, as you extend the upwards stretch of your body from your feet to the tips of your fingers. Allow your heels to lift off the floor. Breathe, holding the stretch for as long as you wish. When you are ready, release the stretch in reverse: lower your heel, relax your body, and lower your fingers, hand and arm back down to your side. With your face now centre, close your eyes as you pay deliberate attention to the sensations flowing through your body and to your breathing. When you are ready, release the stretch, come back to standing and then go through the same movements to 'pick fruit' with your other hand.

Do this sequence once or twice, or as many times as feels helpful.

3. **Sideways bending.** With your hands on your hips, slowly and mindfully bend at the waist towards the left so that your body arcs in a gentle curve that flows from your feet to your hips and torso. Return to a central, upright position on the in-breath. Then, on the next out-breath, bend to the right, repeating the process. Don't worry about how far you can bend. Some people may only be able to bend a slight amount, if at all. The main thing is the quality of the attention you give to the bodily sensations you feel as you do this practice and to any thoughts that may arise.

Do this sequence once or twice, or as many times as feels helpful.

4. **Shoulder rolls.** Bring your mindful attention to your shoulders by exploring how it feels to roll them. There are many ways to roll your shoulders and you can do them here in any order, as many times as you wish, either both shoulders together, or rolling first one shoulder then the other. Dangle your arms loosely by your sides. Then, when you are ready, begin. Allow your breath to set the speed of the rotation. You may, for example, choose to start by raising your shoulders towards the ears, then slowly lowering them,

before beginning again. Or, you could raise your shoulders as before but then choose to roll them backwards, bringing your shoulder blades together before dropping your shoulders completely. Bring awareness and curiosity to these various positions as you explore the sensations they provoke. Listen to any signals from your neck or shoulders around these rolls, doing what feels right to your body.

When you reach the end of the four stages of the Movement Meditation, pause. Allow yourself the space to savour fully whatever bodily sensations, thoughts and feelings you may be experiencing.

Shorter mindfulness practices

Shorter practices are those that can be done in almost any situation, including when you are on the go.

Shorter practice 1: Three-Minute Breathing Space

This is exactly what the name implies: three minutes that you take out of your day to focus on your breathing. Because it takes so little time to do, many people consider this to be one of the most important practices that they learn during the mindfulness course. It can be particularly useful during times of stress, exhaustion, anger and sadness, where your thoughts are spiralling out of control, kind of like an emergency meditation. Doing the Three-Minute Breathing Space enables you to step out of autopilot mode so that you can take a more mindful stance towards whatever is happening.

Adopt an erect posture, sitting or standing. First, ask yourself what your experience of the present moment is right now in terms of your thoughts, feelings, senses and bodily sensations. A word or phrase is fine (for example, 'anxiety', 'tightness in my chest'). Second, gently turn your full attention to your breathing, the uniqueness of each in- and out-breath. Let your attention, as best you can, hold the breath in the foreground as far as possible. In the third and final step, widen the scope of your awareness to include your whole body, your abdomen, facial expression and posture. Include all of your experience in your awareness.

Shorter practice 2: stretching

In any moment, you can bring your awareness to your body and, with clear intention and a sense of self-compassion, make deliberate movements that establish a sense of connection, dignity and awareness of the body. For example, you might be at a meeting and notice you have started slouching and that your neck and shoulders have become tight. Deliberately taking a more upright and dignified posture and releasing the shoulder tension can be one way to respond in these moments. Tai chi, hatha yoga and chi gung all use Mindful Movement and can be adapted into bite-sized everyday stretches.

Shorter practice 3: walking

You might find that your mind and body are too restless or stressed to lie, sit, or stand while focusing on the breath. At these times, doing a meditation that uses movement can help anchor your attention into the present moment. Mindful walking is an everyday and very effective movement meditation that can be done anywhere – inside or outdoors. The destination is not important; instead you are looking for an intentional awareness of the body moving, bringing the torch beam of attention to the feet, legs and body as you walk. It is up to you whether you set aside time for it, or incorporate it into your normal everyday activities, perhaps while walking to work. The intention is to be fully present with each moment, with each step, right where you are.

Mindfulness in everyday life

It can be helpful to keep our 'mindfulness muscles' in shape during the good times, so that when we really need this greater awareness during tough times, they are strong. One great way to give our mindfulness muscles a workout is to pay deliberate attention to our routine, every-day activities. Even doing this once a day can be beneficial.

As mentioned earlier, being on autopilot is risky for people prone to depression, because we can miss the warning signs that may signal a downward spiral. Bringing mindfulness to an everyday activity, such as eating, brushing our teeth, or driving, is another way to pause and check in with ourselves; for as we pay attention in a new way to a routine task, we can sometimes expose thoughts and feelings that we weren't even aware lurked beneath our consciousness. Interestingly, many people also find that practising this gentle, moment-to-moment awareness makes the task itself feel easier, more interesting, less stressful and even enjoyable.

The key to bringing mindfulness to an everyday task is to open yourself up fully to the experience without judgement and with gentle curios-ity. Tune in to your sense of touch, taste, smell, sight and hearing, and the way your body moves. Be aware of your breathing as you perform the task, noticing any feelings such as stress, impatience, anger, sad-ness or joy. You may observe tension in a particular part of your body; perhaps your chest feels tight or your breathing shallow. You can use your breathing to let go of these difficult sensations, or to simply breathe while allowing yourself to 'be' with whatever you are experiencing.

So when can we practise everyday mindfulness? The answer is any time! You might choose a new task to focus on each day, or stick to the same for a week to see how your awareness develops. The list of pos-sible times is endless but here are a few examples:

- *Brushing your teeth.* Where is your mind as you brush your teeth?

- *Showering.* Sense the water on your body, the temperature, the pressure.

- *Preparing food.* Any food preparation is a great opportunity for mindfulness.

- *Eating.* Try having a meal in silence, really focusing on the food and the sensations of eating. This involves attending only to eating (no

TV, radio, or reading!) and the movements and flavours involved in eating.

- *Washing up.* This is an opportunity to pay attention to seeing, moving, and feeling all the sensations associated with washing up, such as the temperature of the water and the sensation of the bubbles.

- *Driving.* Try driving without daydreaming, listening to music or other distractions. Pay attention to the actions involved, the focus of your vision, the sensations in your hands, feet and back.

- *Red traffic lights.* While in your car waiting for the light to turn green, sit quietly, peacefully, and become aware of your breath.

- *Walking.* Pay attention to the sensations of walking, using the bottoms of your feet as anchors for attention.

- *Telephone.* When the phone rings, stop before answering to tune into your thoughts, feelings and body, breathing with these before answering.

- *Email.* Like the phone, before answering your messages, tune into any thoughts, feelings and bodily sensations, breathing with these until your mind is more settled.

Key messages

- Mindfulness practices include focusing on the breath and body through meditation, movement and the development of a more mindful attention to everyday activities.

- We use mindfulness practices to connect ourselves to the present moment so that we are aware of what is happening in our minds, hearts and bodies as they are right here, right now. These practices help us learn to recognize the feelings and patterns of thinking that cause suffering so that we can learn to respond in ways that cultivate wellbeing and happiness.

- Becoming more mindful is not always easy, but if you persevere as best you can, with non-judgemental kindness towards yourself, the rewards can change your life.

- Many find that the Three-Minute Breathing Space is one of the most important gifts that we can give to ourselves. It provides us with a small window of time that we can take to check in with ourselves, particularly during times of stress or unhappiness, at any point in our day.

Tips for supporters

- In addition to trying some of the mindfulness practices yourself, discuss with the person you are supporting ways to bring mindfulness into everyday activities that you could do together. For example, if you are taking a walk together, you can both choose to walk mindfully for part of the time, perhaps sharing how it is for you.

Next step: the eight-week MBCT course

Although you will certainly derive some benefit from doing mindfulness practices on your own, attending an MBCT course for people with recurrent depression can be a life-changing experience. MBCT courses meet once a week for eight weeks, usually in small groups of ten to fifteen people. Generally, before committing to the course, you will have an individual appointment with the mindfulness teacher so that you can find out more about what is involved before you sign up.

It is not recommended that you do an MBCT course while you are experiencing an episode of depression. The programme is intended for people to learn skills to stay well in the long term, and you will be able to engage with the content of the course far more when you are feeling better.

Over the eight weeks, you will learn various mindfulness meditation practices as well as ways to bring mindfulness and awareness into the everyday activities of your life. You will be asked to set aside up to an hour each day between sessions to do formal meditation practice on your own. Although it can be difficult to rearrange your time to accommodate this for two months, this quality of discipline is part of the practice of mindfulness. It can be tempting to let other competing demands and distractions stop you from devoting this time to your practice. You might feel it is selfish to take this time for yourself. You might have to remind yourself, particularly when your 'doing' mind is trying to sabotage you, that you and your happiness are the priority. For those who suffer from depression, that is not selfish, nor time wasting, but a kind and positive gift to yourself.

The mindfulness teacher will gently encourage discussion to help participants deepen their understanding of the practice and to explore each member's experiences with it over the previous week. Although you will be encouraged to participate and talk honestly about your own experiences, it is not obligatory and the sessions are not meant to be 'group therapy'.

Most courses that we do in life have clearly stated goals and learning objectives where we tick off each task before moving onto the next. MBCT, and mindfulness in general, doesn't work like that. The aim is not to strive towards some goal, or even to feel relaxed or more peaceful, though those can be much appreciated results of the practice. The goal is to live a life where we are more fully present and awake, where we can greet whatever arises in ourselves and our lives with kind-hearted openness and where we can be who we already are. That being said, learning awareness through mindfulness practice enables people to recognize and step out of old patterns of thinking and reacting that were part of slipping into depression. The intention of many people starting an MBCT class is to prevent depression coming back, and the research as well as many people's experience is that it works.

Although it can sometimes feel daunting to even think about joining a course, what most people notice straight away is how compassionate, safe and supportive the environment is. This has a lot to do with the mindfulness teacher, for part of their training and their own practice involves developing a mindset of unconditional friendliness to themselves and to others. This kind-heartedness is central to how they run the class. Mindfulness teachers tend to give off a genuine aura of warmth and acceptance. This can feel very supportive, which is particularly important if you are struggling with difficult emotions such as anger, sadness, disappointment or frustration. Seeing kindness in action can be a powerful teaching tool, because developing a sense of kindness towards ourselves and self-care lie at the heart of all mindfulness practices.

It is worth mentioning that, at some point during the eight weeks, you may well struggle because of feelings of impatience, boredom, agitation or doubt. This can happen at any time, but often occurs during the middle sessions. The important thing is to persevere, to keep attending the course and doing the practice homework. As best you can, let go of all your expectations, even the expectation that your depression will get better, and instead try to remain open to each moment as it unfolds. If you can, focus on the present and the rest will take care of itself. Follow that famous advertising slogan 'just do it' and be open to what you learn along the way.

How to find a course?

NICE recommends that people with a history of at least three episodes of depression, who are currently well, and who wish to learn skills to stay well, should have access to MBCT via the NHS. To find a local NHS-run course, contact your GP in the first instance. In some areas, MBCT services are not as well developed and MBCT may be provided through the voluntary sector or in the private sector.

It is important to find an MBCT teacher who has the necessary training and experience. The UK Network for Mindfulness-Based Teacher

Training Organisations is committed to supporting good practice and integrity in the delivery of mindfulness-based courses. They have published good practice guidelines and you might like to check that any teacher complies with these guidelines: *http://mindfulnessteachersuk.org.uk/#welcome*.

Among other things, mindfulness teachers should:

- be familiar with the mindfulness-based course curriculum and have a personal, in-depth experience of the course's core meditation practices.

- have completed a rigorous mindfulness-based teacher-training programme or supervised pathway over a minimum of twelve months.

- have a professional qualification in mental or physical healthcare, education or social care, or have the equivalent life experience recognized by the organization or context in which the course will take place.

- have knowledge and experience of the population that the course will be delivered to. If they are teaching MBCT, the teacher should have an appropriate professional clinical training.

- have their own personal mindfulness practice, including daily formal and informal practice and attending annual residential meditation retreats.

- maintain their own professional development through supervision and professional training.

Beyond the eight-week course

So, you've completed the eight-week MBCT course and you're going home equipped with a range of meditation practices, a small stack of meditation CDs and, hopefully, a new understanding of and relationship with your mind, heart and body. What happens now? Many people end the class with mixed feelings. While you might feel stronger and more hopeful about the future, you might experience some less comfortable feelings. It is common to be apprehensive about how you are going to continue your mindfulness practice without the encouragement of your mindfulness teacher and course members. You might worry that if your practice slips, then you will spiral down into another bout of sadness and depression. You might feel resentful that you now have another task to do in your already busy life.

All of these thoughts and feelings are natural. Whereas in the past you might have tried to suppress them or ignore them, now that you have a new tool at your disposal – mindfulness – you know that your thoughts and feelings are just that: thoughts and feelings. You don't have to act upon them. Instead, you can 'be' with them, observing how your mind and body is in the present moment.

Keeping your mindfulness practice going takes time and effort, so it is important that you find a routine that works for you. There is no 'right' way to maintain your practice, no perfect amount of time to spend on it, no perfect combination of practices. Sometimes, the meditation itself will reveal to you what you need to do to nourish yourself in that moment. There will be days when it feels easy and other days when you'd rather lose a limb than do a mindfulness practice! Those are often the days when we need mindfulness the most. Getting yourself 'on the mat' at those times is a great opportunity for you to explore your resistance and check in with yourself.

You can change your mindfulness routine from day to day depending on what is happening in your life and within yourself. The important thing is to find a realistic routine that works for you on a long-term basis. Often, people find that doing a mix of formal meditation, such as the Body Scan, plus mindfulness in everyday life scattered through-out the day, works well. Some days you might only have time for the Three-Minute Breathing Space, or you might decide to pay deliberate, mindful attention to an activity that you do naturally during your day. Opportunities to bring mindfulness into your daily life are plentiful and grounding. What you have to do is make a commitment to being present, as best you can, with an open mind and heart.

Let's briefly return to Dawn. She was first introduced to mindfulness by reading a book; it gave her a taste that this was a way of being that could be helpful to her. She recognized that what she had been doing to help her depression for many years made sense, but wasn't really working. An eight-week MBCT course was not easy, because Dawn was faced with some of the unwelcome visitors Rumi describes in his poem 'The Guesthouse': negative thinking, impatience and physical agitation. However, she was persistent and, slowly, she was able to stay with it, bringing patience, composure and compassion to her experience, and she learned that this can be transformative. She continues to weave all she has learned into as many parts of her life as possible. Although she still has periods of feeling low, overwhelmed and agitated, she now recognizes them earlier and tries not to let old habits make them worse. Over time, she has found that mindfulness is enabling her to more fully enjoy all that is right with her and her life.

Key messages

- Regardless of whether you choose to do the practices on your own with the help of guided meditation CDs and books, or to attend a mindfulness course, the important thing is to practise regularly, with an attitude of curiosity, patience and non-judgemental kindness.

- For some people, regular practice means doing several Three-Minute Breathings Spaces per day, while for others doing a daily full meditation session is helpful. You can change from day to day, week to week, experimenting with what works for you in terms of your time and wellbeing. Taking care of yourself in this way, to stay well, is a tremendous gift that you can give to yourself and to the people around you.

Tips for supporters

- If the person you are supporting is attending an MBCT course, be aware that they might experience a dip in their motivation, often around the fourth week. They may even wish to stop going. Sometimes it can be helpful to remind them that this is common and that learning to 'sit' with difficult thoughts and feelings, such as boredom, impatience and the desire to give up, can be part of the healing process of mindfulness.

- If the person you are supporting wishes, discuss with them how they plan to maintain their mindfulness practice after their course ends. Some people might value having a set time and place each day for meditation, while others need a more flexible approach. There is no right way, or required amount of time to practise mindfulness. To keep things fresh and to deepen their practice, visit a bookshop or go online to discover the many excellent CDs and books available.

We wish you all the best in this journey.

Acknowledgements

The mindfulness practices described in this chapter have a lineage in contemplative traditions dating back at least 2,500 years. They were formulated for contemporary secular use in healthcare settings by Jon Kabat-Zinn in the 1980s as described in *Full Catastrophe Living*. Many people have since used the essential framework of MBSR set out by Jon Kabat-Zinn. Zindel Segal, John Teasdale and Mark Williams' work in depression has been influential, and their ideas have more recently been applied to a broader range of problems.

Although many sources were used in the writing of this chapter, we were particularly influenced by several ground-breaking works, which are listed in the Further Reading section on page 547 in Appendix 1.

PART 3

Tackling common problems in depression

Introduction

In Part 2 we looked at a number of ideas that could be important to anyone who becomes depressed or low in mood. In Part 3 we move on to discuss particular problems that are very strongly associated with depression. These problems look very different on the surface: sleep, self-esteem and difficulties in close relationships. However, they all have in common that they not only make people vulnerable to depression, but also become much worse if people do get depressed. Melanie Fennell's chapter on low self-esteem shows just how easily this can tip people into depression when things go wrong, and what you can do to boost your self-esteem. Almost everybody has had experience of poor sleep and knows how wretched this can make you feel. When we get depressed, our sleep is very often disturbed, and this makes coping much harder. Similarly, we all know that we feel lousy if we are getting on badly with those closest to us – we need to know how to overcome difficulties, and how to use our close relationships to help us with depression.

18 How to tackle low self-esteem

Melanie Fennell

Introduction

Low self-esteem is one of the problems most commonly experienced by depressed people. Negative thoughts (NATs) about oneself are central to depression (see Chapter 9). Not only that, but people with depression often see it as a sign of personal inadequacy, leading to low self-esteem. They beat themselves up for being depressed, not recognizing the strength and courage it takes to struggle with low mood. It can also work the other way round: long-standing low self-esteem can make you more vulnerable to depression and to other emotional and psychological difficulties. If your negative view of yourself is primarily a part of your depression or a reaction to it, your priority needs to be working on the depression itself. But if your negative perspective on yourself came before your depression, if you tend to doubt and criticize yourself even when you are *not* depressed, and if you find it hard to value yourself or treat yourself with consideration and kindness, then it would probably be helpful for you to try to address your low self-esteem in its own right.

This chapter describes how CBT can help to enhance self-acceptance and self-esteem. This means that you can use and build on the skills you have already acquired: identifying unhelpful thoughts (NATs – see Chapter 9), questioning them, formulating more helpful alternatives and testing them through behavioural experiments (see Chapter 10 for an introduction to these strategies). You can also use these skills with the broader attitudes and beliefs that underpin and feed low self-esteem, working to develop a more accepting and balanced perspective on yourself.

As you read, take time to pause and reflect, and perhaps talk to your supporter if you have one. How do these ideas relate to you? What do you recognize in yourself? How might you change things so as to feel more comfortable in your own skin, happier to be just who you are? In so short a space, this is necessarily something of a 'taster'. If you would like to pursue what you discover in greater depth, you will find more detailed self-help books listed at the end of this book under Further Reading (see page 550).

What is low self-esteem?

Self-esteem means our fundamental sense of our own worth. It is reflected in beliefs about ourselves, which could be expressed as sentences beginning with the words: 'I am ...' Healthy self-esteem is reflected in beliefs like: 'I am OK,' 'I am basically a decent human being,' or 'I am good enough.' In contrast, low self-esteem is reflected in beliefs like 'I am no good,' 'I am inadequate,' 'I am useless,' 'I am unlovable,' and so on.

CBT is based on the idea that it is the *meaning* we attach to things, rather than the things themselves, that is important in shaping how we feel and what we do. This applies to how we feel about ourselves, too. You might actually be a perfectly decent human being with many positive qualities, but if you *believe* that you are inadequate or weak or not good enough, that will affect how you feel and how you lead your life. Among other things, as you will discover, it may make you vulnerable to depression, because thinking badly of ourselves inevitably has an impact on mood.

Understanding low self-esteem

On the opposite page you will find a flowchart showing how low self-esteem develops and what keeps it going. This is a sort of map of the territory of low self-esteem, which you can use to navigate your journey towards self-acceptance. Your map will help you to make sense of your thoughts and feelings about yourself, and to see that there are reasons why they

Figure 27: How low self-esteem works

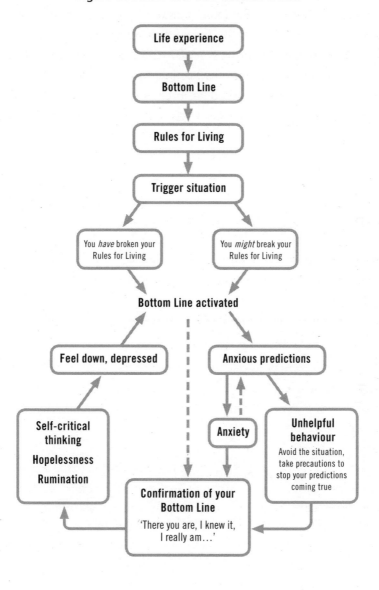

are as they are. It will help you to determine which directions to go in, and to explore how low self-esteem operates, while it is happening. If you can learn to recognize the voice of low self-esteem, rather than automatically believing it, you can say to yourself, 'Uh-oh, there I go again'

– whether it's expecting the worst, putting yourself down, demanding too much of yourself, or whatever it may be. You can begin to see these patterns as no more than old, out-of-date thinking habits, and to discover that you need not engage with them, get sucked into them or do what they say. This is like standing beside a complex mechanism, watching it work and noticing how all the wheels and cogs fit together, but not getting caught up in the moving parts. You can observe what connects to what, what is working as it should, what needs attention and what changes you need to make. So understanding is the first step to positive change.

How does low self-esteem develop?

Figure 27 suggests that your negative beliefs about yourself (referred to here as the 'Bottom Line') are an understandable result of life experiences. Low self-esteem is not something you were born with; it is something you have learned. And what has been learned can be unlearned, and new things learned to take their place.

For low self-esteem to develop three things need to happen:

1. You have life experiences that communicate negative messages to you about yourself.

2. You *believe* these messages – otherwise they would not affect you. This is how you get your Bottom Line.

3. You compensate for feeling bad about yourself by setting yourself extra-high standards (for example, perfectionism, or believing you always have to be in control). These 'Rules for Living' lead you to expect more of yourself than is possible for any normal, imperfect human being.

Let us look at each of these in turn. As you read through this chapter, think back over your own life and see if anything rings bells for you. It might be helpful to keep a record of your thoughts, so write them down in a notebook. It may also be helpful to talk to your supporter about this, especially if looking at the past is difficult or upsetting for you.

1. Life experiences

Painful experiences that lead to low self-esteem often happen during childhood, but not always, as you will see. Here are some possibilities. As you go through the list, consider: which apply to you? Even if these particular experiences are not personally relevant, does scanning them bring events to mind that were important in forming your Bottom Line?

The early years

- Loss of someone important to you (for example, through bereavement, separation, divorce)

- Being ignored, mistreated, neglected or abused

- Failing to meet your parents' standards, or being unfavourably compared to others

- Lacking what you needed in order to develop a secure sense of self-worth (praise; interest; reassurance and comfort; encouragement to express yourself; being taught that making mistakes is a normal part of learning; feeling able to ask for help and support; intimacy, warmth, love and affection)

- Being part of a family struggling with adversity (such as financial hardship, illness, being a target for prejudice or hostility)

School years

- Being teased or bullied or excluded

- Being the odd one out

- Struggling to manage lessons, tests and homework

Transition to adulthood

- Difficulties leaving home and learning how to manage independently, set goals, manage your time and motivate yourself

- Difficulties making new relationships and transforming old ones

- Difficulties establishing a secure sexual identity

Later life

- Experiencing traumatic events

- Experiencing less dramatic, more gradual life changes which impact on things that have been central to feeling good about yourself, such as: loss of work (even through planned retirement); loss of financial security; loss of health, fitness or good looks

- Workplace bullying

- Becoming trapped in an abusive relationship

- Being subject to enduring hardship or stress

Such experiences are painful and distressing in themselves. However, as far as low self-esteem is concerned, the key thing is that you concluded they must in some way be your fault, a sign of something fundamentally wrong with you. This is the origin of your Bottom Line.

2. The Bottom Line

If our experiences are generally positive and we are valued and well treated, we probably feel reasonably okay about ourselves. If not, this can give rise to lasting negative beliefs – the Bottom Lines that sum up how we feel about ourselves and lie at the heart of low self-esteem.

The Bottom Line reflects your attempt to make sense of what happened to you, perhaps early in life. It was your best guess but, if you were very young, you probably lacked enough knowledge or experience to see the bigger picture, view things from different angles, and judge cause and effect. Small children cannot easily recognize that others are responsible for their own bad behaviour, that the unkind things others say may reveal more about them than about us, and that what is happening now will not necessarily continue for ever. So children often reach conclusions that are neither fair nor useful to themselves. Yet the Bottom Line, once in place, continues to influence how we think and feel and what we do, day by day. Over time, it may become an unthinking habit of mind which feels like a simple fact, rather than something learned in the increasingly distant past.

3. Rules for Living

Negative experiences lead to negative beliefs – the Bottom Line. Your Bottom Line seems true to you, yet you still need to negotiate your way through life, to make and keep relationships, to feel more or less okay about yourself. This is where 'Rules for Living' come in. These standards (also learned) sum up what you expect of yourself, how you believe you must act. So long as you follow the Rules, all is well. But if you fall short, up comes your negative Bottom Line. So Rules prevent you from accepting yourself as you *are* and keep you constantly striving to be the person you think you *should* be.

The problem with Rules is that they 'wallpaper over' the Bottom Line. They help you to live with it, but leave it untouched, ready for activation when the circumstances are right. In some ways they are genuinely helpful, but they are also rigid and extreme, expressed in terms of 'I must/I should/I ought', not 'I'd prefer to', 'I'd like to' or 'It would be a good idea to'. The language of Rules is the language of absolutes – 'never, always, everyone, no one, all, nothing'. They make demands no ordinary human being could hope to meet, and take no account of variations in circumstances. So breaking the Rules is inevitable – but when it happens, it feels as if your Bottom Line must be true after all.

Tracey's story

Tracey's Bottom Line was 'I am a failure'. She grew up in an achievement-oriented family, who sent her to a highly competitive school where academic success was paramount. Tracey was intelligent, but the relentless pressure stopped her from performing at her best. She compensated by working extra hard, and this became her Rule: 'I must always perform 110 per cent or I will surely fail.' So long as she could obey the Rule, she felt more or less okay about herself. But if for some reason she *could not* obey it – she was ill, or exhausted, or simply had too much on her plate – then she was in trouble. Sticking to her Rule was not optional – she *had* to do it, no matter what: if not, it just proved she was right: she really was a failure.

What keeps low self-esteem going?

Let us turn now to how the Bottom Line is activated and explore the vicious circle that keeps it alive. The sequence is summarized in the flowchart on page 285. We will follow Tracey's story to illustrate how it works.

Activation of the Bottom Line

Two kinds of situation activate the Bottom Line:

1. Situations where your Rules for Living *might* be broken. In this case, what happens next will have an uncertain, anxious flavour.

2. Situations where you think the Rules definitely *have been* broken. In this case, what happens next will have a low, depressing feel to it.

Figure 28: How low self-esteem works: Tracey's story

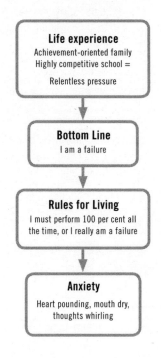

1. Situations where the Rules might be broken (the right-hand side of the vicious circle in Figure 27)

One day Tracey faced a major challenge. She had to give an important presentation at work, in front of a new client and her line manager. She was afraid that she would make a mess of it, in front of everybody. It had not happened yet, but it *might*. Everything that might go wrong raced through her mind – predictions, 'what ifs', and 'supposings'. She saw in her mind's eye an image of herself, stammering, red in the face, everyone staring with disapproval.

Not surprisingly, Tracey's predictions sparked off anxiety. Her heart was pounding, her mouth dry, her mind in a whirl. This prompted even more predictions (the small dotted line) – feeling like this, she was sure to mess up. What could she do to stop her predictions from coming true?

She was tempted to call in sick and avoid the whole thing. In the end she decided she had to do it but took precautions to avert disaster, and stayed up half the night trying to make the presentation perfect in every detail.

Supposing in fact all went well? Rather than feeling pleased, Tracey would probably feel she had had a near miss: had she *not* taken those precautions, what she feared would certainly have happened. So her attempts to protect herself would actually stop her from discovering whether her predictions were valid, thus preventing her from updating her Bottom Line. On the other hand, supposing she was too tired to think straight and things went badly? Once again, her worst fears would seem justified. She really *was* a failure, confirming her Bottom Line.

At this point, anxiety would change to something heavier, gloomier. *Self-criticism* might follow the sense of failure ('Typical. I always make a mess of things. And if I don't, it's by the skin of my teeth.'). Then would come *hopelessness* ('It's always going to be this way.'). With thoughts like these, naturally her mood would dip. She might just feel down for a while or, particularly if she had experienced serious depression in the past, gloom and despondency could persist, and even spiral down into serious depression – the state this book is designed to address. Self-criticism, hopelessness and low mood keep the negative Bottom Line active, and so the vicious circle closes.

2. Situations where the Rules definitely have been broken (the long dotted line left of centre in the vicious circle in Figure 27)

The Bottom Line can also be activated when it seems your Rules definitely *have been* broken. You *did* fail, someone *did* disapprove of you, your feelings *did* get the better of you – or whatever. Because there is no uncertainty, anxiety is not part of the picture. As far as you are concerned, the worst has already happened: the Bottom Line has been activated and confirmed in the same moment, and you may find yourself heading straight for self-criticism, hopelessness and low mood.

Key messages

- Self-esteem develops as a result of our experiences in the world, sometimes when we are very young, but also later in life.

- When these experiences are negative, our self-esteem is affected, but only if we believe that the experiences were our fault, and mean something bad about us – 'the Bottom Line'.

- We cope with these 'Bottom Line' beliefs by developing demanding 'Rules for Living'. Unfortunately, these ask more of us than any normal human being could give. When we cannot meet the demands of our 'Rules for Living', this seems to prove that the Bottom Line is true, and our self-esteem plummets still further.

- 'Rules for Living' create pressure on us to be other than we are, make us vulnerable to depression, and trap us in a vicious circle of anxiety, self-criticism and low mood.

Tips for supporters

- Encourage the person you are supporting to start thinking about things that have happened to them that might have led to the development of their low self-esteem. Can they recognize situations from the list above? Or perhaps other painful situations come to mind. What are they?

- Be aware that the person you are supporting might argue that those things wouldn't have happened to them if they hadn't been so useless, worthless or whatever in the first place. This just shows the power of the old Bottom Line – it doesn't mean it's true. Your 'job' is to encourage them at least to entertain the possibility that there might be a different way of seeing things. They don't have to be convinced of this – just willing to read on through the chapter, try out the strategies it suggests and wait to make up their minds until they've given these new ideas their best shot.

Working with low self-esteem: how CBT can help

Now is the time to tackle the beliefs, thoughts and action patterns we mapped out above. Specifically, the steps you need to take are:

1. Check out your anxious predictions.

2. Question your self-critical thoughts instead of taking them at face value.

3. Learn to appreciate your positive qualities and treat yourself kindly.

4. Change the Rules.

5. Create a new Bottom Line.

Let's look at each of these.

1. Checking out anxious predictions

Fearing you might break your Rules activates your Bottom Line, leading to predictions that, unless you take precautions, something bad is going to happen. Precautions stop you from discovering that what you predict might never happen, that even if it did the consequences might be less bad than you fear, and that you might deal with them better than you think. Checking out anxious predictions involves the following: identifying them precisely, questioning them, finding more helpful and realistic alternatives, and testing them through behavioural experiments (see page 101 for more information on behavioural experiments). Here is an example to illustrate how this might work in practice.

Ed's story

Ed's Bottom Line was 'I am boring'. His related Rule for Living was: 'I must always be the life and soul of the party, or people won't want to know me.' He always had a fund of funny stories and interesting snippets of information, and never stopped talking lest someone realized how boring he really was. Actually this made him rather an exhausting companion. Ed set up an experiment to find out whether, if he was quiet when he had supper with friends, no one would talk to him or want to see him again. He would need to observe his friends carefully, or he would have no idea of their reactions. To his surprise, people were as welcoming as ever. In fact, he enjoyed himself more than usual and one friend said it was nice to see him so relaxed. Ed realized his prediction had been wrong: he had no need to try so hard. He resolved to experiment along the same lines with two other friends the next day.

If you have had your Bottom Line and your Rules for Living for some time, a single experiment will not do the trick. Like Ed, you may well need to experiment in different ways and different situations, repeatedly, for some time.

2. Questioning your self-critical thoughts

When it seems your Bottom Line has been confirmed by experience, self-criticism usually follows. If you can catch self-critical thoughts (NATs) as they happen, you can learn to question them instead of automatically assuming they are true. There are detailed guidelines on how to do this in Chapter 10 (page 88), so all we shall do here is highlight some key points.

Learn to catch yourself being self-critical

What alerts you to the fact that you are being self-critical? Thought patterns (such as making sweeping judgements, comparisons, blaming, 'shoulds')? Mood changes (a drop in confidence, feeling low)? Body sensations (a sinking feeling, tight shoulders)? Or maybe something you do (breaking eye contact, making yourself small)?

Just because self-criticism is loud and compelling, it does not follow that it tells the truth

Self-critical NATs are the voice of the Bottom Line speaking in the present moment. For instance, when your self-critical voice says, 'You see? No one likes you!' this may be the voice of the Bottom Line that developed because your parents were too busy and stressed to pay you attention. Your self-critical NATs may be loud and powerful, but they still represent an old, automatic habit of mind that you no longer need to buy into or take seriously. We saw how, when you were younger, you may have drawn unhelpful conclusions from things that happened around you, because you did not have the ability or knowledge to weigh things up in a more reasoned way. It's important to remember that these conclusions are not the truth – they were just the best understanding you could reach of things at the time. It may also seem as if self-criticism is the only thing that motivates you to meet the standards set by your Rules for Living. If so, letting it go may feel risky. Investigate the real impact of self-criticism on your life. Rather than being motivating, self-criticism actually tends to prevent learning, stifle creativity and paralyse efforts to develop, problem-solve and grow.

Beware the rumination trap

Notice if your mind slips into rumination, going over and over the same ground: wondering why this always happens, what is wrong with you, will it never end, and so on and so forth. Rumination can feel as if it is helpful – if you think things through just one more time, surely you will find the answer – so people often mistake it for problem-solving. In fact, rumination just leads to more rumination and makes you miserable, especially if you are already feeling low. Distraction techniques (see page 175) may be helpful here. Even if self-critical thoughts and ruminations still turn up, perhaps you can learn to let them be like a radio in the background. You can still listen if you want to, but most of the time you would rather pay attention to other things. See Chapter 14 for more on dealing with rumination.

Pacing: the importance of being realistic

If you have had low self-esteem for a long time and it has had a big impact on your life, self-criticism may be an ingrained habit. Do not be discouraged if it is hard to find kinder, fairer views. Your supporter may be really helpful here. Others who know us well and are on our side often have a clearer and more balanced view of us than we do of ourselves. Be persistent, and recognize that however well-rehearsed your self-critical thinking may be, it will still be open to change if you stick at it.

Key messages

- You can use the techniques of cognitive therapy which were described in earlier chapters, as well as this one, to check out anxious predictions, and to stand your ground against self-criticism. By questioning your old habits of thought and checking out whether they really fit the facts and whether they help you or stand in the way of self-acceptance, you can discover fresh, more confident, perspectives on yourself.

3. Learning to appreciate your positive qualities and treat yourself kindly

Being self-critical helps to keep low self-esteem going, but is only one half of the equation. The other half is ignoring or discounting your good points, and failing to treat yourself with kindness, consideration and respect.

Learning to appreciate your good points

Low self-esteem makes you alert for anything negative about yourself at the expense of anything positive. Even if you occasionally notice your good qualities you may discount or forget them, or see them as exceptions rather than as a true reflection of who you are. You might think, 'I know the meal I made was nice, but anyone could have done it, probably better.' Unsurprisingly, these biases against yourself will naturally affect your mood, energy and motivation and make you feel that you are not worth treating with consideration. Learning to value your good points will help you to do yourself justice and develop the feeling that it is okay to be you.

Watch out for 'Yes, but . . . 's

If your low self-esteem is well embedded, the idea of appreciating your positive qualities may seem entirely alien to you. As you try out the strategies outlined below, you will almost certainly have thoughts along the lines of 'Yes, but . . . ': 'Yes, but that would be boasting!' 'Yes, but suppose other people don't agree?' 'Yes, I am generous, but only sometimes.' These will seem more convincing and believable when your mood is low. 'Yes, but . . . 's may seem like barriers to progress, but in fact they are extremely useful. Every time you notice one, you are in fact catching something that keeps you stuck in low self-esteem, right in front of your very eyes. 'Yes, but . . . 's are actually helping you to find out more about yourself.

Identifying good points

It is a good idea to use a notebook for this exercise. Try making a list of your positive qualities. How many come to mind will vary from person to person. If your low self-esteem is not there all the time, or is not very strong, then you might be able to come up with ten or even twenty positive qualities, after giving yourself time to reflect. If your low self-esteem is persistent and long-standing, and no one taught you to value yourself and treat yourself respectfully, you may find it difficult to think of even one. Don't despair. You are developing a new mental muscle. At first you will feel stiff and awkward but, if you keep practising, it will get easier and you will find that you are able to come up with several positive qualities. Do not worry if you can only find one or two good points to start with, and if even *that* takes a while. Stick with it. Take your time, go at your own pace, continue to add things as they occur to you, leave your list and come back to it as many times as you need. If you have a supporter, ask them how they see you: they can probably see good qualities in you that you have trouble noticing for yourself. If you are using this book on your own, you could perhaps seek out someone you are comfortable with and trust, who knows you well, and ask them how they see you.

Making it real: reliving

Recognizing your good points needs to become part of your everyday thinking, not just words written down on a piece of paper. Once you have your list, find a time and place to relax and reflect. Focus on your first item, and recall a recent occasion when you demonstrated this quality in your behaviour. For instance, if your first positive quality is 'I'm helpful', try to bring to mind a recent occasion when you were indeed helpful. It should be recent because you need to remember clearly what happened. Recreate the situation in your mind's eye. Call up a vivid image – what you saw, what you heard, what you felt in your body. Home in on what you did that was helpful and the emotions you experienced at the time.

'Helpful' was the first positive quality on Jenny's list, and she recalled helping her small brother to set up a new game on his computer. She could see his face in her mind's eye and hear his excited squeaks. She could feel his hug, and her love for him. Bringing this vividly to mind made 'helpful' real to her. When you have relived an example of your first positive quality, move on to the next and so on down the list. It's helpful to write down, in detail, the memories you discover, so that you can bring them to mind in future just as vividly.

Making it part of everyday life

It is also important to notice your good points in everyday life. The best way is to record them for a while. Our memories are often unreliable, so write down what happened in enough detail to be able to recall it later. Don't write 'I was honest', but rather: 'I admitted to a colleague that I had forgotten to act on her request'. At the end of each day, review what you have written and call up the memory of what you did as vividly as you can. Let it sink in, and notice how this affects the way you feel about yourself. Later on, especially on days when you feel unconfident and sad and it is hard to remember anything positive about yourself, you will be able to find reminders in your notes.

Once you have become better at recognizing your good points, you may not need to write them down any more (though you may wish to do so). Some people establish this new habit within three or four weeks; others take longer. Part of respecting and caring for yourself is allowing yourself all the time you need.

Exercise: treating yourself with kindness

You may be good at treating other people well, anticipating their needs, being generous and tolerant, and compassionate when they make mistakes or things go wrong for them. But how you treat yourself could be rather different. It may be hard for you to recognize your needs, or act on signs that you are tired, stressed, unwell or depressed. You may rarely (if ever) set aside time to do things you enjoy, that allow you to relax, replenish your resources and be at peace with yourself.

Thinking about how you spend your time may help to bring this into focus. This exercise is similar to activity scheduling for depression (see page 146), but is specifically designed to encourage you to treat yourself kindly.

In your notebook, write down what you do on a typical day. If you work, you could write down your activities for two days – a working day and a leisure day. Start with 'get up' and carry on till you get to 'go to bed'. Then look at each activity and ask yourself if, on balance, it nourishes or depletes you. 'Nourishing' activities lift your mood, energize you, and help you feel calm and centred. This includes purely enjoyable and relaxing activities, as well as things that may not be very enjoyable but give you a sense that you are taking care of business, running your life instead of letting it run you. Depleting activities, on the other hand, drag you down, drain your energy, make you feel tense and uptight. Write 'N' against activities that nourish you and 'D' against those that deplete you. Some activities may do neither, and some will do both, depending on circumstances. See if you can work out what those circumstances are.

When you have given N or D to each activity, look at the pattern. Is the balance between them satisfactory? Would you like to increase your nourishing activities or decrease your depleting ones? For example, you could:

- Add activities you enjoy but have not done lately (such as going to the cinema); take time to care for your body (things like exercise, healthy eating, relaxation).

- Include treats – simple things like buying yourself flowers or a ticket to a football match, taking time to watch a sunset or play with a pet, choosing what TV programmes to watch instead of watching on autopilot.

- Make sure you include activities you have been putting off (writing that email, sorting out that cupboard).

Drop or curtail depleting activities (such as restricting Facebook to the end of the day, limiting how much time you spend on it, and not spending hours talking to people who make you feel bad). As you make these changes, keep writing your activities down. Notice when you start to have more nourishing activities, and see if this makes a difference to how you feel, including how you feel about yourself. You will only benefit from such changes if you focus *attention* on what you do. You cannot savour relaxing activities or feel satisfied with completed tasks if your mind is elsewhere. Even routine tasks can reveal unexpected riches if you pay attention. Consider taking a shower, for example – what a feast for the senses! Experiment with really being present for enjoyable experiences, instead of letting them pass you by. How you pay attention also makes a difference to activities you do not particularly enjoy but have to do. For instance, if you do the washing up with your mind full of 'It's not fair – nobody appreciates what I do', then washing up will deplete you. However, if you experiment with focusing on the warmth of the water, the sensation of bubbles, the texture and weight of the things you are washing, your experience may change. The same careful attentiveness can transform all sorts of routine chores.

Equally, your *attitude* can drain the goodness out of activities that might otherwise nourish you. Self-defeating 'killjoy' NATs (such as comparing how things *are* with how they *should* be) will spoil your pleasure and relaxation and make necessary tasks even more depleting. Experiment with answering them back, acting against them, and observing how this affects your day and how you feel about yourself. For instance, a hardworking businesswoman had to move into a small one-bedroom flat when her business collapsed. For some time she hated being there, and kept thinking, 'I should be in a proper house like I used to be.' It was only when she accepted that this was her reality for the moment that she could look out of the window and realize that she loved seeing the trees outside, and liked being able to chat to her neighbours in the communal garden.

Key messages

- You can discover how to acknowledge your strong points despite 'yes but . . . 's, and you can care for yourself as you would another person dear to you. Gradually, you can learn to appreciate your good qualities and to treat yourself kindly, and make this more accepting perspective part of everyday life.

4. Changing the Rules

Changing your Rules for Living allows you more freedom to be yourself and makes you less vulnerable to getting stuck in the vicious circle of low self-esteem and depression. Unlike the NATs that run through your mind at particular moments, Rules have probably influenced your thinking and actions across a whole range of different situations over a long period of time. So establishing and strengthening a new Rule will take a while, but if you persist it will gradually become second nature. The story of Cathy illustrates how this process works.

Cathy's story

When Cathy was growing up, her mother was chronically ill, weak, and unable to care for her or her little brothers and sisters. It was Cathy's job to look after them, from a young age. Her father naturally worried constantly about his wife's health and what might happen to the family if she became worse. Her mother loved Cathy, but was too unwell to give her time or attention, and her father's preoccupation meant that there was no one to give her the affection and acknowledgement she needed. She learned to be quiet and obedient, to stay in the background, and never to assert her own needs: to do so would be selfish.

Identifying your Rules for Living

What is needed here is detective work. If you find more than one Rule, choose the one you would most like to change. You can use what you learn to address the others later.

Useful sources of information about Rules include:

- *Repeated thought patterns.* Do the same expectations and demands on yourself come up again and again? Do your anxious predictions follow repeated themes? Do the same self-critical thoughts arise repeatedly? Look out for the 'shoulds', 'musts' and 'oughts' that often signal a Rule is around. 'Shoulds' often come with an 'or else' which may not be explicit. See if you can put it into words. Cathy's Rule was 'I must never put myself first'. At first she could not work out what her 'or else' was, so she asked herself: 'If I did put myself first, what would that say about me?' Back came the answer: 'It would mean I was selfish' – a direct reflection of her Bottom Line.

- *Memories.* As a child, what messages did you get about how to behave and who to be? Did you feel that being loved and valued depended on doing certain things, being a certain way? What was expected (or demanded) of you? Cathy had a strong memory from when she was quite a young child. She had caught flu. She could not stop coughing, and lay in bed, feverish, headachy and miserable. Suddenly she heard her mother crying in the bedroom next door, and her father running up the stairs to see what was wrong. As he passed her bedroom door, he shouted: '*Will* you stop that noise! You are upsetting your mother.' Poor Cathy felt consumed with remorse: how could she be so selfish and needy, when her mother was so poorly?

- *Powerful emotions.* When do you feel especially bad about yourself – as if you have fallen short or failed to measure up? When this happens, what Rule have you broken? And what about when you feel really, really *good* about yourself? What Rule might you have obeyed? Cathy often worked overtime if other staff were off sick on her busy ward. She felt absolutely wonderful when the team leader told her that, if it was not for her, the whole place would fall apart.

Questioning the Rules

Once you have a sense of your Rule, take time to find the wording that 'clicks' for you. Keep your draft Rule in mind for a few days and observe whether it ties in with your ideas about what you have to do and be in order to feel OK about yourself. If not, what Rule would better explain the patterns you notice? Stay curious and keep investigating.

Your next step is to question your Rule, and formulate and test an updated version which will give you its advantages without its costs.

Where did my Rule come from?

What experiences led to this Rule and reinforced it over time? Do not worry if its origins remain unclear. Understanding how Rules develop is often helpful, but not essential. The important thing is to change things now and in the future.

Cathy's Rule came from feeling responsible for her younger siblings, for keeping her mother happy as best she could, and taking the pressure off her frantic father. It was up to her to cope, no matter what. Later on, her friends and family automatically expected her to adopt the same role, and she remained unable to assert her own needs.

Is the Rule unreasonable?

Does it consider the realities of being an ordinary, imperfect human being? Are its standards consistent with how the world actually works? How well does it match what you would expect of another person you respected and cared about? In what ways are its demands excessive – even impossible? Your Rule was a sort of contract you made with yourself as a child. Would you choose an inexperienced child to run your life now?

Cathy realized that she would never expect of another person she cared about what she expected of herself. Her history explained why she had these expectations of herself – but that did not mean they were appropriate or good.

What are the benefits?

If there were no advantages to having this Rule, it would not have survived. If you clarify the benefits you gain from living by the Rule, you can ensure you keep them when you create a new one. As well as looking for positive pay-offs, explore what you might risk by letting your Rule go. People often fear that their demanding standards prevent catastrophe from occurring: if they did not try really hard, they would never do anything worthwhile, ever again.

A benefit for Cathy was that she had become extremely good at coping and taking responsibility. This had helped her career, and people really appreciated her efforts. She feared that, if she began to assert her own needs, she would risk the good opinion of people who were important to her.

What are the costs?

How does your Rule restrict your opportunities, colour your relationships, undermine your sense of achievement, pressurize and exhaust you, stand in the way of accepting yourself? Look at its impact in the present and in the past. What have you missed out on, lost or risked because of this Rule? How has it undermined your freedom to have a satisfying career, to relax and enjoy the company of others, to make the most of every experience?

Cathy realized that she was often tired, frazzled and plagued with coughs and colds. She came home too drained to enjoy time with her family – and felt terrible for not putting them first, too. The Rule was unworkable, and it was making her ill.

What new Rule might be more realistic and helpful?

What new Rule would help you feel more at ease with yourself as you *are*, rather than constantly expecting yourself to be something you are *not*? It may take a little while to work out what will suit you best. Take as much time as you need to come up with some guidelines, and to experiment with trying them out and making whatever changes you need.

If it is difficult to think of a new Rule, consider people you know, like and respect. Do they seem to share your Rule? If not, what do you think *their* Rule might be? Can you tell from their behaviour? Or if you know and trust them well enough, you could ask them. Would you advise anyone else to follow your Rule? If an alien from outer space asked you the secret to living a happy and fulfilled life on your planet, what would you advise?

Aim to make your new Rule more flexible than the old one, more responsive to different circumstances. It will recognize that what works on one occasion or with one person may not work with another, and allow you to respond to each situation on its own merits. It will understand that you are not superhuman. 'I must' will give way to 'I'd like', 'I enjoy', 'I prefer', and 'It's okay to'.

Cathy's new Rule was: 'It's okay to take account of my needs too.'

How can you 'road test' your new Rule?

Just creating a new Rule is not enough. You need to put it into practice and see how well it works. Experiment with operating as if it were true, even if you are still unsure, and observe what happens. Have you found a workable alternative, or does your first attempt need revision? You may feel uncomfortable at first but the more you experiment, the easier it will become. There is no need to rush – changing the Rules takes as long as it takes.

Key messages

- Your Rules have probably affected your life for a long time, and in all sorts of situations. So it may take a little while to devise new ones and road test them in everyday life. Step by step, you can learn to clarify exactly what they are, how they affect you, what Rules might work better for you and how best to put your new ideas into practice. Here is a chance to get curious about how you have been going about things, and experiment with doing things differently – allowing yourself the freedom to be exactly who you are.

---

5. Creating a new Bottom Line

The final step towards healthy self-esteem is to tackle your Bottom Line. In fact, even though you have not yet addressed it directly, by now it may seem less compelling than it did. Through the work you have done, you may already be starting to appreciate that it is nothing more than an old opinion – out of date, inaccurate and unfair. Do not worry if this is not yet the case. Changing powerful ideas, especially if they have been around for a long time, takes patience, persistence and practice.

Identifying your Bottom Line

Like Rules, the Bottom Line extends across time and place, a global negative 'I am . . . ' that may have been part of how you see yourself in many situations and perhaps over many years. So it will not change overnight. Look back over the work you have already done on your depression and self-esteem. Have you heard the Bottom Line's voice calling you names ('useless', 'weak', 'a failure'), telling you that acknowledging good qualities is boasting, or that treating yourself kindly is self-indulgent?

Have you found it lurking in the 'or else' behind your personal 'I should'?

These observations can help you work out what your Bottom Line is. When you have identified something that seems to fit, check how well it accounts for your day-to-day reactions. Choose a recent situation when you doubted yourself – one you can still remember clearly. Recall it vividly to mind – relive it in detail if you can. Ask yourself: 'Does my "I am . . . " statement fit how I reacted? Does it feel right?' If not, what statement about yourself would be a better fit? You are seeking a belief that is central and heartfelt, which captures your sense of who you fundamentally are. Check out your best guess in other situations until you feel confident that you have found your Bottom Line.

Cathy's recent situation came out of her work on her Rule about never putting herself first. She had said 'no' to a friend's request to look after her two rather badly behaved dogs over the weekend, as an experiment in meeting her own needs rather than those of others (she had had a frantic work week and needed time to recuperate). Afterwards, she felt terrible, and had to work very hard not to call her friend and say she'd changed her mind. The words that kept coming back to her were: 'You are too selfish to be anyone's friend.' Now she realized that 'selfish' was a word that came up in her mind again and again, whenever she was tempted to give energy to caring for herself.

Undermining your old Bottom Line

The next step is to rethink the Bottom Line. Here are some questions that may be helpful. They resemble questions you have used before to work with NATs, but they cover more ground because of the broad and enduring nature of the Bottom Line.

What 'evidence' appears to support your Bottom Line?

It could be that what you consider supporting evidence for your Bottom Line is actually unreliable, based only on a narrow, negatively biased sample of events. You have full access to the case for the prosecution, but a fair judgement is impossible, because you do not have the evidence for the defence. This is what you will need to seek out.

First, work out what makes you believe your Bottom Line. Evidence can come from different sources, and all can be questioned, reassessed and re-thought. Evidence often lies deep in the past. Thinking about this might be distressing, so make sure that you care for and nourish yourself as you do this work. Make good use of your supporter, especially if looking back is triggering frightening memories of traumatic events or your mood is beginning to slump. They can remind you that, however painful, these events are now in the past, and in fact whatever happened says little about your worth. Take things at your own pace, and feel free to back off and regroup your forces if you need to, before beginning to explore again.

Common sources of 'evidence'

- *How others treated you.* How people are treated by others is probably the single most common root of low self-esteem. Look back at the life experiences outlined on page 287. Have any of these been a part of your life? Such experiences often leave scars, including a lasting sense that there is something fundamentally wrong with you. If being treated badly is at the root of your low self-esteem, and you blame yourself for it, ask yourself what other explanations there might be for the other person's behaviour. If someone you cared about had been subject to the same thing, how would you judge them? If you see things differently when you imagine it happening to someone else, perhaps you could experiment with treating yourself with the same compassion.

- *Judgement of your own shortcomings.* Alternatively, your Bottom Line might be a judgement of your own actions. When you look back, do you see a catalogue of mistakes or things you regret? Are you not living as you would like to? Are you having difficulties in life and then judging yourself for having them or not handling them well, or not overcoming them? Do you judge yourself on the basis of specific shortcomings, such as being unassertive or avoiding challenges, or losing your temper too easily, or not being the weight or shape you think you should be? Do you compare yourself unfavourably with others whom you consider more talented, or clever, or better off than you? Or have you lost something you depended on to feel good about yourself – a job, an important relationship, health or strength or status?

Such difficulties are part of being human. They may seem to define who you are, but in fact it is neither helpful nor fair to condemn yourself *as a person* on the basis of inevitable human imperfection. Nor will it help you to make changes you wish to make in your life. Again, how would you react to someone you cared about who was in the same situation? Would you judge them as you judge yourself, or might you be able to accept and value them, imperfect as they are? Look at Chapter 16 for more information on how to think in a compassionate way towards yourself.

What is the other side of the story?

What evidence contradicts the old Bottom Line and supports a new, more accepting and realistic alternative? What you discover in the past and the present offers the basis for a new Bottom Line, to be consolidated and strengthened by what you do in future.

- *The past.* Review your life again, but this time from a different angle. If there is someone you trust who has known you well for a long time, you could talk to them too. They may remember things that you have forgotten. What experiences (however small) contradict your old Bottom Line and support a kinder, fairer perspective on yourself? These do not have to be major events; short-lived simple things are important too. For example: your teacher smiling as you completed a tough project ('competent', 'accepted'), the cat you had as a child purring as you stroked it ('gentle'), the card a work colleague sent you to thank you for giving her time when she was troubled ('kind', 'good listener'), a guest's comment on how welcoming your house feels ('hospitable'). Include: moments of warmth and appreciation in your relationships; skills that you have acquired, however basic; achievements and successes, however small they might be.

- **The present.** Remind yourself of the work you have done acknowledging your qualities, talents and strong points. Include the fact that you are working through this book. It is a reflection of your courage and resourcefulness. The more you practise noticing and recording your positive qualities, the more hard evidence you are accumulating to support a new Bottom Line.

Identifying a new Bottom Line

Your first draft

Now is a good moment to formulate a tentative new Bottom Line that accepts your inevitable human weaknesses *and* takes account of your good points. Ask yourself: 'If I was *not* inadequate, weak, unlovable, worthless or whatever, how would I *really like* to be?' See if you can turn what comes to mind into a new 'I am . . . ' statement. 'I am adequate, strong, lovable, worthwhile; I am a human being – I am okay.' Whatever fits for you. Write it down to help it feel more solid and real. Does it fit with what you have discovered about yourself, the strengths and qualities you are learning to acknowledge and appreciate? If so, keep going. If not, look for another 'I am . . . ' statement that feels like a better fit. Let it sit at the back of your mind, mull it over, and see what comes to you. Try each possibility on for size until you find one that fits. You do not have to believe it strongly at first – in fact, this would be unusual. You simply have to be prepared to accept it, however tentatively, as a *possible* way of framing the strengths and qualities you have identified.

Incidentally, creating a new, self-accepting Bottom Line does not mean denying that you have weaknesses and flaws, just like every other human being. Nor does it mean that you are ignoring aspects of yourself you would like to change or improve, or pretending they do not exist. This is not about the power of positive thinking; it is about creating and strengthening a balanced sense of yourself, just as you are.

The future

Just like your new Rules, you need to make your new Bottom Line part of your everyday thinking. Be alert to new information that supports it, instead of allowing old negative biases against yourself to screen it out. For example, if your old Bottom Line was 'I'm unlikeable', you need to collect evidence that contradicts this idea and supports the new Bottom Line, 'I'm likeable'. Be as specific as possible. You could look out for people smiling at you, people calling or emailing or asking you to connect with them on social media, people who want to spend time with you. On the other hand, if your old Bottom Line was 'I'm incompetent', you will be looking for signs of competence, for example completing tasks to deadline, responding sensibly to questions, handling crises effectively.

Keeping a record and reviewing it regularly will both sharpen the focus on your strong points and strengthen your new Bottom Line. You can also experiment with behaving differently, and observing and recording the results. Low self-esteem has confined you to a sort of prison; now you have begun to push back the walls. Experiments mean daring to break out, finding opportunities to move more freely and extend your range. What do you need to do in order to treat yourself as a person worthy of attention, respect and love – even if you do not fully believe that yet? Examples include: taking time for yourself; allowing yourself space to relax; standing up for what you believe in; asking for what you need; seeking out people who value your presence and your ideas.

Key messages

- Developing and strengthening a new Bottom Line is the final step in your journey towards self-acceptance, discovering a sense that it is fundamentally okay to be you, without any conditions or demands that you be different.

- In this chapter, you have had an opportunity to investigate how your low self-esteem developed, and to explore the vicious circle of anxious predictions and self-critical thinking that kept it going. By now, perhaps you have been able to begin the process of questioning and testing your unhelpful old habits of thought about yourself, rather than taking it for granted that they speak the truth. Perhaps you have begun to formulate new Rules for yourself, and to establish a new, kinder and more accepting Bottom Line. It would be wonderful if reading a chapter was enough to revolutionize how you feel about yourself, but learning how to treat yourself fairly, with kindness and compassion, is often a lifelong journey. Remember that expecting quick change might be another of those impossibly high standards, especially if your low self-esteem has been around for a long time and has had a big impact on your life.

- If you liked the ideas you found here, have found them helpful, and would like to investigate them in more depth, the self-help books listed in the Further Reading section might be useful to you.

Tips for supporters

- Focusing on low self-esteem can be difficult and depressing, and it may be very hard for the person you are supporting to see a way forward. Encourage them to continue, even when the going gets tough. You may be able to help them travel further than they could on their own. Your continuing kindness, support and encouragement in themselves communicate an enormously important message: it really *is* okay to be them!

19 Overcoming sleep difficulties

Colin Espie

Sleep is a complex, very ordered series of events – yet it's designed to happen naturally without us thinking about it, pretty much the same way that we breathe. Of course, if you have a sleep problem, you become very aware of sleep and wakefulness, and it doesn't seem so easy!

Whether you're a good sleeper or a poor one, it may be useful to find out a little bit about this mysterious thing called sleep. If you are feeling depressed, you will be particularly interested because sleep and depression are closely associated, as we shall see.

In this chapter I will start by talking about sleep, and then go on to talk about insomnia – when sleep goes wrong. Last, I'll describe a CBT programme to help tackle insomnia.

Understanding sleep

So what is sleep? Well, it's a state of greatly reduced awareness, taking up around one quarter to one third of our daily lives, during which the body repairs itself, and our memories and emotions are consolidated. There is a lot of evidence that we need sleep for good mental functioning. It is, if you like, nutrition for the brain – and we simply can't do without it. When we are depressed our sleep is often upset, and this is a two-way street, because having insomnia also makes us more likely to get depressed in the first place.

When we measure sleep we look at three different aspects. We measure the brain's electrical activity with an *electroencephalogram* (EEG), our muscle activity with an *electromyogram* (EMG) and our eye movements with an *electro-oculogram* (EOG).

Together, these measurements are called *polysomnography* (PSG); a short-hand way of describing a full sleep assessment.

Stages of sleep

Figure 29: A typical sleep–laboratory assessment
taking place

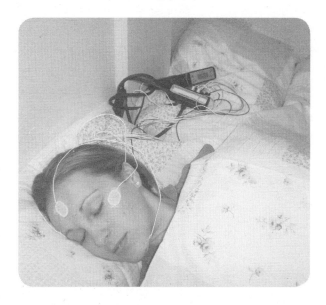

Figure 30 (below) may look daunting, but it just shows the different parts of a night's sleep. Don't worry about the detail. The main thing to understand is that sleep is complex, and that is because each stage of sleep has an important function. You can see in the picture above (Figure 29) that the EEG, EMG and EOG measurements are gathered using sur-face electrodes on the head.

Figure 30: Stages of sleep

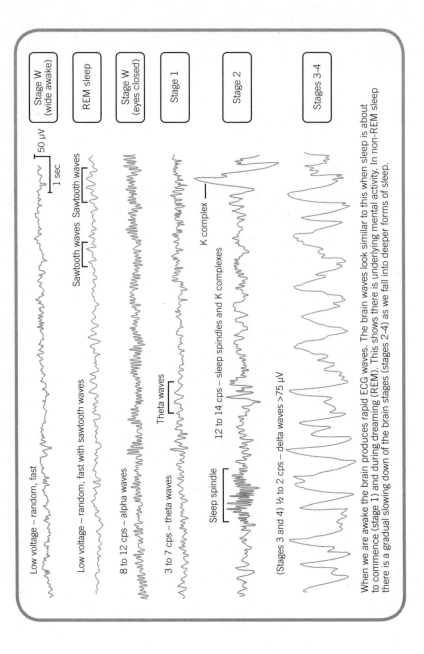

When we are awake the brain produces rapid ECG waves. The brain waves look similar to this when sleep is about to commence (stage 1) and during dreaming (REM). This shows there is underlying mental activity. In non-REM sleep there is a gradual slowing down of the brain stages (stages 2–4) as we fall into deeper forms of sleep.

As we fall asleep we go into a transitional phase between wakefulness (Stage W) and sleep known as Stage 1. Compared with quiet wakefulness, the EEG slows down, and your muscles begin to relax. If someone wakes you up during this very light first stage you might well say, 'Hey, I was just nodding off there!' or you might startle.

After only a matter of minutes, you progress on to Stage 2 sleep. Here the EEG varies a lot with what we call 'mixed frequencies' (some fast, some slow, some high amplitude, some low). However, there are some recognizable parts, called 'K-complexes' and 'sleep spindles'. Different parts of this stage are important for our attention and memory. Stage 2 actually makes up about 60 per cent of our sleep, although when we first go into it we move quickly through it to the next stages.

Stage 3 and Stage 4 are deep sleep, or slow-wave sleep. We have our deepest sleep during the first couple of hours.

I guess most of us would like the idea of having lots of deep sleep, but in fact it makes up only around 10–15 per cent, and less as we get older. Stages 3 and 4 sleep seem important for basic physical recovery, growth and tissue repair.

We can see then that sleep involves not only a loss of consciousness, but also a steady change in the EEG. However, there is a form of sleep during which the eyeballs move rapidly (measured by EOG), whereas the rest of the body is pretty much paralysed (measured by EMG). The term 'rapid eye movement' (REM) sleep was coined to describe this. You can see in Figure 30 that the EEG during REM looks quite like wakefulness. Indeed it is a form of light sleep; it is also important for cognitive and emotional functioning during the day. For example, we know that REM, along with other types of sleep, helps us to consolidate new information and to form memories effectively.

We could easily injure ourselves by acting out our dreams, were it not for the fact that during REM sleep our muscles are very relaxed. You may not have realized before that you are in fact very still in your bed during your dreams, in spite of whatever vivid dream imagery you may experience! Occasional muscle twitches are quite usual, but any movement on a large scale during REM sleep is uncommon. Although some people think that sleepwalking happens when we dream, in fact it is nothing to do with REM sleep. Sleepwalking and night terrors happen in our deep sleep.

What about my personal experience of sleep?

You have probably never been to a sleep laboratory but I'm sure you've tried to measure your sleep – perhaps by working out how long you think you have slept, how long it took you to fall asleep, or how many times you woke up. These are measures of the *experience* of sleep, of what you remember, and of the conclusions that you draw. It isn't easy to calculate these things very accurately!

You may even have tried to keep a sleep diary so that you can see what your sleep is like over a period of time, to work out if there is a pattern. Diaries like this can be useful and I will show you one shortly.

Sometimes it is easier to think about the quality of our sleep, rather than its quantity. Good sleep-quality might be when you feel that you have had a 'great sleep'; and poor sleep-quality might be when you say you have had a 'restless sleep' or 'hardly any sleep' or that it took you a 'long time to get into a proper sleep'. Whether we are trying to estimate quantity or commenting on quality, this is called 'subjective assessment'. We should not fall into the trap of thinking that subjective assessment is less important than objective assessment like PSG (the measures described above). What we think and feel about our sleep is terribly important, not least because it is our experience of it (or lack of it) that relates most closely to the complaint of poor sleep.

Interestingly, when we compare people's judgements of their own sleep with more objective measures, we see that they usually sleep longer than they think they have done. This tells us that people tend to *overestimate* how long it has taken to fall asleep, and how long they have been awake during the night, and to *underestimate* the total amount of sleep that they have had. It's not just people with insomnia who exaggerate their sleep complaint. People who are normally good sleepers also make very similar errors in estimation on those occasional nights when they sleep poorly.

The problem, in fact, may also be with the PSG, since it does not identify subtle EEG characteristics that form part of the underlying pattern in insomnia. For example, the PSG may not always pick up the frequent micro-arousals that intrude into sleep (particularly common in insomnia) which can give us the subjective impression that we are awake.

What controls our sleep pattern?

Two processes work together to regulate our sleep pattern. One is called the *sleep homeostat*, and this controls 'drive' for sleep; the other is called the *circadian timer* and this controls *when* we sleep.

Broadly speaking, the longer we are awake, the sleepier we become. Sleep reduces the drive for sleep, and wakefulness increases it, much in the same way as we become parched if we go without fluid, and thirst increases. Drinking satisfies that thirst and so reduces the drive to drink.

With each hour that we spend awake we accumulate *sleep debt*. In healthy good sleepers this debt is repaid by the night's sleep and they awaken refreshed and 'in balance' the next morning. Pressure for sleep is stronger at the start of a sleep episode than it is later on and this accounts, for example, for why a nap can make us feel much better. Similarly, some people report feeling quite refreshed after a couple of hours of sleep. The restorative value of these early cycles of sleep appears to be proportionally greater. Of course, we might be advised to avoid napping because it has the potential to reduce the drive for sleep at night.

The second sleep process concerns our *circadian rhythms*. The word 'circadian' derives from the Latin words *circa diem*, literally meaning 'around the day'. Sometimes we talk about the 'body clock', meaning pretty much the same thing. The term is used to describe the harmony of the sleep-wake schedule. Other biological functions such as body temperature also follow recognized circadian patterns. We are designed to function in a twenty-four-hour world! This may sound like science fiction, but it is science fact, which is really much more exciting and interesting.

The hormone *melatonin* is largely responsible for the regulation of the body clock throughout our lives. Melatonin is produced in the brain, in the *pineal gland*. Its production rate is dictated by natural light, so that during darkness (the normal sleep period) melatonin production increases, and with the coming of daylight, it is shut down. Of course there is natural variation in circadian alertness during the day. You will probably be aware of the 'afternoon dip' when we feel temporarily more tired. Indeed, in some societies it is normal to have a siesta at this time, because it also coincides with the hottest part of the day. In terms of our circadian tendencies there is something to be said for that lifestyle!

It is important to note that it is the *interaction* of the sleep drive and the circadian timing mechanism that, under normal circumstances, leads to good sleep. This is when the drive for sleep becomes strongest during normal hours of darkness, and results in an absence of pressure for sleep during wakeful, daylight hours.

Why do we need to sleep?

Sleep is not an optional extra in life; it is a fundamental requirement. In fact, you could survive for three times longer without food than you could without sleep. Much of what we know about the importance of sleep comes from the experiences of people who have taken part in sleep-deprivation experiments. When people are sleep-deprived they are simply not able to function properly during the daytime. So, one simple answer to the question 'What is sleep for?' is to ensure good-quality daytime functioning.

We touched earlier on the fact that sleep is required for tissue restoration and for recuperation. During sleep, tired muscles recover and new proteins are synthesized. Equally important, however, is the requirement of sleep for mental purposes. Amongst the most striking effects of sleep loss are inattention, disorientation and memory problems. This is because sleep loss causes fatigue, drowsiness, and ultimately an inability to remain awake during the day. If we are to be alert and mentally fit we need to sleep well. Finally, sleep is extremely important for emotional functioning. When we have not had enough sleep there are likely to be emotional consequences! Irritability is a common one, and perhaps feeling overly anxious or excitable. It is as if the brain is trying to compensate for its own sluggishness by making us more aroused. Finally, people often experience low mood and are depressed after a period of poor sleep.

Owls and larks?

I am sure we all know what an 'owl' is: someone who has a tendency to be up at night. This is the kind of individual who comes to life late in the evening and into the small hours, often having energy and alertness at times when most of us are beginning to feel really sleepy. By way of contrast, the 'lark' is at their best in the morning, preferring to be up early and to make the most of the first part of the day. The owl is not usually good in the morning and the lark is not usually good at night.

People who have one or other of these tendencies simply have a circadian position that is slightly different from the average. Usually people adapt to their body clock, and often they quite like it. They can make it work for rather than against themselves. For others though, their owl or lark tendency can be part of the problem.

How much sleep do I need?

Table 31: Expected amount of sleep at different ages

Age	Typical sleep requirement
Newborn	A newborn baby may sleep up to 18 hours. At first sleep is taken across the 24 hours with no dominant sleep period. By 4–6 months sleep becomes more consolidated at night.
Young child	Toddlers sleep up to 12 hours at night and normally also sleep for $1^1/_2$–2 hours during daytime naps.
Child	By the age of 4 years daytime naps will normally have stopped and the child will sleep 10–12 hours at night. This sleep requirement reduces to around 10 hours during the early school years.
Teenager	During adolescence sleep duration is normally around 9 hours. There is some variation in when sleep is taken, e.g. it is common for young people to stay up late and sleep on into the morning.
Young adult	The young adult typically requires $7^1/_2$–$8^1/_2$ hours' sleep.
Adult	Sleep requirement in terms of total sleep time does not vary greatly during the major part of adulthood. Around 7–8 hours is average.
Older adult	In later life sleep is less consolidated at night, with 6–$6^1/_2$ hours being typical. However, there is a tendency once again to 'top-up' with some daytime naps.

If you are a parent you'll be familiar with checking your child's height and weight against a chart, to see that everything is progressing as expected. However, it's all too easy to get worried if you forget that the charts show a normal *range*. Table 31 provides information on the normal range of total sleep time at different ages. Look at your own age group and see what you think. Of course, even when a value falls outside the normal range, this does not necessarily mean that there is something wrong.

For example, you might expect most adult males will be between five foot six and six foot two tall, but this does not mean that being only five foot four represents a problem. Here we have to introduce what is known as the 'normal distribution'. That is, outside the middle part of the normal range there is *always* a smaller number of individuals with lower and higher scores. Exactly the same applies to sleep. There are people who are long sleepers and people who are constitutionally short sleepers. This does not necessarily mean that their sleep is a cause for concern. If a person is a short sleeper but has no adverse consequences we would have to suppose that a relatively small amount of sleep is in fact sufficient for their needs.

What is the relationship between depression and sleep problems?

Figure 32: Interaction between sleep and low mood

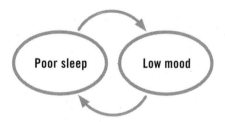

Often when people have a problem sleeping (insomnia), or are sleeping too much (hypersomnia) they also have a problem with their emotions. Most commonly, this is in the form of feeling anxious or down. As you can see in Figure 32, this relationship works both ways. If we become more emotionally upset, then our sleep is likely to get worse, but if our sleep gets worse, we are also more likely to get depressed.

It used to be thought that sleep disturbance was pretty much a symptom – that is, a secondary problem – with depression being the primary or main problem. However, research has now shown conclusively that having persistent difficulty with sleep makes you vulnerable to becoming depressed in the first place. The emergence of sleep problems also makes it more likely that you could have a relapse, or that you might fall back into a further spell of depression.

I don't know what your experience of sleep problems is, but this fits very well with what I have heard from people over many years: 'The doctor didn't take my sleep problems seriously enough,' or 'I always thought my insomnia was a major part of the problem; if only I could sleep well again then I wouldn't feel so depressed.'

It also makes sense when we think about the importance of sleep: it's a fundamental thing, like oxygen and water – not just a symptom or a side issue. The major diagnostic systems that guide us in how to evaluate mental health are beginning to advise that the term *insomnia disorder* should be used whenever people have a major problem with their sleep, and there is new evidence from clinical trials showing that about 20 per cent more people make a good recovery from depression when both the depression and the insomnia disorder are actively treated.

If you are reading this chapter because you have problems with low mood and sleep, then it would definitely be worth checking out other chapters in the book to see if there are ways that you can treat the low mood effectively, too.

Key messages

- Sleep is a very complex state, with many different systems of the body involved.

- Sleep has a number of different stages over the night, and each seems to have a different function.

- Sleep can vary not only in quantity – how much we get, but in quality – how refreshing or restorative it is.

- People differ in the amount of sleep they need, and in the times when it best suits them to sleep.

- Poor sleep can make your mood lower, and low mood can affect your sleep.

Tips for supporters

- The explanations above could be a bit complicated to follow, especially if the person you are supporting is quite low in mood. It might be helpful to go over the main points and make sure that they understand the basics even if they (and you!) don't get all the details.

- Because of the association between low mood and poor sleep, both sides of the cycle need to be tackled. Help the person you are supporting to look at other chapters in the book to see if they could tackle the low mood or depression actively as well.

Insomnia – when sleep goes wrong

Now let's think a bit more in depth about what insomnia actually is, and then we'll go on to think about how it can be helped.

You probably know all too well what it is! But then again, maybe it's useful to confirm whether or not you have a clinical problem. Here's a checklist (Table 33). By working through this list, you'll be able to sum up the nature of your night-time sleep disturbance, its effects on your day-to-day life and, overall, how bad your problem is. You'll also be able to see what type of insomnia disorder you're suffering from.

Table 33: Checklist to show types of insomnia

Night-time (My problem is that . . .)	Check (→)	
I can't get to sleep at the start of the night	→	Sleep-onset insomnia
I can't stay asleep during the night	→	Sleep-maintenance insomnia
I can't get to sleep AND I can't stay asleep	→	Mixed insomnia
Daytime (My poor sleep results in . . .)	Check →	
Fatigue or low energy	→	
Daytime sleepiness	(→)	
Mental impairment (e.g. attention, memory)	→	
Mood disturbance (e.g. irritability, feeling low)	→	Insomnia with daytime consequences
Poor performance (e.g. work, responsibilities)	→	
Problems with others (e.g. family, friends)	→	
Severity (These are problems for me . . .)	Check (→)	
Once or twice a week	→	Mild
3 or more nights a week	→	Severe
For less than 3 months	→	Acute
For more than 3 months	→	Persistent

The example below (Table 34) shows *mild but persistent sleep-maintenance insomnia with daytime effects of fatigue and mood disturbance.*

Table 34: Completed checklist to show mild but persistent sleep-maintenance insomnia with daytime effects of fatigue and mood disturbance

Night-time (My problem is that . . .)	Check (→)	
I can't get to sleep at the start of the night		Sleep-onset insomnia
I can't stay asleep during the night	→	Sleep-maintenance insomnia
I can't get to sleep AND I can't stay asleep		Mixed insomnia
Daytime (My poor sleep results in . . .)	**Check** (→)	
Fatigue or low energy	→	
Daytime sleepiness		
Mental impairment (e.g. attention, memory)		
Mood disturbance (e.g. irritability, feeling low)	→	Insomnia with daytime consequences
Poor performance (e.g. work, responsibilities)		
Problems with others (e.g. family, friends)		
Severity (These are problems for me . . .)	**Check** (→)	
Once or twice a week	→	Mild
3 or more nights a week		Severe
For less than 3 months		Acute
For more than 3 months	→	Persistent

Why don't you write down here what kind of insomnia (if any) you have in this box, or in your notebook if you are keeping one?

How common is insomnia?

There have been many research studies looking at this question. Overall, based on the kind of questions you just looked at, we estimate that one in ten of the population has persistent and severe insomnia with daytime consequences, such as fatigue, mood alteration or poor concentration. This means that 10 per cent of people have difficulty sleeping on three or more nights a week, that this problem has gone on for at least three months, and it is causing them problems such as tiredness and moodiness. Of course many more have less severe problems, and in adults over sixty-five years, the number of people with persistent and severe insomnia could be as high as one in five.

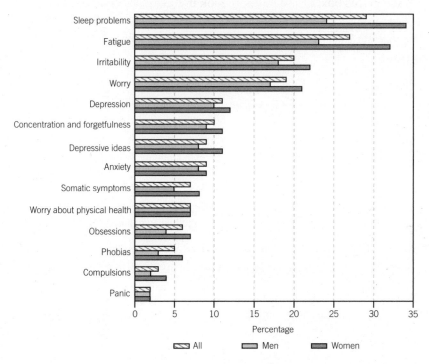

Figure 35: Insomnia is a common problem

(Reproduced from N. Singleton, R. Bumpstead, M. O'Brien, A. Lee and H. Meltzer Kales, *Psychiatric Morbidity among Adults Living in Private Households*. The Office for National Statistics, HMSO, 2001. Crown copyright material is reproduced with the permission of the controller of HMSO and the Queen's Printer for Scotland.)

Almost fifteen years ago, the largest ever survey was conducted of the mental health of the UK population. The graph above (Figure 35) is taken from that survey and reveals just how common sleep problems are. In this case, the questions for each symptom are not very precise, so you get higher rates (more like 30 per cent). The graph shows that for both men and women, sleep problems, tiredness and irritability are by far the most common symptoms of mental distress. Sleep problems are much more common than worry, depression and anxiety.

What causes insomnia?

This is one of the most common questions asked! There are different answers for every individual, but there are also common factors. Let me explain.

Predisposing, precipitating and perpetuating factors

One of the best ways to think about how insomnia develops is to consider the *three Ps*.

The first P refers to *predisposing* factors. This means the types of things that can make it more likely you will develop insomnia. Perhaps your family has a history of poor sleep, perhaps you're the type of person who tends to react to stress or is generally very anxious, or perhaps you've had a lot of upheavals at home or at work.

The second P stands for *precipitating* or triggering factors – events that affect you and stop you sleeping well. You might have been under quite a bit of stress because of an illness, a bereavement, or a period of unemployment. Precipitating factors, however, can also be more everyday things, like noise disturbing your sleep, or having a new baby around. Precipitating factors are not always bad. Any major changes – good or bad – can lead to short-term insomnia.

The third P stands for *perpetuating* factors, meaning things that keep a sleep problem going once it's started. Commonly, people say that they remember when their problem started, but they don't understand what's kept it going for so long! This is exactly what is meant by perpetuation – for some reason the problem remains, even though there may not currently be any major triggers. Often there is a vicious cycle (Figure 36) of not being able to sleep, being concerned and worried about not sleeping, and about the daytime effects of not sleeping well, and then trying (unsuccessfully) to fix things, leading to a continued inability to sleep. This cycle leads to a lot of frustration and anxiety, which of course makes the insomnia worse, not better.

Figure 36: Perpetuating factors

What can we do about your insomnia?

Most people I see with insomnia say they have 'tried everything'. Medication, over-the-counter products from the pharmacy, remedies that people have recommended and even psychological therapies. CBT, correctly applied, is the most effective treatment for persistent insomnia because it deals with the thoughts, behaviour and emotions that build up the problematic vicious cycle.

During the past twenty years, over one hundred clinical trials of CBT in the treatment of insomnia have been conducted, showing that 70 per cent of people gain lasting benefit. There is also some preliminary evidence that mindfulness-based therapies (see Chapter 17) might help insomnia, although there has not yet been a full clinical trial published. I'm going to concentrate, therefore, on CBT – a brief version!

Key messages

- Insomnia is a persistent difficulty in getting to sleep or remaining asleep that results in daytime impairments. The part that insomnia plays in a person's experience has often been overlooked.

- Insomnia is the most common way in which mental distress shows itself, more common even than worry.

- Once established, it is kept going by a vicious cycle of mental and physiological arousal, with an excess focus on sleep itself.

- CBT is the most effective treatment for insomnia.

Tips for supporters

- Sleep can be upset by mental and behavioural processes similar to those that keep other problems going (like negative thinking and excessive generalized worry). Skills learned in one area may help in others too. If the person you are supporting has problems with depression, encourage them to read other parts of the book, particularly the chapters that explain cognitive therapy (Chapters 6–12). See if you can identify chapters that might be particularly relevant.

A brief CBT programme for insomnia

Setting clear personal goals

Before you set out on a journey, it's always a good idea to know what your destination is! Once you know that, then you can plan ahead. Most likely, your personal goal will be pretty much the opposite of what you have been experiencing. For example, if your problem is that you wake up at night, and this affects your mood and your relationships, then your goal might be something like, 'I want to be able to sleep right through, be in a better frame of mind during the daytime, and be able to get on better with other people.'

In the box below, or in your notebook, write down what you think would be the best statement to summarize your goal. If you would like to read more about how to set goals, look at pages 64–5 in Chapter 7 of Part 1.

Keeping a sleep diary

A *sleep diary* is a tool you can use to track your progress. See pages 336–7 for an example of what this should look like (Worksheet 11). Fill in a column each morning soon after you wake up, and keep your diary for around ten days. Over time this will give you a record of how well you are sleeping. If you compare the goal that you wrote in the box to the questions listed down the side of the diary, you will see that some questions are more relevant to you than others. However, keep on filling out all the items in the diary every day until you feel that you have overcome your long-term sleep problem.

Worksheet 11: Sleep diary

Measuring the pattern of your sleep	Day 1	Day 2	Day 3	Day 4	Day 5	Day 6	Day 7	Day 8	Day 9	Day 10
1. Did you nap at any point yesterday? If yes, for how long (minutes)?										
2. At what time did you rise from bed this morning?										
3. What time did you finally wake up this morning?										
4. At what time did you go to bed last night?										
5. At what time did you switch off the light intending to go to sleep?										
6. How long did it take you to fall asleep (minutes)?										
7. How long were you awake during the night because of these awakenings (total minutes)?										

8. About how long did you sleep altogether (hours/minutes)?

9. How much alcohol did you have last night?

10. Did you take sleeping pills to help you sleep last night? If so, how many?

Measuring the pattern of your sleep

11. How refreshed do you feel this morning?

```
0        1        2        3        4
|_____|_____|_____|_____|
not at all      moderately           very
```

12. How would you rate the overall quality of your sleep last night?

```
0        1        2        3        4
|_____|_____|_____|_____|
poor                        very good
```

Calculating your sleep efficiency

Now think about an extra goal, one that you may never have heard about before. This goal is to increase your *sleep efficiency*. People with insomnia are inefficient sleepers. That is, they only sleep for part of the night, whereas good sleepers sleep for most of it. Look at the examples below.

Sarah goes to bed at 11 p.m. and gets up at 7 a.m. She sleeps all of the eight hours between these times. This means that Sarah is a very efficient sleeper indeed – in fact she has 100 per cent *sleep efficiency* because she sleeps absolutely all of the time she spends in bed.

John also goes to bed at 11 p.m. and gets up at 7 a.m. He takes forty-five minutes to fall asleep and is awake during the night for another ninety minutes. This means that John is awake for two hours and fifteen minutes. He sleeps for five hours and forty-five minutes of the eight hours that he is in bed. John's sleep efficiency therefore is only 72 per cent.

Most good sleepers manage around 90 per cent sleep efficiency – and that's pretty good! This would be the equivalent of spending eight hours in bed (480 minutes), and having a total of only forty-eight minutes (10 per cent) throughout that whole time awake. Take a moment just now to work out your own sleep efficiency by putting some numbers into this equation (Figure 37) and calculating your score. Fill in the total time you think you sleep, and divide it by the total time you usually spend in bed. Then multiply by 100 to get your sleep efficiency percentage.

Alternatively you could use the chart below (Figure 38) to calculate it. Your additional goal then is to get your sleep efficiency up to 90 per cent. Why not write this alongside where you've written down your goals?

Figure 37: Calculating your sleep efficiency

Total time you think you sleep ÷ Total time you usually spend in bed × 100

[ ] ÷ [ ] × 100 = [ ] %

Figure 38: Sleep efficiency

Total sleep Time (hours)

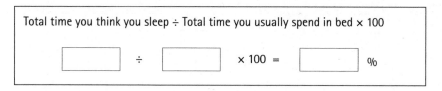

Hours	3	3.5	4	4.5	5	5.5	6	6.5	7	7.5	8	8.5	9	9.5	10
3	100														
3.5	86	100													
4	75	88	100												
4.5	67	78	89	100											
5	60	70	80	90	100										
5.5	55	64	73	82	91	100									
6	50	58	67	75	83	92	100								
6.5	45	54	62	69	77	85	92	100							
7	43	50	57	64	71	79	86	93	100						
7.5	40	47	53	60	67	73	80	87	93	100					
8	37	44	50	56	63	69	75	81	88	94	100				
8.5	35	41	47	53	59	65	71	76	82	88	94	100			
9	33	39	44	50	56	61	67	72	78	83	89	94	100		
9.5	32	37	42	47	53	58	63	68	74	79	84	89	95	100	
10	30	35	40	45	50	55	60	65	70	75	80	85	90	95	100

Time in bed (hours)

Sleep efficiency %

Improving your sleep hygiene

What is sleep hygiene?

Sleep hygiene is quite an odd phrase because it has nothing to do with hygiene. It's a list of the things you can control in order to make a good night's sleep more likely.

Sleep hygiene instructions on their own aren't really effective for treating persistent insomnia. So, if you have tried sleep hygiene and it hasn't really worked, don't become demoralized, because CBT offers many other ways to help! However, sleep hygiene can be used alongside other CBT methods, so here's an illustration of what it is about (see Figure 39).

Figure 39: Factors involved in sleep hygiene

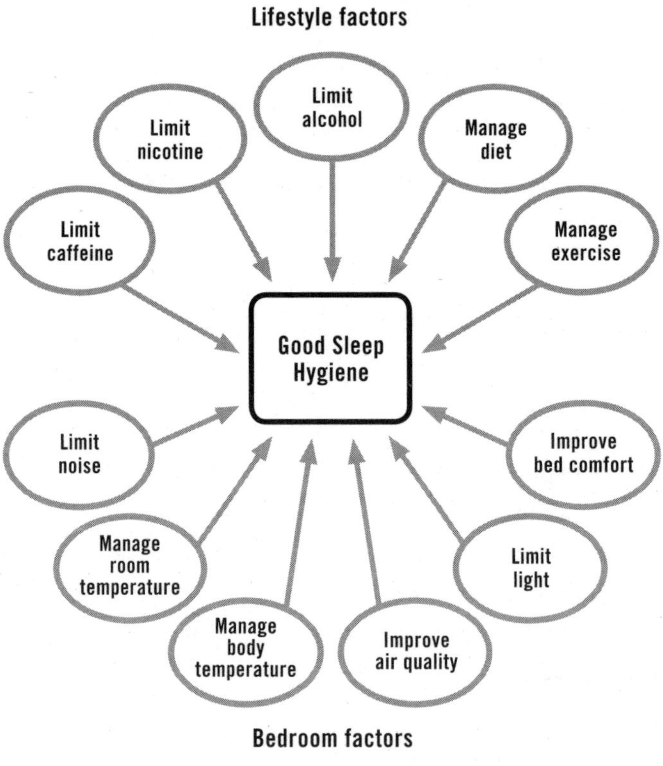

Lifestyle factors

It's best not to drink caffeinated (tea/coffee) or alcoholic drinks, or to have a main meal, within four hours of going to bed. A light meal in the evening, or a small snack a little before bedtime shouldn't be a problem. Likewise, although exercise is good for our physical and mental health, it's best not to exercise within two hours of going to bed because it tends to keep us awake. Smoking, of course, is bad for our health, but if you must smoke, then you should cut down before bedtime and try not to smoke during the night. Not only is nicotine a stimulant drug (like caffeine), but also your body may wake you up craving a cigarette.

Bedroom factors

Most of these factors are about making the bedroom suitable for sleep: limiting noise (not necessarily complete silence), making it dark (not necessarily pitch-black) and making sure that you have a comfortable mattress and pillows. The ideal room temperature is around 18°C (64°F) – not too hot and not too cold. If anything, cool is better, so you shouldn't be too warm, and a hot bath immediately before going to bed is likely to keep you awake.

Improving your preparation for sleep

Bedtime wind-down

You shouldn't expect to fall into bed and go to sleep just because it's bedtime. Developing a *wind-down routine*, so that you can relax and prepare for sleep will help you fall asleep once you are in bed. You can start this routine by putting the day to rest with some 'rehearsal and planning time'; this is discussed in more detail later on page 351, under 'Dealing with a racing mind'.

Figure 40: Example of a winding-down routine

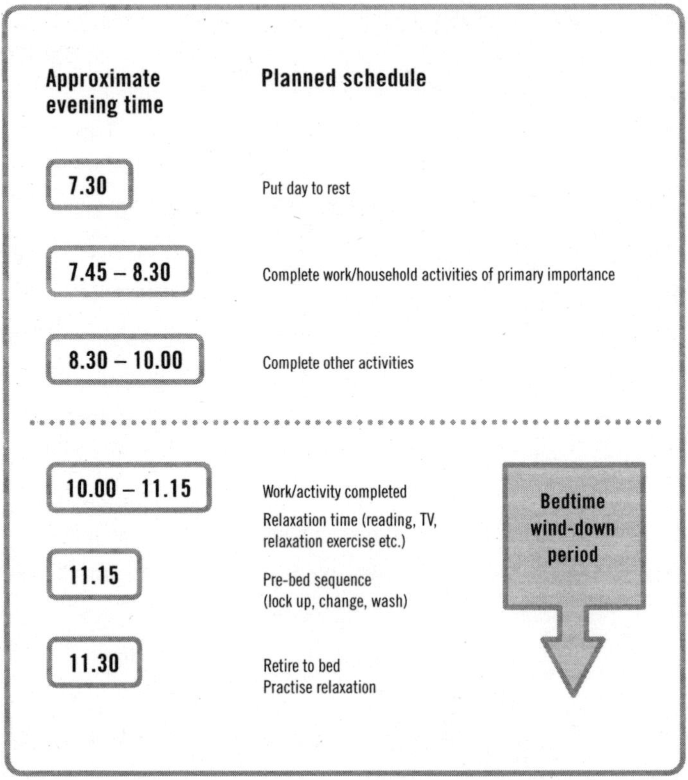

Approximate evening time	Planned schedule	
7.30	Put day to rest	
7.45 – 8.30	Complete work/household activities of primary importance	
8.30 – 10.00	Complete other activities	
10.00 – 11.15	Work/activity completed Relaxation time (reading, TV, relaxation exercise etc.)	**Bedtime wind-down period**
11.15	Pre-bed sequence (lock up, change, wash)	
11.30	Retire to bed Practise relaxation	

Your routine could include things like slowing down your work/activity and then stopping it, and having some relaxation time before you start getting ready for bed. The example routine in Figure 40 covers around four hours, so think about what you'll do throughout the whole evening, but especially the sixty to ninety minutes before you go to bed. The important thing is to unwind during this period.

Learning to relax

Let's first think about the *importance* of relaxation. There are some people who simply don't value relaxation; that's why they don't spend time on it, and they may not even be any good at it.

Our lives can be so full of the words 'should', 'shouldn't', 'must' and 'mustn't' that we don't give ourselves permission to relax. We might even feel that we *shouldn't* just sit and relax, especially when there are 'things that need to be done'. Sound familiar? If so, you could try to learn the value of relaxing.

Figure 41: Different ways to relax

	Active	Passive
Physical	Working out at the gym	Gently strolling
Mental	Doing crossword puzzles	Listening to music

As you can see in Figure 41, there are different ways of getting to a relaxed state. Some people relax by active physical means like exercise, and others through more mental or passive (which means gentle or inactive) pastimes like listening to music. Think about what activities you could do in each of the four areas. What tools do you already have in the relaxation toolbox? What skills do you still need to develop? Some people like to make their own relaxation recordings to help them get in the right mood to go to sleep, and you can download pre-recorded ones (for example at *www.sleepio.com*). But remember, good sleepers are not students of sleep. They just do it automatically and naturally. Nothing more, nothing less. Far from always thinking about how best to get to sleep and stay asleep, they seem quite relaxed about it, despite the fact that sometimes *even they* don't sleep well. So try to have a relaxed or even detached approach to sleep and sleeplessness, rather than thinking and worrying about it too much.

Improving your bed–sleep connection

The good sleeper appears to associate bed with successful sleep. Just like salt and pepper or fish and chips, it's bed and sleep. But clearly this isn't the case for someone with insomnia. If we have sleep problems, bed is associated with anxiety even before going to bed, and with wakefulness and frustration whilst there. So might sleep be helped if the bad bed–sleep connection was changed to a healthy one? Well there are four rules that'll help you to have this healthy connection between sleep and bed:

- The 'bed is for sleep' rule
- The 'quarter-of-an-hour' rule
- The 'sleepy-tired' rule
- The 'saving your sleep' rule

The 'bed is for sleep' rule

Now here's one of the instructions often found in sleep hygiene: 'Don't use your bed for anything except sleep', meaning that activities like watching TV, reading and talking on the telephone are out! When applied correctly, this is not so much a simple set of 'don'ts', but a helpful, positive instruction that means that *bed is for sleep*.

Here's an illustration of getting this rule right. You might think there's nothing wrong with reading in bed. You know plenty of people who do – and they don't have insomnia. Well, there are plenty of people who don't have a fear of dogs; but for some people the presence of a dog means fear. It's an automatic learned reaction: as soon as they see a dog they get scared. It's the same for people with insomnia and reading in bed. For them, reading in bed is associated with wakefulness, whereas for the good sleeper it promotes sleep.

But let's look at this a little more. The good sleeper reads in bed with the intention of reading – that is, their intention is to remain awake in order to read. So reading in bed is associated, if anything, with an effort to remain awake. Contrast that with the poor sleeper, who is actually using reading as a tool to get to sleep and *doesn't* wish to be awake, so again, reading is associated with anxiety and stress.

So, the first rule is to bar all activities (except sexual activity) from the bedroom environment in order to help you fall asleep rapidly after you get into bed.

The 'quarter-of-an-hour' rule

There's very strong evidence that good sleepers fall asleep within fifteen minutes or so of getting into bed. Therefore, if you want to become a good sleeper, you need to train yourself to do this too – the quarter-of-an-hour opportunity.

What is meant by a quarter-of-an-hour opportunity? Well, simply that you don't turn that opportunity into a half-hour or longer! What good is lying awake in bed, tossing and turning, unable to sleep? All that does is strengthen the association between bed and wakefulness. Instead, this rule says that after a quarter of an hour, you should get up, go into another room and do something different until you feel sleepy again. Then you can give yourself another quarter-of-an-hour opportunity – but if you can't get to sleep, you should get up again and repeat this as often as necessary.

If you stick to this, you'll never spend any more than fifteen minutes at a time lying awake in bed, so it stops the bad bed–sleep connection from building up. The quarter-of-an-hour rule will also stop you putting too much effort into getting to sleep.

The 'sleepy-tired' rule

You may feel that you're already an expert in sleepiness, but actually you may be quite poor at telling the difference between tiredness and sleepiness. If you can become really good at it, then you are more likely to fall asleep quickly.

To be clear, you need to learn to recognize when you are what can be called *sleepy-tired*. The usual signs are:

- itchy eyes
- lack of energy
- aching muscles
- yawning
- an involuntary tendency to 'nod off'

This is the way you should be feeling when you go to bed. This is how the good sleeper feels when they are resisting sleep and trying to read their book! *Tiredness* does not mean that sleep is inevitable. *Sleepiness* is a signal from our bodies that it's time to sleep.

So, you should go to bed only when you feel *sleepy*-tired, not simply by habit because it's 'time to go to bed'. Also, following the quarter-of-an-hour rule, you shouldn't go back to bed again unless you feel sleepy-tired. Not easy, I know!

The 'saving your sleep' rule

The connection between bed and sleep is stronger if you save all your sleep for night-time. This means you should avoid napping in the morning, in the afternoon and in the evening. This can be hard, but a nap can reduce the drive for sleep at night.

However, there are exceptions. If you regularly feel sleepy during the day, then you must be careful – particularly while driving or working machinery. You should stop and rest. Having a brief nap (ten to fifteen minutes) under these circumstances, along with a strong caffeinated drink, should allow you to complete your journey or your activities safely. If you continue to feel sleepy in the day, you should see your doctor.

Making your sleep pattern the best it can be

Do you feel like a well-oiled machine, operating at its best? That's the way we're designed to be with good, sound, deep sleep at night, which revives us, and makes us alert, good-natured and productive during the daytime.

Remember the extra goal to make your sleep as efficient as possible? You want good-quality sleep throughout the time you are in bed, and to restore your wellbeing for the daytime. One of the first questions we need to ask, then, is: how much sleep do you need?

How much sleep do I need?

You'll have heard people talking about getting their 'eight hours' as if eight hours is what everyone needs. This simply isn't so, as we discovered earlier.

Take another look at the sleep-efficiency equation from earlier on. What did you estimate your typical sleep to be? No doubt it was less than you wanted, but let's start from where you are at the moment. If you want a really accurate answer about how long you usually sleep, keep your sleep diary for ten nights, and then work out your average sleep time on this chart below.

Worksheet 12: Average sleep time

Night	Amount of time I slept
1	
2	
3	
4	
5	
6	
7	
8	
9	
10	
Total amount of sleep over 10 days = ...	
My average sleep time = ... = ...	

By dividing your total sleep over ten nights, you'll be able to work out the length of your average night's sleep. That is your first step towards getting your sleep as good as it could be.

Setting a regular amount of time in bed

Your challenge now is to work out a way of achieving this *same amount of sleep every night*. One of the problems of insomnia is the difference in the amount of sleep from night to night. So, however much or little sleep you're getting, it's important to work towards getting the same amount every single night.

So decide on a *rising time*, or getting-up time, and write it in the box below. It is best to have a set time for getting up every morning, seven nights a week, until you get your sleep problem sorted.

The next thing is to set a *threshold time* for going to bed – the time at which you go from the living room to the bedroom. You have only got so much sleep to play with, so you can work out your threshold time by subtracting from your rising time. Here's a chart (Table 42) to help you select the best threshold and rising times for you.

Table 42: Selecting your threshold and rising times

Time to bed

Time to Rise	3.00	2.30	2.00	1.30	1.00	12.30	12.00	11.30	11.00	10.30
8.30	5.5	6	6.5	7	7.5	8	8.5	9	9.5	10
8.00	5	5.5	6	6.5	7	7.5	8	8.5	9	9.5
7.30		5	5.5	6	6.5	7	7.5	8	8.5	9
7.00			5	5.5	6	6.5	7	7.5	8	8.5
6.30		Sleep window options		5	5.5	6	6.5	7	7.5	8
6.00					5	5.5	6	6.5	7	7.5
5.30						5	5.5	6	6.5	7
5.00							5	5.5	6	6.5

The period between your threshold time and your rising time is your *sleep window* – the window of opportunity for you to sleep. If you estimate you're sleeping six hours, then you could have a rising time of 7 a.m., and your threshold (going to bed) time would be 1.00 a.m. You are free to adjust in either direction from that – use the chart to help you. So, you might instead set a rising time of 6.15 a.m., and that would make your threshold time 12.15 a.m. The point is you have set a very tight sleep window, *seven nights per week.*

Important note: if you estimate your sleep time as less than six hours, it's best to use a *minimum* six hours as your sleep window.

Changing your sleep window

So what is going to happen if you follow this schedule? Your sleep efficiency will climb rapidly towards 90 per cent. You'll have greatly reduced the amount of time you spend in bed, and that'll force the sleep you do get into the narrow sleep window. You'll have increased the proportion of time in bed that you sleep. This will make your sleep much more refreshing and uninterrupted. Then, once this has worked, it may be possible for you to stretch the window and get a little bit more sleep. You can track your progress over several weeks on your sleep diary.

So here's the 'adjustment rule'. At the end of each week, recalculate your sleep efficiency using the equation on page 339. If it's improving, reward yourself with an extra fifteen minutes in bed for the subsequent week.

To use the example we started with, if you use the adjustment rule this would mean that the sleep window would shift from six to six and a quarter hours in the second week, assuming you have been sleeping well. Again, if you manage to increase your sleep efficiency towards 90 per cent, in the third week you can make the sleep window six and a half hours, and then six and three quarter hours, seven hours, and so on.

It may take several weeks to increase your total sleep, but if you do it gradually it can increase without causing your sleep pattern to break up again.

Dealing with a racing mind

Most people with insomnia feel physically tired, even exhausted, but mentally alert. They complain of a racing mind. Let's look at some things to help with the mental side of the problem.

Putting the day to rest ('rehearsal and planning time')

It's time to think about *putting the day to rest*. Often, the things that keep us awake are our thoughts, especially going over what happened during the day and thinking ahead to the next one. This isn't a bad thing to do, but it could easily be done in the evening, rather than in bed! So here are some suggestions about how you might put the day to rest.

1. Set aside twenty minutes in the early evening, the same time every night if possible (say around 7 p.m.).

2. Sit down somewhere you are not going to be disturbed.

3. All you need is a notebook, your diary and a pen.

4. Think of what has happened during the day, how events have gone, and how you feel about the kind of day it has been.

5. Write down some of the main points. Put them to rest by committing them to paper. Write down what you feel good about and also what has troubled you.

6. Write down anything you feel you need to do on a 'to do' list, with steps that you can take to tie up any 'loose ends' or 'unfinished business'.

7. Now think about tomorrow and what's coming up. Consider things you are looking forward to as well as things that may cause you worry.

8. Write down your schedule in your diary, or check it if it's already there.

9. Write down anything you are unsure about and make a note in your diary of a time in the morning when you are going to find out about it.

10. Try to use your twenty minutes to leave you feeling more in control. Close the book on the day.

11. When it comes to bedtime, if these things come into your mind, remind yourself that you have already dealt with all of them.

12. If new thoughts come up in bed, note them down on a piece of paper at your bedside to be dealt with the following morning.

Accurate thinking

Someone with insomnia might think, 'I am never going to get to sleep tonight.' This can make them feel worried, and then they might go on to think, 'I am not going to be able to cope tomorrow.' This is a vicious circle because it could make them feel down, and then they might have more bad thoughts. A solution to this kind of thinking is to have a close look at it – that is, to *consider how accurate* it is as a thought. Let's take that example and use it in the table below. This table is what we can call a thought evaluator – where we work out whether the thought is really true or not.

The challenge is to have the courage to work out whether your thoughts really are accurate. If you can correct your thinking in this way, it'll be much less threatening and demoralizing. Use a version of this table in a notebook to work out your own negative thoughts and replace them with more accurate and less alarming ones.

Table 43: Thought evaluator

My thoughts about sleep and sleeplessness	How this makes me feel	A more accurate version of my thoughts would be . . .	How this version makes me feel
'It seems as if I am awake half the night and everyone else is sleeping.'	Anxious, annoyed, lonely, jealous	'I probably sleep around six hours and have two hours awake in bed; that's 75 per cent (three-quarters) not 50 per cent. Also if there are 1 million people living in this city and half of them are adults, maybe 50,000 are having serious problems. Everyone else is not sleeping!'	Reassured, more optimistic, less angry
'I'm never going to get to sleep tonight.'	Demoralized, out of control	'Almost certainly I will fall asleep. I always get some sleep. The average in my diary was six hours and I never got less than three to four hours.'	More accepting, relieved, more relaxed
'I'm so tired I just can't concentrate. It's because I slept so badly last night.'	Hopeless, preoccupied with sleep, irritable	'My concentration is not just down to my sleep. I've slept worse than I did last night and felt better during the day. Maybe I'm bored, or doing too much at once, or...'	More in control, able to focus

Stop trying to sleep

This is so important. As soon as you start giving your attention to sleep-lessness, it'll take over your thinking, and will lead to you trying to fall asleep. Sadly, trying to fall asleep doesn't work – you are likely to get anxious and preoccupied, and sleep will elude you. One remedy is to have a more *accepting* approach to your wakefulness. In other words, the problem is not so much being awake; the problem is your emotional response to being awake. If you can correct that, you will feel a whole lot better – and be more likely to get back to sleep.

Evaluating how you feel during the day

We talked about how insomnia is a twenty-four-hour problem. It's important to improve how you feel during the day, as well as how you feel at night. So use the thought evaluator to assess the thoughts you have in the daytime. For example, it might occur to you that you are feeling extremely tired and 'that's because of my poor sleep last night', but think about whether there are any other explanations for feeling tired right now. Perhaps you're overdoing it and need a rest. Likewise, you might have made a bad job of something; it could be all too easy to blame your lack of sleep for that, but maybe you've just made a bad job of it! So you are working on ways to improve your sleep at night, and also to improve the way you cope in the daytime.

Making lasting improvements to your sleep

Before summarizing all of the advice you have been given in this chapter point by point, we should talk about how to make improvements last. There are three headlines here:

1.   Use all the CBT advice in this chapter; try not to pick and choose.

2.   Recognize that it takes time and that it may be tough to make lasting changes.

3. Deal positively with any setbacks.

Keeping it all together

While there's a lot of tightly packed information in this chapter, try to avoid the temptation of treating it like a menu. In other words, it is not really meant for dipping into and selecting items that appeal to you. You are likely to do best if you follow the programme through.

If some parts are completely irrelevant to you, because you simply don't have a problem in that area, then fair enough, but otherwise complete every bit that you can, if you want to make your sleep better in the long term.

It's going to be tough

It can be tough to overcome insomnia. It really does involve breaking up an old pattern and building a new one, completely changing the way you think about sleep, and believing that you too can become a normal sleeper.

While it'll be a challenge, *sticking to the programme* will bear its own fruits in time. You need to be tolerant with yourself if at times you feel that you're failing, and encourage yourself to get back on track. Parts like the new sleep window and the quarter-of-an-hour rule are the most difficult bits for people to carry out. But they're also amongst the best strategies. *Staying motivated* is the key to making a lasting improvement in your sleep.

Dealing with setbacks

There are two ways you might experience a setback. First, you might be able to create a new sleep pattern for a while, but then feel like giving up because it's hard work to keep going. This is *perfectly normal* and to be expected. It's part of human nature, so don't be discouraged. The second thing is that even once your sleep pattern is back to normal you'll have an occasional bad night or a period of poor sleep. The difference between you and the good sleeper at these times is simply that the good sleeper doesn't think that they're developing insomnia. You've had it before, so a change of thinking is definitely required here too – *don't panic*, just go back and work your way through the methods outlined here for a while.

Good luck as you try to overcome your insomnia!

Key messages

- Insomnia can be a stubborn problem. That's why it can hang around for a long time. However it can be overcome using CBT.

- It is important to get your sleep into a new routine and to experiment until you get it right. Remember that your old pattern wasn't working!

- Likewise, managing your racing mind is key and there are many techniques here to help you. Practise makes perfect.

- Remember everyone has the occasional poor night, so don't overreact when that happens.

Tips for supporters

- CBT for insomnia can feel like a lot of things to be doing at once, and the person you are supporting may feel a bit overwhelmed. Remember that being unable to sleep well is a very undermining experience. Helping them to adhere to a structured CBT approach offers them the best opportunity to set their sleep back on a good footing.

20 Couples and depression: improving the relationship and improving depression

Donald H. Baucom, Tamara G. Sher, Sara E. Boeding
and Christine Paprocki

Many of the suggestions in this book focus upon how you as an individual can make changes to address your depression. However, you do not live in a vacuum. Your own wellbeing and how you behave can greatly influence your relationships. That is, if you are depressed now and stay depressed, you are more likely to develop relationship difficulties. The reverse is also true: if you are having relationship difficulties now, you are more likely to become depressed. Of course, it would be overly simplistic to suggest that relationship difficulties cause depression or that depression is the single cause of any relationship problems you might be having. However, difficulties in one of these areas *can* contribute to problems in the other. The important thing for both you and your partner to keep in mind is that working jointly on your relationship can improve it, as well as help alleviate your depression. We recommend that both you and your partner read this chapter, discuss it and apply some of the principles and techniques as you address your depression together.

Although it is very common, obviously not everyone who is depressed is in a bad relationship. Some depressed people have very positive and loving relationships with their partner, and if that is true for you, it will make it easier for the two of you to work alongside each other on your depression. However, even if your partner is fully committed to working with you, many people do not know how to help when their loved one is depressed. Therefore, it can be very valuable to learn together about what you as an individual need to do to get over your depression, and how the two of you can respond to a variety of circumstances related to it. Once you both know how depression works and how to combat it, your partner can become a valuable resource.

Joanne and Ian's story

Joanne and Ian are a couple that got into trouble as Ian tried to help with Joanne's depression, even though they have a respectful and caring relationship. Ian is an accountant; Joanne is a stay-at-home mother to their two daughters, aged eight months and three years. Their younger daughter was born prematurely and has been an exceptionally fussy baby. Joanne became very distressed over this, saying 'I can't even calm my own baby.' She felt like a failure in all aspects of her life because she was no longer a patient mother, and she was often in a bad mood by the time her husband returned home from work. Ian felt terrible when he saw Joanne cry. As a result, as soon as he got home, he told her to go lie down and that he would take care of everything. He then proceeded to clean the kitchen, make dinner and get the kids off to bed. His efforts to 'help out' unfortunately made Joanne feel less competent as a mother and more depressed.

Helping well-intentioned partners know how to be of assistance in treating depression is one of our major goals.

This chapter is therefore divided into two sections: the first looks at communication skills in general, and shows how you can improve them. These skills are important because the lack of them can contribute so strongly to the breakdown of relationships, with all the low mood and depression that this can bring. The second section looks at how to use your relationship in a positive way when one partner is depressed, using the communication tools we discuss in the first section.

Unlike other chapters in the book we have not included tips for supporters, because we are hoping that both of you will be each other's supporters.

1: Using communication skills to improve your relationship

The quality of your relationship with your partner sets the tone for your day-to-day experience at home. If your relationship is distressed, your home is likely to feel negative, and that can be depressing. If you both feel loved and supported by each other, your overall life experience is likely to be more positive, and it will be easier to use your relationship as a resource in combating depression. Therefore, let's focus first on some general principles of what you and your partner can do to improve and enhance the quality of the way things are between you.

The quality of your relationship is influenced by a large number of factors. First, in order for a relationship to work, it needs to meet many of the important needs that each of you has as individuals. For example, you might want a lot of emotional closeness and will feel unhappy if you do not experience that with your partner. Or one of you might find it very rewarding to achieve in your profession and feel frustrated if your relationship makes it difficult for you to be professionally successful.

Second, not only does the relationship need to meet both of your individual needs, but also the two of you need to function well as a unit. Have you worked out how you will deal with limited finances, who will take the children to dance lessons and football practice? Can you communicate with each other effectively, sharing your thoughts and feelings about important topics as well as making good decisions together?

Third, you do not live in isolation as a couple, but rather you are integrated into an environment that includes other people, as well as the physical aspects of your surroundings such as your home and neighbourhood. For a relationship to work, you need to decide how you will operate within this broader environment, which includes giving to others and receiving support from them as appropriate, learning to enjoy the positive aspects of your surroundings, and minimizing the negative impact (for example, having noisy or unpleasant neighbours).

In summary, a successful relationship has three main characteristics: it meets the needs of both individuals; the couple function well as a unit; and they relate well to their environment.

Key messages

- Your relationship can set the tone for how you experience your daily life.

- It can also be a key resource in combating depression.

- Your individual needs, your needs as a couple, and environmental demands must all be taken into account to build a healthy relationship.

The CBT techniques that you have been using to treat your depression can also be applied when focusing on the various aspects of a healthy relationship. That is, both of you have thoughts, feelings and behaviours towards each other as individuals, yourselves as a couple, and the environment. For example, if your partner has a strong need to be professionally successful, they might spend a lot of time at work and/or thinking about work-related issues. You might interpret your partner's long hours at work as meaning that they do not love you and are trying to avoid you, or instead you might believe they want to contribute as much as possible to your family's finances – each belief will have a very different impact. That is, there are important cognitive, behavioural and emotional aspects to how you experience your relationship. These are illustrated in Figure 44 below.

Figure 44. Factors influencing the quality of your relationship

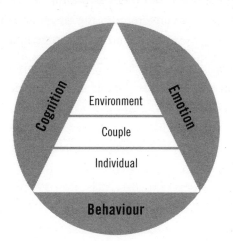

Given that there are so many different factors that influence the quality of your relationship, it might seem overwhelming to think about how to improve it. While we cannot address all factors – whole books have been written on this topic – we will look at some of the major principles that we know help people to have healthy intimate relationships.

Improving your communication

One of the most important aspects in any relationship is how the two of you communicate with each other. In fact, this is one of the best predictors of whether a couple's relationship will be satisfying over the years. When couples sit down to talk to each other, they usually have one of two types of conversation. First, they might want to simply share their thoughts and feelings about some topic. For example, you might routinely talk about how each of your days went, what happened with the children, events in the world, or news from family and friends. When you are speaking, your aim is to share with the other person and to be heard and accepted. When you are the listener, your aim is to understand your partner. If you can develop skills to have these conversations, it is a gift to your relationship because it means that both of you can share and feel understood, whether discussing the good, the bad or the ugly. During this type of conversation, the emphasis is not on making a decision or resolving a problem. That is the second type of conversation, which is critical to keep things organized and get things done effectively.

What are you likely to be talking about during these two types of conversations? Most likely you will be discussing what you both want and need as individuals, what you will do as a couple, or how you will interact with the people and environment around you – the three areas we mentioned above. And good communication is likely to influence how you think, feel and act towards each other. When you communicate effectively, you are more likely to understand each other's intents and desires and less likely to be upset due to misunderstandings. Therefore, you behave in more helpful ways towards your partner, because you both understand what actions would be best. For example, after Joanne began to realize that her depression was tied to feeling less competent as a mother, she was able to express to Ian that what she really needed from him was to listen to her talk about her tough day for a few minutes when he got home from work, rather than him telling her to rest and that he would 'take care of everything'. She was able to share her appreciation for his good intentions in wanting to take care of her, but could also explain that she wanted to feel more competent, as well as feeling heard and understood by Ian.

On the other hand, when couples are not communicating well, problems can mushroom, as Tom and Emily experienced.

Tom and Emily's story

Tom and Emily came to counselling reporting that they didn't understand each other any more and thus had been arguing more and more. Emily complained that Tom didn't listen, and Tom said that Emily talked 'at him' instead of 'with him'. In the counselling sessions, Tom and Emily talked over each other and often rolled their eyes or frowned while the other was speaking. However, when Tom was quiet, Emily used this as evidence that she was the only one who cared about their marriage. Both felt alone, misunderstood and discouraged. Overall, Tom and Emily had both developed bad communication patterns and misinterpreted what the other was trying to say. Although there were many aspects of their relationship that needed to be addressed, they needed to focus on their communication skills early in treatment, so they could talk productively about a wide range of concerns.

Let's first think about guidelines for conversations that focus on sharing thoughts and feelings, and later we will discuss those that focus on decision-making. These guidelines are helpful to people in many different situations, whether they are distressed couples, or happy couples who want to improve their relationships further.

Conversations for sharing thoughts and feelings

Couples share what they think and feel all the time. As we mentioned above, these conversations might be about small things, such as what happened during the day, or about major topics, such as concerns about a parent's health. Whereas it might seem that these conversations just happen, and people don't need to think about them, we know that they can go well, or they can go very badly. Therefore we have developed some guidelines that many couples find useful:

Table 45: Guidelines for sharing thoughts and feelings

Skills for sharing emotions and thoughts (the speaker)	Skills for listening to your partner (the listener)
• Talk about your opinions *subjectively*, as *your own* feelings and thoughts, not as absolute truths. • Include your feelings. • Discuss how you feel about your partner and not just an event. • When you share negative emotions or concerns, try to include your positive feelings as well. • Make your statement as *specific* as possible, both in terms of emotions and thoughts. • Speak in 'paragraphs', not a monologue. Give your partner a chance to respond to one main idea. • Express your feelings and thoughts with *tact* and *timing* so that your partner can listen to what you are saying without becoming defensive.	• **When your partner is speaking . . .** ◊ show that you understand and accept what your partner has to say. Use your tone of voice, facial expressions and posture to show understanding. *Remember, acceptance is NOT agreement.* ◊ try to put yourself in your partner's place. Think about the situation from their perspective to help figure out how they feel and think about the issue. **When your partner finishes speaking . . .** ◊ summarize your partner's most important feelings, desires, conflicts and thoughts. **When you are the listener, do NOT . . .** ◊ ask questions, except for clarification. ◊ express your own viewpoint or opinion. ◊ interpret or change the meaning of your partner's statements. ◊ attempt to solve a problem if one exists. ◊ judge what your partner has said.

The roles of speaker and listener change back and forth during the conversation. You can think of one complete round of conversation as one of you speaking, with the second person listening and then summarizing what they heard the speaker say. Then the cycle repeats, with the two of you staying in those same roles or switching so that you each have a chance to speak. Here is a brief explanation of the guidelines.

How do I speak to my partner?

- **Speak for yourself, not for your partner.** We recommend that you let your partner tell you what they think and feel. One way to maintain this focus on just talking for yourself is to use an 'I' statement that links your own feelings to a specific situation or behaviour. Sometimes we refer to this as an 'XYZ' statement, as in: 'When you do X in situation Y, I feel Z.' For example, 'When you tell me to just get over it when I'm feeling really down and discouraged, I feel even more lonely and depressed.' One advantage to using this approach is that it will help you tie your feelings to specific situations, rather than expressing them as global and potentially more hurtful statements. That is usually easier for your partner to hear, and they are less likely to be defensive in return. For example, Emily tends to do the cooking in the evening, and would like Tom to help, but doesn't think she should have to ask him. She sometimes blows up and says things like, 'You're so lazy it infuriates me.' Obviously this just infuriates Tom back. She could try to say, 'When I'm cooking in the evening and you don't offer to help I get upset.'

  The second, equally important part of this guideline is *not* speaking for your partner. Many people have a tendency to tell their partner what they are thinking or feeling. Even if you believe that you know exactly what they are feeling, your partner is likely to resent it if you speak for them. So speak for yourself about *your* own thoughts and feelings and allow your partner to speak for themselves. For example, Emily has difficulty not talking for Tom and said to him, 'You never listen to me – you just don't care about the things that are important to me.' To express her thought more subjectively, Emily could have said, 'Sometimes I feel like you're not really listening to me, and I start to wonder whether the things I care about aren't important to you.'

- **Express your feelings as your own subjective experience, not as absolute truths.** If you state your thoughts and feelings as facts, your partner is likely to tell you that you are wrong and then tell you their version of the '*real* truth'. Then you proceed to argue about who is right or wrong. However, if you express it in a way that clarifies that this is what you think, feel, or experience, then it leaves room for your partner to have his or her own experience, whether it is the same or different. For example, rather than the many ways that Emily can state that Tom is an uncaring person who thinks only about himself, she can instead focus on describing her own experience of feeling unheard, uncared about, or rejected.

- **Focus on your feelings before moving on to thoughts or opinions.** Feelings provide a lot of information about how you are doing, and that can be valuable to let your partner know what you need or what you are going through. If your partner understands that you are feeling frightened, they can try to help you clarify what feels dangerous and how they might help you feel safer. So share your emotions, not just your thoughts, when you speak. For example, Emily could add an emotion in her statement above to Tom: 'Sometimes I feel like you're not really listening to me, and I start to wonder whether the things I care about aren't important to you. When that happens, I feel frustrated and also pretty rejected and sad.'

- **When expressing negative feelings or concerns, also include any positive feelings you have.** If you can give a balanced expression of both positive and negative feelings, your partner is more likely to hear the negative ones and respond to them in an understanding way. For example, if you tell your partner you are angry because they came home late again, they are likely to try to justify their behaviour. However, if you also add that you love being with them and you were looking forward to being together, your partner might respond very differently and be less defensive. Don't make things up or 'sugar coat' them, but do acknowledge the underlying positive emotions that are often present if you only look for them. Tom has difficulty including positive feelings when he is concerned about an issue. For example, he said to Emily, 'Quit asking me about paying that bill – do you hear yourself? You're such a nag!' He could have put a positive frame around his concern, and said: 'I know how important it is to you to have the bills paid on time, and you being so conscientious really helps us from getting into trouble financially. But when you keep asking me about the same bill, it makes me feel like you don't trust me to do it, and that can be really frustrating for me.'

- **Limit yourself to expressing one main feeling or idea at a time, and then give your partner an opportunity to respond.** Listeners have trouble staying focused when the speaker goes on and on. It becomes difficult to process everything they are saying, and we want your partner to understand what you say. Therefore, limit yourself to just a few sentences, maybe five or six, and then give your partner a chance to respond. You'll have an opportunity to say more; just don't do it all at once. For example, Emily feels overwhelmed and wants to vent everything she is feeling to Tom – this comes out as a steady stream of concerns and complaints and fears that Tom can only listen to for a few minutes before he starts shutting down. If Emily were able to voice her concerns one at a time, giving Tom a chance to respond, the conversation would feel more productive and better for both of them.

- **Choose your words and your timing carefully.** Most of us have 'hot buttons' and when those buttons get pushed, we don't respond well. So think about how you express yourself. You want to be honest, but speak in a way that your partner can hear you without becoming more upset than necessary. So rather than saying that your partner is just like their parent (in some uncomplimentary way), just tell them specifically what is bothering you. Choosing *when* to talk can be as important as *how* you talk. Bringing up a major concern as your partner is going to sleep or leaving the house doesn't allow time to discuss the issue, and they might resent feeling pulled into a conversation at that time. If you're going to raise a difficult issue, do it when you're both available to have a thoughtful discussion. For example, sometimes Tom tries to start a conversation with Emily while she is at her computer checking emails, and she is distracted; as a result both of them feel frustrated. Before starting a serious conversation it can be helpful to check whether it is a good time, or whether it would be better to wait a few minutes to wrap up whatever task is currently being done.

How do I listen to my partner?

Being a good listener can be much harder than being a good speaker. Here are some ways you can show your partner that you want to understand what they are saying. You need to let your partner know you are interested and engaged while they are speaking, and respond constructively after they have finished.

- **Respond while your partner is still speaking.** Engage with them and make sure they know you are engaged! Make certain that you aren't occupied in other ways, so you can focus on the conversation. That means don't have the conversation while you are watching television, are on the computer, or are doing other tasks. For example, Emily gets infuriated when Tom looks down to check his email on his phone while they are talking. You don't want to interrupt your partner, so use non-verbal expressions or body language to show you are listening: maintaining eye contact, turning towards your partner, and avoiding scowling, foot tapping and exasperated sighs. You might occasionally nod, and your facial expressions can demonstrate that you understand what your partner is feeling.

- When your partner is speaking, you should try to just listen and understand their perspective, whether you agree with it or not. You don't have to agree with them, but you can still show that you understand their experience and accept that this is what they think and feel. If they do express ideas and feelings you don't share, you don't need to prepare a rebuttal or a defence of yourself while they are speaking. Your job for now is just to listen. Soon you will be in the speaker role and you can share your own perspective then.

- **Respond after your partner has finished speaking.** The best way to demonstrate that you've heard your partner is to use your own words to summarize or paraphrase what you've heard. This is what we call a *reflection*. For example, 'You'd like us to be more affectionate with each other, just holding hands or snuggling. Your sense is that might help us feel closer. Is that right?' Don't shift the focus by asking lots of questions (except for clarification), interpreting what your partner just said ('You said you want to just snuggle, but I know you're hoping it will lead to sex'), or adding your own opinion. Just listen and let your partner know that you got the message by reflecting.

Reflecting can seem awkward and unnatural at first, but if you listen carefully to conversations around you, you'll find that many people actually do reflect others' comments naturally. The major goal is to create a conversation where you both express yourselves, feel listened to and respected, and have a sense that you understand each other better. This approach to communication applies whether you are just having a brief check-in about your day or are addressing a very important issue.

Conversations for making decisions and solving problems

Conversations for sharing thoughts and feelings can be quite valuable for you and your partner to understand each other. At times, there are also decisions that you will need to make, whether small day-to-day ones, or large ones such as whether to move for a job opportunity. During these conversations, you'll want to continue to use the good communication skills listed above. In addition, there are a series of steps that many couples find useful in reaching a decision, as noted in Table 46 below.

Table 46: Guidelines for decision-making or problem-solving

State the issue.	• State the issue or concern in terms of behaviours. • Break larger problems into smaller issues and deal with them one at a time. • Check that both people agree on the statement and want to talk about it. • Do NOT: ◊ decide who is right and wrong. ◊ try to find the 'truth' about what happened.
Talk about why the issue is important. What do you need?	• Share your understanding of the issue. Include why it is important to you. • Explain what you would like to be taken into account when you make a decision, but do not give any solutions yet.
Discuss possible solutions.	• Focus on the solution. • Propose a solution that takes both people's needs into account. • If you can only think of a couple of solutions, try brainstorming to come up with a lot of different possibilities.
Decide on a solution that is agreeable to both of you.	• Sometimes no solution is perfect and you have to compromise. • Repeat your final decision in terms of specific behaviours. • Do NOT make a decision that: ◊ you will not actually do. ◊ will make you angry or resentful.
Decide on a trial period for the solution or decision.	• Review how the solution is working at the end of the trial period. • You may have to try the new way of doing things several times to make it work.

State the issue in specific terms without blame. Often when there is a problem to be resolved, one or both of you might feel that the other person is behaving badly or not doing their part, and state the problem in terms of how they are causing it. Unfortunately, this is likely to get the conversation off to an unproductive start, with your partner defending themselves and perhaps blaming you in response. Your conversation is likely to be much more productive if you simply state the issue you need to resolve or make a decision about without blaming either person, phrasing the concern in terms of specific behaviours. For example, you might state, 'I think we need to develop a better system for how we clean up the kitchen after dinner – you know, washing up, cleaning the counters and putting away leftovers.'

Clarify why the issue is important. Understanding what is important to both of you can guide you towards a decision that you will both find acceptable. For example, you know that your partner wants to feel you are working together as a team in cleaning up the kitchen, and your partner needs to understand that you want to make certain that you both spend time with the children before their bedtime. Hopefully your solution can incorporate both of these sets of desires. In essence, you will have a small 'sharing thoughts and feelings' conversation in which you both say what you want taken into account in making a final decision together.

Focus on possible solutions. Your goal is to work together as a team to decide what to do in the future. So keep the conversation present and future-oriented. Discuss the past only to clarify what you need to do better as a couple, not to attribute blame.

Couples often become deadlocked when they focus on only one or two possible solutions, usually with each person trying to push for his or her preferences and dismissing the partner's position. When you see that happening, try to brainstorm to develop some more possible solutions. This helps you be creative, and you might come up with new solutions that you had not considered previously.

Decide on a solution that is agreeable to both of you. If you can come up with a solution that you both see as ideal, great; unfortunately, often such solutions do not exist. In that case, look for compromises. The compromise should take into account what both of you said was important to you earlier in the conversation. Compromise means taking into account the needs and preferences of both of you, even though the outcome is not ideal for either of you. For example, Emily would prefer that bills be paid immediately, while Tom is less concerned about this and has the attitude, 'It will get paid eventually; there is no sense worrying about it.' They came to the compromise that Emily will trust Tom to pay the bills he is responsible for within one week of receiving them, and that she won't ask him about it during that week, but can check in after a week has passed to see if he has paid.

Decide on a trial period. Sometimes your solution involves a single instance of what you will do: on Saturday you will take the kids to the park since the weather is nice. However, often your solutions will involve situations that repeat themselves. In those instances, it can be valuable to set up a trial period to see how the solution works out. Even though you made a decision in good faith, often you don't know how it will work until you try it out. Therefore if something occurs daily (for example, washing up), you might decide to try it for a week and then assess the solution. At the end of the week, you might decide to continue with it, change it slightly to make it more effective, or realize that you need a completely different solution. If you need a new solution, you problem-solve again, now taking into account what you learned from your trial period. For example, Emily and Tom decided to implement their plan for paying bills for two months and then check back in to see how it was working for both of them.

To sum up the steps involved in good decision-making: state the issue in neutral terms; focus on the present and the future; clarify why an issue is important and brainstorm a variety of solutions; compromise, and then compromise some more; and remember that your decisions can always be renegotiated if they're not successful initially. Tom and Emily were able to solve their problem by first identifying it (Emily worrying about the bills, Tom feeling that she was asking him about them too often), and deciding it was important because it regularly caused stress for both of them. They brainstormed solutions that would take both Emily's need to be conscientious and Tom's need to have some flexibility into account, and compromised on a solution. They then agreed to check back in after two months, as that would let them evaluate how their plan worked over two cycles of bills.

We have spent a fair amount of time discussing how you communicate because it is one of the most valuable tools that you have as a couple to improve your relationship. If you are already good at it, rejoice and commit to making it even better. If you need to work to improve your communication, as many couples do, take time to practise with each other. These are skills like any others, and you will get better as you talk with each other on a regular basis.

Key messages

- When couples talk, they often have one of two goals – sharing or problem-solving.

- When sharing, link your thoughts and feelings to specific situations or behaviours.

- Prevent 'information overload' by keeping your statements to a few sentences.

- Avoid 'hot button' phrases when discussing emotional topics.

- Show your partner you are listening by using body language and eye contact.

- Reflect your partner's main points so that they feel heard and respected.

- Avoid blaming each other and dredging up the past when making decisions.

- Compromise on one solution that you can implement for a trial period.

Behave in caring ways, day by day

You interact with your partner on a daily basis, beyond the conversations that you have. Your day-to-day actions have a major impact on the quality of the relationship, so it is important to focus on the ways that you behave towards each other. Later in this chapter, we will discuss activities that you might do together for fun, that are productive, or that are particularly meaningful to you as a couple. At this point, we will discuss what small things you can do individually to make life more rewarding and enjoyable for your partner. When people first fall in love, they are naturally thoughtful and nice to each other. They pay each other compliments, buy small gifts, want to please each other. As time goes on and the relationship gets overtaken by the trials and business of daily life, it is very easy for these little things to disappear. As a result, the relationship is much less rewarding and fun. A simple way to improve this is to refocus your efforts on these small ways of showing care and concern for each other.

We recommend that you put emphasis on the word 'small'. Find things that you can keep doing without requiring a large amount of time, money or effort. 'Big ticket' items such as expensive gifts or holidays away together are nice on occasion, but most people can't do them frequently, and often they don't have a long-term impact. It is the small daily things that make up the fabric of your relationship, so focus your effort on being a good partner day-to-day. There is no specific way to accomplish this, but the main thing is to find a concrete way that will help you stay focused on your partner. For example, some couples commit to doing something caring for each other at least once a day, perhaps making a cup of tea or giving them a back rub. Or the small thing could simply be remembering to pay compliments or thank the other person: instead of just eating the evening meal, thank them for taking the trouble to prepare it, or comment on something you liked about it.

It is important that you follow through, regardless of what your partner does. If your partner forgets to do something nice for you on a given day and in response you stop behaving positively, the whole process can break down. What you can control is your own behaviour, so make a plan and stick to it. Whereas you can plan what to do for your partner each day, you can also continually look for opportunities. Try to notice ways that you could be kind or helpful at a given moment; your partner might make comments that spur you to think of things that you can do on the spot. Unhappy couples often miss multiple opportunities to do nice things for each other, so keep your eyes open with the attitude that part of your role is to look for ways to be kind to your partner. Although you will hopefully behave this way simply because it brings out the best in you and will make your partner happy, research is quite clear that over time, if you continue to behave in a positive way towards your partner, they are likely to respond by being nicer to you in return. Therefore, you can improve the overall quality of your relationship if you focus on your own behaviour and the small things that you can do to make it better.

Key messages

- Find small ways to show your partner that you care.

- Make these small caring acts a part of your daily routine.

- Kindness can be contagious – the more you show your partner you care, the more likely it is that they will reciprocate.

Where to go from here in improving your relationship

We have briefly described above some of the major principles that you can adopt to improve your relationship. You can do much of this yourself as a couple, and we have included a list of some self-help books on the subject at the end of this book (see page 551). If your relationship is seriously distressed and efforts on your own are of limited success, you can consider seeing a couple-counsellor or therapist. A number of studies have been conducted that show that when couples in which one person has depression receive couple therapy or marriage counselling, their relationship improves and the depression decreases. However, there are also specific things that the two of you can do together to combat the depression directly, and now we will focus on those.

2. Using your relationship to help

Behavioural activation

If you are depressed, you are likely to have little energy, feel unmotivated, and the world might seem like a rather negative and unrewarding place. As a result, you might withdraw, reducing your contact with other people and doing fewer activities that previously brought you joy and meaning in life. Although you may feel a strong pull to withdraw, we know that doing this makes depression worse, because it removes the opportunity to take part in potentially enjoyable and rewarding aspects of life. In addition, it can be hard on your relationship, because you may no longer be meeting your daily responsibilities, or doing fun things with your partner. Consequently, it is important to get yourself moving and re-engaged in life. In Chapter 13, we looked at how you can do this through a process called behavioural activation. In this chapter, we will discuss how the two of you can work together to use those ideas to reduce your depression and benefit your relationship at the same time. It's a good idea to engage in self-/couple-monitoring (writing down your activities and emotions during the hours and days of each week) and to conduct a functional analysis of your behaviour (studying how your behaviours vary, what triggers them, and what the consequences of these behaviours are). In this chapter, we will focus upon the third step of behavioural activation: activity scheduling.

To some degree, just being active and getting going instead of withdrawing is likely to help your depression. However, a more focused approach can also be valuable. Life tends to be most rewarding when people engage in activities that are enjoyable, that contribute to their sense of achievement, or are consistent with their overall life goals and values. Therefore, it makes sense to focus your efforts on increasing your activity in one or all of these three areas. You might have some sense of which of these will be most beneficial for you to focus on now, or you may need to try out activities in each area and see which have the most positive impact on your depression.

Some activities will focus upon you as an individual – 'individual behavioural activation'. For example, you might decide that you want to exercise more by yourself or spend more time reading. But a significant part of your life involves the two of you as a couple. Therefore, we would also recommend that you engage in what we call 'couple behavioural activation', which involves activities you do together. In both individual and couple behavioural activation, we recommend that you share your thoughts and feelings with each other and make decisions together about how to become more active.

Individual behavioural activation

You probably know what activities will help you feel better about yourself. So why have conversations with your partner about what you need to do as an individual? There are at least three reasons. First, you might not be clear in your mind what activities would be enjoyable for you, but as you talk about it with your partner, you might start to feel clearer about it. Second, your partner knows you pretty well and might have some observations or insights that will be beneficial to you. It is not about your partner taking over and telling you what to do, but they might have useful ideas that you can take into account in deciding on important behaviours to increase. At times we avoid unpleasant situations without even realizing that we're doing it; your partner might be able to share a useful perspective on ways that you have been avoiding that contribute to your depression. Third, even if you are clear regarding which individual behavioural changes you want to make, they might be easier to accomplish if your partner understands what you want to change and can support you in making those changes. For example, if you have decided that you want to exercise more, it might be helpful to have a decision-making conversation in which you conclude that your partner will take care of the children two evenings a week while you go to the gym. In that way, you are working together to make individual changes that could be helpful.

Couple behavioural activation

Couple behavioural activation is just a technical term for suggesting that the two of you increase your activities together. In fact, this is one of the most beneficial things that you can do to combat depression. This can be helpful to the person who is depressed because it increases their activity level, just as individual BA does. Also, for many people, interacting with their partner is one of the most rewarding aspects of life, so we want you to make opportunities for those experiences. And as we mentioned earlier, if your relationship is not as satisfying as you want it to be, then finding positive and rewarding activities to engage in together can also be of great benefit.

Couple behavioural activation activities fall into the same categories that we discussed above, only now you are doing them together: those that are enjoyable, that lead to a sense of accomplishment, or are meaningful in terms of what you value as a couple. To help you think about what kinds of activities could work for you, in Table 47 we have included a list that might help to spur your imagination. Some of these are pleasurable activities such as going out for a meal, going to the theatre, or taking a walk. You might also feel better if the two of you carry out some household projects together. Or you might decide that you want to begin going to your place of worship together because your spiritual lives are important to both of you. In considering this, you might think back to activities you engaged in together in the past that you would like to restart or increase. Try to be bold and creative! Think of something that you haven't done before but might be worth a try. You can probably think of many reasons why you can't do it or why it will take too much effort. Do it anyway – broaden your world; try something new. Being adventurous as a couple can add excitement and energy to your lives.

Regardless of what particular activities you discuss doing together, an important guideline is that you make specific plans and follow through with them. Let's take Will and Elizabeth as an example.

Will and Elizabeth's story

Will has been depressed at various times in his life, but his symptoms became much worse when he lost his job last year. Elizabeth understood that he would feel better mentally and physically if he got out of his pyjamas and out of the house. He resisted her efforts towards this end because, as he said, 'I don't deserve pleasure time if I don't have a job.' With Elizabeth's urging, Will was able to experiment with leaving the house for a Saturday-night date with her as well as attending a weekly watercolour class, since his art had helped him relax in the past. Since starting both, he has remembered that he loves and is good at painting, and he has learned to look forward to his Saturday-night time with Elizabeth as a break from his job search. In addition, as he has become more active and his mood has improved, he has been able to put more energy and confidence into looking for work.

Table 47: Joint activities for couples

		Add your own activities
Taking a walk	Going to a concert	
Going to see a film or play	Attending a lecture	
Going out for dinner	Going to a sporting event	
Cycling	Having a picnic	
Playing golf or tennis	Hiking	
Playing board games or cards	Preparing a special meal	
Going bowling	Taking photographs	
Working on a joint hobby	Going dancing	
Taking a class	Jogging	
Going to a park	Sitting outside	
Having a barbecue	Staying overnight at a hotel	
Camping out	Listening to music	
Playing musical instruments	Going sailing	
Shopping	Going out for dessert	

Going to a museum	Going to the zoo	
Working on a household project	Visiting friends or relatives	
Studying the family genealogy	Making a photograph album	
Going bird watching or star gazing	Volunteering in the community	
Visiting the library	Reading together	
Going out for a drive	Having breakfast in bed	
Getting up to see the sunrise	Giving each other a massage	

Key messages

- Depression can drain your energy and lead to social isolation – this can be tough for your partner, both to witness and to experience.

- In addition to individual-level behavioural activation, couples can engage in it together through joint activity scheduling.

- Focus on increasing activities that are enjoyable, allow you to feel competent and are meaningful to you.

- Use your partner as a resource – they may have good ideas for activities you can try.

- Plan specific and feasible couple activities and make following through on them a priority.

Negative thoughts and the couple

When you are depressed, not only do you withdraw and engage in fewer rewarding activities, you also tend to think about and experience things in a negative way. You do not intentionally decide to do this; it happens automatically, which is why we refer to the thoughts as Negative Automatic Thoughts (NATs). These NATs might be focused upon you as an individual, other people including your partner and the world around you. Chapter 10 discusses how you might challenge these NATs as an individual. In addition, you are likely to express many of these NATs to your partner. For example, you might talk about how worthless and incompetent you are, how your partner does not love you, how the whole world is deteriorating and how things will never get better. This can pose a real challenge to your partner, because in many instances they will disagree with your perspective and recognize that you are being overly pessimistic. They will then have to decide how to respond to these NATs. At times, it might feel to them that whatever they say does not help and even leads to an argument. Here are some suggestions about how, as a couple, you might deal with these situations.

Our recommendation is really rather simple, although it can be difficult to follow. Basically, we suggest that you have a conversation in which you follow the guidelines discussed earlier in this chapter for sharing thoughts and feelings. This means that when the depressed person is expressing their negative thoughts and feelings, the role for the partner is to listen empathically, try to understand how difficult it is for the depressed person, and accept that this is what they are thinking and feeling. It is critical to restate that *acceptance* is not the same thing as *agreement*. The non-depressed partner does not have to agree with the negative perspective of the depressed person. However, we do believe that it can be extremely helpful for the depressed partner if they feel their emotions are understood. Therefore, the role of the non-depressed partner is not to argue about the depressed person's feelings. Arguing about whether they are right or wrong usually does not help; it only makes them believe that they are not understood. We rarely change our minds about something when someone tells us we are wrong and then explains to us how things really are.

However, non-depressed partners also deserve the opportunity to express their own thoughts and feelings. When doing this, they should not try to negate the other person's experience with 'Yes, but . . . ' Instead, when in the speaker role, the non-depressed partner needs to voice their own subjective thoughts and feelings about the situation *as their own perspective*. And the depressed person needs to accept these experiences as their partner's reality. Therefore, the two of you might have very different perspectives, and most likely the depressed person will view things in a more negative way. This is why we stress the importance of speaking for yourself in a subjective way, because then it is quite possible for both of you to understand and accept each other's experience even when it is quite different from your own.

Joanne and Ian, whom we briefly discussed earlier, might have a conversation like this:

Joanne: I just feel like such a failure as a mother. Emma misbehaves, and I don't know what to do. When I try to discipline her, she doesn't listen and looks at me like she just hates me. I had dreamed of these wonderful days at home with our sweet daughter, and instead it seems like a nightmare where I mess it up, and she's unhappy most of the time.

Ian: That sounds just miserable, that you feel like you don't know what to do with Emma, and she's unhappy as well. And it seems to you that she really dislikes you. That's not what you had planned and dreamed of, is it?

Joanne: No, not at all.

Ian: I really do understand what you are experiencing. I agree: I think Emma is hard to handle, and I often don't feel like what I do works either. From my perspective, though, you are a really good mother. I think you are very warm and loving towards her, but you are also willing to say no and set limits on what you will allow. I think that's great, even though she often fights it and gets angry when you do it. I'm sorry it is so hard on you, particularly when you're down, but I personally believe we're doing what we need to do to be good parents.

Key messages

- Hearing you repeatedly express Negative Automatic Thoughts can be difficult for your partner.

- Partners should attempt to understand and empathize with negative thoughts rather than only trying to challenge them.

- Understand that the two of you might see the world differently at this time, in terms of how negatively or positively you view things.

Your physical relationship

Not only does depression influence how you behave, think and feel, it affects you physically as well. One key consequence of depression for couples is that it reduces interest in sex. In addition, one of the unfortunate side effects of many antidepressant medications is that they also decrease your sex drive. Furthermore, if your relationship is generally unhappy, this is also likely to have an impact on your physical relationship. Therefore, it can be quite valuable for you as a couple to talk about the physical aspects of your relationship, so that you can be responsive to each other's needs and understand what you are both experiencing. We know that many couples, both satisfied and distressed, rarely talk about their physical and sexual relationship, and that is fine as long as things are going well. However, if either of you have concerns, then it is helpful to have conversations where you share your thoughts and feelings and make good decisions about how to deal with any issues.

It is worth differentiating between three different aspects of a physical relationship: comfort, affection and sex. Comfort involves reaching out and perhaps touching the other person when they are feeling down or distressed – a pat on the knee or a reassuring hand-squeeze or a hug. Affection is about trying to increase a sense of caring and closeness between the two of you, rather than about trying to reduce distress. You might engage in some of the same activities that you do when comforting your partner, but it will be for a different reason. For example, on a beautiful sunny day, you might take your partner's hand walking in the park just to feel good and close to them. Finally, your sexual relationship involves a most intimate and private way of relating to each other. All of this is not to say that comfort, affection and sex are separate from each other, but it might be worth discussing the three of them separately.

For example, it might be helpful to discuss whether either of you wants physical comfort when you are feeling down. When some people are depressed, they really value being touched and held by their partner, while others need space. It can be helpful to have these conversations so that both of you can understand what the other person needs and not feel rejected if they do not want physical comfort at a given time.

Finally, as we've said, many couples' sexual relationship becomes disrupted during depression. There is no single way to address a depressed person's lower sex drive, and it can be tricky for couples to know what to do. Earlier, we talked about the importance of pushing yourself in general when your motivation is low, making plans and following through with them even if you are not very motivated to do so. However, this can be counter-productive when it comes to sex because most people want to engage in sexual activity only if they are motivated and find the experience rewarding. So we are not recommending that you have sex when one or both of you really do not want to do so. However, you might discuss what you both want and need at this time and, perhaps, discuss small steps that you might take to increase potentially rewarding aspects of your physical relationship. Push yourselves to have conversations about this area and decide how you want to address it. Because this can be somewhat complicated, there are some self-help books listed in the Further Reading section (see page 551) which can assist you. Or you could discuss the problems with Relate (see page 552), the organization that helps couples in distress. Let's take the case of Liam and Margaret.

Liam and Margaret's story

Liam has found that he is really not interested in sex when he is feeling depressed. In order to show understanding and empathy for his situation, Margaret has not initiated sexual contact. She also has resisted sitting too close to Liam on the sofa and cuddling with him in bed because she does not want him to see these gestures as 'pressure to have sex'. However, instead of appreciating this show of empathy, Liam has started to believe that Margaret is no longer interested in him physically, which has made him feel worse about himself. If they were able to talk about it, they might be able to figure out how their physical relationship could work while Liam is depressed.

Key messages

- Depression can reduce sex drive, which can contribute to tension in your relationship.

- Many couples avoid talking about their sexual relationship, but it can be valuable to do so if things aren't going the way one or both of you would like.

- Three important areas to talk about in your physical relationship are: comfort (soothing touch), affection (positive physical closeness) and sex.

Addressing other issues related to depression

Above, we have addressed three specific areas that we know are frequently influenced by depression: a reduction in rewarding/meaningful activity, distorted and Negative Automatic Thoughts, and your physical relationship. In addition, depression can affect many other aspects of a depressed person's life. For example, you might have taken time off from work, which leads to financial complications that you need to address as a couple. You might also be withdrawing from friends and other family members, who do not understand what is happening. It is important that both of you think about how the depression is affecting you both, individually and as a couple. Then, speak to each other about your own thoughts and feelings in these areas, and about how you want to address them. In some cases, your decisions might mean one or both of you taking individual action with the support of the other person. At other times, your decisions might involve both of you working together to carry out a plan. Once you have developed the communication skills discussed earlier in this chapter, you can use them to address any specific issues that are relevant for the two of you.

Key messages

- When you are depressed, almost everything can seem extremely painful and difficult. However, neither you nor your depression exists in isolation. Your depression is affected by your relationship, and your relationship is affected by depression.

- Therefore, it can be extremely helpful to work together as a couple in approaching it. When your relationship is distressed, it can worsen the depression. If your relationship is already rewarding or can be improved, then it can serve as a major source of enjoyment and meaning, which can help to alleviate depression.

- When people are depressed they often feel quite alone. Our hope is that by building a strong relationship and working together, neither of you will feel alone during this process. Your relationship can serve as an invaluable resource for working on depression.

- By communicating effectively with each other, making good decisions, and carrying out those decisions, you can effectively build upon many of the techniques discussed in other chapters.

PART 4

Tackling different types of depression

Introduction

So far in this book we have looked at ways to understand depression that may be relevant to anyone who suffers from it. In Part 4 we move on to look at some special cases, where people have particular conditions that need additional understanding, and for which there are other helpful strategies and techniques. The first of these is bipolar depression, where people swing from depression to its 'polar' opposite, extreme elation and excitement. This requires very different ways of coping, and Warren Mansell and his colleagues describe an approach they find extremely helpful. We then go on to talk about postnatal depression: Lynne Murray and Peter Cooper describe useful ways of thinking about it and suggest techniques to make sure that babies aren't affected by it. Stirling Moorey and his colleagues discuss depression in physical illness, and finally Ken Laidlaw and Dichelle Wong address depression in old age.

21 Bipolar disorders and problematic mood swings

Warren Mansell, Phillip Brawn, Robert Griffiths,
Ben Silver and Sara Tai

Introduction

A lot of people can experience a depressed mood for a few days but do not develop what we call a 'clinical' episode of depression (see the description in Chapter 1 about diagnoses). Similarly, many people may experience a couple of days of feeling energetic, agitated and excitable in a way that is out of character for them but does not cause a big problem. However, some people experience very intense high or low moods for much longer periods, which can be distressing and make it difficult for them to carry on with their normal day-to-day routines. They may swing in mood from high to low very quickly, which can feel unpredictable and overwhelming. We use the term *bipolar disorder* to describe this.

People with bipolar disorder may feel elated and excited, but also feel extremely irritable and agitated. These moods can last for several days, during which the person might sleep very little, have racing thoughts, be hard to interrupt, and do impulsive things that they later regret (such as spending money, starting arguments). These high moods are called *hypomania*.

Mania is similar to hypomania; the main difference is that the symptoms of mania last longer and are extreme enough to impair home or work life, safety or wellbeing. During mania, many people take great financial risks, or extreme risks with their physical safety, or get into fights that bring them into contact with the police. They may become sexually disinhibited and do things that they later regret. Some symptoms of mania might include *psychosis*, and the need to be admitted to a psychiatric hospital. Psychosis is a term used to describe unusual experiences, such as beliefs that other people would find completely unrelated to reality – for example, the idea that you rule the world, or are being spied on by MI5. When people are psychotic they might also have hallucinations – seeing or hearing things that other people cannot.

When a person has experienced both mania/hypomania and depression, this is called *bipolar I disorder* (what used to be referred to as 'manic depression'). You might have heard of different types of bipolar disorders – including *cyclothymia* and *bipolar II disorder*. These are very similar because they also involve significant mood swings, but they are less extreme than bipolar I disorder. Often, the problems that people experience go unrecognized, because they are not so different from normal mood swings. Regardless of whether you have a diagnosis or not, if you are experiencing mood swings that are distressing to you or those around you, you can use the techniques in this chapter to understand and manage them better.

Typical symptoms of bipolar disorders

- Periods of clinical depression (see Chapter 1)

- Periods (over several days at a time) of being in an elated or irritable mood to the extent that you are not your 'normal' self, and you experience:

    ◊ Racing thoughts

    ◊ Talking so fast that other people find it hard to interrupt

    ◊ Being so easily distracted by your own thoughts or things around you that you find it hard to stay focused on anything

    ◊ Not needing to sleep more than a few hours per night over several days

◊   Doing pleasurable things that are risky or might cause future harm such as getting into arguments or fights, spending money you don't have or being sexually active with many partners

Note that people without a diagnosis of bipolar disorder also report some of these experiences, but they do not cause as much disruption to their lives.

This chapter is for anyone who has suffered severe depression and who also experiences periods of highs or irritation that last more than a couple of days, regardless of whether you have received a diagnosis of bipolar disorder or not. The information and exercises described here should help you to manage your moods more effectively and help you on the road to recovery, so that you can regain control of your life.

The TEAMS (Think Effectively About Mood Swings) approach

This chapter is based on an approach that has been tried and tested in a number of research studies involving people who experience mood swings, and has been found to be effective in treating them. It is called TEAMS – Think Effectively About Mood Swings – and is largely based on cognitive behavioural therapy. TEAMS was developed by therapists and researchers who have worked with a great number of people diagnosed with bipolar disorders. Over the years, we have continued to improve the therapy by listening to feedback from those who have received it. We have spoken to people who have recovered from bipolar disorder to find out what helped them, and to people who continue to experience major mood swings on occasion but still manage to live their lives in the way they want. It is also possible to use techniques in this approach through self-help.

For the purposes of this chapter, we will use the terms 'emotions', 'moods' and 'feelings' to mean the same thing, even though some people suggest they are different. In the TEAMS approach, we start from the belief that we can all learn to think about and use our feelings in ways that are more productive to us and increase our chances of achieving what is important to us. As with all aspects of CBT, we believe that it is our thoughts about what is happening to us that are crucially important, and this is true of thoughts about feelings too. Although our feelings can often affect us, it is what we think these feelings mean (how we make sense of them), and how, in turn, we respond to them that determines whether we manage to help ourselves in a particular situation. Sometimes, without intending it, we respond in ways that create more problems for ourselves! For example, feelings of anger (within a certain range) can be perfectly normal, and may actually be helpful in motivating us to change something we are not happy with. However, if we think of anger as a purely bad or even dangerous feeling, we may criticize ourselves or try to suppress our anger, which could then have negative consequences for us.

An underlying principle of the TEAMS approach is that we *all* experience moods; at every moment, we are *always* in one mood or another. Moods are not necessarily a negative thing or something that only happens to people who have 'mood problems' – they are a human thing. Moods always change, and for a lot of the time we do not pay attention to what mood we are in. However, for some people, moods can be distressing and extreme enough to cause problems in their life. Moods sometimes seem to make no sense, and sometimes they seem to be uncontrollable. Hopefully this chapter will help to encourage a better understanding of them. Using some of the key aspects of the TEAMS approach we hope that by the end of this chapter you will:

1. be able to name and describe a number of mood states.

2. see the importance of thinking about your most important goals and values in life.

3. consider that there are both good *and* bad things about each mood you experience.

4. notice that your feelings do change in how intense they are from day to day.

5. be better at describing the different states of mind that you experience.

6. be able to find enough space around moods to take a moment to reflect or contemplate moods and feelings in context with your goals and how you want to be in the world.

7. find a 'healthy self' that helps you to pursue what you really want in life, despite the moods that come and go in the process.

Learning any new skills, such as those described in this chapter, can feel difficult at first. Many of us give ourselves a hard time when we are struggling to learn something new, and this can make the process feel even harder. It is important to take your time with this chapter and to be patient with yourself as you try out the various techniques, because they will take some practice. Try not to criticize yourself if it doesn't come to you straight away. Don't give up if you don't start to feel better immediately. Please keep trying, because we know that this approach has helped many people.

Jamie's story

When I was diagnosed with bipolar disorder I was both disheartened and relieved at the same time. I was afraid of more mood swings coming out of the blue, worried about what other people might do to me in this vulnerable state, and terrified of getting confined to a psychiatric hospital for the rest of my life. I also hoped that I could now get the right treatment or perhaps even a miracle cure that would fix everything. Although the miracle cure didn't appear, when I started psychological therapy it opened up ways of thinking about my difficulties that hadn't occurred to me before.

I finally had a better understanding of myself, about the things that trigger symptoms and what makes them reoccur. My therapist and I went over recent events, and those further back in my past, which helped to make sense of why I was experiencing mood swings. We then looked at the connections between the way I was thinking about my moods and how I behaved when they changed. Once I had a better understanding of the connections between my feelings, thoughts and behaviour, I was able to experiment with different ways of responding to changes in my moods.

For example, sometimes I would feel isolated from others, which would make me think nobody could understand the experience I was having. With my therapist, I spent some time exploring what it was like to have this feeling of isolation. I found that I could tell when I felt isolated because I felt cut off from other people, my thoughts would start to go really fast, I would get a 'cloudy' feeling in my head, I would make quick decisions and my actions felt very speeded up.

I also found that I thought about this isolated feeling in two different ways. Sometimes I would believe I was superior to others because they could not understand what I was experiencing, which made me think I was somehow more advanced in my thinking. However, at other times the isolated feeling made me believe I was inferior and I worried that people might pity me because of how I viewed the world.

When I felt I was superior, I would cut myself off emotionally from people who were important to me. At the same time, I would be much more sociable, go to parties, and do other things that I normally wouldn't do. I would say to myself, 'Keep on going.' I would also seek out people who would confirm the beliefs I had about myself at this time, which would increase the feeling of being different and superior. Eventually, however, I would become exhausted and just couldn't keep on going. Once this happened, the way I thought about this feeling of isolation would change.

When I was exhausted, I would take the isolated feeling to mean that I was inferior to others. I thought that I needed help, but I was too afraid to ask for it because I was worried that people would feel sorry for me. I didn't like the idea of anyone feeling pity for me. So I stayed away from people, shut myself off by staying in bed and avoided answering calls. I would also spend a lot of time thinking about the way I had behaved when I'd been feeling superior. This made me feel embarrassed and I would tend to be overly critical of myself for the things I'd done.

Having therapy helped me to understand this feeling more. I was able to look at my isolated feeling from other angles. I tried to teach myself to let thoughts be in my mind, but not be distressed or act on them in what I now think of as irrational ways. It took a long time for these changes to happen. At times I feared that it may not work at all. However, the more I carried on looking at experiences such as the isolated feeling from other perspectives, the easier it became. It was a bit like doing exercise; the more you do it, the easier it gets.

As obvious as it seems to me now, I realized that other factors were contributing to the intensity of this feeling: trying to block it out with drink and drugs, or intentionally cutting myself off from people who (in hindsight) would've given anything to help me.

Now when these mood changes happen, I can notice patterns and signs before they really come on strongly, and I can change my behaviour so I have more control over them. I have learned that it is helpful to talk to people I trust about how I am feeling, and I try not to be so critical of myself.

Key messages

- Mood swings are very common and they affect people's lives in different ways. Sometimes they are severe enough to be given a diagnosis of bipolar disorder. However, whether the mood swings are mild or severe, people can learn to manage their lives better despite them.

Tips for supporters

- It is possible to spend a lot of time debating whether or not someone fits a diagnosis of bipolar disorder. However, in terms of self-help, if they experience problematic mood swings, including 'highs' or irritability, then the strategies set out in this chapter are likely to be a helpful start to making a recovery.

- Try to help the person you are supporting to think about whether the mood swings are problematic for them, and what they would like to change.

- If you have seen them suffer from very extreme moods, it may be sensible to suggest going to their family doctor to discuss whether they need some professional help.

- Reassure them that this will *not* mean going into hospital for life!

1. Naming and describing moods and feelings

Some feelings are easier to spot than others, and when we do spot them we might do nothing more than give them a name. As with other forms of CBT, this approach is about getting a better understanding of what is happening when we experience a particular feeling or mood.

People describe their moods and mood swings in different ways. Some use words like sad, happy, anxious or angry, but there are many other ways to name and describe them. For example, some people find using colour ('black and murky'), and metaphor ('on top of the world') an easier way to describe how they are feeling. Naming a mood is the first step to understanding it. There is no right or wrong name for a mood; it is whatever it means to you.

We have found that being aware of the different moods we have, or at least the ones we have most often, is really useful for understanding how we control or cope with them. If we can better understand the things that lead to certain mood states it takes away their unpredictability. Figure 48 shows how we can understand one example, by breaking it down into parts to create a more detailed picture of what makes up this mood.

Figure 48: Looking at the feeling 'excited' in more detail

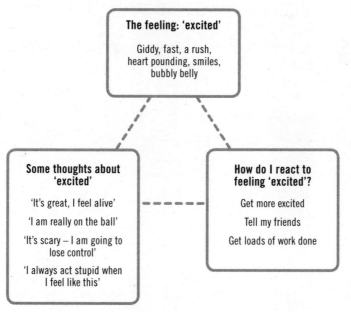

The feeling: 'excited'

Giddy, fast, a rush, heart pounding, smiles, bubbly belly

Some thoughts about 'excited'

'It's great, I feel alive'

'I am really on the ball'

'It's scary – I am going to lose control'

'I always act stupid when I feel like this'

How do I react to feeling 'excited'?

Get more excited

Tell my friends

Get loads of work done

In this case we have named the mood 'excited'. But as well as naming it, we want to think about how a person might experience excitement physically (in the head or body), and what thoughts and behaviours come with it. Try asking yourself the question, 'How do I know when I am excited? What does my body do? What clues are there in the way I am behaving or thinking that tell me that this is how I am feeling?'

Naming and exploring moods can help us to understand what certain feelings mean to us. Doing so develops our awareness of a mood when it is actually happening, so we can more quickly weigh up how we feel and work out how this is helping or getting in the way of moving towards our goals. It can help provide the information we need to work out how best to respond.

Exercise: name and describe a mood state

The aim of this exercise is to help you identify some of the key characteristics of a particular mood. Write the answers out under the questions below. Fill in what you can, and don't worry if you can't complete it all. If you are able to describe this mood, we will be able to use it in the exercise further on in this chapter.

If you are having difficulty thinking of a mood, try thinking about how you are feeling right now, at this very moment as you read this.

Worksheet 13: Name and describe a mood state

1. What do you call this feeling or mood (e.g. angry, high, low, happy)?
2. Describe your mood in as much detail as you can (e.g. its colour or smell, any links to memories, locations or events).
3. What feelings do you get in your body when in this mood (e.g. pain in the head, dry mouth, changes in breathing)?
4. What images come to mind when you think about this mood (e.g. past events or interactions, successes or failures)?
5. How do you explain this mood to others (e.g. use of metaphors like 'black hole', 'stuck in a rut')?
6. What do you feel like doing when you are in this mood (e.g. stay in, do more work, sleep more)?

Key messages

- We all experience a wide variety of moods and feelings.

- Naming and describing mood states helps us have a better understanding of how we think about them.

- We might have certain patterns of physical experiences, thoughts and behaviours/responses with particular mood states. These patterns of thoughts and behaviours could maintain or change that mood state.

Tips for supporters

- Encouraging someone to think about what mood they are in, right at that very moment, can help them identify a mood state they had previously not noticed.

- Sometimes just talking about a mood state might make the feeling or mood appear – it can come online. If you ask about mood, regularly check in with the person that they are OK talking about it and give the person choice about how much they want to say.

- Identify and explore some of your own mood states. Are there similarities with any of the moods that the person you are supporting has?

When to move onto the next section

There are no fixed rules about how quickly you should progress through the different sections of this chapter. People will work through it at different speeds. The key thing is that you work at a pace that feels comfortable for you, allowing yourself time to get the most out of the various exercises. Here are some suggestions to help you decide when to move onto the next section.

- You have had time to practise recognizing and exploring a number of different moods using the tools in this section.

- You are starting to feel more confident at noticing some of the thoughts and feelings that accompany different moods.

- You have started to notice how you react to different moods.

2. Setting life goals

We all have a number of different ways to manage our lives. We might try to avoid certain emotions, such as feeling sad. We can set short-term goals, like 'get all my work done by the end of the day'. We can also set rules for ourselves such as 'I should never make mistakes'. We refer to these as goals, and different goals will vary in how long they may take to achieve and how helpful they might be. Yet, if we really want to move our lives in the right direction, we need to think about what our long-term goals are.

Identifying long-term goals can be difficult. Sometimes it might help to reflect on what is important to us and what we really value. This could be what we value in our relationships with others, the activities we choose to invest in, and the direction in which we want our lives to travel. One way to think about these long-term goals, or values, is as the settings on a compass. Following a compass setting does not take us to a specific destination, but it can guide us in the right direction. Similarly, we can value things that may never even be reachable, but will nevertheless guide us in a direction that makes it more likely that we live a meaningful life, closer to the way we want it to be. For example, a person may value 'being a good parent' and work towards that goal throughout their life. This goal is unlikely to have a specific end point, but there is certainly a sense of what is important.

There may be specific short-term goals we can set ourselves that will help us live according to the values we want. For example, taking your child swimming at the weekend (even if sleeping late often seems much more appealing) might be a short-term goal that you could set for yourself in order to work towards being a good parent. When planning short-term goals, it is useful to think about whether they fit with your longer-term goals and values, such as how you would like your life to be, and your relationships with the people around you.

It is not always straightforward to know what you really, really want out of life, but the questions below can help you start to think about the short-term and long-term goals you might want to set yourself.

- What do I hope to get out of this self-help book?

- What makes reading this important to me?

- What kind of life would I like if the self-help is successful?

- How would I actually know that I am making progress?

- What do I want in the long term?

- How would I like my life to be?

You may find that these questions are all you need to generate your life goals. If not, it is okay to start to think of shorter-term goals in the here-and-now that would make a difference to you, and build from there. Worksheet 14 below is designed to help you think about your goals in more detail. Don't feel that you have to complete every row, just complete as many as you can when prompted by the questions. Make a copy of the table so that you can complete it as many times as you wish. It may be worth getting a notebook for this purpose, paper or electronic, so that you can keep a record and refer back to it in the future. We will return to these life goals later in this chapter.

Worksheet 14: Generating your life goals

Arena	Questions	Your life goals
Short term	How will you know that doing this self-help guide is making a difference?	I will notice that I am . . . *. . . feeling like I have more control over my moods*
Myself	How do you want to see yourself in the future?	I want to . . . *. . . be creative, productive and less critical of myself*
My relationships with family, friends and partners	How would you like your relationships to be in the future?	I want to . . . *. . . have positive relationships with my family where we respect our differences of opinion.*
Other goals	Any other goals you have in the long run that are important to you?	I want to . . . *. . . work in a job that I find meaningful and enjoyable*

Key messages

- Spending time thinking about what really matters to you in the long term can help you use this self-help chapter more constructively.

Tips for supporters

- Sometimes it is tempting to use the first answer someone comes up with – for example 'to cope better'. But the questions need to go further. For example, if the person you are supporting says, 'I want to cope better', you could ask, 'What would be different for you if you could cope better?' This may reveal deeper goals, such as 'to get on better with my family' or 'to manage to keep my job'. Other examples of questions you could ask are 'What makes this important for you?' and 'What would you be doing differently if you were coping better?' In this way, the goals will eventually become more detailed and in the end be more relevant to the everyday life of the person you are supporting.

When to move onto the next section

Here are some suggestions to help you decide when to move on to the next section.

- You have had a chance to think about the differences between short-term and long-term goals.

- You have had time to reflect on what is really important in your life.

- You have generated a number of different life goals using the table provided.

3. The pros and cons of different feelings

Our feelings can sometimes help us to achieve our life goals, but at other times they might block us from doing so. In this section, we will help you to identify the feelings you are experiencing and the different ways in which they can be helpful and problematic. It is often tempting to think about moods as extremes – low moods versus highs, and slowed-down feelings versus sped-up and activated feelings. Similarly, there are 'negative feelings' such as fear, sadness, anger, shame and guilt, which we can separate from 'positive feelings' such as happiness, joy, excitement and comfort. However, even though negative feelings can be unpleasant, they usually have a *purpose*.

Fear helps us to be prepared for a threat, and anger alerts us to situations of injustice around us. But if we are too frightened, then we are unable to face our fears at all. If we are too angry, then we can go off the rails without being able to tackle the injustice itself. So these emotions have both pros and cons to them. It is the same with positive emotions. Feeling happy and excited can make us energized and optimistic about achieving our goals, but if you are too excited then you may not be able to concentrate well enough to get anything done.

We might also have positive and negative ideas about our emotions. For example, we might think that it is 'bad' to feel angry or 'weak' to feel sad. We might think that we 'ought' to feel happy. If you have trouble with mood swings then these ideas can be particularly strong. If you feel happy, for instance, you might think 'Oh no, I am going high again – it'll be disastrous.' If you feel sad you might start to panic and think 'Oh no, the depression is starting again – I won't be able to stand it.' These ideas about your emotions can make it much harder to cope with them.

Jamie's experience of anger

When I was depressed I felt that my anger was kind of suppressed because I was pushing away all kinds of negative feelings. Through therapy I began to understand that these feelings can also be helpful in dealing with a difficult time or event and it changed how I viewed anger. I realized, for example, that if somebody shouts at you it will eventually make you angry – that is normal. But an appropriate amount of anger is very natural and does not have to get out of hand; it doesn't have to lead to a low or depressed state of mind. There have been situations where I have been able to use my anger in a productive way to stand up for myself. Now I see it as being like a burglar alarm – it goes off to let me know that something isn't the way I want it to be. For example, if someone is being abusive, but you don't do anything about it, the abuse will just carry on. Getting angry doesn't mean being violent or abusive back, but it is a warning sign that I might need to do something; it tells me I need to find a way of letting the other person know that I'm unhappy with how they are treating me.

Why weigh up the pros and cons of moods and feelings?

The exercise that follows can help you to look under the surface of what a feeling means to you, in order to understand why you might respond in certain ways. For example, Beth realized that she had tried to suppress her anger all her life because she did not want to end up being a critical person like her mother. However, in doing so, she had not stood up for herself at work, or in her relationships. When she looked under the surface of what anger meant to her, she concluded that her high moods might have been a way of trying to stand up for herself without getting angry. Another reader found that she was worrying so much that her feelings of happiness signalled another episode of mania that she would feel worse when good things happened to her. She learned to notice the difference between normal feelings of happiness, which did not signal an episode, and the feelings of increasingly agitated excitement that did cause her more difficulties.

Worksheet 15 below is designed to help you to notice the range of feelings you experience, and to identify the beliefs you hold about them, which might be positive or negative. Look at the worksheet below (or make a copy in your notebook) and fill in each of the columns. You can see Jamie's example afterwards in Table 49. The aim of this exercise is to help you to start considering the negative and positive beliefs you have about different emotions. They don't have to be equal – it might be that the negative beliefs you hold about feeling sad, for example, outweigh the positives at the moment. Nevertheless, seeing both sides may give you a little more choice about how you manage these emotions – for example, they may be okay if they are quite mild but less okay when they are extreme. In the next section, we will see how thinking about emotions on a sliding scale can be helpful.

Worksheet 15: Considering the pros and cons of different emotions

Feeling	Pros	Cons
Can you think of a time when you have had each of these experiences below? Try to imagine the feeling. Where is it in your head or body?	What can be achieved with this feeling? Does it tell you anything useful if you feel this? Try to think of at least one advantage for each feeling.	What are the problems with this feeling? What are your worst fears about too much of this feeling? Try to think of at least one problem for each feeling.
Angry		
Excited		
Afraid		
Sad		
Happy		

Guilty		
Agitated		
Relaxed		
Fast thinking		
Slow thinking		
Very active		
Doing nothing		

Table 49: Part of Jamie's completed worksheet

Feeling	Pros	Cons
Can you think of a time when you have had each of these experiences below? Try to imagine the feeling. Where is it in your head or body?	What can be achieved with this feeling? Does it tell you anything useful if you feel this? Try to think of at least one advantage for each feeling.	What are the problems with this feeling? What are your worst fears about too much of this feeling? Try to think of at least one problem for each feeling.
Angry: I feel this in my head, hands, and arms. I notice a 'hotness' in my head and a trembling feeling in my arms and hands.	A controlled, appropriate amount of anger helps me stand up for myself when I feel like other people are being disrespectful or abusive.	It feels dangerous to have too much of this feeling. I might become abusive towards other people. Maybe I will say or do something I regret later on.
Excited: I notice my heart going fast, my thoughts are racing, and I get an 'electrified' feeling in my chest.	This is a fun feeling that I really like. I'm able to do more things, I feel more confident, and I can take on lots of projects and be more creative.	If it goes too far, I take more risks and do things that I regret later, like drinking lots or spending too much money. It also means I neglect important relationships.

Key messages

- Emotions are not only normal but can often be useful to us. Yet, in some situations, depending on the intensity of the emotion, they can be unhelpful because they make us feel out of control or overwhelmed. It can help to understand the negatives and positives of different emotions if we are to manage the ups and downs of everyday life better.

Tips for supporters

- Weighing up the pros and cons of moods and feelings can help people consider how they perceive things and challenge ideas about what is a helpful or unhelpful mood. It is surprising how many positives one can generate about low moods and negatives about high moods, given a chance!

- We have also found that people use pros and cons to weigh up other things in their lives besides moods, such as their views about their medication, or practical decisions like where to live.

- Using these ideas, help the person you are supporting to think of their own ideas about pros and cons. Sometimes it can be hard for people to think in a new way about problems with their mood, so if they don't come up with suggestions try out a few of your own and see what they think.

When to move onto the next section

Here are some suggestions to help you decide when to move on to the next section.

- You have had a go at weighing up the pros and cons of several different moods using the table provided.

- You have had time to reflect on what the process of weighing up different moods felt like.

- You have had a chance to think about how different moods might be relevant to some of the important life goals you have.

4. Thinking about our emotions on a sliding scale

When we think about the negatives and positives of different emotions, we can consider how intense a particular emotion is, or how long it lasts. If we just see an emotion as either 'on' or 'off' then we are faced with a basic choice of either continuing to have it, or trying to get rid of it. When the emotion is unpleasant, our tendency is to want to get rid of it. However, if we instead think of emotions as being on a sliding scale, rather like a volume control from 'very mild' at 1 out of 100, to 'extreme' at 100 out of 100, then we have some other choices. We may find that we can endure a certain level of the emotion.

One reason why it is useful to think about our emotions as being on a sliding scale is that it is very hard to get rid of an emotion completely, and the harder we try, the greater the impact on other parts of our lives. For example, someone who feels anxious around other people may avoid every kind of situation that might involve being around others because they think it will make them anxious. This makes them increasingly isolated. They also don't find out that they can manage to see certain people close to them without the anxiety being overwhelming. Some people use alcohol, drugs or medication to try to numb or get rid of their feelings, and this can make things worse, too.

Another reason to think about emotions being on a sliding scale is that there are usually advantages to having some level of a particular feeling. For example, feeling a little excited might give you the motivation you need to get up in the morning and see people. It might only be extreme levels of excitement that you need to be concerned about, especially if they don't go down. Similarly, some level of fear keeps us alert to real dangers in the world; only extreme levels compromise our ability to think logically. By thinking about emotions in this way, you can learn to experience the range of different feelings that you need in your life.

Jamie's experience of the sliding scale

The sliding-scale exercise helped me enormously. It made me feel more positive about my emotions instead of thinking they were purely negative. I used to worry about feeling excited because I thought it was a sign that I was getting ill again. I tried to avoid situations that could make me excited and this would make me panicky and anxious. The sliding scale helped me understand that excitement is still very important in life and that it is not a bad thing to experience to some degree. I don't want to switch the feelings off completely! For example, if I'm playing a gig, feeling excited can really help me get into the right frame of mind and perform better. I might even do things to help the excited feeling get stronger, like socialize with friends beforehand. Noticing where I am on the scale means that I can adjust what I am doing to give me more control over this feeling. If I feel like I'm getting too excited, I can go somewhere quiet or do something less stimulating to turn the feeling down.

Sliding-scale exercise

This exercise (Worksheet 16 below) is designed to help you identify your current experience of a particular mood and see if you can notice how much it varies in intensity. This may enable you to notice it better in future and to work out the level of this mood that is okay for you. First we need to identify a feeling – you could use one that you described earlier in Worksheet 13 or go through that process again and think about how you are feeling right now.

As a rule it is best to generate the two extremes on the sliding scale first – so, once you have located that mood or feeling and described it a little bit, ask yourself, 'Can you imagine how life would be with none of this feeling at all at 0?' and then 'Can you imagine this feeling at its most extreme – at 100?' Then, circle the number that represents how intensely you are feeling it right now.

Worksheet 16: Sliding–scale exercise

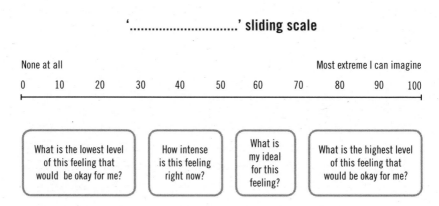

After you have done that, ask yourself the following questions and circle the numbers that match your answers:

- What is the lowest intensity of this feeling that is okay for me?

- What is the highest intensity of this feeling that is okay for me?

- What is my preferred or ideal level of intensity for this feeling?

Then ask yourself again . . .

- How intense is that feeling for me right now?

- Has it changed or stayed the same?

Try revisiting this as you work through this chapter, or even later today or tomorrow. See what happens to the level of intensity of that feeling.

The great thing about this exercise is that it helps us to see that moods are not something we should try to just turn on or off in a rigid way. Moods can change slowly without us seeming to notice, as well as changing suddenly. When you first do this exercise, you might find that there is quite a narrow range of what feels okay to begin with. The aim is not to try to face the extremes, but to really think about the variation in how intense any feeling can be. This is the main way in which we can experiment with moods and encourage you to develop a wider range of moods with different intensities that are acceptable to you.

Once you get used to the idea of putting moods on a scale, you realize that any felt sense, mood or feeling can go on there – tiredness, sadness, contentment, anxiety and pain, just to name a few.

Here are some examples of people using the sliding scale. Jess feels guilty a lot of the time when she is depressed (a very common symptom in severe depression) and when she is high has a lot of problems with her thoughts racing. She used the sliding scale to try to help herself.

Figure 50: Jess's 'guilty' sliding scale

'Guilty' sliding scale

None at all								Most extreme I can imagine	
0	10	20	30	40	50	60	70	80	90	100

5 — What is the lowest level of this feeling that would be okay for me?

20 — What is my ideal for this feeling?

50 — What is the highest level of this feeling that would be okay for me?

70 — How intense is this feeling right now?

Jess's brief summary about why she selected those places on the scale: 'I am feeling guilty at the moment, but it is not the most I could imagine, or have felt in the past. I don't want to feel this guilty – maybe I could manage a fifty. I do recognize that some guilt is useful some of the time – it tells me that I have done something that might have upset someone I love, and I can make sure I don't do it again. I do need to feel some guilt at the moment, so maybe twenty is about right, not five.'

Figure 51: Jess's 'fast thinking' sliding scale

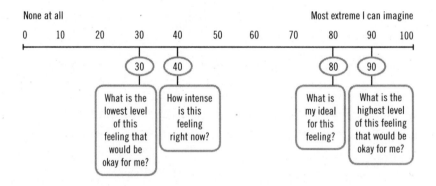

Jess's brief summary about why she selected those places on the scale: 'When I think fast, I can get so much more done and stave off the depression, so my ideal is an eighty. Because I am only on a forty right now I am feeling frustrated and a bit low. But forty is manage-able. Thirty would be getting too slow, like being depressed. I have put ninety not one hundred as the highest, as I know that I can get too fast – there is a limit. The problem is that an eighty can become a ninety just like that.'

At the end of this book there are more spaces where you can complete a sliding scale about different moods or feelings you are experiencing. Remember to describe the feeling first. Using the questions from earlier, put it on the scale and work out the different intensities that are okay or difficult for you to cope with.

Key messages

- Moods are not simply there or not there. They can vary in intensity.

- It is helpful to think of moods as being on a sliding scale – we can experience very extreme forms of any emotion, but we can also experience it to a much less intense degree.

- We may often only be aware of the extremes, but we can learn to notice when we experience much lower intensities of emotion.

- This can make emotions more acceptable to us so that we don't react badly to the idea of them.

- It can also help us to make the best use of our emotions, for example by speaking out when we are angry.

- We find that as people start to accept a wider range of moods, they become better at dealing with them and at managing their life as a whole.

Tips for supporters

- It can be particularly useful to remind a person about times when they were experiencing emotions that they are finding difficult to remember at the moment. As a supporter, you can also ask questions about the subtle differences between the different levels on the scale, as it may help them become more aware of their broad range of moods.

When to move onto the next section

As you have now completed a few sections of this chapter, you are probably developing your own sense of when to move onto the next section, but here are some suggestions to help you make this decision.

- You are starting to feel confident about noticing different intensities of moods.

- You have used the sliding scale to notice how intense your moods are right now.

- You have also used the sliding scale to measure the highest and lowest levels of certain moods you would like.

- You have begun to think about your ideal level of different moods.

5. Thinking about yourself on a sliding scale: different 'self-states'

We rarely get just one feeling by itself. We usually have a number of different emotions that come together – a mixed mood. We will call this a 'self-state'. For example, depression often involves feelings of tiredness, guilt, worthlessness and slowed thinking. High moods frequently involve feelings of excitement, confidence, rapid thinking and being very active, but can also include irritability, agitation, panic, worry and anger. This whole collection of feelings, thoughts, physical signs and behaviour makes up your self-states. Unlike moods, a self-state can last for days rather than a few minutes. The particular mix of feelings and emotions in a certain self-state will be different for everyone but they make up who you are at a particular time. For instance, Jamie sometimes thought of himself as a very dull and boring person. The spider diagram below shows his self-state for when he felt like that. Jamie called it 'dull me' and was able to list a range of feelings, thoughts and behaviours that were involved. These included: feeling numb, feeling calm, feeling sluggish, not feeling quite real, waiting for something to happen and thinking he was the same as everyone else. Using the sliding scale, Jamie also rated how much he was feeling the self-state of 'dull me' at that moment – 45 out of 100.

Figure 52: Jamie's self–state 'dull me'

It can be beneficial to think about your different self-states, and to produce a sliding scale of these in the same way that you did with your emotions. This time the sliding scale looks at the whole experience of being 'high' or 'low', so the extremes are the highest and lowest 'self-state' you have ever been in. Try to identify at least three of your own self-states. Figure 53 below shows some more of Jamie's different self-states, from quite low to very high.

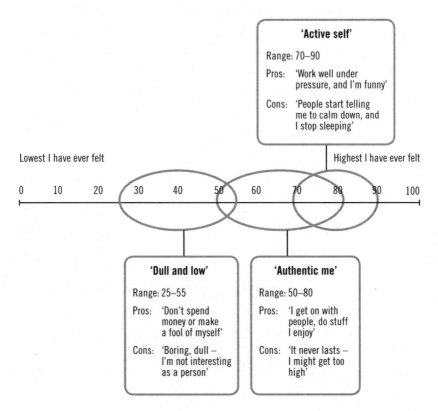

Figure 53: An example of Jamie's self-states shown using the sliding scale

When you are marking the intensity of your 'self-state' on the sliding scale, it may help to step back and try to view the different self-states you have – they all make up who you are. In this exercise, try to recognize as many different states you experience in your everyday life as you can, and reflect on why you seem to be in them in some situations and not in others. You might find that some situations are more related to your important life goals and that is why they affect your self-state more. We have asked you to identify at least three self-states; however, try to use your notebook to identify even more.

You can also think about the advantages and disadvantages of different self-states, just like we did with your feelings. From this you can then start to make choices – maybe being your 'active self' for a few days is a way to manage tough times at work, so it's okay in small bursts. Maybe being 'worried and upset' is okay now because you have just split up with your partner and you can't expect to feel good right now – but you can manage this situation without returning to your 'depressed self'.

It is often easier to notice the self-states that exist at the extreme ends of the sliding scale than those that appear in between. This exercise is a useful way of identifying the range of different ones that exist along the scale. Recognizing that there are self-states that exist between the extremes has been very helpful to many people.

Finally, although you might only experience some of your self-states for a short while, by doing this exercise every week you may be able to notice them more often when they do occur. Becoming aware of your different self-states might help you to notice ones that you'd like to experience more in your life.

Below is a blank scale, which you can use to plot your own self-states, their location on the scale and the pros and cons of each self-state. There are more at the back of this book.

Worksheet 17: Examining self–states

Self-states

Lowest I have ever felt
Highest I have ever felt

| 0 | 10 | 20 | 30 | 40 | 50 | 60 | 70 | 80 | 90 | 100 |

Key messages

- Noticing and describing different self-states helps us to see our moods with more colour and depth. This can enable us to work towards making things more as we want them to be, and to understand our moods in relation to our goals.

Tips for supporters

- It is important to help people describe not only their most obvious extremes of self-states, but also the ones in between that they might not otherwise notice, even if they appear only very briefly.

When to move onto the next section

Here are some suggestions to help you decide when to move on to the next section.

- You have described several different self-states in detail.
- You have mapped where these different self-states occur on a sliding scale that goes from 'lowest I have ever felt' to 'highest I have ever felt'.

6. Finding time for contemplation

Many people have described how a really useful part of therapy is having the opportunity to take a step back and look at themselves – what they are doing, feeling and thinking. The exercises in this chapter are designed to help you to do that, and to become more aware of the different sides of yourself (your different 'self-states').

As you do this, you may find that you start to develop a different mindset in which you can see the bigger picture, shift your awareness, change your perspective, or observe things more carefully. You may find that you are able to weigh things up and consider them more easily in this mindset. On the one hand, being very immersed in our feelings means that they can be hard to manage and control; however, on the other hand, being too distant and cut off from them may mean that they are suppressed or that we do not give ourselves the opportunity to understand them. Instead, it is better to be able to 'hold them in mind', not too close and not too far – just the right distance to maintain an objective perspective on them.

This 'observing' mindset is very different from another mindset that is much more familiar to us – the 'autopilot' mindset, which Chapter 17 discussed. Most of us can think of times when we have been on autopilot. How many times have you driven a car and then suddenly arrived at your destination with no recollection of how you got there? Where was your mind all this time? Because our minds are so clever at thinking about past events or things that might happen in the future, it is easy to become lost in our thoughts and disconnected with what is happening *right now*. This ability of our minds – to throw themselves back into the past or forward into the future – can be a mixed blessing. Whilst it means we can reflect on and learn from our experiences, and plan for the future, it also means that we can get caught in a cycle of ruminating about difficult past experiences and worrying about future events that might not even happen. Sometimes it is useful to step back from this constant stream of thoughts and notice what is happening right now instead. Stepping back from memories doesn't mean that they will happen again – instead, it gives you the chance to reflect on what happened in the past, so that you might deal with things differently when they happen now.

Jamie's tips for an observing mindset

When I'm trying to cultivate an observing mindset, I imagine my mind sitting at a bus stop and watching cars go past (the cars being my emotions and thoughts). I feel that I'm able to observe these cars from a distance without being fearful of them. I can watch them without getting involved with them in any way. Contemplating my thoughts like this allows me to work through them calmly. In the past, I often tried to block out difficult thoughts and feelings, or I would criticize myself for having them. Just allowing the thoughts to be there gives me some space to decide how I want to respond. Before, I would use things like drinking to get away from these thoughts and feelings. Now I have healthier ways of dealing with them. I might speak to someone I trust about my worries or do other things to look after myself, like getting an early night.

You may or may not have had an observing mindset before reading this chapter. If you haven't, don't worry: it is normal to need a bit of practice before being able to cultivate one easily. As you start to work through the exercises it might start to emerge. If you have experienced an observing mindset, either as you read this chapter or in the past, think about when this mindset is most useful for you, and what you could do to bring it about when you need it. We don't tend to automatically be in an observing mindset; we tend to be immersed in whatever we are doing, or worrying about the future or the past. So the challenge is to find a way of switching into it sometimes, to provide space for contemplation – just enough for you, in your life, to make a difference.

Cultivating an observing mindset

There are various techniques and exercises that you can use to cultivate an observing mindset. Some people find regular meditation a good technique for bringing it about.

However, like many other things that we know are probably good for us – such as eating five portions of fresh fruit and vegetables a day, or exercising regularly – it can be a struggle to fit it into our busy lives. Fortunately, there are other techniques for bringing your mind into the here and now. Chapter 17 on mindfulness talks about this in more detail. One way is to practise noticing *what is happening right now*. For example, while you are reading this book, what do you notice? What can you see and hear? If you are sitting down, can you notice where your body touches the chair or where your feet touch the floor? Can you notice how the book feels in your hand? What sounds can you hear around you? Perhaps you can hear the TV in the room next door, or maybe you can hear the sound of traffic or birdsong outside? It is worth taking a few seconds to try this. Have you noticed anything you weren't aware of beforehand?

Like most things, bringing our awareness into the present moment becomes easier the more we practise it. The observing mindset can be very beneficial as it gives us some space to reflect on our experiences. Making space for our thoughts in this way makes it easier to think about what we want to do, rather than just being on autopilot and going through the motions, not really being aware of why we are doing what we're doing. Try the exercise above and experiment with cultivating an observing mindset, bringing your awareness into the present, and see if it is useful for you. If you do find it helpful, can you use it to reflect on different self-states?

Use the worksheet below to think about and describe your observing mindset. Consider the advantages that it might offer you and make a note of any difficulties you have had trying to cultivate it. Think about *when* in your everyday life you could put time aside to practise this. Try to anticipate anything that might get in the way of practising this technique – like doing chores or watching TV – and plan how you can make time for it in your daily routine.

Worksheet 18: My observing mindset

How would I describe a mindset that helps me to weigh up things and contemplate my thoughts and emotions at the right 'distance'? What words would I use?
What would be the benefits of cultivating this mindset?
What would be the disadvantages of cultivating this mindset?
What could I do to bring about this mindset when I need it? Often it helps to build a 'When . . . then' plan. For example, 'WHEN I have finished my dinner THEN I will spend ten minutes weighing up my options.'
WHEN

THEN

Is anything likely to get in the way of this plan? If so, what?

What plan do I have for dealing with any obstacles?

WHEN

THEN

Key messages

- Cultivating a mindset that helps us to observe how we respond to our different thoughts and feelings, or to people or particular events, can be an excellent idea. It can help us to see how our reactions to different situations or feelings might make things better or worse. This new perspective can enable us to start to respond differently. This in turn should help us with our goals.

Tips for supporters

- One of the best ways to work out what an observing mindset feels like is to try to identify it in our everyday lives. People will often be able to 'step back' at some point, but are often too busy or stressed to do it very often. Help the person you are supporting to fill in the worksheet by helping them to think of times when they have been be able to cultivate an observing mindset, however briefly. If they struggle to think of any examples, try to think of some examples from your own life and describe them.

- You may also find that the person you are supporting says they are more able to use their mental imagery in this state – without getting too distressed by it. For example, they may be more able to hold distressing memories or imagined future scenarios in mind to work through them.

- Some people will be unable to think of times when they have experienced an observing mindset and therefore they are unable to describe it. The opportunity may arise in the future as they work through self-help, or talk freely with people they know.

When to move onto the next section

Here are some suggestions to help you decide when to move on to the next section.

- You have had a chance to consider what your helpful mindset is.

- You have given yourself time to weigh up the advantages and disadvantages of cultivating it.

- You have got a clear plan to help you develop this mindset.

7. Your 'healthy self' – putting it all together

There is only so much time in our everyday lives for contemplating and reflecting on things, so what happens in the long term? Earlier in this chapter we discussed the different self-states that people with bipolar disorder may have, such as 'the depressed self', 'the manic self', 'the irritable and worried self', and so on. When you are in any one of these self-states you may experience a range of different feelings.

The last stage of this chapter is to consider which self-state you would like to experience more. Some people call this 'my healthy self', 'my real self', or 'me on an even keel'. The name of this state is up to you, but it represents a state that you can see will help you manage day to day and pursue the life goals that you identified on page 405. When people are able to visualize their healthy self, it becomes much easier to move towards it. Often our healthy self will contain elements of our other states, including a range of negative and positive emotions. It may also include being able to contemplate and weigh up your life. If we recognize the value of all our different self-states and feelings, it makes it easier to consider what kind of self-state we would like to have more of.

Some people find it easier than others to imagine their healthy self. You may have had times in your life when you have felt like 'the real you' and so you can bring this image of yourself to mind quite easily. On the other hand, it may need to be built up over time, starting with something quite vague and becoming gradually more vivid and defined. In therapy, people often think of particular situations, such as being on holiday, or talking to certain people, when they feel closest to their healthy self. Using that as a starting off point, the therapist then helps them to develop their understanding of what it means to be their healthy self – the emotions and thoughts that go with it, the way they relate to other people and to themselves in those situations. The richer the description and the more detail you can come up with, the easier you will find it to recognize what you are looking for.

The following questions are designed to help you start to think about what being your healthy self means to you.

Table 54: Identifying your healthy self

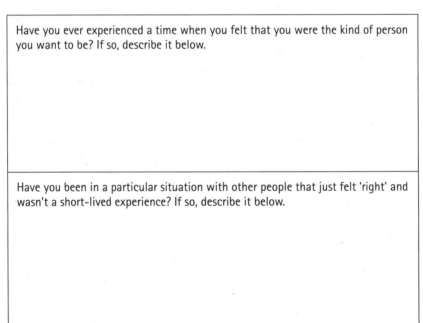

Have you ever experienced a time when you felt that you were the kind of person you want to be? If so, describe it below.

Have you been in a particular situation with other people that just felt 'right' and wasn't a short-lived experience? If so, describe it below.

Do you have an idea of the 'real you' that isn't too high or too low? If so, describe it below.

Are there other people, either real or fictional, whom you want to be more like? If so, describe them below.

Naming the healthy self

What would you call the self-state you would like to experience more? (e.g. 'my healthy self', 'my real self', etc.)

What emotions do you associate with this self-state? How strong would they be and how long would they endure? Most people find that although their healthy state may include quite a wide range of both positive and negative emotions, they feel more 'grounded' and not overwhelmed, despite still having these feelings. Write down the emotions that would be acceptable to you in your healthy self-state. If they are negative emotions, describe what would make them acceptable to you.

What now?

By now you have:

1. thought about and written down your life goals, or the direction you wish to move in your life.

2. weighed up the pros and cons of the different emotions you experience.

3. considered how your emotions can move on a sliding scale.

4. started to recognize the different kinds of self-states and long-term moods you experience.

5. learned about the observing mindset and made a plan to set aside time to practise cultivating yours.

6. identified what your 'healthy self' feels like.

From now on, it is important to keep focused on this approach. When you experience difficult emotions in the future, or when you become stuck in a particular mood state, or you feel you have lost sight of your goals, return to the notes you have made while reading this chapter to see how they can help. Try to break down problems in the same systematic way. Ask yourself: what do I want from this situation? How is it making me feel? What are the positives and negatives about this feeling? How strong is it? What self-state am I in right now? Depressed? High? Healthy? On autopilot? Is it helping me achieve my goals? If not, would some time to step back from the situation help me to weigh up my options? How can I get back on track and be more the kind of 'self' that I want to be?

If you experience a difficult feeling, rate how strong it is right now and compare it to other times when you have felt the same in the past. Did you feel it more or less extremely then? Consider both the advantages and disadvantages of feeling like this. Is this feeling telling you something about your life goals? For example, does anger signal that someone is denying you what you need? Would it help to step back and notice what is going on with your observing mindset? What would your healthy self try to do to get your needs met?

It can take time to change the way we deal with our moods and to get back in control of our lives, but many people have benefited from the approach described in this chapter. It may or may not work for you, so the best way to find out is to try it and see.

Key messages

- In everyday life we experience a range of feelings, which are often useful to us but can also develop into 'states' that lead to problems. If we can be clear about what we really want in the long term, it is easier to manage our feelings in ways that help us achieve our long-term goals. We may also notice that we get more time to reflect and contemplate and we experience more of a healthy balance of feelings that helps us genuinely connect with the people that are important to us.

Tips for supporters

- It is important that the healthy self is not seen as the only self-state that should be experienced. There are many reasons why people get into depressed, anxious or high states and they are not always easy to get out of once you're in them. The challenge is to notice the state – which can mean switching on the observing mindset described on page 426 – and this will give the person you are supporting more mental space to consider alternative self-states.

Final word

The self-help guide in this chapter is based on the principles of the model used in TEAMS during face-to-face therapy. The therapists in TEAMS are very open with their clients about the model and encourage them to use what they learn outside the therapy session extensively, so it seems only right to make these ideas available to whoever might benefit from them. They also fit closely with what people who are recovering from problems with their mood swings tell us has helped them. Nevertheless, only you know what is going to help you right now and this self-help guide is just one of many sources of support. You can draw on any of these at the same time as you are using this book. Most people with bipolar disorder say that they have brought together influences from all kinds of areas and made their own sense of them to help build a life that works for them.

Acknowledgements

Thank you to Sondos Ghalayini for her helpful contributions to this chapter.

22 Postnatal depression

Peter J. Cooper and Lynne Murray

There has, over the years, been a lot of confusion about what exactly postnatal depression (PND) is, how common it is, and what sort of treatment is best for people who have it. PND occurs sufficiently commonly to have attracted widespread attention and to appear often in newspapers and magazines and on radio and television programmes. It is one of those issues that attracts rather strong opinions, and unfortunately ideas about the causes of PND and how best to treat it have, at times, taken hold without much evidence to support them. In fact, over the past forty years or so there has been a steady stream of solid research about PND and, while several questions remain to be answered, we now know a lot about the condition. In this chapter we will provide a summary of what we know about PND. We'll help you to identify whether you might have it, how it might affect you and your family, and what you can do to overcome it. Finally, we'll describe the effects of PND on parenting and how you can tackle common difficulties.

What is PND?

It may be helpful to begin by describing two conditions that are *not* PND. First, PND is not the 'maternity blues'. The 'blues' is a term used to refer to a disturbance in mood that affects women a few days after delivery (typically day five). It is characterized by rapid mood swings (from elation to tearfulness), with some mild feelings of anxiety and depression. The blues affect around half of women at some point in the first week or so following delivery. The troubling swings in mood usually stop spontaneously after a week or two. Although the blues were once thought to be largely caused by hormonal changes, it now seems that factors such as tiredness and sleep deprivation may be more important. Although the blues can be quite distressing, for the vast majority of women who experience them the feelings go away naturally and are not a sign of a serious problem.

The second condition that is not PND is a *puerperal psychosis*. This is a major mental illness which usually starts within a few days of delivery. It can arise in several different forms. Sufferers can appear withdrawn, confused, apparently distracted by auditory hallucinations (voices in their head); or they can be elated, rambling in their speech, agitated and excessively active, with marked mood swings. Typically, sufferers have strange beliefs, commonly focused on childbirth and concerns about the baby. A puerperal psychosis occurs in something like one in 500 to 1,000 women after childbirth. While this may seem like a rare condition, in fact the chances of a woman having a psychotic episode immediately after childbirth are thirty times higher than at any other time of her life. What is more, women who have had one such episode are quite likely to have another episode following subsequent deliveries: the risk of a puerperal psychosis for someone who has had one before is at least one in four. If you have had a puerperal psychosis in the past and are thinking about having a baby, or if you are pregnant again, then it is very important that you discuss the help you will need with your doctor. If you do have a puerperal psychosis, then you will certainly need to receive medical care. Similarly, it is crucial that anyone suspected of having a puerperal psychosis is assessed by a qualified professional and, if the diagnosis is confirmed, then they should receive immediate clinical care. This usually means being in hospital for a while (from a few weeks to a few months) but, encouragingly, a very good recovery can be expected.

So, if PND is not the baby blues and it is not a puerperal psychosis, then what is it? It was once thought that it was a specific psychiatric disorder, quite different from depressions occurring at other times, with its own special set of symptoms. In fact, PND is just like depression occurring outside the postnatal period. The main features are low mood that last for most of the time over at least a two-week period and, over the same period, a loss of enjoyment or interest in anything. If you are experiencing PND you may have several other symptoms too, but these vary in nature from person to person. They include feeling excessively tired, not sleeping or eating normally, being irritable, and feeling guilty and lacking in self-esteem. The severity of PND and how long it lasts are the same as one would find in other people suffering from depression. None of this, of course, diminishes the importance of acknowledging it when it is present, and of obtaining appropriate help.

How common is PND?

If you have PND you might look about you and see only blissfully happy mothers with perfectly contented babies, and feel that you are the only one for whom motherhood is a struggle. In fact, it is not at all uncommon. A recent review found that almost one in five women had some level of depression at some point in the first three months after birth, and about one in ten had a more severe depression. What this means is that around 70,000 women in the UK suffer from PND every year. In some other countries, where socio-economic conditions are particularly harsh, as many as one in three women who have recently delivered a baby experience PND.

How long does PND last?

For the majority of women, PND improves significantly within a few months. This is not to say that these women all become very happy (although some certainly are), and some of them will still show symptoms of depression. But only a third of those who had PND at three months postpartum remain significantly depressed by six to nine months. This raises two important questions. First, why do the majority of those who have PND feel so much better a few months later? There is no single answer to this question, because several factors could contribute to the improvement in mood. Some of these could be related to developments such as the baby having more settled sleep or starting to interact more with its parents. Others could have nothing to do with the baby; perhaps there has been an improvement in the marital relationship, or the mother has benefited from support from a health visitor or from family and friends. Whatever the reasons, for most women, the depression improves substantially within a few months.

The second question concerns the women whose depression does not improve by around nine months: what is known about them? The honest answer to this question is 'not much'. However, it does seem that these women, in the main, suffer from a particularly severe form of depression that requires professional help.

Key messages

- PND must be distinguished from the maternity blues and puerperal psychosis.

- The symptoms of PND are the same as those in depression occurring at other times.

- It is a common problem, affecting about one in ten women following delivery in the UK.

- Those with PND typically recover within a few months, but for around a third the disorder persists beyond six months, and these people are particularly likely to need professional help.

Tips for supporters

- You may be reading this chapter because a friend or relative has asked you for help, or it may be that you are close to someone who has recently had a baby and are worried about them.

- If that is the case, then read through the next few sections, particularly the one headed 'How do I know if I have PND?' Encourage the person you are supporting to look at that, too.

Who is likely to develop PND?

There is no such thing as a typical woman who will develop PND. Several factors have been found to increase the risk of developing the condition, but the increase associated with each one of them is generally quite small. This makes it very difficult to predict exactly who will have PND. The following factors may all play a part: a previous history of a depressive disorder; low mood and anxiety during pregnancy; general low self-esteem; marital difficulties; recent adverse life events; and poor social support. However, although these factors make it more likely that someone will become depressed, it is possible to have one or even all of them without developing PND.

It is worth noting that most of these risk factors for PND are very similar to those that would increase the risk of depression at any time. However, there are factors that do seem to be specific to women in the period from birth to about six weeks. First, it has been found that if you have had a difficult birth experience (such as pre-eclampsia, prenatal hospitalization for a variety of complications, or having an emergency caesarean), this makes it more likely that you will get depressed, especially if you have been depressed at some time before this delivery. Second, although the baby blues are very common, and usually mild and fleeting, if you experience severe blues which persist, you are more likely to become depressed. Finally, there are some characteristics of the new baby that can be important. Having a baby with health problems can, understandably, increase the risk that you will feel depressed. In addition, even some healthy babies are born extremely sensitive to what happens around them, and when they get upset they take a long time to calm down. So they seem to fall apart with every nappy change or bath or loud noise, and are then difficult to comfort. Almost one in five babies are like this, and they are in general more difficult to care for in these early weeks than less sensitive babies; this presents challenges to mothers over and above the already considerable demands of ordinary parenting. Unsurprisingly, where a mother is already under stress, and especially if she lacks good support from her partner or family, then having a baby with these sorts of sensitivities increases the likelihood of her becoming depressed.

If a woman has her first ever episode of depression after having a baby, then she is at increased risk for being depressed after her next baby. It has also been found that if one of a pair of sisters has PND, the chances of the other sister having it too are increased. These findings suggest that some women have a very specific vulnerability (possibly with some biological basis) to depression at this time.

What causes PND?

Childbirth is associated with big changes in hormone levels, especially substantial decreases in *oestradiol* and *progesterone*. It used to be thought that this drop in hormone levels caused PND; however, research has not supported this conclusion. It has also been suggested that some women become depressed when they stop breastfeeding because of hormonal changes related to that. However, studies that have looked carefully at the relationship between breastfeeding and mood over time have concluded that the causal relationship goes in the other direction: that is, women who become depressed are likely to give up breastfeeding, just as they are likely to give up on other activities they find taxing, *because* they are depressed.

So there is no clear and simple cause, and for any woman who develops PND, it is likely to be the result of the interplay between a number of different factors. These may include a biological vulnerability, but more commonly the important factors are social and psychological. Difficulties like housing problems, marital conflict and a lack of social support all raise the risk of postpartum depression, and can even be said to *cause* a woman to become depressed. Similarly, if a woman is expecting a wonderful experience of motherhood with an easy, happy child, and she finds that her baby is in fact highly sensitive and difficult to manage, the profound sense of loss provoked by this dashed expectation can cause her to become depressed.

Key messages

- It is not possible to predict in pregnancy – with any great accuracy – who will become depressed postnatally.

- There is no good evidence that PND is caused by the hormonal changes associated with birth or stopping breastfeeding.

- Some women may have a biological vulnerability to PND, but the evidence for this is not strong.

- A severe and persistent episode of the maternity blues raises the chances of a woman developing PND, as does having a highly sensitive baby, if the mother has poor support.

- The factors that make it more likely that a woman will become depressed are, in the main, the same ones that cause women to become depressed at other times, but how they combine in any one person is complex.

How do I know if I have PND?

If you have recently had a baby and feel much more unhappy than is usual for you, then you may have PND. If you are at all concerned that you might have it, then talk to your midwife, health visitor or GP. They may ask you to fill in the questionnaire below. This is the Edinburgh Postnatal Depression Scale, or the EPDS.

Table 55: The Edinburgh Postnatal Depression Scale

In the past 7 days:

I have been able to laugh and see the funny side of things

- ☐ 0   As much as I always could
- ☐ 1   Not quite so much now
- ☐ 2   Definitely not
- ☐ 3   Not at all

I have looked forward with enjoyment to things

- ☐ 0   As much as I ever did
- ☐ 1   Rather less than I used to
- ☐ 2   Definitely less than I used to
- ☐ 3   Hardly at all

I have felt scared or panicky for no very good reason

- ☐ 3   Yes, quite a lot
- ☐ 2   Yes, sometimes
- ☐ 1   No, not much
- ☐ 0   No, not at all

Things have been getting on top of me

- ☐ 3   Yes, most of the time I haven't been able to cope at all
- ☐ 2   Yes, sometimes I haven't been coping as well as usual
- ☐ 1   No, most of the time I have coped quite well
- ☐ 0   No, I have been coping as well as ever

I have been so unhappy that I have had difficulty sleeping

- ☐ 3   Yes, most of the time
- ☐ 2   Yes, sometimes
- ☐ 1   Not very often
- ☐ 0   No, not at all

I have blamed myself unnecessarily when things went wrong

- ☐ 3   Yes, most of the time
- ☐ 2   Yes, some of the time
- ☐ 1   Not very often
- ☐ 0   No, never

I have been anxious or worried for no good reason

- ☐ 0   No, not at all
- ☐ 1   Hardly ever
- ☐ 2   Yes, sometimes
- ☐ 3   Yes, very often

I have felt sad or miserable

- ☐ 3   Yes, most of the time
- ☐ 2   Yes, quite often
- ☐ 1   Not very often
- ☐ 0   No, not at all

I have been so unhappy that I have been crying

- ☐ 3   Yes, most of the time
- ☐ 2   Yes, quite often
- ☐ 1   Only occasionally
- ☐ 0   No, never

The thought of harming myself has occurred to me

- ☐ 3   Yes, quite often
- ☐ 2   Sometimes
- ☐ 1   Hardly ever
- ☐ 0   Never

It is important to appreciate that the EPDS was developed as a *screening* questionnaire. That is, it cannot tell you definitely whether you (or anyone else completing it) are actually suffering from PND; but if you have a high score, then it is *likely* that you have PND, and if you have a low score it is likely that you do not. The figure on page 446 shows, for a UK sample, how likely someone is to have PND at various scores on the EPDS. So, if someone has a score above 16, then the chances that they have PND are more than 90 per cent (in other words, out of 100 people who have this score, more than 90 of them will have PND). In clinical practice, we regard scores of 12/13 as the significant boundary: that is, women with scores under 13 are, on average, unlikely to have PND (only around 5 per cent); and people who score 13 or more are likely to be depressed (more than two thirds).

Your health visitor, midwife or GP are also likely to ask you two further specific questions. (Note that in some clinics, practitioners do not use the EPDS, and will instead just ask the questions below.)

- During the past month, have you often been bothered by feeling down, depressed or hopeless?

- During the past month, have you often been bothered by little interest or pleasure in doing things?

If you have answered 'yes' to either of these two questions, and your score on the EPDS is 13 or over, this suggests that you are probably suffering from PND. However, a diagnosis can only be made by a clinician making a full assessment. If you are concerned that you might have PND then it would be sensible to discuss this with your GP or health visitor. However, the advice in this chapter is likely to be helpful for you, whether you have a diagnosis of PND, or are low in mood but not clinically depressed.

Figure 56: The chances of having PND at a given EPDS score

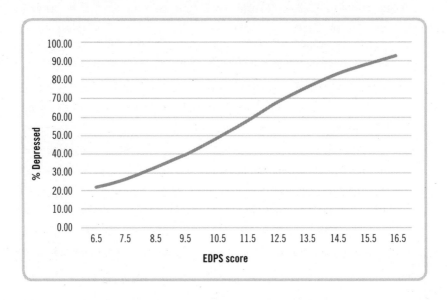

Key messages

- The EPDS score and the answer to the two questions above can tell you whether it is likely that you have PND.

- If you think you might have PND you should talk to your GP or health visitor.

- The advice in this chapter will be relevant to you whether you are suffering from PND or just have low mood.

> ### Tips for supporters
>
> - If you are supporting someone who might have PND, then encourage them to complete the EPDS and think about the two other questions above. If they have a high score on the EPDS or say 'Yes' to either of the two key questions, encourage them to visit their GP.
>
> - Sometimes mothers can be concerned about what people will think of them if they acknowledge feelings of depression, or they can be frightened that if they admit to such feelings their baby will be taken away from them. Reassure them that these concerns and fears are unfounded and that health professionals are in fact very supportive of the large number of mothers in this position.

What is the impact of PND?

As with all depression, PND makes it difficult for people to function. This can occur in a range of areas, including the relationship between the parents, the experience of motherhood, and the mother's relationship with her baby.

Impact on the parents' relationship

Relationship difficulties are often present in women who have PND and, as mentioned above, such problems are one of the main risk factors; a lack of support from her partner, and the presence of conflict can tip the mother into depression. It is also true that relationship difficulties can sometimes come about as a *consequence* of the mother being depressed. This can happen, first, because the partner cannot understand why the mother is not happy now that she has the baby she so wanted, and this lack of understanding and sympathy can lead to conflict. Second, depression is often accompanied by feelings of irritability, meaning that a postnatally depressed mother may have a short fuse, and be more prone to being argumentative with her partner than she otherwise would. Unfortunately, the mother, who is feeling unhappy and may be struggling with caring for her baby, then has a further problem of having an unsupportive and critical partner. Chapter 20 talks a lot more about the association between relationship problems and depression.

Impact on the experience of motherhood

Being depressed is always an unpleasant experience. We feel bad about our lot in life, about the prospects of our circumstances improving, and especially about our own value. It is particularly unpleasant when we are supposed to be feeling good, like on our birthday or when on holiday. So it is with being depressed after having a baby. The experience of motherhood has been so romanticized that there is an almost universal expectation that every mother must be ecstatically fulfilled and enjoy every moment of mothering. So if you are feeling depressed and unable to gain pleasure from caring for your baby, it is understandable that you might feel guilty and blame yourself for not being happy. In this case you are doubly burdened: you feel depressed, with all the unpleasant symptoms that accompany low mood – and you also feel guilty that you are not enjoying motherhood as you should, which makes you feel even more depressed.

Impact on the mother-baby relationship

A core feature of being depressed is that we turn inwards and focus on our negative thoughts. So you are preoccupied with thinking about your problems – such as financial problems or housing difficulties, relationship issues, and so on – and this preoccupation creates a vicious circle: the negative thoughts can go round and round in your head, and focusing on them in an unproductive way seems to take up all your mental energy, and makes you even more upset. Just as this can make it difficult for you to relate as you normally would to your partner, it can also make it hard for you to enjoy being with your baby. Of course, this is not always the case, and there are many instances where a mother is depressed, and the one positive aspect of her life is her relationship with her baby. But it is unfortunately the case that depression can make it much harder to manage the job of parenting – a very demanding job at the best of times – and this can feel particularly so if the depression is more severe and long-lasting.

In general, there are three key ways in which PND can make it hard for you to respond to your baby. First, depression generally makes you withdraw into yourself. So, when you are feeling depressed and have little energy, and are focusing on your own negative thoughts, this makes it hard for you to notice what is happening around you and engage socially, and this difficulty can extend to engaging with your baby. Second, depression is associated with feeling irritable, and so it is common to have a short emotional fuse. Third, your negative thinking can distort your perceptions of your parenting, and interfere with your ability to see things as they really are. Each of these three features of depression can interfere with parenting.

It must be stressed that although the chances of these parenting problems arising are increased where a mother has PND, in many cases depressed mothers and their families manage to support the development of their children extremely well. However, being aware that you may be depressed, and knowing that it can affect your responses in certain ways is an important first step in changing things for the better; this awareness can give you the opportunity to take stock and think about what is happening with your baby from a fresh perspective.

The treatment of PND

A number of forms of psychological treatment have been shown to help women with postpartum depression, including counselling, Interpersonal Psychotherapy (IPT) and CBT. In the following section, after saying a few words about the role of antidepressant medication, we show how you can use CBT to overcome PND, and offer strategies to improve the mother's provision of care for her baby.

A note on medication

There is a good deal of evidence showing that a variety of antidepressant medications are helpful to people who are depressed. Although the research is limited, there is every reason to expect the same benefit postnatally as is seen at other times. However, in the UK, women who have just had a baby are generally unwilling to take medication for mood problems. This is partly because they do not see themselves as 'ill' and therefore do not believe that this form of treatment is appropriate; and sometimes it is because they are concerned about the medication passing through breast milk and getting to the baby. The position with antidepressants in breast milk is complicated, and needs careful consideration by the mother and the doctors and health workers involved. Since antidepressant medication and psychological intervention have been shown to be equally effective, the case for antidepressants being the *first* choice treatment is weak. Having said this, where the depression is severe and persists, especially when other forms of help have been provided and not proved sufficiently helpful, antidepressant medication should be seriously considered.

The cognitive behavioural approach

Since, as we have already said, PND is essentially the same as depressions arising at other times, the cognitive behavioural principles outlined in this book apply just as much to PND as they do to depression at any other time. Below, we highlight four particular features of depression that are especially problematic aspects of PND, and for which specific strategies are known to be helpful. Where appropriate, we refer you back to the relevant earlier chapters.

Isolation

It is very common for women with PND to become socially isolated. This is partly because when you are depressed it is difficult to muster up the energy and the motivation to see friends and family. For many women, it is also because they do not wish to parade in public the difficulties they feel they are having with their baby and thereby open themselves to public scrutiny and possible criticism. In this way, many women with PND become more or less housebound. This would be a depressing state of affairs for anyone! If you have become socially isolated, there are two important courses of action to take.

First, it is enormously helpful to find someone with whom you can talk. This could be a professional, like a health visitor, a counsellor or a practice nurse. Tell your GP how you are feeling and that you understand that it might help you to be able to talk to someone. An alternative (or something to do in addition to regularly seeing a professional) is to find a friend or relative in whom you can confide. This can be a difficult thing to do, if you feel that you ought to be managing better, and you may worry that telling someone that you are not coping will open you up to criticism. However, ask yourself this question: if a close friend or relative were to turn to you, in confidence, and tell you that they were having difficulties coping, would you be critical of them or would you be kind and sympathetic? Surely you should allow yourself to expect the same kind of response as you would give someone else? Having identified someone to talk to – and, no doubt, having found that they are keen to help – it is important that you see them regularly, at least once a week. You should use these times to talk to them about how you have been feeling and what you have been thinking. The simple fact of being heard and understood can, in itself, be extremely helpful.

The second course of action is to schedule specific activities that involve social contact. This could be going for a walk in a park, arranging to visit a friend, or organizing for a friend or relation to visit you. Make a list of, say, five or six such activities, and rank them in terms of how difficult they would be for you. So, for example, going for a walk in the park where you might meet someone to chat to might seem not too daunting; whereas, going to a tea party of mothers and babies might seem much more difficult. You should then start planning to do the things that are relatively easy and work your way up your list doing things that are increasingly difficult. The important thing is to recognize that being isolated is unhelpful to you and to decide to begin doing something about this.

Self-denigration

It is an almost universal feature of depression that sufferers blame themselves for their problems and feel guilty about not being able to solve them. In particular, they are highly self-critical and self-denigrating. In PND, the guilt and blame and general self-criticism commonly focus on feelings of inadequacy as a mother. In the last part of this chapter, we present specific strategies you might use to help you in your relationship with your baby. However, here we are concerned to focus on your self-critical thoughts and how you might learn to be more kind to yourself.

In Chapter 16 of this book, Professor Gilbert shows how important it is that we learn to be more compassionate to ourselves when we are depressed. Certainly, if you are depressed, there will be many factors that have contributed to it. Perhaps you have been having difficulties in your relationship with your partner. Perhaps, for one reason or another, the support that would be of such help to you from your family has not been there. Perhaps you feel sad and disappointed that the experience you are having with your baby is not anything like what you were expecting. Whatever the reasons are, it is certainly the case that you did not *choose* to be depressed. This is not something you wanted to happen, and it is a state you would very much like to end. So being depressed is not something that you should blame yourself for, as if it were your fault. It is not your fault. It is just something bad that has happened to you, by dint of circumstance, just as it has happened to 69,999 other women who had a baby in the UK in the past year. Having said that, there are things you can do to overcome these feelings. We discussed above the importance of putting your isolation behind you and of finding someone in whom you can confide. You can also tackle your self-denigratory tendencies head on.

In Chapter 16 Professor Gilbert provides a number of strategies for promoting such a state of kindness. Here we will reiterate just two of these (but we urge you to read his chapter in full). The first is the technique of inducing a sense of calmness by controlling your breathing, described on page 230. You should practise doing this; and, indeed, when you are good at doing it you will see below that you can use this technique to pre-empt other difficulties.

The second technique is that of remembering a time when someone was kind to you. Professor Gilbert calls this a 'compassionate image'. He describes several ways in which you can create a compassionate image. On pages 238–9 he describes remembering an occasion when someone was particularly kind to you or supportive towards you and you felt affirmed by this. (Of course, as Professor Gilbert notes, if the image that first comes to you makes you feel sad, because, for example, the person who was kind to you has since died, then this is not the right image to use). The important thing is to find for yourself an image of kindness that you remember with fondness and appreciation, and then to practise bringing this image to mind and focusing upon it. You should try to make this image as detailed and as concrete as possible, recalling the actual words, the behaviour, the facial expression, and so on. Many people have found that by making time, preferably every day, to calm themselves through the breathing technique, and bringing to mind a compassionate image on which to focus, their depressive feelings and thoughts have lessened in frequency and reduced in intensity.

Avoidance and limiting positive experiences

When you are depressed, there is a natural tendency to avoid anything that might make you feel upset or uncomfortable. And the relief you feel when you have avoided these is encouragement to continue avoiding. The problem with this is that the avoidance becomes a habit: you avoid more and more things, and that leads to fewer opportunities for pleasure and enjoyment. So, you become even more depressed. One way to help yourself break this vicious circle is to fight against the avoidance and thereby provide yourself with more opportunities for positive experiences.

In Chapter 13, Dr Richards gives an account of how to increase your opportunities for positive experiences. He suggests that you keep a record of your activities and your mood to help you think about the sorts of things you could do to improve how you feel. What sorts of things are you avoiding doing, which, if you could face them, might improve your mood? On pages 146–158 Dr Richards describes what he calls 'activity scheduling'. What this boils down to is deciding to do certain things either because you know they will improve your mood or because you know that not to do them will worsen your mood. For example, if you were to notice that when you do manage to take your baby out to friends or the park, or wherever, your mood improves, then you would plan more of these trips. Similarly, if you were to see that avoiding doing the washing up in the evenings made you feel bad about the house being a tip, you would plan to make yourself (hopefully with some help!) do the washing up before going to bed.

On page 147 Dr Richards suggests that setting up a routine can be useful. This can include ordinary chores, like housework and cooking, but also activities like taking your baby out for a walk. This works well because, though you may not feel like doing these things, if you plan to do them and then carry through the plan, the fact of your having done them will itself be rewarding. The routine will also provide you with a solid structure around which your day can be organized, and this too can be helpful.

Finally, you should consider what sorts of things you are doing that make your mood worse. For example, it may be that if you stay at home on your own for a whole day, by the evening you feel lonely and particularly sad. In this case, you need to think how to break this cycle – that is, how you can plan not to be at home all day on your own. On pages

148–50 Dr Richards has some helpful suggestions about how you can come up with alternative behaviours which can replace the ones causing you difficulty.

There are two aims here: first, to help you see what you are doing (or not doing) that is making you feel worse, so that you can find alternative things to do; and second, to help you increase your opportunities for doing pleasurable things so that you can break the vicious cycle into which you may have slipped.

Rumination

As detailed in Chapter 14 of this book, particular ways of thinking can be a problem in depression. People with PND, as with many others who are depressed, commonly slip into what is called 'rumination'. This refers to repetitive thinking about problems, or feelings, or unhappy past events. Typically, there is a kind of 'script' to rumination, in which people go over the same ground again and again without reaching any kind of resolution. This makes negative thoughts and feelings much worse, and makes you feel even more depressed.

In Chapter 14 Professor Watkins provides an account of the nature of rumination and what to do to overcome it. He makes the important point that thinking about your problems and about bad events that have happened is a perfectly normal and appropriate thing to be doing. However, if such thinking becomes excessive and uncontrollable, it becomes a serious problem in itself. Further, depressive rumination causes particular trouble in the postnatal period because it interferes with a mother's ability to focus on her baby. So, overcoming rumination will create a virtuous cycle: it will make you feel less depressed, this will help you more able to engage well with your baby, and this will lead to more times of closeness and enjoyment together which, in turn, will improve your mood.

On page 164 Professor Watkins lists a set of questions you can ask your-self to decide whether rumination is a problem for you. Do look at these questions and try to answer them for yourself. If you decide that it is a problem for you then you should read Chapter 14 in full and follow the steps that are set out for dealing it. The essential message is that the way to change the habit of ruminating is to spot the early signs – the triggers – of it, and then interrupt the habitual chain by doing something else, incompatible with ruminating. If you practise doing this repeatedly, the rumination will gradually wane. On page 172 a list of common triggers is provided. Look at these and consider how they might apply to you. You might, as suggested, keep a diary of when you ruminate, to help you become aware of what is happening just before it starts. Once you are aware of the precursors to rumination, you will be in a position to intervene and pre-empt it. On pages 171–5, Professor Watkins makes several suggestions for what you could do to pre-empt rumination. You should study these carefully and think which of them might be of most help to you. We have already mentioned two techniques that could be useful: controlled breathing, and using your compassionate image. Indeed, you might find that using both techniques together – the controlled breathing and the compassionate image – works best for you. You need to be experimental about this: try a strategy and see how it works for you. If it doesn't work, read pages 171–5 again, and think of another strategy to try. When you have hit on something that seems good to you then, if you practise it whenever the opportunity arises, the ruminations should fade.

There is one further strategy that could be added in the case of PND. If you find that one of the triggers to ruminating is when you feel things are not going well with your baby, then focus your attention wholly on your baby (see the section below for how to do this). Concentrating on the details of your baby's activities and experience, as described, could well be an effective pre-emptive strategy.

Key messages

- Find someone to talk to – a professional, or a friend or relative – and tell them how you are feeling and what difficulties you are having.

- Try to see people more.

- Use the controlled breathing technique and your compassionate image to combat your feelings of guilt and self-denigration.

- Find ways of increasing your opportunities for positive experiences.

- Develop a strategy for intervening early to prevent yourself ruminating.

Tips for supporters

- Overcoming social isolation is an important element in dealing with depression. You can help with this, by being available yourself and by helping organize regular opportunities to participate in social occasions.

- Another important aspect to overcoming depression is finding ways of engaging in activities which, before the depression, were found pleasurable. Again you can help by finding out what activities the person you are supporting previously enjoyed, and helping to bring them about.

PND and parenting

PND can affect different aspects of a mother's parenting. Below, three particular ways are discussed, together with suggestions about how you can overcome the difficulties.

'Contingent responding'

The first aspect of parenting that can be affected by depression is what has been termed 'contingent responding' – that is, noticing what the baby is experiencing, and then responding to his interest and signals. This kind of responding is of general benefit to babies, but it is particularly helpful in supporting their ability to learn, as it helps them pay attention for longer and become more involved in what they are doing. It teaches them about the connections between their own actions and things around them, and the parent's responses can also help the baby become more competent, as he is supported to do things that he could not manage on his own.

Maggie and Harry's story

Baby Harry was looking around and spotted something interesting across the room (a soft squeaky toy) that was out of reach, and he was too young to crawl to it. His breathing quickened as he focused on it, his face looked very concentrated, and he moved his arms excitedly. Maggie spotted the change in his behaviour and turned to follow his interest. She saw what Harry was looking at, and brought it across to him, holding it up within his reach so that he could explore it. Harry enjoyed playing with it for a good few minutes and learned a lot about its texture, weight and what he needed to do to make it squeak.

If a mother is feeling depressed, it might be more difficult for her to respond in this way. This can happen for three reasons. First, if she is feeling very withdrawn and preoccupied because of her depression, she may not notice her baby's signals. If her baby is looking around and sees something that he would like to explore, and the mother does not notice and respond, he might lose interest if what he wants is out of reach. Or if her baby is looking at her and making cooing sounds to attract her attention, she may not notice what he is doing and not respond, and he may then give up trying.

The second kind of problem also involves the mother finding it difficult to notice the baby's signals, but in this case, rather than not engaging at all as described above, she may try hard to get him to follow her own agenda, perhaps trying to get his interest in something that she thinks will entertain him, even if he doesn't seem keen. This second pattern of parenting can be quite common when a mother wants very much to engage with her baby, but is perhaps feeling anxious and that things are out of her control. These feelings can be overwhelming and can cause the mother both to miss the baby's cues, and also to become somewhat over-stimulating or demanding in an effort to engage with him, perhaps trying repeatedly to get her baby to look and smile at her, even when he is happily absorbed in something else. This style of behaviour can make it difficult for the baby to attend well to what is going on, and can cause him to become distracted and uncomfortable, something that can then make it even harder for the mother to have the kind of positive interaction with him that she is seeking.

Finally, a mother's negative thinking can cause her to feel that when her baby is not attending to her, it is not because he is simply interested in something else, but because he isn't interested in *her* and doesn't care about her response. This might make her reluctant to start a game, or respond, as she may be convinced that there is no point.

Of course, mothers who are not depressed do not behave contingently all the time (indeed, perfect contingency isn't altogether helpful for the baby), but mothers with PND do seem quite commonly to find it much harder to take note of their baby's behaviour and respond to them in this way. Think about whether there have been times when feeling depressed has interfered with your ability to respond contingently with your baby. If this is the case, there are simple things that you might want to try so that you can become aware of your baby's signals, try some contingent responding and see its effects.

Tips about observing and responding contingently

Although it's not always easy when you're feeling depressed, it can be useful to practise observing your baby when you are not busy with other things, and when she seems to be in a calm state. Try to take just a few moments when you simply watch what she is doing, for example, as she tastes the food you have just given her, and try to imagine what she feels about it, how she might be exploring its texture, moving it around her mouth, or perhaps squashing it between her fingers. Or perhaps you could take a few moments to watch her as she sits on the floor with a few toys nearby, noticing how her interest is caught by the different objects, what she tries to do with them, how she might explore them by putting them in her mouth or banging them against the floor. If you can manage to set aside even a brief time for simply observing your baby in this way, you may see things that you might not have noticed before, or find that behaviour that seemed before to be merely random and uninteresting, starts to be fascinating. And once you begin getting used to observing your baby, her behaviour and expressions will begin to make more and more sense to you and help guide you in how to respond. (For a detailed description of how you can understand more about your baby's behaviour see *The Psychology of Babies* by Lynne Murray: see page 554.)

One tip that can help you become a good observer of your baby's interest in her environment, and also help her engage contingently with you, is to *imitate* her. So, for example, if your baby is old enough to sit up and handle objects, you could place a few objects within her reach, and if you can manage to find doubles (like two wooden spoons, or two plastic cups), or even several examples of these objects (like several wooden bricks), you could take a few minutes to copy whatever your baby does, no matter how silly it might seem (such as sucking on the spoon yourself if this is what your baby has done). Because you are imitating your baby, she will have the experience of your responses being 'contingent'. You might find that she notices that there now is a connection between what she has done and your response, and if so, she is likely to become quite interested in what is happening and start to enjoy the connection with you while you play an imitation game together.

If your baby is younger and is not yet able to handle toys, you can be contingent in other ways. Again it can be helpful to take some moments to just watch her when she is calm and alert, for example, after a nappy change. Even small babies (say around two months old) can make different facial expressions, active mouth movements and some vocal sounds, and if you notice these and either imitate them back, or give her some other sign that you have seen what she has done, then she will also get a sense of the connections between her own experience and what happens around her. This is something babies enjoy, and it will help her learning too.

'Emotional scaffolding'

Another set of parenting skills that can be affected by depression is what is termed 'emotional scaffolding' – that is, the capacity to remain warm and give consistent support to a baby, even in stressful situations where the baby is upset or angry. Providing this emotional scaffolding can help babies to develop the ability to manage their difficult feelings themselves, and to develop positive ways of coping with stress. As we saw earlier, this area of emotional responsiveness is one where babies can differ markedly from one another, even from birth. For some particularly sensitive young babies, even everyday experiences like being undressed, or being hungry or tired, can be very hard to tolerate, and they may cry easily and be hard to soothe. As babies develop, it is quite normal for them to show anger when they are frustrated, as well as distress. The baby, of course, does not understand *why* he might need to do the things his parents want (such as change his clothes), and nor can he know that what is difficult for him in the moment might soon end, and this lack of understanding is part of the reason he can become so worked up. The box below provides an illustration of how emotional scaffolding can make a difference to the baby's response to a situation of frustration and anger.

Harry now has his first teeth and Maggie has started to use a toothbrush to clean them. As he is quite often reluctant, she does it while Harry has a bath, when he can play with his toys in the water at the same time. On the last occasion when she showed Harry the toothbrush he looked unhappy about it, and as Maggie brought it towards him he got agitated and batted her hand away crossly. Maggie wanted to find a way of getting his teeth brushed, but she also wanted to avoid a head-on confrontation, as she knew that this would just escalate his anger. So she found a toy in the bath that would squirt water, filled it, and then playfully directed a jet of water at the plastic cup that Harry was holding. Harry's anger lessened and he looked on with interest as his cup began to fill with water. Maggie dipped the toothbrush in the cup so that Harry could see it, and then pretended to brush her own teeth. This fascinated Harry and he was soon reaching out for the brush himself and brought it to his mouth. Maggie praised him warmly, and when she offered to help him, Harry's mood had recovered and he was happy to let her brush his teeth. Harry's difficult feelings did not escalate out of control, but he also had the chance to realize that being angry wouldn't stop his mother doing what she needed to, and that joining her could be a positive experience.

When faced with a very distressed, frustrated or angry baby, it can be difficult for any parent to remain calm and continue to support their baby in a helpful way, but for a parent who is depressed this can be very challenging indeed. One problem can be having depressive thoughts about these issues. For example, a depressed mother may imagine that her baby is the only one who cries a lot, that it is her fault that her baby gets upset, or that her baby is crying deliberately to be 'naughty' or to 'wind her up'. She might also, as a consequence of feeling depressed, feel helpless to do anything about her baby's crying or angry mood, and as a result she may give up trying to find a way through the situation; or she may feel irritated or angry with her baby. Both these kinds of response can make it harder for the baby to learn how to cope with challenges, and also leave mothers feeling disheartened because the difficult time she had with her baby wasn't resolved.

Again, mothers who are not depressed by no means get emotional scaffolding of their baby right all the time, but mothers with PND do generally have more difficulty with this. Try reflecting on whether there have been times when feeling depressed has interfered with your ability to provide emotional scaffolding for your baby. If this is the case, there are a number of things that you might be able to do.

Tips for emotional scaffolding

First, it can be helpful to realize that anyone, no matter how competent they feel as a parent, can find these baby behaviours stressful, and that it is completely reasonable to want more support. If you have a baby who is more sensitive than others, you are particularly likely to need the support of someone else to take the pressure off. Having someone to talk to can not only give you support, but can also give you a different perspective, so that some of the negative thinking (such as that your baby deliberately cries to wind you up) can be considered afresh.

There may be limits to what you can do to reduce a sensitive baby's crying in the early weeks – some babies just do seem naturally more prone to cry. But knowing that this is not your fault, that it is just unfortunate for you that your baby has this difficulty, may help you reduce any feelings of self-blame and make it easier for you to seek support from your partner, a friend or a professional. You might also feel reassured to know that just because a baby is 'difficult' in the early weeks it does not mean that they will continue to be so. In fact, such babies can develop particularly well if they do have good support.

Aside from these considerations, it can also be helpful to notice what kinds of situation your baby finds difficult to manage. As you observe her habits you may be able to pick up a good sense of situations that are particularly tricky for her. Then, at a time when you can take a few minutes out, it will be worth thinking about whether there are things you can do to reduce her chances of getting into situations that are likely to lead to extremes of distress. Here, some problem-solving work might be helpful (see Chapter 11). If she seems to hate having her nappy changed, for example, it might be worth setting up something she is likely to enjoy to accompany the nappy changing, like putting up a mobile over the changing mat, or giving her a toy she enjoys holding before you begin, or playing some music she likes.

A second problem-solving technique is to ask yourself whether the goals you have are really that important. For example, if your baby becomes very upset every time you put her in her bath, it is worth questioning whether this is something you really need to do at this stage, or whether perhaps you could clean her by 'topping and tailing'– that is, washing one half of her while she is still wearing clothes on the other half, so that she doesn't have to be completely undressed. Or you may decide that you could have her in the bath with you, so that you can help her feel comfortable.

For babies of nine months and older, you can begin to do things that are likely to reduce any tendencies for difficult, angry or oppositional behaviour. This is an age when babies start to be keen to join in activities with you, and it is a good idea to look for opportunities to have positive times with your baby to help her develop the idea that cooperating with you can be fun. You might, for example, set up small projects with her that are easily within her capabilities, like putting things into the washing machine with you (even if they are sometimes pulled out again as you turn your back!). The more opportunities you can create that involve doing something enjoyable together with your baby, and the more she senses your praise and approval as she joins in, the more she will be keen to go along with your suggestions generally, and therefore be less likely to become angry when you need to get her to do something she doesn't particularly want to do.

Supporting the baby's attachment needs

Babies form attachments to the people who care for them, but attachments are not all the same: the kind that is most helpful for a baby to develop in terms of helping him to cope with future challenges and develop satisfying close relationships himself is what is termed a 'secure attachment'. This means that the baby feels that he can trust his parent (or other important carer) to understand and respond to his needs, by giving him comfort and support when he is feeling vulnerable. This might be in the context of feeling ill, or tired, but the clearest signs of a baby's attachment needs are usually when he experiences some challenge that makes him feel vulnerable or frightened. This often occurs in babies at times when they are separated from their parent, but attachment needs can also be seen when someone or something unfamiliar is present and alarms them. Generally, babies start to show clear signs of their attachment needs from around six months, when they begin to realize how important their parent is to them. At this age they might start to cry if you leave the room, or if someone they don't know tries to pick them up. Sometimes parents worry that if they respond to the baby's signs of distress in these moments the baby will become overly dependent on them. Research shows that just the opposite is true: babies who are responded to sympathetically and supportively when they are distressed are more likely to become confident and independent than babies whose attachment needs are not met.

An illustration of a situation where a baby's attachment needs are prominent and meeting them can make a baby feel secure is given below.

Jenny and Iris's story

Baby Iris is six months old. She has been having a difficult day, and is crying more than usual. Her mother, Jenny, isn't sure what the matter is. She has checked Iris's nappy, and fed her, and now she wonders if Iris is bored, so she places her in her baby seat and attempts to play. Iris recovers a little, but then starts to cry again. Jenny changes tack, and lifts Iris from her seat and tries to attract her interest in her mobile hanging over her changing mat. Again Iris calms a little, but soon starts to cry again. Even though Jenny still doesn't know for sure what the matter is, she is able to remain calm herself, and decides that this is just 'one of those days' and that she will put Iris in her sling and provide her with the comfort of being held and rocked a little as she gets on with some simple tasks in the kitchen. Eventually Iris is a little calmer, but Jenny realizes she will just have to adjust her expectations for the day and try to give Iris what support she can. Since walking around with Iris in the sling seems to help, she decides this will be a good day for a walk across the park, and phones a friend to invite her to join them.

Iris will have the sense that her need for comfort from her mother will be met, and that her mother tries hard to understand and respond to her in a helpful way. She will develop the feeling that she is lovable and that other people will support her.

Being postnatally depressed, or overburdened with other problems, can make it difficult for mothers always to meet their baby's attachment needs. Part of this difficulty may arise because the mother herself has not had a good attachment experience – something that is more likely in a depressed mother than other mothers – which leads her to interpret her baby's distress in a particular way. When this happens, it may be hard for her to see her baby's attachment signals for what they really are. A depressed mother might imagine that her baby does not really need her support, or even that it is good for him to have to manage on his own without her responding to his distress. Sometimes she will think that her baby does not like her, and that she isn't important to him. All these beliefs and interpretations can lead a mother to ignore her baby's distress, or even feel irritated by it and reject his bids for comfort when he really needs it. This can lead to the baby feeling insecure and becoming wary of expressing his needs in case he is rejected. Sometimes a mother might find her baby's neediness and distress upsetting or confusing, stirring up difficult feelings about her own needs not having been met. This may lead her to respond inconsistently to her baby, sometimes managing to give comfort and support, but at other times withdrawing. As a result the baby may feel uncertain about whether the mother will respond or not, and this in turn can lead him to be even more demanding in an effort to get a response.

It must be stressed that mothers who are not depressed also often find it hard to respond well to their baby's attachment needs, but, as with contingency and emotional scaffolding, having PND can make this area more difficult to manage. It is worth reflecting on whether there have been times when feeling depressed has made it difficult for you to respond to your baby's attachment needs, and then considering the suggestions below.

Tips for handling the baby's attachment needs

Just as with the other areas where parenting can be affected by depression, it is very worthwhile trying to notice and understand your baby's attachment signals. Once you realize what is really going on, it is likely to make it easier for you to give the support that your baby needs. For example, you might not be aware of how important you are to your baby, and of how much she values your responsiveness when she is feeling vulnerable. You can get a better understanding of this if you try to notice what happens if something alarms her – for example, if she is shown a new toy that she finds quite scary, or if a strange dog comes up to sniff at her in the park. At such times it could be helpful for you to notice your baby's reactions and offer support and reassurance. This will make her feel secure and able to rely on you when facing new challenges. It can also be helpful to keep in mind that babies do *not* become overly dependent if their needs are met, so there is no need to worry that you may do harm by responding to your baby when she is distressed.

Aside from noticing your baby's behaviour, and responding by giving her comfort and support in situations when she needs this, it develops a baby's sense of security if you show your understanding of her experience in the way you talk to her. Obviously, small babies don't understand words, but they can still pick up emotional meanings from the tone of your voice. Later, as your baby does start to understand words, then hearing you talk about her experience, and feeling that you understand her, will contribute even more to her sense of security.

More help with parenting issues

It can be very difficult to think that your depression might be making it harder for you to respond to your baby than you would like. It can make you feel even more guilty and depressed. But being aware of the problem is a really good starting point for breaking unhelpful cycles of engaging with your baby. And as babies are naturally keen to connect with people, particularly you, they are very likely to respond positively when quite simple strategies are followed. This in turn can help you begin to enjoy the experience of being with your baby more. Much more information is given on these parenting issues in two books: *The Social Baby*, which covers the first three to four months and focuses on aspects of care like feeding, crying and sleeping; and *The Psychology of Babies: how relationships support development from birth to two* (both written by Lynne Murray). This second book (see page 554) shows in detail how parenting can support the different areas of babies' development outlined above – that is, their learning, emotions and self-control, and their attachment security. Both books are highly illustrated with photographs derived from video material showing the value of observing babies closely, and these photograph sequences give commentaries to help you understand babies' signals and experiences better.

Key messages

- Observe your baby closely so you can understand better how he experiences his world.

- When you are in face-to-face engagement with a baby of around two to three months, follow and imitate his expressions and social signals. As he grows and begins to explore, help his efforts by attending to what he wants to do and supporting his efforts, and practise imitation games.

- Notice the triggers for your baby's distress so that you can try to avoid them until he is more mature and able to handle these situations, and note the kinds of things that he finds soothing so that you can support him as much as possible.

- Notice how when your baby is scared or uncertain he turns to you for security, and how when you provide that security he becomes more confident and independent.

- Talk to your baby about his experience.

Tips for supporters

- As noted above, in many cases depressed mothers and their families manage to support the development of their children extremely well. Nevertheless, being depressed can make this more difficult.

- You can help by listening as the person you are supporting talks about these experiences, and thinking about what sorts of help the depressed mother might find beneficial.

- Remember that it is very difficult for mothers to reflect on the care they give to their baby without blaming themselves. Every mother wants the best for her baby and if a mother feels that her doing something, or not doing something, is not doing the best for her baby, this can be very distressing for her. It is, therefore, extremely important to stress that, in so far as a mother is having difficulties, it is her depression that is responsible, and that in dealing with her depression she is doing the best she can for both herself and her baby.

Conclusion

This chapter has attempted to provide you with an understanding of the nature of PND, and of how it affects sufferers and their families. It has also provided some general guidelines on the sorts of strategies you can use to overcome your depression and to help you in your relationship with your baby. We very much hope that you will find this useful. However, some people's depression will be too severe for this chapter to be of much use to them. For others, for various reasons, their efforts to use this chapter will not be successful and their depression will persist. If either of these applies to you, we urge you to seek professional help. There are effective treatments for PND and it is important that anyone whose depression persists receives the help they need.

23 Depression in physical illness

Stirling Moorey, Kathy Burn and Lyn Snowden

Aims of this chapter

Everyone learns to deal with illness in their own individual way, bringing their unique strengths and resources to the process of coping. This chapter is about helping you to find what works best for you, and in particular what works in managing low mood associated with illness. This may mean exploring new ways to think about the illness and its impact on your life, trying new methods to cope, or even just getting back to some of the things you used to do before you became ill. The methods for overcoming depression described in earlier sections of this book can all be applied to the low mood that may be triggered by any diagnosis such as diabetes, cancer, multiple sclerosis, heart disease or respiratory disease. In this chapter we will look at some of the special challenges you and those who support you might come across when tackling depression where there are ongoing physical symptoms and disability. We will also look at how the basic methods for dealing with thoughts and behaviours can be adapted to meet these challenges. In our experience most depression in physical illness responds well to the CBT techniques described in this book.

We will first consider what is known about depression in those who are physically ill, and then introduce you to Sonia, a patient with advanced cancer whose story will illustrate how CBT can help people in this kind of situation. We will then help you to identify the sorts of problems you want to work on using this self-help book, and show you how you can map these problems in a way that takes account of physical symptoms as well as thoughts, feelings and behaviours. We will help you to identify your strengths and resilience so that you can create a more positive view of how you can cope. Using Chapter 13, we will consider the power of activity or 'doing' as an antidepressant in physical illness. Although being active may be the last thing you feel like, we hope to show you that you *can* become more active (within the limits of your illness), and that by 'doing', many aspects of your mood and your life will improve. Then we will discuss some methods you can use to cope with negative thoughts (to be used with Chapters 9 and 10) and finally we will look at how to put it all together as a coping plan (building on Chapter 12).

CBT for depression in physical illness

People with physical illness will often have added psychological and emotional needs resulting from the burden of living with their symptoms and added disability. Depression is common and has significant implications for both the patient and their family. As depression is more likely to develop in people with physical illness, there is a Department of Health Strategy – No Health Without Mental Health: A Cross-Government Mental Health Outcomes Strategy for People of All Ages (2013) aiming to address the issue. The reference is in Appendix 1 (page 555) at the end of the book. When depression is present it can affect a person's motivation and their ability to make use of treatment or rehabilitation for their illness. We have included a number of other references in the Other Resources section at the end of the book, for readers who'd like to know more.

Cognitive behavioural therapy is an effective treatment for depression in physical illness. A number of studies have shown that people who have CBT improve more than those who have other treatments, particularly if their depression is more severe. CBT can be effective in a range of different diseases, even severe life-threatening illness such as breast cancer. Furthermore, self-help treatments based on CBT, such as reading books, or working on computerized CBT, have also been found to be effective. As a result of the research, the governmental organization that reviews treatment effectiveness (the National Institute for Health and

Clinical Excellence, or NICE) recommends guided self-help based on CBT for patients with low mood and a chronic physical health problem, and a course of CBT with a therapist for moderate or severe depression or anxiety.

Understanding your reactions to illness

People cope with illness in many different ways. The key to understanding the impact of disease on someone's life is through their thoughts, interpretations, images and beliefs about it. The meaning that your illness has for you will have a major effect on how you feel and therefore the coping methods you use. There are no right or wrong ways to think about the disease and its effects on your life. But if you understand how you are thinking about your situation, you may find that you have choices: choices that may let you look at it differently and cope with it differently. Now we will illustrate how CBT can help people with physical illness by introducing Sonia, who has cancer. You may have similar problems to Sonia, or your own illness may not be as severe or life-threatening, so it may be the themes or common symptoms and reactions that you can relate to.

Sonia's story

Sonia had breast cancer with secondary cancer in her bones. She was having considerable difficulty with pain. The medical staff tried some different medicines and they seemed to work well when she was in hospital but when she went home, the pain seemed to break through the painkillers and Sonia would find that she needed to take more. This made her feel drowsy and she found that she was spending more time in bed. When Sonia thought that her pain was increasing, she would start thinking about her cancer and would get very worried that having the pains meant that it was getting worse. In bed, she had nothing to take her mind off the pain and so she focused on it even more. It seemed to get worse and worse. Being in bed for long periods was uncomfortable; she began to notice new pains that she started to worry about. She saw these pains as more proof that her disease was progressing faster.

Below we show two vicious circles: the first illustrates how staying in bed increased her worry and anxiety, and the second shows how it increased her depression. Of course, in reality both of these were going on at the same time, but we have separated them for clarity.

Figure 57: Sonia's worry cycle

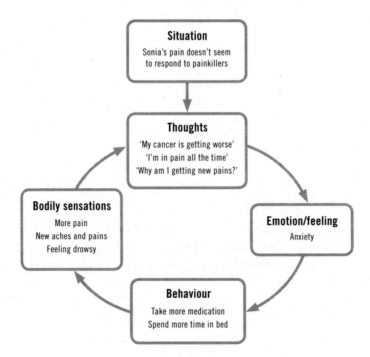

Figure 57 shows how Sonia was stuck in a vicious circle of anxiety and pain. The things she was doing to cope – going to bed and taking more painkillers – made perfect sense, but in her case were actually contributing to her anxious thinking and increasing her pain.

On top of this, Sonia's withdrawal to bed was ruining her days, making her feel depressed and overwhelmed. This is a map of what was going on for Sonia:

Figure 58: Sonia's depression cycle

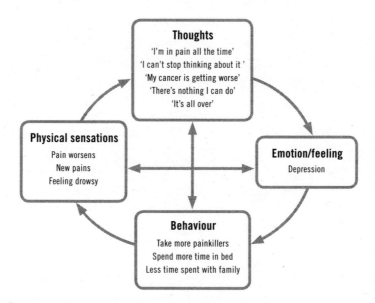

The more time Sonia spent in bed, the more time she had to dwell on how she felt, and she had fewer opportunities to do the ordinary everyday things that give satisfaction in people's lives, such as seeing family and friends. Research also tells us that depressed mood makes physical pain worse.

CBT sessions helped Sonia not only by giving advice about pain relief, but also by making her more aware of her pain and mood. The therapist asked her to keep a 'diary' of her pain, because she originally believed that she was always in pain over a twenty-four-hour period, unless she was asleep. However, when she started keeping a pain diary and monitoring its severity during the day, from 0 to 10, with 10 the worst, she found that there were differences. For example, she discovered that when she was busy with activities, or occupied with friends and family, she was much less aware of her pain and rated its level much lower. It appeared to be more acute and more difficult to manage when she was on her own and she was surprised to learn that going to bed actually seemed to make it worse rather than reduce it. With her therapist, Sonia tried experimenting to see whether increasing her activity during the day had any effect on her pain. She discovered that the more she did activities that distracted her from thinking about the pain, the better she felt and the more she was able to do. She came to realize that although she had very real physical pain, psychological factors made it worse and, using the diary and the experiments, she was able to learn some coping strategies to help her to manage it and have a more normal day.

The work she did with her therapist created 'coping' cycle that made her feel better emotionally and physically:

Figure 59: Sonia's coping cycle

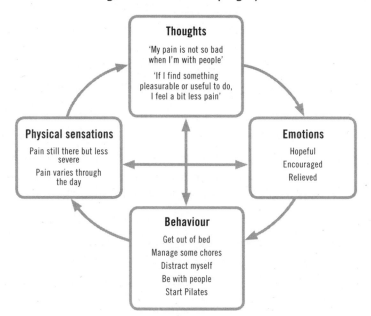

'It's the thought that counts' in CBT

Before therapy, Sonia's pain and way of coping with it by resting robbed her of chances to put enjoyment, distraction and company into her day and she had no way of getting pleasure from life. Her pain and her day seemed intolerable. For her, increased pain meant her disease was worsening and led to extreme anxiety. With the help of CBT, she discovered that her thoughts were certainly unhelpful, but also unrealistic. After she worked with her diary and her supporter she discovered her pain was still present, but it was less overwhelming and did not take up all her waking life.

When our thoughts are focused on threat or danger we feel fear or anxiety, and when they are focused on loss we feel sadness. This is a very natural reaction and is of course realistic when, like Sonia, you are confronted with a disease that will limit your life. It may be difficult for you to separate anxiety and depression when you are ill, and in fact the two often go together. From the CBT perspective you are more likely to feel anxious when you focus on what is uncertain about your illness. For example, someone with multiple sclerosis or rheumatoid arthritis may worry about when the next relapse might occur; someone with cancer may worry about recurrence; and someone with chronic obstructive pulmonary disease (COPD) may worry about the effects of infection or increased breathlessness. Although it is hard sometimes not to worry – and some worry is natural – depression is likely to follow from focusing on what could go wrong next or what you have lost in your life.

When you were diagnosed with your illness you may well have gone through a whole range of emotional reactions. This is a normal part of adjustment to a major change in your life. You might initially have felt confused, disbelieving or numb because the news was unexpected and bore no relation to what you had planned. This may have been followed by feelings of anger ('Why me?'); anxiety ('How am I going to cope?'); and grief ('I've lost my old life.'). These emotions may fluctuate and change during the first few weeks or months after you have been diagnosed with a serious illness. Over time these feelings are likely to settle as you come to accept some of the difficult realities of your situation. Since you are using this self-help book to cope with depression and low mood, you are probably finding your negative thoughts about your illness difficult to manage. People who are depressed tend to have a lot of very negative thoughts, about themselves, the future, or the world. Some examples of this are:

Table 60: Negative thoughts in physical illness

You
'I'm not a normal person any more.'
'I'm useless now.'
'I'm weak. I shouldn't be so upset about this illness.'
'I'm a burden to my family.'
World
'There's no pleasure in life any more.'
'There's nothing anyone can do.'
'People don't want to know me because of my illness.'
Future
'I've only a future of increasing pain to look forward to.'
'I'll never be cured.'

The techniques described in Chapters 9 and 10 and later in this chapter can help you to notice and examine these thoughts to identify whether they might be unrealistic or unhelpful, then find alternative, more helpful ways to approach the situation.

One action is worth a thousand words

Sonia tested her negative thoughts about her pain by collecting information and experimenting with a different approach to it. She discovered that being a little more active not only distracted her from her pain but also gave her constructive things to do which lifted her mood. Keeping as active as you can be (within the limits imposed by your disease) is one of the most effective ways to beat depression. The helplessness and hopelessness associated with low mood generate negative thoughts that make us want to do less and just give up – thoughts like 'What's the point? My life's over anyway. If I can't do everything I used to do, it's not worth doing anything.' Unfortunately, if we're not aware of these thoughts, we might not bother, do less, and then the trap is that by doing less, we are achieving less and feeling even more miserable and hopeless. This inactivity and avoidance keeps the depression, and the negative thoughts, going. Try to think of meaningful activities that you can still do to break this cycle of depression. If you are still able to get about reasonably well, this will mean reminding yourself of what you used to enjoy and experimenting with the effect of returning to those activities. If you are physically less well you may not be able to do some of the things you did in the past. In this case, think about alternative ways to still make progress towards your valued goals: if you used to walk the dog in the woods, start by walking the dog around the block, or finding a wheelchair access path so you can enjoy watching the dog playing.

We often feel anxious and lose confidence when we are depressed and this can easily lead us to avoid situations we find difficult. We might have thoughts like 'My friends won't know what to say to me; we'll all be embarrassed,' or 'How will I cope if I get too tired?' Concern about meeting people is normal, but turning down visitors often leads to ongoing avoidance and this makes things more difficult for us. Avoiding social situations makes us feel more isolated, and feeling isolated keeps the depression going. In the same way, fears of hearing bad news, or what might be ahead, may prevent you from discussing things with your doctor and finding out the facts, or what help would be available to you.

One of the best ways to deal with anxiety is to carry out an experiment, where you test your fear by doing something different to overcome your avoidance. For example, Sonia tested her belief that being more active would make the pain increase by noticing what happened to the pain if she spent a little more time out of bed each day. This proved to her that she could cope without so much rest and also without as much medication.

Key messages

- Depression and physical illness often interact together in a vicious circle to make each other worse.

- The way that we think about our illness makes a huge difference to the way we feel.

- Although illness and depression both make us want to stop doing things, this is bound to make the depression, and the experience of illness, far worse. Reversing this inactivity is a very good way to start tackling both.

- Experiment with doing a little more, and see how it makes you feel.

Tips for supporters

- It can be very difficult for people who are unwell to believe that the way they think and behave can make a difference.

- Try to make sure they don't think the book – or you – are saying it's all in their mind.

- Encourage them to start doing very small things differently, and point out any changes that you notice.

Where to begin: identifying target problems

You may feel that you have so many problems associated with your illness that you do not know where to start. This is a very common feeling. So a sensible beginning may be to make a list of all the problems that are troubling you. Just writing everything down can be a relief, because at least you know what you have to tackle. Some people also find that seeing everything on a bit of paper helps to give some distance from the problems – they are 'out there' rather than rattling round your head. Perhaps a family member or friend can help you with the list. Try to make the problems on your list as specific as possible. It is easier to find a solution if the problem is phrased specifically: 'My husband and I argue two or three times a week over whether he does enough to help around the house,' rather than 'We row all the time – he never helps out.'

You may want to consider your problems under some of the following headings:

Table 61: Identifying target problems

Problem area	Sonia's example
Problems with emotions	Crying every day
	Depressed and not interested in answering the phone or seeing people
Problems with activity/behaviour	Staying in bed all day
	Shouting at the children when they play noisily
Physical problems	Tiredness limits what I can do
	Waking up at night and worrying so I can't sleep well
Relationship problems	Feeling like I am a burden to my family
	Feeling guilty for being too ill to have sex with my partner

You could use a form like this to help you to write everything down. You could use the same categories as above, or use different ones if they are relevant to you.

Worksheet 19: My problem list

Problem Area
Problems with emotions
Problems with activity/behaviour
Physical problems
Relationship problems
Other problems

Now look at your list to see if any of the problems are linked, in which case maybe two could be tackled together? Choose a problem that you would like to work on first. This may be the one that is the most important for you, but might also be the one that you would find easiest to tackle.

The problem I would like to work on is . . .

Now that you have identified the problem that you'd like to work on, think about how you would like it to be better. What would you like to achieve? Try to make this as specific as possible. For example, 'I'd like it if my husband and I could sit down and agree what he is going to do to help, so we won't need to row about it,' rather than 'I want him to do more.'

What I would like to achieve is (my goal is) . . .

Key messages

- Make a start on tackling your depression by making a problem list.

- Choose one of the problems to start working on, and make it as specific as possible.

- Think about what you'd like to change, and again, make this specific so you'll know when you've achieved it.

Tips for supporters

- It may be hard for the person you are supporting to be specific about the problems affecting them. This is a common difficulty. If they identify a problem like 'depression' you can help them by asking, 'What aspect of depression is most troubling? Are there particular symptoms that are really upsetting?'

- In the same way it can be helpful to make the goal for therapy as specific as possible. You could help by asking:

   ◊   'How would things be different if you overcome the problem?'

   ◊   'What would you be doing more of that you're not doing now?'

   ◊   'What would you be doing less of?'

   ◊   'Are there things you would no longer be avoiding?'

Understanding the 'depression trap'

Angela's story

Angela had been feeling depressed since having a heart attack a few months previously. Nothing gave her pleasure any more. She felt that all she ever talked about was her illness; her mood was so low she didn't want to 'inflict' herself on anyone. She stayed at home, and often stayed in bed or didn't even bother to dress. When people telephoned she would tell them she had a hospital appointment to avoid them coming to visit. Angela identified feeling miserable as her main problem. She was trapped in a vicious circle of low mood and inactivity.

Figure 62: Angela's low mood and inactivity vicious circle

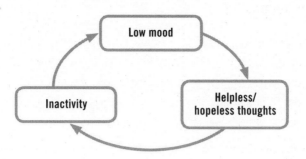

Angela knew the best way out of depression is to become active again, but she was worried that if she exerted herself she would put too much strain on her heart. Her negative thoughts were 'I can't risk anything happening again. If I overdo it I'll become a complete invalid.' Her supporter helped her to look at these fears, which she had not shared with anyone before. They were able to examine them and see that there was no evidence for such caution: all the information Angela had been given suggested that gentle exercise was actually very beneficial. She could also see that she was behaving like an invalid already, so her efforts to protect herself were hardly paying off.

Her supporter suggested that she gradually increase her activities as an experiment to see what happened to her mood, and also what happened to her heart. She discovered that she did not feel any worse physically and she did not feel like her heart was strained. Doing these small tasks meant that she was able to succeed at each step and this motivated her to go further. She realized that the more things she did, the more she had to talk about, and she could therefore meet her friends without having to discuss her illness all the time.

Figure 63: Effect of Angela's increased activity

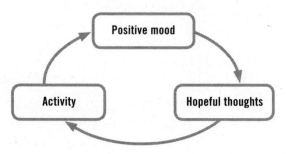

The depression trap does not only lock you into cycles of low mood; it can also have a direct effect on your physical state. Pain and tiredness are both made worse by depressed mood, and activity can help you to escape.

Figure 64: Low mood/inactivity/hopeless thoughts/ pain vicious circle

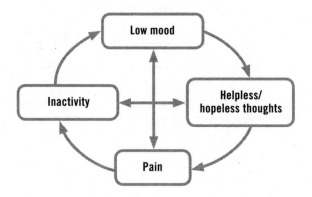

Derek's story

Derek suffered from frequent migraines. He got so fed up with them that every time he noticed a migraine starting he would sink into angry despair. His negative thoughts were 'I can't stand it! This is another day ruined! I have no life any more.' He would then take the day off work and do nothing. Monitoring the migraines revealed that sometimes they really could only be managed by spending time quietly in a dark room, but at other times Derek's withdrawal and negative thinking just created a self-fulfilling prophecy that made the pain and depression worse. By noticing this pattern and recording his headaches Derek got better at separating serious migraines from tension headaches.

Mapping your unhelpful patterns

Now that you have seen some examples of how thoughts, feelings, behaviours and bodily sensations can interact to trap you in depression, you may want to map some of your own negative patterns. This is often difficult at first. Do not worry if this is the case. There is another example below to help you. Here are some tips:

1. Start with the problem you want to work on and a recent situation that has been difficult.

2. What emotions or feelings did you have in the situation – depression, anxiety, panic, anger?

3. What did you feel in your body – tight chest, breathless, muscle tension? Did you have other physical sensations that were associated with your disease – pain, nausea, tiredness?

4.   What thoughts did you have? Try to write down the actual thoughts that went through your mind – for example: 'My friends won't want to know me.' 'I'm going to have a heart attack.' 'This pain means I'm going to have a relapse.' 'I can't cope.' Did you have any images in your mind? For example, a patient with cancer commonly saw a neon sign saying 'Poison' whenever she thought of the chemotherapy she was having.

Here is a different example to guide you:

Tom's story

Tom was devastated when he learned that his stomach cancer had returned only two years after its first onset. He worried that this would mean his cancer was incurable and that he was going to die. Tom felt hopeless about his future and thought that there was nothing good left in his life. He had stopped working as soon as he received the bad news and spent most of the day in bed or watching TV. He stopped going out to any of his usual weekly activities and made excuses when his friends tried to encourage him to come out with them. Tom thought that staying home made him feel better, but came to realize with the help of his supporter that the less he did, the worse he felt. Often, during the day, he would not get dressed, but would just sit on the sofa and feel overwhelmed by sad thoughts, which lowered his mood. He would sometimes spend time crying and feeling angry or low.

Below is Tom's unhelpful patterns map – have a look at it and then fill in the blank version which follows.

Figure 65: Tom's unhelpful patterns map

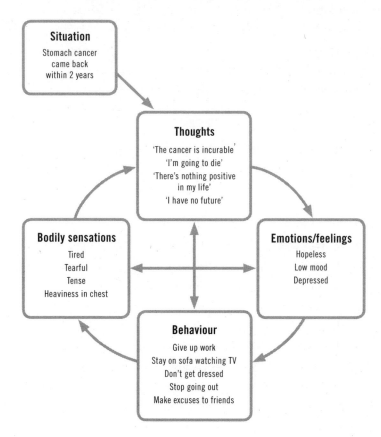

Situation
Stomach cancer
came back
within 2 years

Thoughts
'The cancer is incurable'
'I'm going to die'
'There's nothing positive
in my life'
'I have no future'

Bodily sensations
Tired
Tearful
Tense
Heaviness in chest

Emotions/feelings
Hopeless
Low mood
Depressed

Behaviour
Give up work
Stay on sofa watching TV
Don't get dressed
Stop going out
Make excuses to friends

Worksheet 20: Unhelpful patterns map

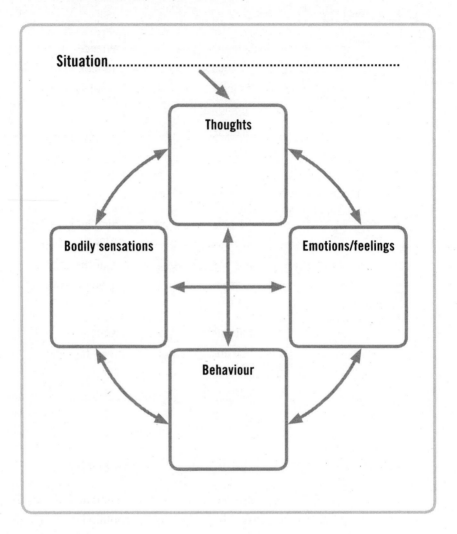

Key messages

- Thoughts, feelings, behaviour and physical experience interact together in a very understandable way. Starting to look in detail at how this works can help you to understand what is keeping your own vicious circles going.

Tips for supporters

- You might like to help the person you are supporting by filling in the thoughts, feelings, behaviours and physical symptoms with them. This should help you both make some sense of the confusing mass of thoughts and feelings that can swamp you when you are depressed.

- You might ask them what is the best place to start – this will often be the physical side – and then draw the arrows together to see how vicious circles are created.

Breaking unhelpful behavioural patterns

The paralysing effect of depression on our motivation and activity levels is one of the themes of this book. Chapters 8 and 13 contain lots of advice on how activating yourself can help you break out of depression. This applies as much when your depression is linked to physical illness as it does to any other type. The depression can fool you into thinking you are not able to do things that will give you pleasure and/or a sense of achievement. Challenging some of these negative beliefs can help you to become more active again.

'If I can't do what I used to do there's no point in doing anything'

This thought is a bit like throwing the baby out with the bathwater. Your illness may be limiting you in many of the things you can do, but we find that depression makes people underestimate what they are still capable of. If you draw out the vicious circle arising from this belief you will discover that you are depriving yourself of opportunities to get pleasure and achievement from things you *can* still do.

'I'm too tired/too ill/in too much pain to do anything'

We generally trust our body to tell us when it is safe to do things. The challenge you face with low mood and physical illness will be in distinguishing real signals (when your body is telling you it's best to rest) from negative signals (when your depression is telling you it's best to do nothing). The thoughts that are characteristic of depression tend to be helpless and hopeless. They are very negative and overwhelming – 'there's no point', 'it'll never get better'. They tend to lead to an 'all or nothing' approach to activity, which may mean you overdo things when you are feeling a little better, but then avoid doing anything when you are more unwell. The way to deal with this is to explore whether this feels like the depression talking (with practice you may be able to distinguish physical tiredness from the mental tiredness of depression), and to test the thoughts by using a step-by-step approach to activity as described below.

Graded activities

Breaking tasks down into small steps is a great way to overcome mental lethargy, and to pace yourself if you are physically ill. Things that are usually easy to do when you are well can seem like insurmountable obstacles when you are unwell. Cutting them down to size by dividing them into small steps will help you to manage them one at a time.

Joan's story

Joan was experiencing a lot of joint pain and stiffness from rheumatoid arthritis. In the past she could clean her house in just a few hours, but now even a few minutes' housework tired her out. She decided to concentrate on just one room and take the work at a steady pace. She knew she could manage to dust for about ten minutes before feeling pain, so she did as much as she could in this time, then rested. When she felt ready she began where she had left off and in this way managed to cover the whole room in less than an hour. She realized she had been avoiding the dusting because she had felt so overwhelmed, but in fact by doing it step by step she could still get there, and the rest periods helped to prevent her feeling too much pain.

Increasing activity when your illness limits what you can do

When we are depressed we tend to focus on the tasks we can no longer do and forget what we can still achieve. Even if your illness limits you physically, there may be other activities that still give you pleasure. For instance, you may still find enjoyment in talking to your family on the phone, even if you are not well enough to visit them; if you can't go out to the cinema you might nevertheless enjoy watching a DVD. Many people find that they now have time for reading, or a talking book, which in the past had to be put off because they were too busy. Of course, if you are depressed, your concentration may be a problem, and you might need to gradually build up the amount you can read.

It may be helpful to identify what you got from the activities you can no longer engage in, to see if there are other ways you can get the same value. You can ask yourself:

- What was it about the activity that gave me pleasure?

- What was it about the activity that gave me satisfaction, and helped me towards my goals?

- Can I achieve this in another way?

For example, a young man who became paralysed after a rugby accident might have loved many other things about sport as well as the game itself – such as the social camaraderie. So he might explore other group activities, such as volunteering for a charity or taking up wheelchair rugby.

Key messages

- We often have thought blocks to becoming more active which can get in the way of making a start. Try to think about whether you share any of the ones described above, or have different ones of your own.

- Start off in a graded way, or look for alternative activities that provide the same kinds of pleasure and satisfaction.

- Try not to compare it to what you used to be able to do, but appreciate things for what they are now.

Tips for supporters

- If you know the person you are supporting well, you might be able to remind them of things they used to enjoy doing. When you are ill and depressed it is easy to forget these things.

- Help them to think about *all* the reasons that they enjoyed that activity, not just the obvious ones. What was it about, for example, walking along the seafront for the newspaper in the morning?

It may be that if the real tonic was feeling the wind and spray on their face they can still have this pleasure, even though they are less mobile.

- You can help them to identify steps towards their goals. Sometimes we set ourselves unrealistic goals that might be appropriate when we are well, but too ambitious when we are ill. When they have suggested some first steps, you might ask 'Do you feel able to do that at the moment? Do we need to break it down into smaller steps?'

- Make sure that you and the depressed person notice any small achievements. These small steps can be really hard and so need to be fully recognized and credited.

Managing unhelpful thinking patterns

Coping with illness can sometimes mean facing major changes in your life and dealing with uncertainty about the future. Many of your thoughts about your illness and the changes you are facing may be constructive and help you cope, but sometimes your thoughts may be unhelpful and lead to distress. Understanding what you are thinking and how your thoughts can affect your emotions, as well as affecting what you do during your day, is very important in enabling you to manage distress. Some examples of thoughts that can make it more difficult for people to cope are:

- 'I won't be able to manage.'

- 'I must have done something really bad to deserve this.'

- 'What's the point?'

- 'Nothing is worth doing any more.'

- 'I have lost control of my life because of my illness.'

These are the Negative Automatic Thoughts (NATs) referred to throughout this book. They are unrealistically gloomy, seem to come from nowhere and pop unbidden into your mind. We may not always be aware of them because they happen so quickly that we don't pay very much attention to them. But these thoughts are very important to our mental wellbeing. As we've seen, when we feel depressed we tend to think negative thoughts about ourselves, others, our situation and our future. When we learn to recognize them, we can begin to look at them more closely. We can think about whether they are realistic, or if they are being coloured by depression, and need to be questioned and changed. Recognizing unhelpful thoughts and starting to think in different ways can help us to begin to feel better.

Keeping a diary

The first step in changing your thinking is to begin identifying your NATs, as described in Chapter 9. They can be difficult to spot to start with (you are probably not even aware that they are there most of the time) but try to recognize what is going through your mind at times when you are feeling depressed. You may find it helpful to keep a diary of times when you are aware that your mood has changed. You could write down what might have triggered the mood change, what you are thinking, and what you feel and do when these thoughts come into your mind. Many people find that just recognizing their NATs and writing them down helps them to realize how unhelpful they are and they begin to feel more in control.

Recognizing unhelpful patterns of thinking (thinking traps)

When you start to feel overwhelmed or demoralized, you can fall into the trap of unhelpful patterns of thinking, or 'thinking traps'. One example of a thinking trap is making negative predictions. It is realistic to consider that the future for many people with cancer is uncertain, but it is not helpful to predict the worst without any evidence that the worst is going to happen, for example:

- 'I know the treatment won't work.'

- 'My partner will no longer find me attractive.'

- 'My pain won't be controlled.'

- 'My future is very bleak.'

Realizing that you can get into unhelpful patterns of thinking will help you to examine your thoughts more closely and consider how you might avoid making such automatic judgements without any evidence.

When people feel overwhelmed or demoralized they often get things out of proportion. This can lead them to exaggerate the real problems they are facing, and to underestimate their ability to cope with them. Some of the examples below may help you to notice the distortions in your negative thoughts.

1. **Overgeneralization**

    You see a single negative event as the never-ending pattern of defeat. For instance, if you have a row with your partner the day after you get back from hospital you think: 'We'll always be arguing – things will never be the same again. We might as well split up now and get it over with.'

2. **Magnification and minimization**

    You exaggerate some things, such as other patients' strengths and coping abilities, while at the same time playing down your own methods of coping. You may say to yourself: 'Everyone is coping better than me. I'm just a mess.'

3. **All-or-nothing thinking**

    The world is seen in absolute terms. For example, a man who had been told that he could not be cured of cancer said: 'If I can't be cured, there's no point in doing anything. I might as well die now.' However, with appropriate treatment he could have had months or years of active life.

4. **Selective attention**

   If you feel depressed you are only able to think about the negative parts of your life. You selectively attend to these while ignoring all the positive things that are happening to you. For example, 'I'm no use: I can't cook as I used to, I can't do the housework, I can't get to the shops – what use am I?'

5. **Negative predictions**

   The future for many people with physical illness is uncertain. But you can turn this into a negative certainty by assuming the worst: 'I know this treatment won't work.' 'Even if I'm cured I know something else will come along to cause problems for me.'

6. **Mind-reading**

   You jump to conclusions about what other people are thinking. For example, someone might think, 'Now that I'm ill my friends won't want anything more to do with me.'

7. **Shoulds and oughts**

   You try to motivate yourself with 'shoulds' and 'oughts', but end up feeling guilty. For example, 'I should be able to do everything I did before I got ill. Even though I don't feel well, I should still be looking after my children.'

8. **Labelling**

   You apply a critical label to yourself instead of accurately describing the situation. You might say, 'I'm just a useless cripple now.' Or if you find it difficult to concentrate because of the stress you are under you say, 'I'm an idiot.'

9. **Personalization**

   You see yourself as the cause of some negative event for which you are not necessarily responsible. If friends cancel a visit you say, 'It must be because of my illness.'

Recognizing the difference between a realistic and reasonable thought and an unhelpful and distressing thought

Once you have begun to recognize and identify the automatic thoughts that are running through your mind when you are feeling low or anxious, you can begin to examine them to see whether they are realistic and reasonable or unhelpful and distressing (as described in Chapter 9).

Sometimes it is difficult to distinguish between a realistic thought and a negative one. You may like to consider the 'Serenity Prayer' to help you make the distinction between the two.

> *God grant me the serenity to accept the things I cannot change . . .*
>
> *The courage to change the things that I can . . .*
>
> *And the wisdom to know the difference*

Thoughts that are realistic are:

- 'I have emphysema/heart failure/cancer and this has altered my life.'

- 'I do feel more tired some days but this doesn't mean I can't do anything.'

Unhelpful and distressing thoughts might be:

- 'I have emphysema/heart failure/cancer and now my life is not worth living.'

- 'I'm always tired so I may as well just curl up and stay in bed.'

Challenging and changing your unhelpful and distressing thoughts

Once you have identified the thoughts that are unhelpful and distressing, the next step towards making you feel better is to identify a different and more realistic thought about the same situation. Finally, see if you can develop a new belief that will help you to change the way you are thinking.

Here are some examples:

Table 66: Changing unhelpful thoughts

Unhelpful and distressing thoughts	Realistic thoughts	New belief
If I wake up in the morning feeling more panicky and sad than usual, then I know the rest of the day is going to be dreadful. Emotion: sad and anxious	Everyone feels sad and anxious some days. I cannot expect to be perfect. No one is perfect. Just because I wake up feeling bad it doesn't mean my whole day will be dreadful.	Some days are better than others. I need to work on some ways that will help me to cope better when I wake up feeling panicky and sad.
I will never be able to do this! Emotion: defeated	I might not be able to do all of this but I can do something. I am doing better on some days than I was before so that is an accomplishment!	I need to try and take little steps – I will just start with some easy things and build up to the more difficult things.
I could not get out of bed until quite late today and now I have wasted the whole day. Emotion: frustrated	It is hard to get out of bed when you are feeling sad, but I know I will feel better if I make the effort.	Today, I will make a plan that will help me to get out of bed tomorrow.

If you find it difficult to think of realistic thoughts or new beliefs, here are a few suggestions that you may find helpful:

- What evidence do you have that this thought is true? Do you have any evidence that it isn't?

- What might you say to a friend if they came to you and told you the same unhelpful and distressing thought?

- Imagine you are talking to someone you know who always seems to give good advice. What do you think they would say to you?

- If you were not feeling anxious or depressed how might you view the situation differently?

- How might you have considered this thought before you became ill?

Changing your thinking really will help you to feel better

It can be very difficult to start making changes. Your negative thoughts are likely to be present and may interfere with you even trying. You might say to yourself, for example, 'This is just too complicated for me, I'll do it later,' or, 'It would be better if I just try to ignore or forget all about this,' or, 'This book is not relevant to me because I know my symptoms stop me from going out.' Perhaps you might find that it is too frightening to look at your thoughts in great depth.

It is quite natural to want to avoid thinking through unpleasant experiences, particularly when you are feeling low or anxious, but doing this is the best way to combat your anxiety and depression. Ignoring your thoughts won't make them go away.

If you are struggling to make changes, then it might be because you are having powerful negative thoughts which are getting in the way. When you are contemplating changes but just can't face making them, then stop and write down what you are thinking. If you can identify negative thoughts that are getting in the way of change, you can start to tackle them. Talk to your supporter, or a friend or family member about your difficulties and see if they can help you identify the negative thoughts.

Testing thoughts through experiments

Sometimes it may be difficult to believe your alternative thoughts, or you may not have enough information to decide if they are correct. In this case you could set up an experiment to test them. We usually assume our thoughts are pretty accurate about the way things are, and so we act on them accordingly. But when you are in a depression trap, thoughts like 'What's the point? I can never be well again,' may lead you to stop doing things you used to enjoy and rob you of pleasure that might still be open to you. Or thoughts like 'If I go for a walk today, I'll be in even more pain,' might keep you sitting in your chair all day. One way to challenge these thoughts is to set up an 'experiment' to test if your predictions are correct. There are more details about these experiments in Chapter 10.

Step one – identify the fear

What do you fear will happen? *If I walk to the end of the garden I'll pay for it and my pain will be worse.*

How strongly do you believe this will happen? *90 per cent.*

Step two – examine the fear

What evidence do you have that your prediction will come true?

Have you had to walk this far before – for example to the outpatients clinic?

Is this a pattern of avoidance you have identified with your supporter that might be keeping you stuck in your house?

I'm frightened I could get stuck out there away from the house, but I have been regularly walking to the toilet, and when we couldn't get a parking space near the hospital. I managed to walk a little.

Step three – plan an experiment

Decide what you need to do to test your fear. Plan when and where you will do the experiment. What will you need to know to find out if your prediction has been disproved?

I will take a painkiller at lunchtime and if my pain is less than 4/10 severe, I will walk down the garden. I will see how bad my pain feels when sitting at the end of the garden, after five minutes to recover.

What do you need to do to make it more likely there will be a positive outcome?

I will ask my husband to leave a chair halfway.

I will take a painkiller so I am comfortable when I set off.

I will increase my walking in the house today and count how many steps I can take comfortably.

We do have a wheelchair, so I know I could get back.

How will you cope if your fear is proved correct?

If I can't walk that far, I'll at least get to the chair, and we can plan how to make the garden more accessible, or talk to the physio/doctor to see if it's something I can work on, or not.

Step four – evaluate the outcome

What happened? Were your fears upheld? How strongly do you believe your prediction now?

Make sure you are objective about the result. It may be that a prediction partly comes true, but don't let your negative thoughts label the experiment a complete failure. Examine your prediction.

It was lovely to get out in the fresh air. I felt very shaky at first, but I sat and smelt the flowers. I enjoyed being in the open and even dead-headed a few roses. My pain was no worse than a 4/10, same as indoors. My prediction was 0 per cent accurate.

Step five – decide what you need to do next

Sometimes an experiment disproves your fear completely. In this case you may want to set up an action plan to build on it and ensure you don't fall back into avoidance. At other times you may not be fully convinced and so need to set up more experiments.

I'm going to do this twice more to regain my confidence and then I'm planning to walk to the postbox!

Figure 67: Testing a thought by experiment

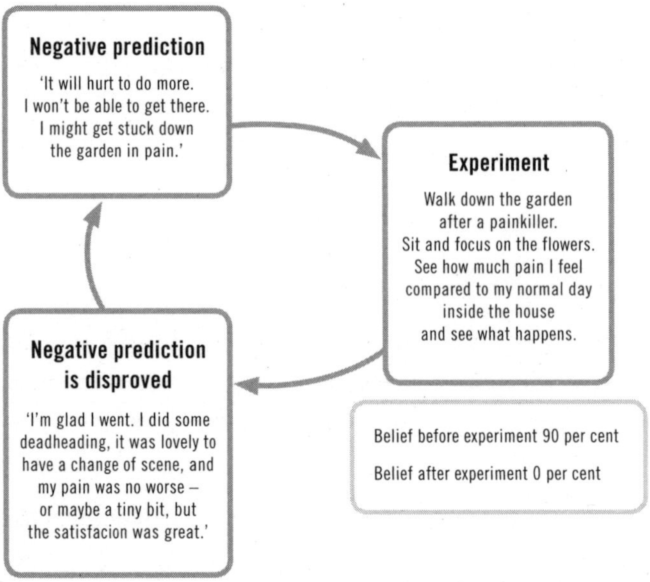

Negative prediction

'It will hurt to do more. I won't be able to get there. I might get stuck down the garden in pain.'

Experiment

Walk down the garden after a painkiller. Sit and focus on the flowers. See how much pain I feel compared to my normal day inside the house and see what happens.

Negative prediction is disproved

'I'm glad I went. I did some deadheading, it was lovely to have a change of scene, and my pain was no worse – or maybe a tiny bit, but the satisfacion was great.'

Belief before experiment 90 per cent

Belief after experiment 0 per cent

Key messages

Experiments can be a source of real learning, but are a novel approach to many. To help you start off it may help to refer back to the section on behavioural experiments in Chapter 10 on experiments. Important messages are:

- Practice makes perfect; don't give up after the first attempt!

- Think of a particular problem you have, and a particular thing you wish to find out.

- Be specific about what you predict will happen. For example, 'If I'm tired I need a nap in the afternoon.'

- Follow the step-by-step guide above and plan a different afternoon. Plan twice or three times and measure how it affects your tiredness if you do something different.

- Be patient; it takes time.

- You can write down your experiment and its outcome on the behavioural experiment worksheet that follows.

Tips for supporters

- Testing thoughts is a new process and can take time to learn. Be supportive and understanding of the patient's negative thoughts – they often have a basis in reality, even if they contain some thinking traps.

- Try to let the person find their own answers, even though it can be tempting to give advice or answers because you're so keen to see change. People often believe their own advice and if they can find out for themselves how the world works for them, with their own experiments, they will achieve lasting change. You might use some gentle questioning along the lines described above to help them explore how helpful and realistic their negative thoughts really are.

- Behavioural experiments are wonderful opportunities for you to help the person you are supporting. You can be a resource to go out with them if they are testing a negative belief.

Worksheet 21: Behavioural experiment

Step one – identify the fear

What do you fear will happen?

How strongly do you believe this will happen?

Step two – examine the fear

What evidence do you have that your prediction will come true?

Step three – plan an experiment

Decide what you need to do to test your fear.

Plan when and where you will do the experiment.

What will you need to know to find out if your prediction has been disproved?

What do you need to do to make it more likely there will be a positive outcome?

How will you cope if your fear is proved correct?

Step four – evaluate the outcome

What happened? Were your fears upheld? How strongly do you believe your prediction now?

Make sure you are objective about the result. It may be that a prediction partly comes true, but don't let your negative thoughts label the experiment a complete failure. Examine your prediction.

Step five – decide what you need to do next

Creating effective coping patterns

Earlier, we met Tom, who had learned that his stomach cancer had returned only two years after diagnosis; he had thoughts that this would mean his cancer was incurable and that he was going to die. Here's what happened when he began to try CBT.

Tom felt hopeless about the future, had stopped working, and spent most of the day in bed watching TV. He couldn't be bothered to shave or get dressed and made excuses when his friends asked him out.

He initially thought that staying in bed made him feel better. With the help of his supporter he started keeping a diary of what he was doing during the day when he felt depressed. He discovered that the less he did, the worse he felt. Tom found that after increasing the amount he did and starting to add some social activities into his week, his mood started to lift. He engaged more in life and in CBT techniques and then was able to learn to challenge some of the negative and unhelpful thoughts that had often led him to feeling more depressed. Tom could see that he had coped before and although it was unpleasant and frightening, there was nothing physically different about the way he felt now from the way he had felt during his first bout of the illness.

Figure 68: Tom's helpful thought patterns

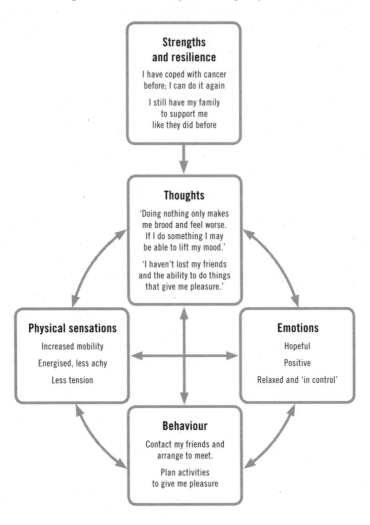

Your plan for coping

You might like to think what a more helpful pattern of coping might look like for your problems. You could summarize your old way of coping under Plan A and your new way under Plan B.

On the sheet below, describe your Plan A – that's the unhelpful aspects of how you are coping at the moment. Describe the things that you might avoid, the unhelpful thoughts you have, or the times you withdraw and give up. Under Plan B describe things you are doing now that work, and what you can do in the future to maximize your quality of life.

After the blank sheet, there is an example to show how you might fill it in.

Worksheet 22: Old and new plans

Plan A	Plan B

Table 69: Example of old and new plans

Plan A	Plan B
Rest a lot. Stay in bed. Don't get out into the garden.	Experiment to find out how much rest I need and how much more my pain will allow me to do in the day. Get up and dressed every morning, write down how my mood and pain is compared to being in bed. Walk around the house until I can manage fifty steps, then experiment by walking down the garden.

Key messages

- In this chapter you have been introduced to the idea that the physical symptoms of an illness can lead you to think differently, do less and feel depressed.

- Hopefully you have some new ideas about how these are inter-linked and how changes in either your thinking, or what you do, can be beneficial.

- Hopefully you have been able to map out your negative thinking or activity patterns and found some ways you might break these by doing a little more within your limits, or by experimenting with doing things differently.

- We have also looked at how noticing and questioning your thoughts and beliefs about your illness can make you more aware of the impact they have on you. Taking the time to loosen up your think-ing and alter what you do can not only break the vicious circles but also create positive circles of increasing hope, self-confidence and energy. This in turn will promote more effective coping.

Acknowledgements

Some sections of this chapter were taken from the self-help manual used in a clinical trial of CBT in palliative care. We would like to thank St Christopher's Hospice, London, and Kings Health Partners Biomedical Research Centre for permission to use extracts from this manual.

24 Depression in later life

Ken Laidlaw and Dichelle Wong

Introduction

Depression is not as common in later life as people assume, and in fact, older people are less likely to be depressed than working-age adults (people under the age of sixty-five). Researchers in the US have produced interesting results that seem to fly in the face of what many people believe happens to us when we get older. They interviewed almost 200 people aged between nineteen and ninety-four years of age over a period of ten years and found that people's emotional wellbeing *increased* as they aged. Perhaps equally interesting is the fact that those who experienced more positive than negative emotions tended to live longer.

As people get older, certain medical conditions such as dementia become more common, but researchers who study ageing report a common 'ageing paradox'. That is, despite the challenges later life can bring, older people typically report high levels of life satisfaction. We can therefore deduce that, happily, it is not necessarily the case that life gets worse as you get older. People tend to become more accepting of change and loss, as they are seen as being 'on time' – expected as part of growing older.

While it is obviously good news that clinical depression affects only a minority of older people, it is still the most common mental-health problem in later life. Depressive *symptoms*, rather than clinical depression, may be more common for older people. This just means that people can experience a lack of motivation, feeling blue or downhearted, feeling hopeless about the future, and so on – but would not be diagnosed by a doctor as having 'clinical' depression. As mentioned briefly in Chapter 1, this is called dysthymia (pronounced diss-thigh-mee-ahh) or 'subclinical' depression and shouldn't be underestimated or ignored as it can make your life unnecessarily miserable. Furthermore, it can be effectively treated. If you feel you may have a problem with subclinical depression, then you've probably been feeling sad, low or just not your 'usual self' for a number of months, or even for the last couple of years. You may have noticed that you have less of an interest in hobbies or activities than before and you find it hard to motivate yourself. You might have experienced a disturbance in your sleep or appetite; you may be sleeping or eating too much or too little. *These are not symptoms of old age, but symptoms of depression.* Later on in this chapter we are going to tackle a few myths and misunderstandings about depression in later life, but before we go on would like to be clear about the following:

Depression is not part of normal ageing, and if you are feeling low you should not just accept it. Depression in older people, irrespective of cause, is just as treatable as it is at any other age. Medication is helpful, and there are a range of psychological interventions that can make a big difference. CBT has been shown to be very effective with this age group, and so has interpersonal psychotherapy, or IPT, mentioned in Chapter 5. These treatments are just as effective for older people as they are for younger ones, so there is no reason not to ask for them. These therapies, particularly CBT, can also be adapted for self-help use, so that you don't need to talk to a professional if you don't want to, but can use the ideas and techniques described in this book.

Although it does seem to be true that rates of depression increase in certain circumstances, such as after a major physical event like a stroke, or the onset of diabetes, depression does not automatically result from a physical illness. Chapter 23 on depression and physical ill health talks in a lot more detail about this. One of the crucial differences seems to be the way that we think about what has happened to us, and the way we respond to it. This is a constant theme in cognitive therapy, and we will remind you of it a little later in this chapter.

Overall, the good news is that you can do something to take back control. Parts 1 and 2 of this book describe many things that can help you, so if you have not done so already, read through and see if they do. You can also try out the ideas in this chapter, which are specifically designed to help those experiencing depression in old age.

What to do when anxiety accompanies depression

Depression often has an evil sidekick: anxiety. On page 9 in Chapter 1 we talked about how to tell if you have a significant anxiety problem that needs tackling in its own right. Anxiety is a common experience and everybody worries from time to time, but when it is very severe and goes on for a long time it may need additional help.

Anxiety can make life very uncomfortable and it can make us fearful about a lot of things we were not concerned about before. It can often lead to changes in our behaviour: we may start to avoid certain situations, or activities, or other people. In the short term, avoidance may make us feel less pressured, but it has an unfortunate longer-term side effect: we never learn that what we were anxious or worried about is well within our coping capabilities. In the end, we lose confidence because the more we avoid something, the less chance we have to find out that we were worrying about something unnecessarily. In reality, the only thing you need to fear is the one thing most anxious people don't seem to fear: avoidance itself. *Avoidance always makes your problems worse.*

Pat's story

Pat is a sixty-eight-year-old retired plumber who has become anxious that he may have a life-threatening disease. He has seen a few of his mates from the building trade die recently. Pat has always been health-conscious and has never smoked. He developed a chest infection and was convinced that he had cancer; as a result, he stopped going out and meeting his friends. He became so concerned that something bad was going to happen that he stopped going to work. Pat stopped going too far from his house in case he became ill. These days he is almost housebound and instead of going out and filling his day with pleasant activities, Pat has filled his day with worry and frustration.

Pat has fallen victim to what is called 'emotional reasoning': we feel so bad and worried that we emotionally reason there is good cause for our concerns. That makes us feel more anxious, and we convince ourselves we are facing an impending catastrophe, which makes us more anxious, and so on.

President Roosevelt said, 'The only thing we have to fear is fear itself' – but we beg to differ. If you avoid something you never give yourself the chance to see that you can cope; therefore avoidance is the biggest thing you have to fear.

If you are worried about feeling anxious, it would be helpful to review your recent activities. Have you noticed that you've stopped doing things you previously enjoyed? Do you keep yourself to yourself more now? If so, perhaps you might want to make some changes.

- Take it easy, and if you set targets for yourself, make them easy steps.

- If you haven't seen your friends for a while, think about calling up one or two of your closest friends and ask them to come round to visit you.

- Arrange to go somewhere local, with a friend. This could be a café you used to visit frequently before you felt low.

- Do you feel guilty about asking your friends for help? What would you do if you knew someone you cared about was not asking you for help?

- When you plan to make a change, choose something easy to do and set limits for yourself. If you go out, make sure to give yourself some sort of reward for doing this.

- Remember, anxiety affects many people and is *not a sign of weakness*. The fact that you are looking to help yourself shows that you have great courage and strength.

- Finally, try to remember that in difficult circumstances, criticizing yourself only makes life more difficult for you *and* it never helps find solutions. It does result in demoralization and upset. Instead consider these points:

  ◊ What would you say to someone you cared about if they were attempting to do something they found difficult? Would you say to them, 'You'll never do it' or 'You're not good/smart/strong/ clever enough'?

  ◊ Remember, athletes prepare for competitions by giving themselves positive statements. Try that for yourself. Athletes don't go it alone, so neither should you. Get yourself a coach – this should be someone you can trust to be supportive.

  ◊ Make a shortlist of people you might want to recruit to be your coach. Try to have a list of three or four people you know will be able to help and provide you with the understanding and motivation to help you make some positive changes.

Key messages

- Depression in older people is treatable and self-help strategies like those described in this book have been shown to work, as have other evidence-based treatment options such as IPT, should you need these.

- All the ideas and helpful strategies outlined for people in the first two parts of the book are equally applicable to a person aged nineteen or ninety. Please read the first sections of this book and then use this chapter where there are gaps.

- Depression is often accompanied by worry. Avoidance is a very common response to anxiety, which tends to make both it and the depression worse. Tackling avoidance is a very good start to overcoming your difficulties.

Tips for supporters

- It's best to be honest now: agree what you can and can't do and how often you can be there to help. Keeping to what's agreed, even if it is less frequent than your partner might like, is going to be better for you both in the long run.

- When people feel low it can be difficult to know what to do to help. A useful strategy may be to get the person you are supporting to be more active; get them out and about to distract them for a short time. Encourage them to make some changes. The first step is to work out a plan together. Start small, with easier things to do.

- If you can persuade them to go out with you, plan a very short trip somewhere local at first. It can sometimes help if you ask the person you are supporting to rate their mood (how sad, upset, blue or fearful they feel on a 1–10 scale, where 10 means they are feeling very depressed and 1 means not at all depressed) before and after they go out, to see if the activity has helped.

Depression in later life: myth busting

There are a number of commonly held beliefs about depression in later life. Very often these beliefs are very inaccurate, giving a biased view of depression and the possibility of overcoming it. Below we describe some of the most common myths, and why they are inaccurate.

Myth one: what do you expect? Old age is a depressing time of life!

There is a very common belief that depression and anxiety are inevitable in older life, that they are understandable reactions to the challenges that ageing can bring. It is certainly common for people to have lost someone they love, to have more restrictions in what they can do, to no longer be working. *It is normal and appropriate that people feel upset and need time to adjust to the loss of a loved one, but this grief is not the same as depression.* It is normal to experience loss and longing when we lose any member of our family. Grief can also extend to pets, as they are often part of the family. Grief is the price we pay for loving someone, and while we may need time to adjust, most people find a way to accommodate to the loss over time. This does not mean we ever 'get over' our loss. We will always miss our loved ones, but in time we find a way to place them in our hearts so we can love them without forgetting them. Feeling sad and grieving is not the same as depression.

But although there are times when we need to grieve, *growing older does not need to mean being downhearted and miserable.* Sadly, because of this myth, depression in older people can often be overlooked, because healthcare professionals and older people themselves believe depression and anxiety are inevitable. Viewing them as understandable and inevitable is dangerous, because it means people are more likely to put up with a much poorer quality of life and a more miserable existence than is necessary. Life is precious and short and anything that makes it unhappy isn't something you should just accept. So if you are feeling low, don't accept that this is how it's going to be. There is a lot that you can do to make things better.

Busting the myth

There are a number of very good examples of older people who achieved a great deal when they were somewhat past the first flush of youth – we give a couple in the section below. Another example is the novelist Mary Wesley, whose first novel was published when she was in her seventies, and who went on to write many more. And again as we saw, there is good evidence to show that life satisfaction tends to *increase*. Think of the agonies of youth, the fears about sexual identity and attractiveness, the struggle to get qualifications and employment, the scramble up the career ladder, the impossibility of juggling children and work. How nice that so many of these struggles are behind us.

Myth two: depression is weak and selfish

For many people, depression still carries a stigma, so it can be difficult to ask for help. Older people grew up in a time when one had to 'grin and bear it', and often people believed that it was wrong to talk about these things outside the family, or even within families. In fact, depression is not a sign of weakness, nor of laziness, nor is it a flaw in your character. Simply, depression is an illness, and it is not a question of choice. No one would ever choose to be depressed.

Mrs Arnott's story

Mrs Arnott sees her depression like this: 'Along the way I have understood if you're depressed then you must be a selfish person . . . I was always brought up to put other people first and to put myself last.' She doesn't want to seek help for her depression, and thinks about it in quite a negative and harsh way. People would be surprised to hear her talk this way as she is an exceptionally kind and considerate person (to everyone but herself). Thinking about depression in this way creates a vicious circle for Mrs Arnott. It leads to her withdrawing from those around her as she doesn't want to 'burden' them.

Do you agree with Mrs Arnott that it is selfish to be depressed? Her vicious circle is illustrated below:

Figure 70: Mrs Arnott's vicious circle

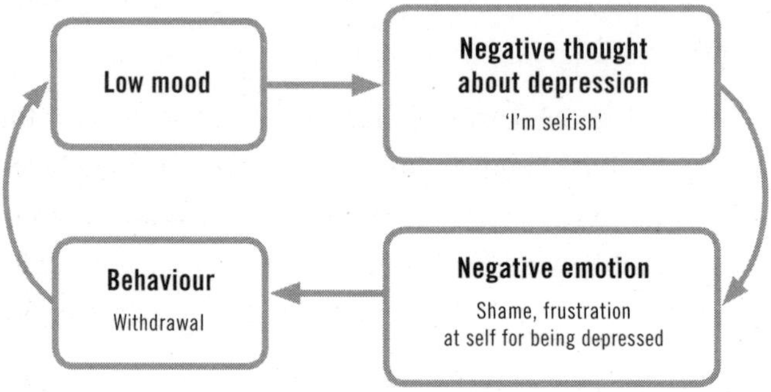

Busting the myth

Can you imagine talking to Mrs Arnott as if she were a very good friend of yours? What would your attitude be towards her? Would you feel sympathetic and compassionate? What might you say to her so that she might feel less ashamed about being depressed?

Write down what you would say to her. You could start by saying that being depressed is not selfish because . . .

Now that you can see what you would say to someone else, you can apply the same ideas to yourself – you are not weak and selfish because you are depressed.

Myth three: you can't teach an old dog new tricks

'You can't teach an old dog new tricks' is a common saying that is *not* true for humans – nor, as it turns out, dogs! If it were true, that would mean people can never change, and their habits can never change either.

The possibilities for change are more linked to our willingness to try to do something different, and to persevere with new strategies, than to do with age.

Did you know that Colonel Sanders, the founder of Kentucky Fried Chicken, was sixty-five years old when he came up with his business idea? Nelson Mandela was seventy-four and well past retirement age when he became president of South Africa.

Age shouldn't hold you back from making changes in your life. Most often it is fear of what others might think or, unfortunately, our own negative thoughts that hold us back. So make a resolution: if your reason for *not* doing something is because you believe you are too old, either find a better reason for not doing it, or just do it and see how you get on!

Ageing is not necessarily good or bad, and the age of a person tells us very little about them. Usually, people don't feel their age. It is very common for people to describe feeling many years younger than their real age. Evidence suggests that people who maintain an active interest in the things that have meaning for them are likely to report better overall satisfaction with the quality of their life. Staying active means more than just staying *physically* active. Stronger, more diverse social networks are also important for staying well. Research has shown that older people who have more positive thoughts about ageing tend to live longer, by an average of seven-and-a-half years, compared to people with more negative age perceptions. Remember, age is just a number and it does not define you, nor should it constrain you.

Busting the myth

Is there something you could do that may require a little effort on your part, but which you know will be enjoyable and will take up your attention, distracting you from depression or worries? Make a plan and do it soon. Don't be too rigid but set a target range of time when you will complete this task. Once you have done it, make a note of it in your diary and make sure you reward yourself. Rewards can be small but personal.

For example, Mrs Johnstone found it very difficult to get herself out of her home on her own after her husband died, and thought she'd never be able to do things alone. However, she started to go down to the local shops, and to reward herself she would always buy herself a second-hand penny-romance book. Her library soon built up and she was able to see her success for herself.

Use the form below to help you if you think you can't do something. Your low mood may make you more negative in outlook, so this form may help you defeat the negative.

Worksheet 23: Planning an enjoyable task

Make a prediction before you do something. Write it here:

I am going to ....

I think (prediction of how it will turn out) ....

Afterwards, write down how it turned out.

I did ....

I can be proud of myself because ....

Below is an example from Pam, who had always wanted to learn Italian but never had the time when she was younger. She had been putting it off because she thought she was too old, but used this form to help her.

Figure 71: Pam's enjoyable task

Make a prediction before you do something. Write it here:

I'd like to learn Italian but there's no point me going to classes because I won't be able to follow it.

I am going to . . . *make myself sign up to evening classes at the local college . . .*

. . . .

I think (prediction of how it will turn out) . . . *I'll go to one lesson and then have*

to give up because I can't do it and it will be a complete waste of time and money

. . . .

Afterwards, write down how it turned out.

I did go, and actually it went much better than I expected. I'd forgotten how much it has in common with French. I am a bit slower than some of the young ones there, but I have more time for homework!

I can be proud of myself because . . . . *I really didn't think I could do it, but I*

signed up anyway – and I'm really proud I made myself go. . . . .

. . . .

Myth four: nothing good comes with ageing – it's a depressing time of life

It is unlikely that we can live a life free from some sort of challenge or indeed some setbacks. But life can teach us valuable lessons and we can gain in wisdom if we use our past experiences of dealing with adversity to help us cope with current problems.

Learning to challenge automatic ways of thinking, and realizing that there are many different ways to think about any situation, is a step in the right direction to developing personal wisdom. Wisdom is probably most often used when we are facing uncertainty or dealing with situations where there is not an easy answer or readily available solution. As Leonardo da Vinci said, 'Wisdom is the daughter of experience.' Can you look back over your life and look for your own personal wisdom? For instance, Alice went back to work after her husband died, and realized how much time she'd spent worrying about little things. She was able to use her greater grief to help herself, and her younger colleagues, to get some perspective when things were tricky, and to help them to think about what was good. When difficult life experiences make us wiser and help us to better cope in the here and now, this can be the silver lining to the clouds that have caused us pain in the past.

One important strategy is to keep ourselves attached to the facts of an experience rather than our feelings about it. Keeping ourselves 'grounded' in what we did rather than how we feel about a past event may open us up to new possible ways of seeing ourselves – such as a resilient survivor. People who are depressed tend to recall past events in an over-generalized way. In other words, they think back to when things were difficult and often see their actions in a very negative light. They are likely to think they failed, or were mean, unkind, selfish. In reality, life is rarely black and white. Being honest and *specific* in your recall of past events, especially painful ones, can help you to see this more clearly.

Pete's story

Pete and his first wife split up after four years together. He blamed himself and said he became quite guarded afterwards until he met and married his second wife. He has a good, supportive relationship now. Although Pete may well have contributed to the end of his relationship, there were other reasons too. To begin with, he would beat himself up for his marriage ending, but when he was encouraged to think more concretely about the past, he could see that there was a different story to be told. Beating himself up also meant that he was ignoring evidence suggesting he is good at sustaining relationships, because he is still married to his second wife.

Busting the myth

1. Think of a person you would consider wise. What was it that made you think of them? How would you describe them? What are their characteristics? What did they do that made them wise in your eyes?

2. Now think back to a difficult situation in your own life. (If this causes you great distress, stop and distract yourself and perhaps return to this task later. It is a good idea to start with more minor, less upsetting events from your past first.) It can be from the recent or more distant past. What did you do to help yourself cope? What was the outcome at the time? Looking back on it with the benefit of hindsight, what do you think about how you coped?

3. Now, recall the wise person and try to imagine what they would have done in that situation. How differently would they do things from the way you did? Looking back, how would you do things differently now?

If you are depressed right now and feeling hopeless about the future, and if you are worried that this is how your life will be from now on, can you use the wisdom you have gained over the years to challenge your fears? If you were depressed before, what happened?

Let's look at an example.

Eve's story

Eve is seventy-eight years old and she was feeling very depressed, to the extent that she was admitted to hospital for a short respite. While she was in hospital she convinced herself that she was never going to leave. Her CBT therapist asked her if she had thought that she would not recover the previous time she'd been depressed (Eve had experienced depression once before). She replied that she had thought this very strongly. Eve was able to draw on her personal wisdom about depression and think, 'Well, maybe I was wrong then, and I'll be wrong this time.' Thankfully Eve *was* wrong and, with help, she made a full recovery from her depression and returned to her own home. As she recovered she found that all her favourite activities and hobbies provided her with the same pleasures she had always experienced. The more she did, and the more she pushed herself to take part in her old hobbies and activities, the more she noticed her old confidence and ease returned to her.

Key messages

- There are a number of myths that can make the experience of depression much more difficult to identify and tackle. Bringing the myths out into the open and seeing how they can be 'busted' can make it easier to do what you need to do to make changes.

- So what we've seen is that:

  ◊ depression in older age is *not* inevitable.

  ◊ depression is *not* weak and selfish.

  ◊ older people *can* change – you *can* teach an old dog new tricks.

  ◊ wisdom doesn't necessarily come with age, but personal wisdom comes from looking at our life experience and learning from it.

Tips for supporters

- Sometimes people can hold these ideas without really knowing that they do so. Encourage the person you are supporting to have a really good chat with you about what they think about depression, and what they might have been told about it in the past. If you recognize some of these ideas yourself, then talk about how you feel about it too.

- If you and the person you are supporting have known each other for a long time, the 'wisdom' exercise may relate to an event you yourself witnessed or even were involved in. Once your friend/partner has completed the task above, give your own perspective on what happened, especially if you feel your additional information will be helpful and constructive.

Starting to tackle depression

If you recognize any of the symptoms of depression, then you can start to make a plan. It is time to do something about your low mood when you feel it is getting in the way of enjoying your retirement years.

Setting goals

The first step is to set some goals for yourself and make sure they are *manageable* and *realistic*. Doctors often use the mantra 'start low and go slow' when it comes to medication for depression, and you can use this when it comes to planning goals. Often we want things to change instantly and it can cause us to lose confidence if we don't feel better straight away. Give yourself time and you will get there. Work up to it by setting easily manageable steps towards your eventual target. Tick off each step and be sure to give yourself praise and encouragement along the way.

When setting goals for yourself think in terms of long-term and short-term ones.

- A short-term goal may be to 'get up and going' earlier in the day.

- Set a plan the night before. For this goal to be achieved you need to build in steps. So if you have been staying in bed till 11 a.m. and you are unhappy about this, plan to be up at 10.45 a.m. and see if you can stick to this consistently over a week or so.

- For the following week trying getting up at 10.30 a.m., and so on.

For longer-term goals the same principles apply of setting manageable steps and monitoring your progress.

- When starting out on this plan make sure you appreciate your achievements. Prioritize giving yourself praise and encouragement.

- Perhaps you may also want to consider what makes this an especially important goal for you and how your life will be improved once you achieve it.

Using a notebook or computer, keep a note of your mood. When you have a day with pleasant events in it (in other words, when you did things you enjoyed) compare it with when you had a day with very little activity. Most people find that their mood (by this we mean sadness, fearfulness, and so on) improves as they do more. The more you do the easier it will get. Look at the information about exercise and lifestyle changes below. Are there certain things you do that make you feel better? Can you find a way to increase the things you enjoy? Set a target to review your progress every week at first. If you don't notice improvement remind yourself that you may need to keep at it for a while, and keep reviewing progress weekly. It will take a bit of perseverance and may be hard work, but the more you do the better you will feel. As suggested above, set yourself some short-term goals to increase your exercise and activities.

Depression often leaves you feeling that things just won't work out for you. When we are depressed we think negatively and by believing our negative, depressed thoughts we become more depressed. Thoughts are not facts, but they can become self-fulfilling prophecies. If we have the thought that nothing will change and we believe it, then we feel worse and we do less. You don't have to believe your thoughts and it is helpful to talk back to those nasty negative ones. Think about what you'd say to someone else going through the same thing. You'd probably be supportive of them. Now apply that to yourself.

Take it easy on yourself. Perfectionists often strive to be perfect in every way, but the reality is that we are all human and therefore can't be perfect all the time. Perfectionism is destructive and increases the chance that we will feel depressed as we strive to never make a mistake or get it wrong. Let it go, be kinder and more accepting of yourself, and you may surprise yourself with how much better you feel.

Exercise and lifestyle changes

Recent evidence suggests that modifying your lifestyle can be an effective way to prevent and, in some cases, self-manage depression. Exercise can have psychological as well as physical benefits and can improve our mood.

Evidence is still being collected comparing the benefits of exercise to the benefits of medication for depression, but a review in the *British Journal of Psychiatry* in 2012 suggested that structured exercise programmes (such as tai chi, resistance training, and so on) may be *as effective* as antidepressant medication or therapy. Exercise also has added health benefits such as lowering the chance of heart disease, reducing high blood pressure and obesity, and lacks the side effects found with medication, so it is something you may wish to discuss with your GP as an alternative treatment option.

If you are interested in doing more exercise, could you persuade a friend or family member to go to the gym or to a class with you? Perhaps you could sign up for a taster session before you take out membership. Your local library or your GP's surgery may have leaflets on local council-run gym facilities. If you can, go at a time when it is less busy. Some people go to the café at the local gym first as a way of checking it out.

Tackling your negative thoughts

One idea has been talked about throughout this book, and we reiterate it here:

It's not your experiences but the meaning you give them that counts.

This idea is a simple but powerful one. It means that an experience by itself doesn't necessarily cause us upset. Usually we are upset because of the meaning we are giving the consequences or importance of a situation. So for example, if you go to the shops and forget to buy the one thing you were going for, you may feel a bit frustrated but you will probably soon forget about it. However, if you are concerned about your memory and fear you may be developing forgetfulness (or worse!), you may become very upset about it, because it seems to be more important and to indicate some consequences you fear. If you continue to dwell on this event, you may notice that your mood changes for the worse and you become flat and more hopeless about the future. Therefore, whether or not a difficult situation or event causes us distress depends on our point of view and the way we make sense of it. This is a very old idea, known since the time of the ancient Greeks, when Epictetus famously said: 'People are not disturbed by things, but by the view they take of them,' and 'It's not what happens to you, but how you react to it that matters.'

So if thinking about a particular situation or event gives rise to negative emotions in you, it is important to ask yourself, 'What is it about this particular event, situation or interaction that makes me upset?' Are your own personal stress points being activated? If so, which ones, and what does that mean?

So, in situations when you feel sad or afraid, think back to when you first started to experience this and look at your thoughts about events. As Hamlet said: 'There is nothing either good or bad but thinking makes it so.'

Most people who have made it to their seventh or eighth decade and beyond will have experienced a few 'speed bumps' along the way on life's journey. These setbacks often teach us some valuable lessons as we learn things about ourselves. Perhaps you can think about what you learned about coping with setbacks?

Jack's story

Jack is eighty-two and a retired civil engineer. He has always been a worrier. He lives on his own as his wife died two years ago. Over time, his worries became overwhelming and started to really get him down. He'd wake in the morning and dread getting out of bed as the day ahead was always full of demands he didn't think he could cope with. Jack started to get very depressed. Because he doubted his ability to cope, he avoided doing anything, and started to feel that he was useless and 'past it'. Eventually Jack felt so bad, and his life had got to such a stuck point, that he realized he would have to start to tackle it. He made a huge effort to think about what might help, and realized that he needed to do things differently. By talking to other people about what had helped them, he realized that he was likely to be able to manage his worrying better when he was more active, and had much less time to concentrate on his worries.

Jack used to enjoy painting and while many people admired his art, he tended to dismiss their compliments as he thought they were just being polite (they weren't, he is really very good). When he was besieged by worries he learned that he could use sketching and painting as a distraction technique. The first time he painted as a way of focusing on something other than

---

his worries, he found it very difficult; he felt agitated and was sure that something catastrophic was going to happen to him. He couldn't identify anything tangible that was about to go wrong immediately, so there was no need for special action on his part; nonetheless he was left feeling ill at ease. He decided to experiment with painting. It took him a week to build up to doing it. It took him ninety minutes to paint a picture and while he found it tiring, he also achieved a real sense of satisfaction. While he was painting, he was distracted from his usual worries. Jack also thought about other things that he used to enjoy before his mood became so low that he avoided everything. He arranged to start meeting friends at the local swimming baths again, and he joined a gym.

By keeping a record of his fears, Jack started to realize that his worries never happened, at least not in the extreme forms that caused him so much distress. Jack has learned a new trick to help him manage his anxiety and tackle his sense of foreboding. He's learned there is nothing to fear from fear itself.

This is an important lesson about worry: the consequences we worry about rarely occur, at least to the extent we fear. In the event that an experience we fear happens, anxiety rarely provides us with any help in working out a good strategy. Here's a useful question to ask yourself when you notice yourself worrying: are you able to do something, right now, about this? If the answer is yes, then do it now and get rid of the worry. If not, distract yourself until you can do something about this event. When you feel agitated, doing something to distract yourself takes your mind away from your worries. You focus on what you are doing and put yourself back in control of your thoughts. It's not easy but it can be done. It also gives you a sense of satisfaction.

Key messages

- There are a number of different ways in which you can start to tackle the depression. Firstly, think about what you would like to be doing differently if you *weren't* depressed, and set yourself some achievable goals.

- Being more active can make a huge difference to how you feel, particularly if you have stopped most activities, so think about exercise that you might be able to start doing.

- Tackle your thoughts! Thinking in an unfair and unrealistic way is a major part of depression, and learning to think in a more fair and realistic way can help a lot.

- Watch out for worry! Worry can make low mood much worse, and can be tackled in its own right.

Tips for supporters

- Help the person you are supporting with these changes. Encourage them to set reasonable goals, which they can start to tackle step by step, and help them think about activities that they might be able to increase.

- Watch out for the negative thinking that might get in the way – they may say they can't think of anything, or that there's no point doing anything differently because nothing will work. If they say this, then encourage them to try it and see! Some people like the idea of an experiment – they could try to do things differently and see if it makes a difference.

- If they are unable to think of something they can praise themselves for, make suggestions but be aware that they may dismiss what you say because they assume you are biased. Make it clear that you are there to help them, not to flatter, so that they feel able to trust what you say.

Staying well: what to do to maintain your recovery

Below are things that you can think about to make sure you stay well once the depression has started to get better. They will help to prevent it occurring or getting worse if it has started to develop a bit.

Step one: accept yourself and become your own best friend

The term 'redemptive sequence' is sometimes used to describe what happens after a traumatic or difficult event, when something bad leads to a good or positive emotional outcome, although the positive outcome may not be apparent immediately. For example, someone might have a heart attack and realize they need to make lifestyle changes. Once they make changes they realize that this event 'saved' their life. Although they would not recommend the experience, it has a positive outcome for them. This is both a 'recovery' and a 'growth experience' in that the person recovers, and the event leads them to make changes that benefit their lives in a whole variety of ways. For instance, they might start to take exercise, go for walks with their partner or friends, and enjoy the country. Another kind of redemptive sequence might involve a sacrifice which leads to a positive outcome. For example, a woman may make sacrifices to support her family, such as giving up her own job to relocate when her husband has a new job. This may not be her first choice, but once she makes this sacrifice and moves to a new area, she makes new friends and discovers a better quality of life. While this act may have been done at the time primarily for the benefit of others, it ultimately has a good outcome for the individual.

Can you think of examples of redemptive sequences from your own life?

You could start to make use of your experiences to help you cope better with the sort of problems you may be facing right now. Think back to some of the challenges you have faced in the past. Try to think of one experience in particular – it doesn't need to be the most difficult experience of your life, but it should be a difficult or traumatic event that led to an unexpectedly positive outcome (however small). Use the form below to describe the event. Try to provide as much detail as you can, as you will be more likely to come to a more realistic and even-handed summary, and this will provide you with more helpful insights. Perhaps it was the loss of a business you had high hopes for, or a breakdown in an important relationship, or a serious health challenge? Don't just write, 'My business went bust in 1986.' Write down exactly what happened – the sequence of events – and what you did afterwards. Stick to the facts, rather than how you felt at the time.

- Now, take some time to think about how you coped in that situation. With the benefit of hindsight, can you see that you coped well in difficult circumstances?

- Are there any aspects of how you coped that deserve praise? What did you do well at the time?

- What did you learn about yourself from the experience?

- Looking back, was there a silver lining to the cloud? Did it change your life for the better in any way (however small) or lead to a change that you welcomed later?

If you think back over what happened, you may be able to see that although the immediate outcome was uncertain, you took the decisions you did because that was what you thought was the right thing to do. Regardless of the outcome, you did the best you could at the time.

Step two: recognize your own personal resilience

Sometimes it can be useful to review our lives in order to see how resilient we are. Resilience can be measured by how well we overcome adversity and challenges. As we go through life we will all face challenges, both good and bad. You could think of resilience as your bounce-back ability. Of course, what is challenging to an individual is very personal and, as we have read above, an important factor will be our attitude. How we view our ability to cope may also be important. As you cast your mind back to difficult experiences you have faced in the past, watch out for emotional reasoning; sometimes we can draw the conclusion that because we experienced emotional distress it must mean we didn't cope well. This is not the case, however. Think of a difficult experience from your past and look at it from the point of view of an outsider. If it had happened to a friend, what would you say to that person about how well they had coped? Apply that logic to yourself.

Eric Farraday has mobility problems and has been depressed for a year or more. He and his third wife are separated and he is alone. The marriage had been in trouble for more than a year and while he is sad about its end, he has a sense of relief at now being in a position to make plans. He has a social worker and contacted his psychologist for more support. (Note: You may not need the help of a psychologist, but we can all do with a helping hand sometimes.) With this help, he got through a difficult time. However, as he was upset and had sought help he feels that he has not coped.

Do you agree? In reality, it was Mr Farraday who helped himself. He was the one taking the decisions to do things to make his life better and he showed real strength, character and resilience. It is true that he sought help, but we all need help from time to time. If we didn't need other people we'd all be off living life as hermits. You can ask for help and still be strong. Admitting that you need help is one of the bravest things you can do.

Occasionally it is not possible to find an especially positive outcome from a difficult experience. Sometimes the aim is not to eradicate all negative aspects. Sometimes it is to achieve the best outcome in the circumstances. As not all external events are under our control, we are seeking to make the best of a bad situation. For Mr Farraday, the worst outcome could have been very bad indeed, but he is a strong survivor, even though he finds it hard to believe at times.

Key messages

- When we re-evaluate past events based on the eventual outcome it may not reflect the facts of the situation *at the time*.

- It is important to remember that, *at the time*, there was no way for you to know how things would turn out.

- Take a longer view: over time what have you learned from past mistakes and past challenges?

- It is important to remember that you are a survivor; you have been through difficult times and you carried on. (How can we know this? Well, you are here reading this chapter and regardless of the outcome you have carried on with your life!)

Tips for supporters

- It can be very difficult to re-evaluate the way you view events in your life, especially if you have been thinking about things in a particular way for a long time. Help the person you are supporting by encouraging them and giving them prompts.

- Sometimes re-evaluating important things can cause quite a bit of emotional turmoil, so be on hand with comfort and tea, but don't worry – it will calm down.

A note on medication for depression in later life

There are many types of antidepressants that can help depression, either used on their own or when used alongside CBT. Different antidepressants have different potential side effects and your doctor will be able to discuss these with you so that you can choose the one that suits you most, should you both feel you would benefit from a trial. There is a little more about antidepressants on page xx in Chapter 5. In addition to improving your mood, they may improve your alertness, concentration, sleep, or appetite.

Your GP will know about which antidepressants are better for older people. There are no age-specific ones, but doctors often use the medication in lower doses, or choose ones according to whether the individual has other existing health problems and other medication. This will avoid potential side effects worsening the other health problems, and prevent different types of medication interacting with each other in unhelpful ways. Dose adjustments and slower increases of medication may be needed for older people, depending on what health problems co-exist and what else has been prescribed.

Key messages

- Depression in later life is not something you should expect as an outcome of growing older – don't just accept it.

- It can be treated and if you or a loved one become depressed it's important to look for support and treatment.

- Staying connected to activities that make life pleasurable for you, and being around friends and family is an important preventative strategy. You may also decide to take up exercise, as this has important physical as well as psychological benefits.

- We wish you good health and many more years of it.

Appendix 1: Further reading, references and other resources

Part 1: Introduction to depression and CBT: the basics

Further reading

The following are some books you may find helpful if you want to find out more about how CBT self-help can aid your fight against depression. Many of these are available in both paperback and eBook formats, and should be available from any good bookshop or online booksellers. They all have slightly different styles and approaches, so it's a good idea to have a look at them if you can, and see which one might suit you best:

For depression

Burns, D., *Feeling Good* (New York: Avon Books, 1980).

Butler, G., and T. Hope, *Manage Your Mind* (2nd edition, Oxford: Oxford University Press, 2007).

Gilbert, P., *Overcoming Depression* (3rd edition, London: Robinson, 2009).

Greenberger, D., and C. Padesky, *Mind Over Mood: Change How You Feel by Changing the Way You Think* (New York: Guilford Press, 1995).

Williams, C., *Overcoming Depression and Low Mood: A Five Areas Approach*, London: Hodder Arnold (2012).

For anxiety

Kennerley, H., *Overcoming Anxiety* (London: Robinson, 1997).

Shafran, R., L. Brosan, and P. Cooper, *The Complete CBT Guide for Anxiety* (London: Robinson, 2013).

For anger

Bloxham, G., and W. Doyle Gentry, *Anger Management for Dummies* (Chichester: Wiley, 2010).

Davies, W., *Overcoming Anger and Irritability: A Self-Help Guide Using Cognitive Behavioural Techniques* (London: Robinson, 2013).

For information about Interpersonal Therapy (IPT)

Law, R., *Defeating Depression: How to Use the People in Your Life to Open the Door to Recover* (London: Robinson, 2013). A self-help guide using IPT ideas.

Stuart, S., and M. Robertson, *Interpersonal Psychotherapy: A Clinician's Guide* (2nd edition, London: CRC Press, 2012).

References

The following classification tools and guidance are also referred to in Part 1:

DSM-V The Diagnostic and Statistical Manual of Mental Disorders, 5th Edition, is the 2013 update to the American Psychiatric Association's classification and diagnostic tool.

The ICD-10 Classification of Mental and Behavioural Disorders, 10th Edition, published by the World Health Organization.

NICE Guidance and website: *www.nice.org.uk/CG90*

Other resources

Websites

If you have internet access (most main libraries offer access if you do not have it at home), you might like to check out some of these sources of information and advice:

Depression Alliance, a national UK charity: *www.depressionalliance.org*

NHS information about depression: *www.nhs.uk/conditions/depression*

Information from MIND, the national mental-health charity: *www.mind. org.uk/information-support/types-of-mental-health-problems/depression*

Information from the Royal College of Psychiatrists: *www.rcpsych.ac.uk/ mentalhealthinfoforall/problems/depression/depression.aspx*

Samaritans (24-hour helpline): *www.samaritans.org*

Papyrus (help aimed specifically at young people with suicidal thoughts): *www.papyrus-uk.org*

Citizens Advice Bureau (CAB). This is an organization that gives advice about a whole range of issues, and has offices in most reasonably sized towns in the UK: *www.adviceguide.org.uk*

NHS website with information about the effects of exercise: *www.nhs.uk/ Conditions/stress-anxiety-depression/Pages/exercise-for-depression.aspx*

Further help

If you want to get further help with your depression, and you are not already seeing a mental-health professional, you need to talk to your GP to discuss what kind of referral might be possible and appropriate. For further advice on medication, you will need to see a psychiatrist. Psychological treatments, like CBT or IPT, may be offered by a number of different members of the mental-health team. Unfortunately a lack of NHS resources means that there are often long waiting lists for psychological treatments. Your GP will be able to advise you on what treatments are available in your area and what the waiting time is likely to be.

If you are considering getting CBT independently, the British Association for Behavioural and Cognitive Psychotherapies (BABCP) has a directory of accredited CBT therapists. These are people who have had approved training and supervision in CBT. You can find out about accredited therapists by visiting the BABCP website at *www.babcp.com* and clicking on 'Find a therapist', or by going straight to the CBT Register of accredited therapists at *www.cbtregisteruk.com*.

Alternatively you can contact BABCP at:

BABCP, Imperial House, Hornby Street, BURY, BL9 5BN.
Telephone: 0161 705 4304
Fax: 0161 705 4306
Email: *babcp@babcp.com*

Part 2: Further strategies for tackling depression

Chapter 13: Using activity to combat depression: more about behavioural activation

Further reading

Addis, M.E., and C.R. Martell, *Overcoming Depression One Step at a Time: the New Behavioral Activation Approach to Getting Your Life Back* (Oakland, CA: New Harbinger Publications, 2004).

Jacobson, N.S., C.R. Martell, and S. Dimidjian, 'Behavioral activation treatment for depression: returning to contextual roots', *Clinical Psychology: Science and Practice*, 8 (2001), 255–70.

Martell, C.R., M.E. Addis, and N.S. Jacobson, *Depression in Context: Strategies for Guided Action* (New York: WW Norton & Co., 2001).

Veale, D., and R.Wilson, *Manage Your Mood: Using Behavioural Activation to Manage Your Mood* (London: Constable & Robinson, 2007).

References

Dimidjian, S., S. Hollon, K. Dobson, *et al.*, 'Randomized trial of behavioural activation, cognitive therapy, and antidepressant medication in the acute treatment of adults with major depression', *Journal of Consulting and Clinical Psychology*, 74 (2006), 658–70.

Ekers, D., D.A. Richards, and S. Gilbody, 'A meta-analysis of randomized trials of behavioural treatment of depression', *Psychological Medicine* 38 (2008), 611–23.

Ekers, D., D.A. Richards, D. McMillan, J.M. Bland, and S. Gilbody, 'Behavioural activation delivered by the non specialist: phase II randomised controlled trial', *British Journal of Psychiatry*, 198 (2011), 66–72.

Chapter 14: Thinking too much: dealing with rumination in depression

Further reading

Nolen-Hoeksema, S., *Women Who Think Too Much* (London: Piatkus, 2004). This provides a good overview of what rumination is and potential means to reduce it.

References

For more information on the relevant research underpinning these self-help suggestions and the evidence from randomized controlled trials that these approaches work, please see the following scientific papers.

These papers also provide more information relevant to professionals acting in a supportive role:

Watkins, E.R., 'Constructive and unconstructive repetitive thought', *Psychological Bulletin*, 134 (2008), 163–206.

Watkins, E.R., C.B. Baeyens, and R. Read, 'Concreteness training reduces dysphoria: proof-of-principle for repeated cognitive bias modification in depression', *Journal of Abnormal Psychology*, 118 (2009), 55–65.

Watkins, E.R., J. Scott, J. Wingrove, K.A. Rimes, N. Bathurst, H. Steiner, S. Kennell-Webb, M. Moulds, and Y. Malliaris, 'Rumination-focused cognitive behaviour therapy for residual depression: a case series', *Behaviour Research and Therapy*, 45 (2007), 2144–54.

Watkins, E.R., E.G. Mullan, J. Wingrove, K. Rimes, H. Steiner, N. Bathurst, E. Eastman, and J. Scott, 'Rumination-focused cognitive behaviour therapy for residual depression: phase II randomized controlled trial', *British Journal of Psychiatry*, 199 (2011), 317–22. Doi:10.1192/bjp.bp.110.090282.

Watkins, E.R., R.S. Taylor, R. Byng, C.B. Baeyens, R. Read, K. Pearson, and L. Watson, 'Guided self-help concreteness training as an intervention for major depression in primary care: a phase II randomized controlled trial', *Psychological Medicine*, 42 (2012), 1359–73. Doi:10.1017/S0033291711002480.

Other resources

The Mood Disorders Centre, University of Exeter, has developed a number of rumination-focused CBT treatments, including a guided self-help treatment and an internet-based treatment. For further information on these go to www.exeter.ac.uk/mooddisorders.

For more information on supporting CBT interventions for rumination and for therapists working with patients with rumination, please see the treatment manual shortly to be published by Guilford Press, *Rumination-Focused Cognitive Behavioural Therapy*.

Chapter 15: Using images to help with depressing memories

Further reading

Hackmann, A. and J. Bennett-Levy, *Oxford Guide to Imagery in Cognitive Therapy* (Oxford: Oxford University Press, 2011).

Rosen, T., *The Positive Power of Imagery: Harnessing Client Imagination in CBT and Related Therapies* (Chichester: Wiley-Blackwell, 2011).

Life Choices and Life Changes through Imagework, Dina Glouberman (London: Unwin-Hyman, 1989).

Chapter 16: Compassion-focused therapy for depression

Further reading

Gilbert, P., *The Compassionate Mind* (London: Constable & Robinson, 2009).

Gilbert, P. and Choden, *Mindful Compassion* (London: Constable & Robinson, 2013).

See also:

Baer, L., *The Imp of the Mind: Exploring the Silent Epidemic of Obsessional Bad Thoughts* (London: Plume, 2002).

Germer, C., *The Mindful Path to Self Compassion: Freeing Yourself from Destructive Thoughts and Emotions* (New York: Guilford Press, 2009).

Neff, K., *Self-Compassion: Stop Beating Yourself Up and Leave Insecurity Behind* (New York: Morrow, 2011).

Panksepp, J., *Affective Neuroscience* (New York: Oxford University Press, 1998).

Sapolski, R., *Why Zebras Don't Get Ulcers* (New York: Henry, Holt and Company, 2004).

Siegel, D., *Mindsight: Transform Your Brain with the New Science of Kindness* (New York: Oneworld, 2010).

Weil, A., *Spontaneous Happiness: Step-By-Step to Peak Emotional Well-Being* (London: Hodder & Stoughton, 2011).

You can read about how to use this approach to dealing with other problems too:

Goss, K., *The Compassionate Mind Approach to Beating Overeating* (London: Constable & Robinson, 2011).

Kolts, R., *The Compassionate Mind Approach to Managing Your Anger* (London: Constable & Robinson, 2012).

Lee, D., *The Compassionate Mind Approach to Recovering from Trauma* (London: Constable & Robinson, 2012).

Tirch, D., *The Compassionate Mind Approach to Overcoming Anxiety* (London: Constable & Robinson, 2012).

Welford, M., *The Compassionate Mind Approach to Building Your Self-Confidence* (London: Constable & Robinson, 2012).

Other resources

Websites

Many of the following websites have downloads for you to listen to and practise:

Paul Gilbert's website is at *www.compassionatemind.co.uk*

See also

www.compassionatewellbeing.com

www.self-compassion.org

www.mindfulselfcompassion.org

Centre for Compassion and Altruism Research and Education at: *ccare. stanford.edu*

The Greater Good: *http://greatergood.berkeley.edu*

NHS website with information about the effects of exercise: *www.nhs.uk/ Conditions/stress-anxiety-depression/Pages/exercise-for-depression.aspx*

Chapter 17: Mindfulness: befriending depression

Further reading

Books that have been acknowledged as major influences on the authors

Williams, J. M. G., and D. Penman, *Mindfulness: A Practical Guide to Finding Peace in a Frantic World* (London: Piatkus, 2011). The included CD contains these practices: Mindfulness of Body and Breath; the Body Scan; Mindful Movement; Breath and Body; Sounds and Thoughts; Exploring Difficulty; Befriending; and the Three-minute Breathing Space.

Williams, J. M. G., J. D. Teasdale, Z.V. Segal, and J. Kabat-Zinn, *The Mindful Way Through Depression: Freeing Yourself from Chronic Unhappiness* (New York: Guilford Press, 2007). The included CD contains these practices: Body Scan; Mindful Standing Yoga; Mindfulness of the Breath; Mindfulness of the Breath and Body; Mindfulness of Sounds and Thoughts; and the Breathing Space.

Kabat-Zinn, J., *Full Catastrophe Living: How to Cope with Stress, Pain and Illness Using Mindfulness Meditation* (New York: Delacorte, 1990).

Other books and CDs

Johnstone, A. and M. Johnstone, *Living with a Black Dog: How to Take Care of Someone with Depression While Looking After Yourself* (London: Robinson, 2009).

Johnstone, M., *Quiet the Mind: An Illustrated Guide on How to Meditate* (London: Robinson, 2012).

Kabat-Zinn, J., *Wherever You Go, There You Are: Mindfulness Meditation in Everyday Life* (London: Piatkus,1994).

Kabat-Zinn, J., *Coming to Our Senses: Healing Ourselves and the World Through Mindfulness* (London: Piatkus, 2005).

Stahl, B., and E. Goldstein, *A Mindfulness-Based Stress Reduction Workbook* (Oakland, CA: New Harbinger Publications, 2009). The included CD contains twenty-one practices such as: Mindfully Eating a Raisin; Mindful Check-in; Mindful Breathing; Walking Meditation; Body Scan; Sitting Meditation; Mindful Lying Yoga; Mindful Self-Inquiry for Stress and Anxiety; Mindful Standing Yoga; and Loving-Kindness Meditation.

Guided meditation CDs

When starting to learn mindfulness many people find the support of a set of guided practices really helpful. The authors recommend the practices below:

Brejcha, C., *Guided Mindfulness Practices* (2013). (Available from *www.exeter-mindfulness-network.org/about-useful-resources.php*) Practices include Body Scan; Mindful Movement; Breathing Space; Short Sitting Meditation; and Full Sitting Meditation.

Kabat-Zinn, J., *Full Catastrophe Living: Using the Wisdom of Your Body and Mind to Face Stress, Pain and Illness*. Audio book and CD (Random House Audio Assets, 2008). Practices include Body Scan; Sitting Practice; and Mindful Movement/Yoga.

Kabat-Zinn, J., *Guided Mindfulness Meditation* (Sounds True Inc., 2005). Includes four CDs of the following practices: Body Scan Meditation; Mindful Yoga 1; Sitting Meditation; and Mindful Yoga 2.

Kabat-Zinn, J., *Guided Mindfulness Meditation Series 3* (Sounds True Inc., 2012). Includes four CDs of the following practices: Breathscape and Bodyscape Meditations; Soundscape, Mindscape and Dying Before

You Die Meditations; Nowscape (Choiceless Awareness) and Walking Meditations; and Heartscape (Lovingkindness) and Lifescape (Everyday Life) Meditations.

Two books already listed in full above include guided practice: *Mindfulness: A Practical Guide to Finding Peace in a Frantic World* and *The Mindful Way Through Depression: Freeing Yourself from Chronic Unhappiness.*

Other resources

Websites

www.youtube.com/watch?v=PEJGPuPFIvc

This link to the *Healing Within* video shows Jon Kabat-Zinn working with a group of people with pain and physical health difficulties.

Jon Kabat-Zinn has many other talks on YouTube – simply use the search function and maybe use the number of views as an indication of the talk's popularity.

Exeter Mindfulness Network, University of Exeter: *www.mindfulness-network.org*

Mindfulness-Based Cognitive Therapy, University of Oxford, Department of Psychiatry: *http://mbct.co.uk*

The Centre for Mindfulness Research and Practice, Bangor University: *www.bangor.ac.uk/mindfulness*

Part 3: Tackling common problems in depression

Chapter 18: How to tackle low self-esteem

Further reading

Fennell, M., *Overcoming Low Self-Esteem: a Self-Help Guide Using Cognitive Behavioural Techniques* (London: Robinson, 2009).

Fennell, M., *Boost Your Confidence* (London: Robinson, 2011).

Palmer, S. and C. Wilding, *Beat Low Self-Esteem with CBT: Teach Yourself* (London: Hodder, 2013).

Other resources

Website

Centre for Clinical Interventions workbook on Self-Esteem:

www.cci.health.wa.gov.au

Chapter 19: Overcoming sleep difficulties

Further reading

Carney, C., and R. Manber, *Quiet Your Mind and Get to Sleep: Solutions to Insomnia for Those with Depression, Anxiety or Chronic Pain* (Oakland, CA: New Harbinger, 2009).

Espie, C., *Overcoming Insomnia and Sleep Problems: A Self-Help Guide Using Cognitive Behavioural Techniques* (London: Robinson, 2006).

Espie, C., *An Introduction to Coping with Insomnia and Sleep Problems* (London: Robinson, 2011).

Glovinsky, P., and A. Spielman, *The Insomnia Answer: A Personalized Program for Identifying and Overcoming the Three Types of Insomnia* (New York: Perigee, 2006).

Website

www.sleepio.com

There is also a Sleepio app available for download from this website.

Chapter 20: Couples and depression: improving the relationship and improving depression

Further reading

Crowe, M., *Overcoming Relationship Problems* (London: Constable & Robinson, 2012).

Johnstone, M., and A. Johnstone, *Living With a Black Dog: How to Take Care of Someone with Depression While Taking Care of Yourself* (London: Robinson, 2009).

Markman, H.J., S.M. Stanley, and S.L. Blumberg, *Fighting for your Marriage: A Deluxe Revised Edition of the Classic Best-seller for Enhancing Marriage and Preventing Divorce* (San Francisco: Jossey-Bass, 2010).

McCarthy, B., and E. McCarthy, *Sexual Awareness: Your Guide to Healthy Couple Sexuality* (5th edition, New York: Taylor & Francis, 2012).

Snyder, D.K., D.H. Baucom, and K.C. Gordon, *Getting Past the Affair: A Program to Help You Cope, Heal, and Move On – Together or Apart* (New York: Guilford Press, 2007).

Other resources

Relate is an organization that offers advice, relationship counselling, sex therapy, workshops, mediation, consultations and support face-to-face, by phone and through their website: *www.relate.org.uk.*

Part 4: Tackling different types of depression

Chapter 21: Bipolar disorders and problematic mood swings

Further reading

Jones, S., F. Lobban, A. Cooke, J. Hemmingfield, P. Kinderman, W. Mansell, M. Schwannauer, A. Palmer, E. Van der Gucht, K. Wright, and J. Hanna, *Understanding Bipolar Disorder: Why some people experience extreme mood states and what can help* (British Psychological Society, 2010). Free to download at *www.bpsshop.org.uk/Understanding-Bipolar-Disorder-P1280. aspx.*

Jones, S., P. Hayward, and D. H. Lam, *Coping with Bipolar Disorder* (Oxford: Oneworld Publications, 2002).

Mansell, W., A.P. Morrison, G. Reid, I. Lowens, and S.J. Tai, 'The interpretation of and responses to changes in internal states in bipolar disorder: an integrative cognitive model', *Behavioural and Cognitive Psychotherapy*, 35 (2007), 515–39.

Mansell, W., S. Powell, R. Pedley, N. Thomas, and S. A. Jones, 'The process of recovery from Bipolar I Disorder: a qualitative analysis of personal accounts in relation to an integrative cognitive model', *British Journal of Clinical Psychology*, 49 (2010), 193–215.

Scott J., *Overcoming Mood Swings* (London: Robinson, 2001).

Other resources

Useful organizations

For further information about TEAMS, including how to get involved in local trials and research, go to: *http://teamstrial.net*

TEAMS Trial, c/o Dr Warren Mansell, School of Psychological Sciences, University of Manchester, Coupland One, M13 9PL. *warren.mansell@ manchester.ac.uk*

Bipolar UK

A well-recognized and active charity supporting people with bipolar disorder and related difficulties. Used to be known as the Manic Depression Fellowship.

www.bipolaruk.org.uk

Victoria Charity Centre, 11 Belgrave Road, London, SW1V 1RB.
Tel: 020 7931 6480
Email: *info@bipolaruk.org.uk*

Rethink

A longstanding mental-health charity focused on supporting people with serious mental health problems and their families.

www.rethink.org

Rethink Mental Illness, Head Office, 15th Floor, 89 Albert Embankment, London, SE1 7TP.
Tel: 0300 5000 927
Email: *info@rethink.org*

Chapter 22: Postnatal depression

Further reading

Murray, L., *The Psychology of Babies: how relationships support development from birth to two* (London: Robinson, 2014).

Williams, C., R. Cantwell, and K. Robertson, *Overcoming Postnatal Depression: A Five Areas Approach* (London: Hodder Arnold, 2008).

Other resources

Leaflets on postnatal depression are available from the Royal College of Psychiatrists:

www.rcpsych.ac.uk/healthadvice/problemsdisorders/postnataldepression.aspx

or from:

Royal College of Psychiatrists, 21 Prescot Street, London, E1 8BB.

Chapter 23: Depression in physical illness

References

Beltman, M.W., R.C. Oude Voshaar, and A.E. Speckens, 'Cognitive-behavioural therapy for depression in people with a somatic disease: meta-analysis of randomised controlled trials', *British Journal of Psychiatry*, 197 (2010), 11–19.

De Jonge, P., F. Bel Hadj, D. Boffa, C. Zdrojewski, Y. Dorogi, A. So, J. Ruiz, and F. Stiefel, 'Prevention of major depression in complex medically ill patients: preliminary results from a randomized, controlled trial'. *Psychosomatics: Journal of Consultation Liaison Psychiatry*, 50 (2009), 227–33. De Jonge and colleagues showed that a nurse-led intervention halved the likelihood that rheumatology inpatients and diabetes outpatients would develop depression over the following year.

Freedland, K., M. Rich, J. Skala, *et al.*, 'Prevalence of depression in hospitalized patients with congestive heart failure', *Psychosomatic Medicine*, 65(2003), 119–28.

Grassi, L., P. Malacarne, A. Maestri, *et al.*, 'Depression, psychosocial variables and occurrence of life events among patients with cancer', *Journal of Affective Disorders*, 44 (1997), 21–30.

NICE Guideline CG91 (2009), *The Treatment and Management in Adults with Depression and a Chronic Physical Health Problem*.

Rudisch, B., and C. Nemeroff, 'Epidemiology of comorbid coronary artery disease and depression', *Biological Psychiatry* 54 (2003), 227–40.

Savard, J., S. Simard, I. Giguere, H. Ivers, C.M. Morin, E. Maunsell, P. Gagnon, J. Robert, and D. Marceau, 'Randomized clinical trial on cognitive therapy for depression in women with metastatic breast cancer: psychological and immunological effects', *Palliative and Supportive Care*, 4 (2006), 219–37. Savard and colleagues demonstrated that cognitive therapy was an effective treatment for depression in women with metastatic breast cancer.

Zabora, J., K. BrintzenhofeSzoc, B. Curbow, *et al.*, 'The prevalence of psychological distress by cancer site', *Psycho-Oncology*, 10 (2001), 19–28.

Other resources

No Health Without Mental Health: A Cross-Government Mental Health Outcomes Strategy for People of All Ages (Department of Health, 2013): *www.gov.uk/government/publications/no-health-without-mental-health-a-cross-government-mental-health-outcomes-strategy-for-people-of-all-ages-a-call-to-action*

Chapter 24: Depression in later life

Other resources

Useful organizations

Dementia Action Alliance

www.dementiaaction.org.uk

Alzheimer's Society

www.alzheimers.org.uk

Dementia 2010, a report by the Alzheimer's Research Trust in the UK

www.dementia2010.org

Appendix 2: Blank worksheets

Part 1

Chapter 2

Table 1:
Patient Health Questionnaire (PHQ-9) to assess depression

Over the last 2 weeks, how often have you been bothered by any of the following problems?	Not at all	Several days	More than half the days	Nearly every day
1. Little interest or pleasure in doing things	0	1	2	3
2. Feeling down, depressed, or hopeless	0	1	2	3
3. Trouble falling or staying asleep, or sleeping too much	0	1	2	3
4. Feeling tired or having little energy	0	1	2	3
5. Poor appetite or overeating	0	1	2	3
6. Feeling bad about yourself – or that you are a failure, or have let yourself or your family down	0	1	2	3
7. Trouble concentrating on things, such as reading the newspaper or watching television	0	1	2	3

8. Moving or speaking so slowly that other people could have noticed; or the opposite – being so fidgety or restless that you have been moving around a lot more than usual	0	1	2	3
9. Thoughts that you would be better off dead or of hurting yourself in some way	0	1	2	3
Add each column's scores:				

Add together all column scores to get TOTAL SCORE: _____

	Not difficult at all	Somewhat difficult	Very difficult	Extremely difficult
Finally, if you checked off **any** problems, how difficult have these problems made it for you to do your work, take care of things at home, or get along with other people?	❏	❏	❏	❏

If you scored at least 'Somewhat difficult' on that last question, then your score can be interpreted as follows:

0–4	No depression
5–9	Mild depression
10–14	Moderate depression
15–19	Moderately severe depression
20 or more	Severe depression

Table 2:

Generalized Anxiety Disorder Questionnaire (GAD-7) to assess anxiety

Over the last 2 weeks, how often have you been bothered by any of the following problems?	Not at all	Several days	More than half the days	Nearly every day
1. Feeling nervous, anxious, or on edge	0	1	2	3
2. Not being able to stop or control worrying	0	1	2	3
3. Worrying too much about different things	0	1	2	3
4. Trouble relaxing	0	1	2	3
5. Being so restless that it's hard to sit still	0	1	2	3
6. Becoming easily annoyed or irritable	0	1	2	3
7. Feeling afraid, as if something awful might happen	0	1	2	3
Add each column's scores:				

Add together all column scores to get TOTAL SCORE: _____

Finally, if you checked off **any** problems, how difficult have these problems made it for you to do your work, take care of things at home, or get along with other people?	Not difficult at all ❏	Somewhat difficult ❏	Very difficult ❏	Extremely difficult ❏

If you scored at least 'Somewhat difficult' on that last question, then your score can be interpreted as follows:

0–4	No anxiety
5–9	Mild anxiety
10–14	Moderate anxiety
15 or more	Severe depression

Chapter 8

Worksheet 1: Weekly Activity Schedule (WAS)

Time	Monday	Tuesday	Wednesday	Thursday	Friday	Saturday	Sunday
5–6 a.m.							
6–7 a.m.							
7–8 a.m.							
8–9 a.m.							

9–10 a.m.	10–11 a.m.	11–noon	Noon–1 p.m.	1–2 p.m.	2–3 p.m.

Time	Monday	Tuesday	Wednesday	Thursday	Friday	Saturday	Sunday
3–4 p.m.							
4–5 p.m.							
5–6 p.m.							
6–7 p.m.							
7–8 p.m.							

8–9 p.m.	9–10 p.m.	10–11 p.m.	11–midnight	Midnight–1 a.m.

Chapter 9

Worksheet 2: Basic thought record

Date / time	Situation	Emotion and severity (0–100)	Negative thoughts and belief at the time (0–100 per cent)

Chapter 10

Worksheet 3: Testing the evidence about NATs

Date / time	Situation	Emotion and severity (0–100)	Negative thoughts at the time (0–100 per cent)	Evidence that *supports* the thought	Evidence that counts *against* the thought	Balanced thought

Chapter 11

Worksheet 4: Behavioural experiments

Date	Target cognition(s)	Experiment	Prediction	Outcome	What I learned
	What thought or belief are you testing? Is there an alternative perspective? Rate belief in thoughts (0–100 per cent).	Design an experiment to test the thought/belief (e.g. facing a situation you might avoid, behaving in a new way, finding something out).	What do you predict will happen?	What actually happened? What did you observe? How does the outcome fit with your predictions?	What does this mean for your original thought/belief? How far do you now believe it (0–100 per cent)? Does it need to be modified? How?

Chapter 12

Worksheet 5: Relapse-prevention worksheet

How did my depression start?
What kept my depression going?
What are my most painful and unhelpful thoughts and beliefs? What alternatives did I find to them?

What else have I learned in this self-help book that has been useful?

What situations might lead to a setback? How can I cope with them differently?

How will I know if I am getting depressed again? What will I do differently?

Part 2

Chapter 13

Worksheet 6: Monitoring activity and mood

In each box write the activities you engaged in during the hour, and how you felt. Rate your mood on a scale of 1 to 10, with 1 being the least intensity of feeling and 10 being the most.		
Day and Date:		
Time:		
Midnight–1 a.m.	Activity	
	Mood	
1–2 a.m.	Activity	
	Mood	
2–3 a.m.	Activity	
	Mood	
3–4 a.m.	Activity	
	Mood	

	Activity	
4–5 a.m.	Mood	
	Activity	
5–6 a.m.	Mood	
	Activity	
6–7 a.m.	Mood	
	Activity	
7–8 a.m.	Mood	
	Activity	
8–9 a.m.	Mood	
	Activity	
9–10 a.m.	Mood	
	Activity	
10–11 a.m.	Mood	

11 a.m.–noon	Activity	
	Mood	
Noon–1 p.m.	Activity	
	Mood	
1–2 p.m.	Activity	
	Mood	
2–3 p.m.	Activity	
	Mood	
3–4 p.m.	Activity	
	Mood	
4–5 p.m.	Activity	
	Mood	
5–6 p.m.	Activity	
	Mood	

6–7 p.m.	Activity	
	Mood	
7–8 p.m.	Activity	
	Mood	
8–9 p.m.	Activity	
	Mood	
9–10 p.m.	Activity	
	Mood	
10–11 p.m.	Activity	
	Mood	
11 p.m.–midnight.	Activity	
	Mood	

Worksheet 7: Triggers, behaviours and consequences

Triggers	
Behaviours	
Consequences	

Worksheet 8: Activity planning

Time	Monday	Tuesday	Wednesday	Thursday	Friday	Saturday	Sunday
Midnight–1 a.m.							
1–2 a.m.							
2–3 a.m.							
3–4 a.m.							
4–5 a.m.							

Time	Monday	Tuesday	Wednesday	Thursday	Friday	Saturday	Sunday
5–6 a.m.							
6–7 a.m.							
7–8 a.m.							
8–9 a.m.							
9–10 a.m.							
10–11 a.m.							

11–noon	Noon–1 p.m.	1–2 p.m.	2–3 p.m.	3–4 p.m.	4–5 p.m.

5–6 p.m.	6–7 p.m.	7–8 p.m.	8–9 p.m.	9–10 p.m.	10–11 p.m.	11 p.m.–midnight

Chapter 15

Worksheet 9: The emotional bridge technique

How do I actually feel right now?
How do I feel in my body when I feel this way?
What thoughts am I having when I feel this way?
Do I have any mental pictures in my mind?

What am I afraid might happen next? What is the worst thing that could happen?

When in my life do I first remember feeling this way?

Were there key times in my life when I felt like this?

Worksheet 10: Changing unhelpful beliefs

What conclusions might I have drawn (as a child, or at the time of the event) based on my experience?
What sense did I make of the experience at the time?
Are these beliefs still around with me today?
How would I rate the strength of these beliefs?
What do I think about this event now, from my current perspective?
What would a compassionate friend say?
How could I update my old beliefs based on my adult perspective and the views of people who care about me?
How would that change my unhelpful beliefs?

Part 3

Chapter 19

Worksheet 11: Sleep diary

Measuring the pattern of your sleep	Day 1	Day 2	Day 3	Day 4	Day 5	Day 6	Day 7	Day 8	Day 9	Day 10
1. Did you nap at any point yesterday? If yes, for how long (minutes)?										
2. At what time did you rise from bed this morning?										
3. What time did you finally wake up this morning?										
4. At what time did you go to bed last night?										
5. At what time did you switch off the light intending to go to sleep?										
6. How long did it take you to fall asleep (minutes)?										

7. How long were you awake <u>during</u> the night because of these awakenings (total minutes)?

8. About how long did you sleep altogether (hours/minutes)?

9. How much alcohol did you have last night?

10. Did you take sleeping pills to help you sleep last night? If so, how many?

Measuring the pattern of your sleep

11. How refreshed do you feel this morning?

```
     0     1     2     3     4
     └─────────┴─────────┘
 not at all   moderately    very
```

12. How would you rate the overall quality of your sleep last night?

```
     0     1     2     3     4
     └─────────┴─────────┘
   poor                  very good
```

Worksheet 12: Average sleep time

Night	Amount of time I slept
1	
2	
3	
4	
5	
6	
7	
8	
9	
10	

Total amount of sleep over 10 days = ...

My average sleep time = ... = ...

Part 4

Chapter 21

Worksheet 13: Name and describe a mood state

1. What do you call this feeling or mood (e.g. angry, high, low, happy)?
2. Describe your mood in as much detail as you can (e.g. its colour or smell, any links to memories, locations or events).
3. What feelings do you get in your body when in this mood (e.g. pain in the head, dry mouth, changes in breathing)?
4. What images come to mind when you think about this mood (e.g. past events or interactions, successes or failures)?
5. How do you explain this mood to others (e.g. use of metaphors like 'black hole', 'stuck in a rut')?
6. What do you feel like doing when you are in this mood (e.g. stay in, do more work, sleep more)?

Worksheet 14: Generating your life goals

Arena	Questions	Your life goals
Short term	How will you know that doing this self-help guide is making a difference?	I will notice that I am . . . *. . . feeling like I have more control over my moods*
Myself	How do you want to see yourself in the future?	I want to . . . *. . . be creative, productive and less critical of myself*
My relationships with family, friends and partners	How would you like your relationships to be in the future?	I want to . . . *. . . have positive relationships with my family where we respect our differences of opinion.*
Other goals	Any other goals you have in the long run that are important to you?	I want to . . . *. . . work in a job that a find meaningful and enjoyable*

Worksheet 15: Considering the pros and cons of different emotions

Feeling	Pros	Cons
Can you think of a time when you have had each of these experiences below? Try to imagine the feeling. Where is it in your head or body?	What can be achieved with this feeling? Does it tell you anything useful if you feel this? Try to think of at least one advantage for each feeling.	What are the problems with this feeling? What are your worst fears about too much of this feeling? Try to think of at least one problem for each feeling.
Angry		
Excited		
Afraid		
Sad		
Happy		

Guilty		
Agitated		
Relaxed		
Fast thinking		
Slow thinking		
Very active		
Doing nothing		

Worksheet 16: Sliding-scale exercise

'..............................' sliding scale

None at all   Most extreme I can imagine

| 0 | 10 | 20 | 30 | 40 | 50 | 60 | 70 | 80 | 90 | 100 |

| What is the lowest level of this feeling that would be okay for me? | How intense is this feeling right now? | What is my ideal for this feeling? | What is the highest level of this feeling that would be okay for me? |

'..............................' sliding scale

None at all   Most extreme I can imagine

| 0 | 10 | 20 | 30 | 40 | 50 | 60 | 70 | 80 | 90 | 100 |

| What is the lowest level of this feeling that would be okay for me? | How intense is this feeling right now? | What is my ideal for this feeling? | What is the highest level of this feeling that would be okay for me? |

'..............................' sliding scale

None at all   Most extreme I can imagine

| 0 | 10 | 20 | 30 | 40 | 50 | 60 | 70 | 80 | 90 | 100 |

| What is the lowest level of this feeling that would be okay for me? | How intense is this feeling right now? | What is my ideal for this feeling? | What is the highest level of this feeling that would be okay for me? |

'.............................' **sliding scale**

None at all   Most extreme I can imagine

0   10   20   30   40   50   60   70   80   90   100

| What is the lowest level of this feeling that would be okay for me? | How intense is this feeling right now? | What is my ideal for this feeling? | What is the highest level of this feeling that would be okay for me? |

'.............................' **sliding scale**

None at all   Most extreme I can imagine

0   10   20   30   40   50   60   70   80   90   100

| What is the lowest level of this feeling that would be okay for me? | How intense is this feeling right now? | What is my ideal for this feeling? | What is the highest level of this feeling that would be okay for me? |

'.............................' **sliding scale**

None at all   Most extreme I can imagine

0   10   20   30   40   50   60   70   80   90   100

| What is the lowest level of this feeling that would be okay for me? | How intense is this feeling right now? | What is my ideal for this feeling? | What is the highest level of this feeling that would be okay for me? |

'.............................' sliding scale

None at all   Most extreme I can imagine

| 0 | 10 | 20 | 30 | 40 | 50 | 60 | 70 | 80 | 90 | 100 |

| What is the lowest level of this feeling that would be okay for me? | How intense is this feeling right now? | What is my ideal for this feeling? | What is the highest level of this feeling that would be okay for me? |

'.............................' sliding scale

None at all   Most extreme I can imagine

| 0 | 10 | 20 | 30 | 40 | 50 | 60 | 70 | 80 | 90 | 100 |

| What is the lowest level of this feeling that would be okay for me? | How intense is this feeling right now? | What is my ideal for this feeling? | What is the highest level of this feeling that would be okay for me? |

'.............................' sliding scale

None at all   Most extreme I can imagine

| 0 | 10 | 20 | 30 | 40 | 50 | 60 | 70 | 80 | 90 | 100 |

| What is the lowest level of this feeling that would be okay for me? | How intense is this feeling right now? | What is my ideal for this feeling? | What is the highest level of this feeling that would be okay for me? |

Worksheet 17: Examining self–states

Self-states

Lowest I have ever felt   Highest I have ever felt

| 0 | 10 | 20 | 30 | 40 | 50 | 60 | 70 | 80 | 90 | 100 |

Self-states

Lowest I have ever felt   Highest I have ever felt

| 0 | 10 | 20 | 30 | 40 | 50 | 60 | 70 | 80 | 90 | 100 |

Self-states

Lowest I have ever felt   Highest I have ever felt

| 0 | 10 | 20 | 30 | 40 | 50 | 60 | 70 | 80 | 90 | 100 |

Self-states

Lowest I have ever felt   Highest I have ever felt

| 0 | 10 | 20 | 30 | 40 | 50 | 60 | 70 | 80 | 90 | 100 |

Self-states

Lowest I have ever felt   Highest I have ever felt

| 0 | 10 | 20 | 30 | 40 | 50 | 60 | 70 | 80 | 90 | 100 |

Self-states

Lowest I have ever felt   Highest I have ever felt

| 0 | 10 | 20 | 30 | 40 | 50 | 60 | 70 | 80 | 90 | 100 |

Self-states

Lowest I have ever felt   Highest I have ever felt

| 0 | 10 | 20 | 30 | 40 | 50 | 60 | 70 | 80 | 90 | 100 |

Self-states

Lowest I have ever felt   Highest I have ever felt

| 0 | 10 | 20 | 30 | 40 | 50 | 60 | 70 | 80 | 90 | 100 |

Self-states

Lowest I have ever felt   Highest I have ever felt

| 0 | 10 | 20 | 30 | 40 | 50 | 60 | 70 | 80 | 90 | 100 |

Self-states

Lowest I have ever felt   Highest I have ever felt

| 0 | 10 | 20 | 30 | 40 | 50 | 60 | 70 | 80 | 90 | 100 |

Worksheet 18: My observing mindset

How would I describe a mindset that helps me to weigh up things and contemplate my thoughts and emotions at the right 'distance'? What words would I use?
What would be the benefits of cultivating this mindset?
What would be the disadvantages of cultivating this mindset?
What could I do to bring about this mindset when I need it? Often it helps to build a 'When . . . then' plan. For example, 'WHEN I have finished my dinner THEN I will spend ten minutes weighing up my options.'
WHEN

THEN

Is anything likely to get in the way of this plan? If so, what?

What plan do I have for dealing with any obstacles?

WHEN

THEN

Chapter 23

Worksheet 19: My problem list

Problem Area
Problems with emotions
Problems with activity/behaviour
Physical problems
Relationship problems
Other problems

Worksheet 20: Unhelpful patterns map

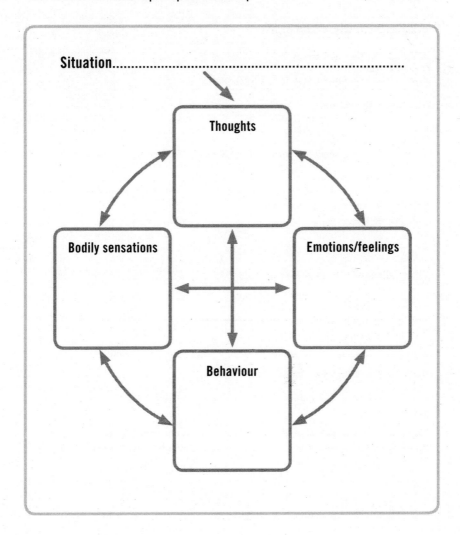

Worksheet 21: Behavioural experiment

Step one – identify the fear

What do you fear will happen?

How strongly do you believe this will happen?

Step two – examine the fear

What evidence do you have that your prediction will come true?

Step three – plan an experiment

Decide what you need to do to test your fear.

Plan when and where you will do the experiment.

What will you need to know to find out if your prediction has been disproved?

What do you need to do to make it more likely there will be a positive outcome?

How will you cope if your fear is proved correct?

Step four – evaluate the outcome

What happened? Were your fears upheld? How strongly do you believe your prediction now?

Make sure you are objective about the result. It may be that a prediction partly comes true, but don't let your negative thoughts label the experiment a complete failure. Examine your prediction.

Step five – decide what you need to do next

Worksheet 22: Old and new plans

Plan A	Plan B

Chapter 24

Worksheet 23: Planning an enjoyable task

Make a prediction before you do something. Write it here:

I am going to ....

I think (prediction of how it will turn out) ....

Afterwards, write how it turned out.

I did ....

I can be proud of myself because ....

Index

abstract thought 178, 180–1, 183
abuse 211
acceptance 231–3, 382–4, 534–5
Accident and Emergency (A&E)
  departments 19
achievement 70–1, 76–7
achievement-orientation 290
activity 69–78, 129–61, 376–7
  changing your patterns of 76–7
  depleting 300–2
  and depression in physical illness
    472, 476, 479, 485–6, 491–5, 507
  graded 492–3
  in later life 521–3, 526, 528, 529–32
  monitoring 69–75, 572–5
  nourishing 300–2
  pleasurable 300–1, 377–81, 493–4,
    522–3, 526, 528, 531–2, 602
  and rumination 176–7
  social 54, 60, 451–2
  stimulating 237–8
  see also inactivity
activity planning 577–80
activity scheduling 144, 146–58, 454
  introducing alternative behaviours
    148–50, 156
  making a plan 150–1
  reducing avoidance 147–8
  'What if ... then what?' plans 156
actors 234
adulthood, transition to 288
Affect Regulation Systems 220
affection 384–5
ageing paradox 512

agitated depression 9
'all-or-nothing' thinking 91, 492, 497
alternative behaviours 148–50, 156,
  175–83, 455, 502–4
American Psychiatric Association 10
anger 13–15, 205, 225, 408–9, 412
  behavioural 14
  cognitive 13–14
  emotional 13
  masking depression 14
  physical 14
  productive 408, 412
anhedonia (lack of pleasure) 43, 53,
  129–30, 224, 438
antidepressant medication 34–6, 384,
  450
  and addiction 35
  how long to take 35
  in later life 513, 538
  masking true problems with 36
  monoamine oxidase inhibitors
    (MAOIs) 34
  over-focus on 23
  for postnatal depression 450
  selective serotonin reuptake
    inhibitors (SSRIs) 34, 36
  serotonin norepinephrine reuptake
    inhibitors (SNRIs) 34
  side effects 35
  tricyclic antidepressants 34
anxiety 12–13
  accompanied with depression
    12–13, 14–15, 514–16
  behavioural 13

cognitive 12–13
diagnosis 19–20
emotional 12
in later life 514–16, 518
physical 13
and physical illness 473, 474, 475,
  477, 479–80
and rumination 163, 164, 168, 172,
  176, 177, 180
and sleep problems 344
social 414
appetite problems 8
appreciation 240, 298–303
arthritis, rheumatoid 493
attachment 465–9
attention
  and acts of self-kindness 302
  mindful 231
  selective 498
  switching 228–9
attitude 151, 302
autopilot mode 253–4, 271, 425
avoidance strategies 130–1, 139–40,
  142–4, 147–8, 168, 453–4, 479–80,
  514–15
awareness
  developing 248
  and mindfulness 254–7, 270
  of rumination 169–71
  of your breath 265–6

babies
  difficult/sensitive 358, 441–2,
    461–4, 466
  sleep requirements 324
baby blues 437–8, 441
'bad person, a', believing yourself to
  be 200–1, 203–4, 212
Baer, Lee 232
bathing 464

'bed is for sleep' rule 344–5
bed time 349–50
  wind-down 341–2
bed-sleep connection 344–7
bedroom factors 340, 341
behavioural activation 129–61, 376–81
  activity scheduling 144, 146–58
  avoidance strategies 130–1, 139–40,
    142–4, 147–8
  background 129–31
  behavioural triggers 131, 141–7,
    149, 156, 158, 160
  'boom and bust' 134
  for couples 377, 378–81
  functional analysis 140–7
  how does it work? 131
  individual 377–8
  and negative reinforcement 130,
    139–41
  'outside-in' principle 131, 148
  and positive reinforcement 130,
    133, 141, 147, 148
  programme structure 132–58
  progress monitoring 134
  and rumination 156, 158–61
  and self-monitoring 133–41
behavioural experiments 101–9, 313,
  502–6, 568–9, 600
behavioural patterns
  breaking 491–5
  mapping unhelpful 487–91, 599
  study of 140–6
behavioural symptoms of depression
  9, 44
behaviours 46, 576
  alternative 148–50, 156, 175–83, 455,
    502–4
  caring 374–5
  consequences of 141, 143–5, 147,
    149, 158, 160, 164, 576

and depression in later life 519–20

and depression in physical illness 475, 481–2, 487–91, 507–8

function 129, 131, 141–6, 158, 160

as interacting system 46–7

and your relationships 360–1

beliefs

about rumination 168–9

about the self 186, 202–4, 206–15

about your emotions 408–12

about your relationship 360

alternative helpful 121, 583

biology 27–8

bipolar disorder 11, 389, 391–436

bipolar I disorder 392

bipolar II disorder 392

case examples 395–7, 408–9, 412, 415, 417–18, 420–2, 426

cyclothymia 11, 392

symptoms 392–3

TEAMS (Think Effectively About Mood Swings) approach to 393–436

blame 371

see also self-blame

bodily sensations

and depression in physical illness 473–7, 480, 486–92, 503, 508

mindfulness of 256, 263–4, 266–9, 270–1

and Mindfulness-based Cognitive Therapy 250

and rumination 171–2, 175, 178

body

mind-body link 227

working with your 230–1

see also mindfulness practices (mind-body-based trainings)

body compassion 242–3

Body Scan technique 263–4

bone cancer 473–7, 480

boring, feeling 295, 420–2

Bottom Line, The 286, 288–90, 290–6, 304, 308–14

brain 27–8, 217, 226, 227, 234–6

and emotion 220–1, 234

and nutrition 243

and sleep 316–17

brainstorming 114–15, 371, 372, 373

breast cancer 473–7, 480

breastfeeding 442

breathing techniques 230–1, 265–71, 453

Breath Practice 265–6

mindfulness of the breath 249

Three-Minute Breathing Space 269–70

British Journal of Psychiatry 529

Buddhism 262

bullying 190, 192, 194, 209, 210

CAB *see* Citizens Advice Bureau

caffeine 341, 346–7

calmness, sense of 453

Campbell, Alistair 22

cancer 213, 473–7, 480, 488–9, 507

caring behaviour 37, 374–5

causes of depression 27–33

biological 27–8

life experiences 28–9

CFT for depression *see* compassion-focused therapy (CFT) for depression

child carers 303–7, 309

childbirth 441, 442

childhood sexual abuse 211

children, sleep requirements 324

Churchill, Winston 23

circadian rhythms 321–2, 323

circadian timer 321–2, 323

Citizens Advice Bureau (CAB) 115
clarifying 371
classification of depression 9–11
clinically depressed 5
cognitions (thoughts) 44–6, 46–51
    about your relationship 360–1
    as interacting systems 46–7, 48–9
    interpretations of 45
    see also thoughts
cognitive behavioural therapy (CBT)
    37–8
    basic ideas of CBT 43–8
    and depression in later life 513
    and depression in physical illness
        472–3, 475–510
    identifying negative thoughts
        79–87
    increasing activity levels 69–78
    and insomnia 333–56
    and low self-esteem 294–315
    and maintaining factors 32
    and meaning 284
    model of depression 43–61
    NHS availability 18
    and postnatal depression 449–57
    problem-solving 111–18
    relapse prevention 119–25
    and relationship difficulties 360
    starting the process 62–8
    tackling negative thoughts 88–110
    see also behavioural activation;
        TEAMS (Think Effectively About
        Mood Swings)
cognitive symptoms of depression
    7–8, 43–4
cognitive therapy 202–6, 514
    see also Mindfulness-based
        Cognitive Therapy
Cohen, Halley 231
comfort 384–5

compassion 127, 241–2, 257–50
compassion candle 244
compassion-focused therapy (CFT)
    for depression 216–46
    body compassion 242–3
    compassionate behaviour 241–2
    and the compassionate image 233,
        238–40, 453
    and the compassionate self 234–6
    compassionate writing 240–1
    mindful attention 231
    practicing compassion 243–5
    recognition and acceptance 231–3
    and stimulation 237–8
    working with your body 230–1
compromise 372
concentration difficulties 7
concrete, being 178–82
conflict 56
confrontation 156
consequences 141, 143–5, 147, 149,
    158, 160, 164, 576
contemplation 424–31
contingent responding 458–61
conversations
    about sexual problems 385–6
    for making decisions and solving
        problems 369–73
    for sharing thoughts and feelings
        363–9
coping cycles 476, 507–10
counselling 449
couples and depression 357–88
    and communication skills 358,
        359–76
    and the environment 359–60
    functioning as a unit 359
    and individual needs 359
    and physical illness 481–2
    and physical relationships 384–6

using your relationship in a
    positive way to overcome
    depression 358, 376–88
courage 241
crises 110
cyclothymia 11, 392

daily stresses/hassles 29
daytime naps 346–7
decision making 369–73
defining depression 3–15
dementia 512
Department of Health Strategy – No
    Health Without Mental Health... 472
'depression about depression' 55
'depression traps' 484–91, 502
deservingness, lack of a feeling of 23
development of depression
    examples of 49–51, 58–9
    factors affecting 30–2
diagnosing depression 16–21
*Diagnostic and Statistical Manual of
    Mental Disorders*, Fifth Edition
    (DSM-5) 10
diaphragm 230–1
diaries
    pain 475–7
    rumination 169–72
    sleep 320, 335–7, 584–5
diet, poor 242–3
disappointment, feelings of 142–3
disconnectedness, feelings of 224
disruption 148–9
distraction techniques 88–9, 297, 476,
    531–2
'doing' *see* activity
domestic chores, mindful practice of
    271–2
downward spirals 236, 247, 251, 254,
    258, 269, 271, 277, 292

dreams 319–20
driving, mindful 272
DSM-5 (*Diagnostic and Statistical
    Manual of Mental Disorders*, Fifth
    Edition) 10
dysthymia 11, 513

early life experiences 28, 50, 51, 58, 67,
    204–5, 212
    accuracy of memories regarding
        188
    and Rules for Living 304
    and self-esteem 287–9, 303–4
early warning signs
    of the onset of depression 122, 254
    of the onset of rumination 171–2,
        174, 175, 181–2
early warning systems 191
early-morning awakening 8
eating, mindful 271–2
ECT *see* electroconvulsive therapy
Edinburgh Postnatal Depression Scale
    (EPDS) 443–7
EEG *see* electroencephalogram
Einstein, Albert 189
electro-oculogram (EOG) 317, 319
electroconvulsive therapy (ECT) 37
electroencephalogram (EEG) 316–19,
    321
electromyogram (EMG) 317, 319
emotional bridge technique 197–9,
    581–2
emotional reasoning 91–2, 515, 536
emotional scaffolding 461–5
emotional symptoms of depression
    7, 43
emotions
    about your relationship 360–1
    and attention 228
    in behavioural activation 143

counter-emotions 177–8

and depression 220–3

and images of memories 194–5

incentive/reward system 220–1, 222, 228, 230

as interacting systems 46–7, 48–9

and Mindfulness-based Cognitive Therapy 250

negative 112–13, 220–1, 223, 224, 226–9, 250, 512

non-wanting/affiliative system 220–1, 222–3, 228, 230

painful 112–13

and poor diet 242–3

positive 512

recognition and acceptance 231–3

and Rules for Living 304–5

self-monitoring 133

and sleep 322–3

sliding scale of 414–20, 591–3

and thought records 81

threat system 220–1, 223, 224, 226–9

when thoughts push out of balance 226–8

see also feelings

encouragement 241–2

energy levels, low 8

engagement 368, 458–61

enjoyment, return of 76

see also pleasure

environmental influence 217–18

EOG *see* electro-oculogram

EPDS *see* Edinburgh Postnatal Depression Scale

escape behaviours 142–3

everyday life

and mindfulness 270–3

and self-esteem 299, 300

evidence 92–8, 309–11, 501

evolution 217

excitement, feelings of 399–400, 412, 414

eye movement, measurement 317, 319

facial expression, friendly 235

facts about depression 22, 25

failure

memories of 187

sense of 290, 292

family adversity 287

fathers

stay-at-home 102

strict/authoritarian 204–5

fatigue 8, 329–31

fear 502–4, 506, 514, 515, 530, 532

feelings 45–6

acceptance 382–4

of bipolar disorder 393–8, 407–13

communicating your 365–9

conversations for sharing 363–9

and depression in later life 519–20

and depression in physical illness 475, 477–8, 481–2, 487–91, 495, 507–8

how depression feels 3

informing other people how you feel 365–6

mindfulness to 277

naming and describing 398–403

negative 366–7, 407, 408

positive 366–7, 407

pros and cons of 407–14, 589–90

sharing 366–7

see also emotions

'felt sense' 233

fortune telling 92

'found out', fear of being 204

Frankl, Viktor 255

Freud, Sigmund 187

friends, becoming your own best friend 534–5

Fry, Steven 22
fun, compassionate 244
functional analysis 140–7
functions of behaviour 129, 131, 141–6, 158, 160

General Practitioners (GPs)
  and antidepressant medication 34
  and exercise schemes 243
  and postnatal depression 443, 445, 451
  referrals 18, 19, 275
  and suicidal thoughts 110
Generalized Anxiety Disorder questionnaire (GAD-7) 19–20, 559
genes 27, 217, 218
goal-setting 403–7, 588
  and depression in later life 527–9
  identifying the goals of therapy 64–5
  and insomnia 334–5
  long-term goals 403–4, 406, 528
  short-term goals 403–6, 528
  SMART goals 65
gratitude 240
grief 518, 524
growth experiences 534–5
guilt 417–18, 452–3

habits 166–7
hallucinations 392
  auditory 438
hatred 232
'head-heart' lag 207
health
  fears about 515
  see also physical illness, depression in
health visitors 443, 445, 451
heart attack 484–6

help
  asking for 536
  feeling you don't deserve 23
  helping others 241
  see also professional help
helplessness, feelings of 204–6, 463, 479, 492
heredity 27
hopelessness 187, 479, 486, 488, 492, 507, 525, 530
  vicious circles of 54–5, 292
'hot cross bun' 47, 51
hypersomnia 325
hypomania 391, 392
hypothyroidism 28

'I' statements 365
ICD-10 (International Classification of Diseases, Tenth Revision) 10
ideal compassionate other 238–9
identification, with depression 24
identity, and memory 186–93
'If ... then' plans 174–7, 181–5
imagery, of compassion-focused therapy 233
images
  changing the perspective of 209
  compassionate 233, 238–40, 453
  and depressing memories 186–215
  skill of working with 213–14
  talking to 210
  'travelling back in time' with 210–11
imagination 207, 209, 212, 226–8
imitation 460–1
inactivity 479, 484–6, 507
  see also activity
inadequacy, feelings of 156
incentive/reward system 220–1, 222, 228, 230

incompetence, feelings of 358, 362, 383–4
inferiority, feelings of 397
insomnia 316, 321, 325–37
    accepting approach to 354
    and the bed-sleep connection 344–7
    calculating sleep efficiency 338–9, 350
    causes 332–3
    CBT for 333–56
    dealing with setbacks 255–6
    evaluating how you feel during the day 354
    goal-setting for 334–5
    improving sleep hygiene 340–1, 344
    improving sleep patterns 347–50
    making lasting improvements to sleep 354–6
    mixed insomnia 328
    perpetuating factors 332–3
    precipitating factors (trigger events) 332
    predisposing factors 332
    and preparation for sleep 341–3
    prevalence 330–1
    and racing minds 351–4
    and sleep diaries 335–7
    sleep-maintenance insomnia 328–9
    sleep-onset insomnia 328
    tackling 333–56
    types of 328
insomnia disorder 326, 327
interacting systems 46–9
interdependence 218
International Classification of Diseases, Tenth Revision (ICD-10) 10
Interpersonal Psychotherapy (IPT) 38, 449, 513
interpretations 45, 394, 513–14
    about your relationships 360
    finding alternative 121
    and memories 188
    negative 188
irritability 13–15, 225, 323, 331, 448–9

judgementalness 310–11
    see also non-judgemental approaches

K-complexes 318–19
Kabat-Zinn, Jon 248, 249, 250, 255
Keyes, Marian 24
kindness 244, 275
    see also self-kindness
Kukyen, Willem 231

labelling 498
later life, depression in 389, 512–38
    depression with anxiety 514–16
    goal setting 527–9
    myth busting 518–27
    staying well 534–7
    tackling depression 527–33
learned behaviours, rumination as 166–7
legal problems 115
letter-writing, compassionate 240–1
life events 29
life expectancy 513, 521
life experience 524
    and beliefs about ourselves 186, 200
    and how other people treat you 310
    and memory 186, 189, 191–2, 200
    and self-esteem 286, 287–9, 291, 310–11
    see also early life experiences
life goals
    long-term 403–4, 406
    setting 403–7, 588
    short-term 403–6

lifestyle 340, 341, 529–30
light therapy 36–7
listening skills 364–5, 367–9
loss 187, 287, 518

magnification 497
maintaining factors 30–1, 32, 49–51, 66
   CBT's focus on 66–7
   examples of 60–1
   identifying 120–1
   and relapse prevention 120–1
   see also vicious circles
major depressive disorder 5, 10
Mandela, Nelson 521
mania 11, 391–2
MAOIs *see* monoamine oxidase
  inhibitors
MBCT *see* Mindfulness-based
  Cognitive Therapy
MBSR *see* Mindfulness-based Stress
  Reduction
meaning 284
meditation 262, 266–70, 274
melatonin 322
memories 186–215
   are memories facts? 188–9
   changing the ending of 211–12
   changing the meaning of 202–6
   dealing with 127
   and depression 186–7
   distorted 192
   general 192
   as ghosts from the past 189–91,
     196–201, 209
   how they influence the way we see
     ourselves and the world 186–93
   as images 194–6
   mood-congruent 189
   negative self-defining 189
   recurrent intrusive 191–2, 200

and reducing our sense of suffering
  211
and Rules for Living 309
and sense of smell 190
and sense of taste 190
specific 192
thinking through 196–207
using imagery to place in a wider
  context 213
using images to help with 186–215
working with 194–215
mental function 322–3
midwives 443, 445
migraine 487
mind
   depressed 223–5, 240
   'holding it in mind' 226, 425
   nature's mind 231–3
   racing 351–4
mind-body link 227
mind-reading 92, 498
mindful attention 231
Mindful Movement 266–9
mindfulness 127–8, 244, 247–80
   and autopilot mode 253–4, 271
   and awareness 254–7, 265–6
   and compassion 257–50
   definition 248–9
   in everyday life 270–3
   and help for people with
     depression 251
   and non-judgemental approaches
     257–50
mindfulness practices (mind-body-
  based trainings) 248
   Body Scan technique 263–4
   Breath Practice 265–6
   defining 261–3
   examples 263–73
   Mindful Movement 266–9

mindfulness of the breath 249
stretching 270
Three-Minute Breathing Space
  269–70
walking 270
mindfulness-based approaches
  249–50
  efficacy 252
  eight-week Mindfulness-based
    Cognitive Therapy course 273–6
  for insomnia 333
Mindfulness-based Cognitive
  Therapy (MBCT) 248–50, 263
  beyond the eight-week MBCT
    course 276–9
  efficacy 252
  eight-week MBCT course 273–6
  teachers 275–6
Mindfulness-based Stress Reduction
  (MBSR) 249–50, 252, 263
minimization 497
mobility problems 536
moment, being present in the 66, 222,
  244, 248, 254, 274, 277, 427
monoamine oxidase inhibitors
  (MAOIs) 34
mood
  and bipolar disorder 391, 392,
    393–433
  and breastfeeding 442
  diurnal variation 8
  and having a baby 437–8
  improving with activity scheduling
    454
  and insomnia 329, 330
  low 4, 6, 43, 49, 127
    combating through behavioural
      activation 130–1, 133–40, 142,
      149, 156, 158
    and depressing memories 188–9

and depression in later life
  519–20
and dysthymia 513
identification of the reasons for a
  worsening of 80–1
and low self-esteem 292
maintenance through negative
  thinking 187
and negative automatic thoughts
  79
persistence 5
and physical activity 53
and physical illness 477, 479,
  484–6
and postnatal depression 438
and self-harm/suicide 18
severity of 5
and sleep problems 325–6
as symptom of depression 7
using imagery to lift 206–15
vicious circle of 52, 53, 56, 60
see also sadness; unhappiness
and memory 188
monitoring 572–5
naming and describing 398–403,
  587
mood records 102–3, 528
mother-baby relationship 448–9,
  458–70
motherhood, experience of 448
mothers
  critical 188, 200–1
  feeling incompetent 358, 362,
    383–4
  ill 303–6
  unloving 58–9
movement, mindful 266–9
'musts' 304, 498
myelinated parasympathetic nervous
  system 230

myths
  about depression 22–5
  about later life 518–27

napping 322, 346–7
National Health Service (NHS) 34, 275
National Institute for Health and
  Clinical Excellence (NICE) 34, 252,
  275, 472–3
nature's mind 231–3
needs, attachment 465–8
negative automatic thoughts (NATs)
  50–1, 77
  automatic chains of 163, 178–9
  and behavioural experiments 101–9
  characteristics 79–80
  and the couple 382–4
  evidence for 92–8
  focusing on, and feeling worse 86
  identification 79–87
  looking at alternative views to 99,
    102–3
  and physical illness 496–9
  plausibility 79
  pros and cons of 98–9
  and rumination 163, 178–9
  self-critical 295–6
  and self-esteem 283, 302, 303, 309–10
  tackling 88–110
negative beliefs, about yourself 189,
  206–15, 286, 288, 289
negative reinforcement 130, 139–41
negative thoughts 7–8, 48–53, 56–7,
  60–1, 186–7
  about physical illness 477–9, 485,
    487, 491, 492, 495–506
  and activity 77
  beginning the CBT self-help battle
    against 62–3
  and behavioural activation 131

and the couple 382–4
and depression in later life 530–2
distracting yourself from 88–9
identification 79–87
mindfulness to 257–8
and monitoring your activity levels
  69
and parenting 459
of postnatal depression 449
and problem-solving 111–13
and recurrent depression 251
tackling 88–110
testing out (tackling method)
  90–100, 566–7
see also negative automatic
  thoughts; suicidal thoughts
nervous system, myelinated
  parasympathetic 230
neurotransmitters 27–8
NHS see National Health Service
NICE see National Institute for Health
  and Clinical Excellence
nicotine 341
Nolen-Hoeksema, Susan 166
non-judgemental approaches 257–50
  see also judgementalness
non-prescription drugs 36
non-wanting/affiliative system 220–1,
  222–3, 228, 230
normal distribution 325
nutrition 242–3

observation
  observing babies 460–1
  observing mindset 425–31, 596–7
oestradiol 442
one step at a time, taking things 62–4
onset of depression 120
opinions 51
opposite action strategies 177–8

optimism 98
other, ideal compassionate 238–9
'oughts' 304, 498
'outside-in' principle 131, 148
over-generalizing 91, 178, 192, 497, 524
overwhelmed, feeling 113, 492, 496–7

pacing 297
pain
　pain diaries 475–7
　physical 473–7, 480, 486, 487, 492, 503
parasympathetic nervous system, myelinated 230
parental relationships, and postnatal depression 447–8
parenting
　and attachment 465–8
　and contingent responding 458–61
　and emotional scaffolding 461–5
　and postnatal depression 458–70
parents
　critical 287
　fighting 212
　see also fathers; mothers
pathetic, feeling 22–3
Patient Health Questionnaire (PHQ-9) 16–17, 557–8
pause, power of the 255–6
'people pleasing' behaviour 206
perfectionism 200, 259, 529
personalization 498–9
perspective (of images) 209
perspectives 368–9, 382–4
pessimism 98, 382
PHQ-9 see Patient Health Questionnaire
physical exercise 36, 53, 77, 243, 341, 529–30

physical fitness levels 77
physical illness, depression in 389, 477–511, 513–14
　breaking unhelpful behavioural patterns 491–5
　CBT for 472–3, 475–510
　coping patterns 507–10
　the depression trap 484–91, 502
　identifying target problems 481–4
　managing unhelpful thinking patterns 495–506
　mapping unhelpful patterns 487–91
　understanding your reactions to physical illness 473–80
physical relationships 384–6
physiology 44, 46–7
pineal gland 322
plans, making 150–1
pleasure
　loss of 43, 53, 129–30, 224, 438
　pleasurable activities 300–1, 377–81, 493–4, 522–3, 526, 528, 531–2, 602
　rating your feelings of 70–1, 76–7
polysomnography (PSG) 317, 320, 321
positive experiences, limiting your 453–5
positive qualities, learning to . appreciate your 298–303
positive reinforcement 130, 133, 141, 147, 148
postnatal depression (PND) 437–70
　causes 442
　definition 437–9
　duration 439–40
　impact 447–9
　and parenting 458–70
　people at risk from 441–2
　prevalence 439
　recognition 443–7
　severity 439

symptoms 438–9
treatment 449–50, 449–57
powerlessness, feelings of 210
prayers 499
precipitating factors (triggers) 30, 50, 120, 122
prediction making, negative 496–7, 498, 504
predisposing (vulnerability) factors 30, 120
prescription drugs 34–6
present moment, being in 66, 222, 244, 248, 254, 274, 277, 427
prevalence of depression 25, 216
problem-solving 111–18
    action plans for 115–16
    in activity scheduling 149–50
    brainstorming solutions 114–15
    choosing a solution 115
    conversations for 369–73
    deciding on the first target 114
    defining the problem 113
    evaluating the results of your 116
    helpful and unhelpful thinking about problems 182–3
    and parenting 464
    planning the next steps 116–17
processes of depression 49–51
professional help, seeking out 109–10, 376
progesterone 442
protective factors 31
PSG see polysomnography
psychomotor agitation 9
psychomotor retardation 9
psychosis 392, 438
puerperal psychosis 438
'putting the day to rest' 351–2

'quarter-of-an-hour' rule 345

questions, unanswerable 183

racing minds 351–4
rapid eye movement (REM) sleep 319–20
realism 63–4, 69, 90, 499, 500
reality checks 217–18
reasoning, emotional 91–2, 515, 536
recovery from depression
    incomplete 25
    see also relapse prevention
recurrent depression 251–2, 274
'redemptive sequences' 534–5
reflection 369
reinforcement
    negative 130, 139–41
    positive 130, 133, 141, 147, 148
relapse prevention 119–25, 570–1
    identifying maintaining factors 120–1
    identifying the onset of depression 120
    identifying setback triggers 122
    recognizing onset warning signs 122
    worksheet 123–4
    and your interpretation of events 121
relationship counsellors/therapists 376
relationships
    building 223
    and communication skills 358, 359–76
    and depression 357–88
    difficulties 281, 357–88, 481–2
    and the environment 359–60
    functioning as a unit 359
    and individual needs 359
    mother-baby 448–9, 458–70

parental 447–8

physical 384–6

and physical illness 481–2

using it to overcome depression 358, 376–88

with yourself 223

relaxation 342–3

reliving 299–300

REM (rapid eye movement) sleep 319–20

resilience 192, 508, 535–7

responsibility 218–19

rising time 349–50

routines 454

'Rules for Living' 286, 289, 290–5, 303–8

advantages of 306

costs of 306

identifying your 304–5

questioning 305–7

'road testing' 307

trying out new 307

Rumi 258–9, 278

rumination 127, 131, 147, 162–85, 251, 254

alternatives to 175–83

as avoidance 168

awareness of 169–71

becoming specific and concrete 178–82

and behavioural activation 156, 158–61

bodily responses to 171–2, 175, 178

common triggers for 172

consequences of 164

definition 162–3

diaries 169–72

discriminating between helpful and unhelpful thinking about problems 182–3

early warning signs 171–2, 174–5, 181–2

as habit 166–7

'If … then' plans 174–7, 181–5

and low self-esteem 296–7

normal and helpful 164–5

overcoming 169–71, 455–6

positive beliefs about 168–9

and postnatal depression 455–6

why it is hard to stop 168–9

sadness 518

natural 112–13

see also mood, low; unhappiness

safety behaviours 13

St John's wort 36

Samaritans 110

Sapolsky, Robert 226

'saving your sleep' rule 346–7

school years 287

Seasonal Affective Disorder (SAD) 37

secure attachment 465–6, 468

Segal, Zindel 250

selective attention 498

selective serotonin reuptake inhibitors (SSRIs) 34, 36

self

compassionate 234–6

healthy 431–3

how memory influences the way we see ourselves 186–93

negative beliefs about 189, 206–15, 286, 288, 289

self-acceptance 534–5

self-appreciation 298–303

self-blame 24–5, 212, 232–3, 452–3

self-care 37

self-criticism 216, 223, 227, 235–6, 258–9, 292, 310–11

questioning 295–7

self-denigration 452–3
self-esteem, low 56, 281, 283–315
    and anxious predictions 291–2,
        294–6
    and changing the rules 303–8
    definition 284
    learning 286
    maintenance 290–3
    process of development 286–90
    and 'Rules for Living' 286, 289,
        290–5, 303–9
    and self-appreciation 298–303
    and self-criticism 292, 295–7
    and self-kindness 298–303
    and The Bottom Line 286, 288–90,
        290–6, 304, 308–14
    understanding 284–6
    working with 294–315
self-fulfilling prophecies 54–5, 529
self-harm 18–19
    see also suicidal thoughts
self-kindness 200, 204–6, 223, 236–7,
    257–8, 260, 454
    and low self-esteem 298–303, 313
    treating yourself with 300–1
self-monitoring 133–41
    eight main questions 133–4
    exercises 134–40
self-states
    healthy 431–3
    sliding scale 420–5, 594–5
self-support 236–7
self-worth 287
selfishness, depression seen as 519–20
'Serenity Prayer' 499
serotonin norepinephrine reuptake
    inhibitors (SNRIs) 34
severe depression 5, 10, 18
sex lives 9, 384–6
shame 216, 232

'shoulds' 304, 498
siestas 322
sleep diaries 320, 335–7, 584–5
sleep homeostat 321–2
sleep hygiene 340–1, 344
sleep problems 8, 281, 316–56
    average sleep time 586
    bed-sleep connection 344–7
    and CBT for insomnia 333–56
    deep sleep 319, 320
    functions of sleep 322–3
    larks 323
    owls 323
    preparation for sleep 341–3
    quality of sleep 320
    quantity of sleep 320–1
    rapid eye movement (REM) sleep
        319–20
    relationship with depression 325–6
    sleep efficiency 338–9, 350
    sleep pattern control 321–2
    sleep requirements 324–5, 347–50
    stages of sleep 317–20
    understanding sleep 316–27
sleep spindles 318–19
sleep window 350
'sleepy-tired' rule 345–6
sliding scales 414–25, 591–3
slowed down, feelings of being
    (psychomotor retardation) 9
'slowing things down' strategy 176,
    234–7
SMART goals 65
smell, sense of 190
smoking 341
SNRIs see serotonin norepinephrine
    reuptake inhibitors
social activities 54, 60, 451–2
social anxiety 414
social isolation 396–7, 451–2

social networks 521
social withdrawal 187, 376, 449, 459, 519–20
specific, being 178–82
SSRIs *see* selective serotonin reuptake inhibitors
stigma 519
stimulation 237–8
stomach cancer 488–9, 507
strength, sense of 236, 508
stress
    daily stresses/hassles 29
    and memory 190
    and rumination 167, 171, 174, 176–8
stress hormones 229
stretching 266–8, 270
stuckness, feelings of 208
subclinical depression 513
subjective assessment 320
subjectivity 366
suffering, sense of 211
suicidal thoughts 8, 18–19, 109–10
summarizing 364
superiority, feelings of 396–7
support 516
symptoms of depression 6–9, 11, 43–4, 513
    behavioural 9, 44
    cognitive 7–8, 43–4
    emotional 7, 43
    physiological 44

'taking a dislike to someone' 190
tasks, breaking down 177, 182
taste, sense of 190
TEAMS (Think Effectively About Mood Swings)
    and bipolar disorder 393–436
    contemplation 424–31

healthy self (putting everything together) 431–3
    naming and describing moods and feelings 398–403
    pros and cons of different feelings 407–14, 589–90
    self-states sliding scale 420–5
    setting life goals 403–7
    sliding scale of emotion 414–20, 591–3
Teasdale, John 250
teeth brushing 462
terminology 11
thinking
    about yourself 420–4
    abstract 178, 180–1, 183
    fast 418
    managing unhelpful patterns 495–506
    physical symptoms 8
    processes of 7
    realistic 49
thinking errors/traps 90–2, 496–9
thought evaluators 352–4
thought patterns, repeated 304
thought records 80–6, 496, 564–5
thought-testing 90–100, 502–6, 566–7
    see also behavioural experiments
thoughts
    of bipolar disorder 393–8
    communicating your 365–9
    content of your 7–8
    conversations for sharing 363–9
    and depression in later life 519–20
    and depression in physical illness 475, 477–80, 485, 487–491, 495–510
    distinguishing from feelings 81
    finding alternative 121
    and insomnia 351–4
    mindfulness to 255, 257–8, 277

and Mindfulness-based Cognitive
Therapy 250, 251
as pictures 82
realistic and reasonable 499,
500
recognising unhelpful/distressing
499–501
recognition and acceptance 231–3
recording 286–7
and self-esteem 286–7, 298
telling other people how they think
365–6
which push emotions out of
balance 226–8
'yes, but ...'s 298
see also cognitions (thoughts);
negative automatic thoughts;
negative thoughts
threat 209, 477
threat system 220–1, 223, 224, 226–9
time
getting a clear idea of how you
spend your 69–75
structuring 66–7
'time travelling' technique 210–11
tiredness 8, 331, 345–6, 354, 438, 439,
486, 492
tissue restoration 323
'topping and tailing' 464
treating depression 34–9, 37–8
see also specific treatments
treats 301, 313
tricyclic antidepressants 34
trigger situations 30, 50
identifying 120, 122
for insomnia 332
for rumination 172
for setbacks 122
trigger-behaviour-consequence cycle
147, 149, 160, 576

'turning to others' 242
Twain, Mark 101

UK Network for Mindfulness-Based
Teacher Training Organisations
275–6
under-valued, feeling 162
unhappiness 5–6
see also mood, low; sadness
useless, feelings of being 119–22

vicious circles 52–61, 81
breaking 62, 69
CBT's focus on 66–7
and depression in later life
519–20
and depression in physical illness
474–5, 484–5
identifying 121
and insomnia 332, 333, 352
and low self-esteem 290–2, 303
of negative thinking and low mood
187
and postnatal depression 448–9,
454, 455
and relapse prevention 121
vocal tone, friendly 235–6, 244–5

walking, mindful 270
weakness 22–3, 210, 312–13, 519–20
Weekly Activity Schedule (WAS)
69–70, 560–3
weight gain 218
weight loss 8
wellbeing, emotional 512
Wesley, Mary 519
'What if ... then what?' plans 156
Wilde, Oscar 186
Willliams, Mark 250
wisdom 236, 241–2, 524, 525, 526

World Health Organization (WHO)
  216
worrying 473–5, 531–2
worthlessness, feelings of 58–9

'XYZ' statements 365

'yes, but...'s 298